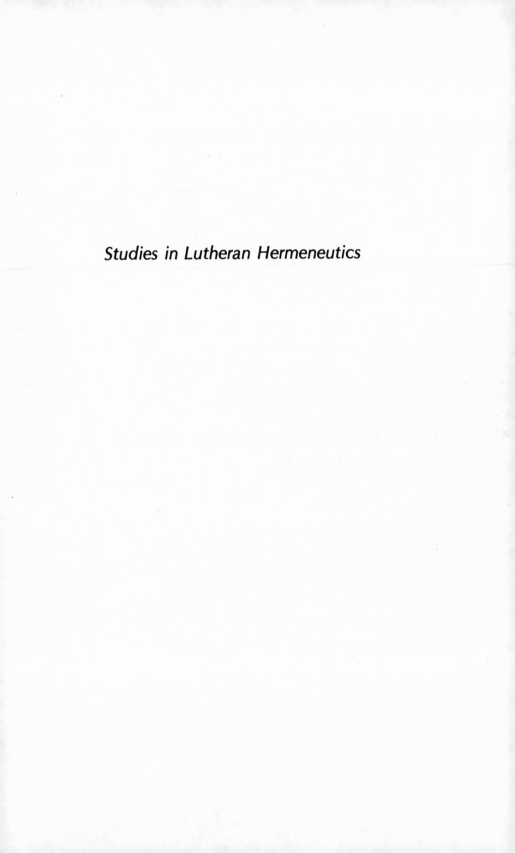

Studies in Lutheran Hermeneutics

STUDIES
in
LUTHERAN
HERMENEUTICS

edited by
JOHN REUMANN

in collaboration with
SAMUEL H. NAFZGER
and
HAROLD H. DITMANSON

97706

FORTRESS PRESS   PHILADELPHIA

COPYRIGHT © 1979 BY FORTRESS PRESS

Library of Congress Cataloging in Publication Data

Main entry under title:

Studies in Lutheran hermeneutics.

    1.   Bible—Hermeneutics—Addresses, essays, lectures.
2. Theology, Lutheran—Addresses, essays, lectures.
I. Reumann, John Henry Paul. II. Nafzger, Samuel H.
III. Ditmanson, Harold H.
BS476.S84   220.6′3   78-14673
ISBN 0-8006-0534-9

7408K78   Printed in the United States of America   1–534

Contents

Contents

III. METHODS OF INTERPRETATION—
THE HISTORICAL-CRITICAL METHOD AS HERMENEUTIC?

Preface

PAUL D. OPSAHL

Executive Director
Division of Theological Studies
of the Lutheran Council in the U.S.A.
New York, New York

The Division of Theological Studies of the Lutheran Council in the U.S.A. has existed since 1967 to help Lutherans in America "grow together theologically."[1] It shares in a particularly significant way one of the purposes of the entire Lutheran Council, which is "to seek to achieve theological consensus in a systematic and continuing way on the basis of Scripture and the witness of the Lutheran Confessions."[2] To accomplish this goal, the Division is mandated to undertake programs of study and research in areas of concern in contemporary Christianity and in areas where the attainment of a specifically Lutheran consensus is desirable.

Early in its history (1968) the Division launched a series of six regional conferences on a subject considered critical for the faith and life of the church—hermeneutics, or how we understand and use Scripture. Discussion of the general theme at each of those conferences was opened up by papers presented on methods in studying the biblical texts today, the authority of the biblical texts today, and the hermeneutical problem in communicating the texts today.[3] Although no volume of essays was published at the conclusion of this study series, some of the papers appeared individually in theological journals.[4]

The Division did not return to a special study of hermeneutics until 1975. In the meantime, however, problems of scriptural interpretation surfaced repeatedly in a number of other studies. This was particularly true in a series of conferences on "The Function of Doctrine and Theology in Light of the Unity of the Church" convened by the Division between 1972 and 1977 and involving representatives of the participating churches.[5] Among other things, that study reflected differences which had developed among Lutherans in the United States on "the nature, function, and legitimacy of the historical-critical method of biblical interpretation." In this study process, theologians representing The American Lutheran Church (ALC) and the Lutheran Church in America (LCA) affirmed the appropriateness of this method. Representatives of the Lutheran Church—Missouri Synod (LCMS), on the other hand, rejected its legitimacy.[6]

Hermeneutical issues had gained prominence among Lutherans in America in recent years, especially through the conflicts within the Lutheran Church—Missouri Synod and the appearance of "A Statement of Scriptural and Confessional Principles."[7] While the understanding and use of Scripture came to be of burning interest within the LCMS itself, the issue became increasingly crucial also for relationships between the LCMS and other Lutheran churches in the United States.

In 1975 the Division began its second major consideration of hermeneutics. To help shape a possible study program Karlfried Froehlich of Princeton Theological Seminary was invited to present a paper on hermeneutical problems confronting Lutherans. A study committee of the Division consisting of John Reumann (LCA), Samuel H. Nafzger (LCMS), and Harold H. Ditmanson (ALC) was then given special responsibility for developing, with staff, an entire study process.[8]

It was early decided that Division committee members and staff should involve themselves fully in this project and not simply administer a study program done by others. Therefore, in addition to three national conferences to which the Division invited participants from the church bodies, theological forum discussions within the Division took place at several of its regular meetings.[9] Papers presented and discussed at Division forums (f) and at the national conferences (c) included the following:

I. *Lectionary (Canon) as Hermeneutic:* James A. Sanders (f), Claremont School of Theology, Claremont; Victor R. Gold (f), Pacific Lutheran Theological Seminary, Berkeley; Arland J. Hultgren (c), Luther Theological Seminary, Saint Paul; Stanley D. Schneider (c), Saint Paul's Lutheran Church, Toledo; Carl L. Bornmann (c), Saint John's Lutheran Church, Luxemburg, Wis.

II. *Confessional Propria as Hermeneutic:* Horace D. Hummel (f),

Concordia Seminary, Saint Louis; Edwin D. Freed (f), Gettysburg College, Gettysburg; Warren A. Quanbeck (f), Luther Theological Seminary, Saint Paul; Robert H. Fischer (f), Lutheran School of Theology at Chicago; Foster R. McCurley (c), Lutheran Theological Seminary at Philadelphia; Joseph A. Burgess (c), Lutheran Theological Seminary at Gettysburg; Ralph A. Bohlmann (c), Concordia Seminary, Saint Louis.

III. *Methods of Interpretation:* George W. E. Nickelsburg, Jr. (f), School of Religion, University of Iowa, Iowa City; Ronald M. Hals (f), Trinity Lutheran Seminary, Columbus; Walter A. Maier (f), Concordia Theological Seminary, Fort Wayne; David L. Tiede (c), Luther Theological Seminary, Saint Paul; James W. Voelz (c), Concordia Theological Seminary, Fort Wayne; Duane A. Priebe (c), Wartburg Theological Seminary, Dubuque; Kurt E. Marquart (c), Concordia Theological Seminary, Fort Wayne; Martin H. Scharlemann (c), Concordia Seminary, Saint Louis; Donald H. Juel (c), Luther Theological Seminary, Saint Paul.

The Division of Theological Studies realizes that it is not possible to issue a statement of consensus at this time in an area that is still so sensitive and controversial. Yet it feels that the materials produced in this study process can be of real importance to contemporary theology in America. Therefore the Division authorized the publication of these papers and commissioned introductory essays by the editorial group of John Reumann, Professor of New Testament, Lutheran Theological Seminary at Philadelphia; Samuel H. Nafzger, Executive Secretary, LCMS Commission on Theology and Church Relations; and Harold H. Ditmanson, Professor of Religion, Saint Olaf College, Northfield, Minnesota. It is hoped that this volume will help create the climate and provide clarification and insight for continued discussion in which Lutherans take seriously one another's commitment to Scripture and the witness of the Confessions.

NOTES

1. See the "Statement of Purpose" developed by the Standing Committee of the Division of Theological Studies of the Lutheran Council in the U.S.A. in 1969 and 1970, printed in the Division minutes for 28–29 March 1974 as Exhibit C-1.

2. Lutheran Council Constitution, Article IV.

3. Essayists included Edgar M. Krentz, Robert W. Bertram, Walter J. Bartling, and Norman C. Habel of the Lutheran Church—Missouri Synod; John Reumann, Jack L. Clark, and Arnold E. Carlson of the Lutheran Church in

America; Ronald M. Hals, Duane A. Priebe, and Wendell W. Frerichs of The American Lutheran Church.

4. Edgar Krentz, "A Survey of Trends and Problems in Biblical Interpretation," *Concordia Theological Monthly* 40, no. 5 (May 1969): 276–93; John Reumann, "Methods in Studying the Biblical Text Today," *Concordia Theological Monthly* 40, no. 10 (November 1969): 655–81; Duane A. Priebe, "Communicating the Text Today," *Dialog* 7 (Autumn 1968): 266–74.

5. The report and papers from the study "The Function of Doctrine and Theology in Light of the Unity of the Church" have been printed in the "Studies" series of the Division of Theological Studies, Lutheran Council in the U.S.A. (New York: Lutheran Council in the U.S.A., 1978), and are available from the Division, 360 Park Ave. South, New York, N.Y. 10010.

6. Ibid., p. 11.

7. The study edition of "A Statement . . ." was published in 1972, and is available from the Commission on Theology and Church Relations of the LCMS, 500 North Broadway, St. Louis, Mo. 63102.

8. Other standing committee members of the Division of Theological Studies who have been involved in this study process include: ALC—Charles S. Anderson, Joseph A. Burgess; LCA—Lloyd E. Sheneman, H. George Anderson; LCMS—Ralph A. Bohlmann, Theodore F. Nickel, Karl L. Barth. Staff included Paul D. Opsahl and William G. Rusch.

9. The national conferences on hermeneutics were held 2–3 June 1976; 10–11 December 1977; and 3–5 May 1977. Division theological forum discussions on hermeneutics took place at the regular standing committee meetings in March and October of 1975, March and October of 1976, and March of 1977.

The Lutheran "Hermeneutics Study":
An Overview and Personal Appraisal

JOHN REUMANN

Professor of New Testament
Lutheran Theological Seminary
Philadelphia, Pennsylvania

"Lutherans Split," the headline screamed. A one-sentence story followed on the religion page of the *Philadelphia Evening Bulletin* for 29 April, 1978:

> BUENOS AIRES—(AP)—The Lutheran Diocese of Costa Rica and Panama has decided to sever relations with the Lutheran Church—Missouri Synod, saying it employs "rigid and unrealistic concepts of biblical interpretation," a Lutheran agency reports.

Biblical interpretation and splits—if such they be—over how people use Scripture is what this volume is about. It is a case study of U.S. Lutherans during the years 1975–78.

The Diocese of Costa Rica and Panama is a tiny body with just three congregations and four church workers, in the small Council of Lutheran Churches in Central America and Panama, an agency of the Lutheran Church—Missouri Synod for mission in that part of the world. But the issue of interpretation of the Bible is a big one, and it has wracked Missouri Synod–related churches in Papua New Guinea, Hong Kong, India, and throughout the world—and the parent body itself. In the United States the issue led to the formation of the Association of Evangelical Lutheran Churches (AELC), which is made up of more than 240 local congregations numbering some 110,000 members that left the Missouri Synod. The AELC joined the Lutheran Council in the U.S.A. in 1978.

While biblical interpretation, or hermeneutics, was not the only issue,

1

it is the issue at the heart of what has been called a U.S. Lutheran civil war that split what once was the largest seminary in the United States, Concordia Seminary in Saint Louis, and led for the first time to a conservative "takeover," as journalists put it, of a major denomination.[1]

The chapters that follow show that even when Lutherans disagree vigorously over issues at the heart of things they can continue to discuss fervently and explore together under the aegis of the Lutheran Council in the U.S.A. (LC/USA). They thus exhibit scholarly and fraternal theological endeavors that may be of help to other groups facing similar problems or to those who need to face or are unaware of these issues in the relationship of the historic Christian faith to how Scripture is to be read today. Needless to say, these pages may be of help to Lutherans themselves and of immense value to students and all who deal with Scripture.

A MORE-THAN-LUTHERAN PROBLEM

Hermeneutics is not, of course, a peculiarly Lutheran discipline. The "art and science of interpreting" is widespread and very much current, even if the traditional term is not always used. Columbia University in New York has among its University Seminars one entitled "Hermeneutics," which is secular and not religious at all. The more modern term *communications* picks up many of the traditional hermeneutical concerns.

Hermeneutics, in fact, applies to any document from the past. Where religious writings are concerned, however, especially writings venerated highly or deemed inspired by a community, debate is most likely to arise. How to interpret the ancient Torah has long been a Jewish concern, and how to apply and reapply papal or council statements is a matter of perennial Roman Catholic interest. It is historical criticism and the refinements of hermeneutical method that have introduced new dimensions into the age-old process.

The so-called historical-critical method has arisen especially in the last century or two, with widely agreed-upon rules for interrogating documents from the past to get at their intent and meaning more fully and clearly.[2] As a method, it has been regarded as an ally or a threat, or both, to biblical understanding. There are of course different definitions of the historical-critical method, and some of the essayists in this volume seek to identify what the term means to them. Some practitioners seemingly stress one adjective in "historical-critical" more than the other. To be "critical" of the Bible is precisely what bothers some. Historical-critical methods—plural—would be more accurate, others say, and the debate then is over which methods are acceptable and which are not, and with what degree of rigor, for believers. The fact is that, however defined, the historical-critical methods have affected the way religious texts, such as the Bible, are read, and there are varying opinions on the appropriateness of this widely used methodology. In the pages that follow, American Lutherans will speak pro and con, conservatively, radically, and moderately, on these methods and what they presuppose.

The discussion about historical criticism and the Bible which Lutherans here are baring to others is not, however, an isolated dispute in one denomination or one nation. The controversy rages, recognized or not, in many churches and countries, as a few examples will show.

To begin with, it is not simply a rerun of the Fundamentalist-Modernist controversy of the 1920s, as if Lutherans isolated in linguistic-ethnic ghettos were catching up belatedly half a century later. For one thing, all parties in this Lutheran debate espouse a confessional position reflecting the faith affirmed in the symbolical books of the Reformation period, something decidely not true of the 1920s liberals. Indeed the "radical party" in Missouri, known as the moderates, will certainly seem conservative to many Christians, and most Lutheran voices in these discussions will sound far from avant-garde. The simple factual difference is that in the 1970s "conservatives" were not forced out to form new seminaries and denominational alignments but rather came to control almost every leadership position and institution in the Missouri Synod.

On the surface a parallel case might be seen in the polemic voiced by Walter Wink in his *The Bible in Human Transformation: Toward a New Paradigm for Biblical Study*.[3] His now famous opening sentence reads: "Historical biblical criticism is bankrupt." It is, he goes on—and this from an associate professor then at New York's Union Theological Seminary—"no longer able to accomplish its avowed purpose . . . so to interpret the Scriptures that the past becomes alive and illumines our present with new possibilities for personal and social transformation."[4] (That of course is already a hermeneutical program.) But the "shift in paradigm" Wink calls for, so as to effect our transformation, still employs, along with a communal, psychoanalytical approach, the full panoply of all "the criticisms"—form, source, textual, and redaction.[5] So this personalistic line is not raising the same hermeneutical questions that Lutherans face in this volume.

A clearer parallel can be seen in what has been occurring within American Protestantism, especially among the currently significant Evangelicals. When the United Presbyterian Church in the U.S.A. put forward its "Confession of 1967" one of its architects, Edward A. Dowey, Jr., said that while church theology need not reflect every ripple of history it "must respond when it crosses over a major watershed"—which Oswald T. Allis took to be "evolution, higher criticism, development in theology."[6] What is surprising is not that Auburn or Union Seminaries in New York or Princeton Seminary should have accepted some or all of "the higher criticism" as a method of biblical studies (that was already decided in the case of C. A. Briggs in the 1890s or the exodus of J. Gresham Machen from Princeton in the 1920s) but that conservative schools of the Southern Baptist Convention or Fuller Theological Seminary in California should now embrace enough of the historical-critical approach to have their orthodoxy impugned.

The Battle for the Bible is what Harold Lindsell, a former editor of *Christianity Today*, entitled his broadside in favor of biblical inerrancy.[7] In case after case, he contends, individuals and groups in Southern Baptist circles, North Park Theological Seminary (of the Evangelical Covenant Church, a denomination of Swedish background), and Fuller Theological Seminary, in altering its statement of faith, represent a trend away from inerrancy brought on by use of the historical-critical method. Lindsell also devotes a chapter to the Missouri Synod battle capped by a long quotation from Walter A. Maier on the "blasphemous views arising from the modern, scholarly use of historical-critical methodology."[8]

Alongside these Protestant examples a similar story can be told of the impact of modern biblical scholarship in the Roman Catholic church and the subsequent reaction of its right wing against the Bible-study movement and the use of historical tools. Familiar is the story of how Pius XII's encyclical *Divino afflante spiritu* opened the way in 1943 for the beginning of more precise scriptural study using methods and techniques that the Protestant world had been sharpening for decades. Much of the fruit of Vatican II can be said to be a result of advances in biblical studies among Catholics. One could among Catholics speak of "our new approach to the Bible," though there was a period in the early sixties when some sought to turn back the clock.[9]

The Jerome Biblical Commentary (1968) provided a landmark work "written by Roman Catholics according to the principles of modern biblical criticism."[10] With his 1977 study *The Birth of the Messiah*, Raymond E. Brown, in taking up the narratives of Jesus' birth and infancy, has traversed what he calls "the last frontiers to be crossed in the relentless advance of the scientific (critical) approach to the Gospels."[11] Yet it is also well-known that publications of the Catholic right inveigh against such work—condemning it as "Protestant"—while rightist Protestant papers reprint such condemnations approvingly!

Our debate rages not only in U.S. Protestant-Evangelical circles and in Roman Catholicism but also, most surprisingly, in German theological and church circles. Of course German scholarship, perhaps more so than scholarship anywhere else in the world, is perpetually reflecting upon and seeking to improve its methodology. One could cite a number of articles proposing reexamination of the Synoptic problem or of the form-critical method. One can also cite discussions that go farther and point to the limitations of the historical-critical method and the lack of clarity about the goal of hermeneutics.[12] But we have in mind debate that goes further and seeks a yes or no answer to the question about historical-critical method.

Peter Stuhlmacher, a pupil of Ernst Käsemann, the well-known German exegete in New Testament studies, has been in the forefront of those contending for the indispensability of the historical-critical method as a tool in scientific study of texts.[13] That he distinguishes such criticism from theological acknowledgment of truth and sets it within the framework of biblical theology and places the whole within the framework of the Third Article of the Creed is not enough for some. Gerhard Maier, who once did a dissertation at Tübingen (where Stuhlmacher is now professor) on man's free will according to various Jewish groups prior to Paul, has undertaken a frontal assault in a book entitled *The End of the Historical-Critical Method* (1974).[14] Its English translation has been enthusiastically recommended by a Missouri Synod professor Eugene F. Klug, who holds that the historical-critical method buries the Word of God because it lets scholars "determine what that Word or 'message' is" and thus creates a "canon within the canon," a "Word of God . . . separated from the Scriptural text."[15]

Maier's book in actuality does focus on that principle, found in Luther, of a canon within the canon. Maier contends that exegetes never agree on what that is (Luther had shown a preference for certain books in the New Testament as central and he demoted others as marginal) and that systematicians retreat into "spiritual experience." Besides, the Confessions do not themselves endorse a canon within the canon. Therefore one needs to approach the whole of Scripture, he goes on, by means of a "historical-*biblical* method." When one adds, however, that this method for Maier includes finding the text (through textual criticism), translation, historical background, and attention to "other (contemporary) religions surrounding Scripture," and even literary criticism and form criticism and classification within the epochs of salvation history,[16] Maier's approach is not far from that of many who would call themselves practitioners of the historical-critical method.

Stuhlmacher, in setting forth his own program in *Historical Criticism and Theological Interpretation of Scripture*, has incorporated a reply to Maier.[17] He scores Maier for rejecting any inner canon while accepting "Christ as the center and the heart of scripture," since Luther's test for measuring books in the Bible was whether or not they "bring Christ" (*Christum treiben*) to the reader. Above all, he holds that "Maier's half-hearted dependence on historical criticism will bring the expositors he leads into the greatest difficulties"; how can one be against form criticism but allow investigations into hymns and parables?[18]

The discussion in Tübingen—and at stake is the practice of historical-critical theology in the heartland of German Pietism in Württemberg—continues.[19] It not only shows how the issue exists in German theology, but also points to the underlying question of the scriptural canon.

SHAPING THE LUTHERAN COUNCIL STUDY

Given the many issues interrelated under "hermeneutics," how to forge a study for U.S. Lutherans on what was a problem for other Christians too was the task faced by the Lutheran Council's Division of Theological Studies in 1975.

Lines had already been drawn in 1972 when the president of the Lutheran Church—Missouri Synod, J. A. O. Preus, issued "A Statement of Scriptural and Confessional Principles." (The longest section, Section IV, on Holy Scripture, and other portions will be discussed below.) "A Statement . . ." was subsequently declared "in all its parts, to be Scriptural and in accord with the Lutheran Confessions" by the 1973 Missouri Synod convention in New Orleans, and its use led to the disruption at Concordia Seminary in February 1974, when a large majority of faculty and students left the Saint Louis campus to form "Seminex," a seminary in exile. The Missouri Synod's Commission on Theology and Church Relations (CTCR) had published an annotated study edition of "A

6

Statement . . ." in 1972 and also "A Comparative Study of Varying Contemporary Approaches to Biblical Interpretation" in 1973.[20] The latter describes in parallel columns the preferred "Historical Grammatical (Traditional) View" and "The Historical-Critical View" (in "Radical" and "Mediating" versions). The year 1975 saw publication of another CTCR report on "The Inspiration of Scripture," as well as of Paul G. Bretscher's book, *After the Purifying*, which is written from a different ("moderate") point of view.[21] Bretscher argued that some Missouri Lutherans like himself had come to see *the gospel* as the Word of God and not all of Scripture infallibly and automatically. (His view is often dismissed by others in Missouri as "gospel reductionism," that is, reducing Scripture to the gospel.) Thus we did not lack for statements or controversies on the Scripture issue.[22]

Our actual starting point on 21 March 1975 lay in a scholarly analysis by Karlfried Froehlich, Professor of Church History at Princeton Seminary, of a controverted verse in the Reformation and the history of the papacy and the exegetical history of that verse. The standing committee (which consists of three persons from each of the major Lutheran bodies in the United States—The American Lutheran Church [ALC], the Lutheran Church in America [LCA], and the Lutheran Church—Missouri Synod [LCMS]) had for some time included a "theological forum" in its semiannual meetings. Froehlich's paper was intended to provide an initial airing of hermeneutical problems confronting Lutherans. A layman of the LCA teaching in a non-Lutheran seminary, he had done his doctoral dissertation at Basel under Oscar Cullmann on medieval exegesis of the Matthean passage about Peter and the rock on which the church will be built (Matt. 16:18).[23] Co-author of a widely used New Testament introduction,[24] he was also knowledgeable about theology over the centuries and had specialized in the history of biblical interpretation. Froehlich was known personally to several members of the standing committee and staff for his contributions to the Lutheran-Catholic dialogue in the United States.

In his paper, to illustrate the problems of Lutheran hermeneutics, Froehlich focused on Matthew 16:18 as it has been assessed by representative exegetes, measured by three interests that the Reformation inherited from the Middle Ages and spread into the modern world. Those interests are (1) the literal sense, (2) the clarity of Scripture, and (3) historical continuity—exegesis is to bring out the true meaning always there. Broadly speaking, the history of exegesis can be divided into two periods: the "premodern" period, covering up to the seventeenth century or so, a long span of centuries when the emphasis was on the divine authorship of Scripture and often on the allegorical sense; and the "modern" period, where interpreters stress the human authorship and the nonallegorical, literal sense of Scripture.

Premodern interpreters of Matthew 16:18 considered by Froehlich were Robert Bellarmine (1542–1621), Jesuit theologian of the Counter Reformation and "Doctor of the Church"; and Martin Luther (1483–1546), Reformer, who shares many of the same presuppositions. Modern interpreters (all "Lutheran" or, in European terms, *evangelisch*) considered were H. J. Holtzmann (1832–1910), professor at Heidelberg and Strasbourg; Adolf von Harnack (1851–1930), church historian, Berlin; Albert Schweitzer (1875–1965), Strasbourg 1902–12; Ethelbert Stauffer (1902–   ), Erlangen professor; Oscar Cullmann (1902–   ), Basel and the Sorbonne; and Theodore Hoyer (1883–1963), to represent a Missouri Synod view. (It was difficult to locate in print a detailed "traditionalist" treatment of the passage from this perspective.) The version included in this volume limits itself to five of these interpreters.

The chief finding in the paper was that presence of a common view on inspired Scripture and a divine author did *not* prevent rifts in the sixteenth century, while stress on the human author has made the exegete more humble in his goals and more aware of biblical variety and therefore perhaps of the need to live together with some nonuniformity. Above all, Froehlich raised the question of the scriptural author's "horizon" (which includes historical-literary and theological factors). But inevitably in our discussion the *Echtheitsproblem* arose ("Did Jesus historically speak the words in 16:18 at Caesarea Phillippi?"),[25] as well as questions concerning the authoritativeness of the final text (that the Missouri Synod's statement on biblical interpretation avers) and whether "the Lutheran view" extends also to the "horizon of the Confessions" about Scripture.

The actual design for the LC/USA study on hermeneutics, planned in the summer of 1975, was one of staged advance into the thicket of problems. As noted above in the Preface, it was first of all agreed that members of the standing committee would themselves tackle a topic with presentation by an outside expert and then share in a nationwide conference involving fifteen to twenty invited specialists on the topic. These invited participants varied with the subject matter, but there was a core of half a dozen invited to all three two-day (or longer) meetings.[26] A second major decision was to tackle the subject of the lectionary as a hermeneutical influence first, then the Confessions and their influence, and finally methods of historical interpretation. Underlying the whole was awareness of the "canon question" and the fact that all three stages deal with hermeneutics. Thus, in outline:

	FALL 1975	SPRING 1976	FALL 1976	SPRING 1977
Standing Committee	Lectionary, Canon	Confessional Propria	Methods of Interpreting	Methods of Interpreting
National Conference	—	Lectionary	Confessional Propria	Methods of Interpreting

Committee sessions took place in October and March in New York, national conferences in December and June in Chicago. The subcommittee monitored the process throughout and made changes in its course, such as scheduling additional papers on "methods" for the committee in March 1977 and examining publication possibilities. While the option of three "program packets" for clergy groups was considered, the final choice was for this volume of selected essays, with interpretative chapters by committee members.

The decision to begin at the first session with something other than what everyone recognized to be the neuralgic issue (namely, application of the historical-critical method to the New Testament) was not just a pragmatic one. We chose not merely to honor the possibility that emotions and divisions might run highest here but also to recognize that (1) the pericopes are where the average Lutheran churchgoer week-in and week-out is confronted with Scripture and that where the average clergyperson must expound them is in connection with the lectionary and its "shape," and that (2) the role of the Confessions and their dominant themes in biblical interpretation is an issue for Lutherans. The attractiveness of the topic of lectionary as hermeneutic was enhanced by the fact that Lutherans by that time were completing the first full round of use of a new three-year cycle of lessons based on the Roman Catholic *Ordo Lectionum Missae*[27] and it was an appropriate time for appraisal. Furthermore, enough questions existed about how the Confessions themselves are to be interpreted and about how their themes hold up and apply in scriptural exegesis today that Confession as hermeneutic seemed to be a necessary topic, as well.[28] There was also a feeling that the

9

historical-critical method should be examined in its application first to noncanonical documents, then as a whole by systematicians for methodology, and finally as applied to each Testament. It was a deliberate decision to mix exegetes, dogmaticians, historians, liturgical experts, and parish clergy throughout the process.

LECTIONARY AS HERMENEUTIC

What is read Sunday after Sunday, year by year, is de facto a canon within the canon for any denomination. The body of scriptural writings bound between two covers is already a hermeneutical given for a church that takes the Bible seriously. We began our study, therefore, with attention to the influence of the pericope system used during the church year which Lutherans share with most liturgical Christians. Consistently underlying the study was the "canon question."

To begin, James A. Sanders, then Professor of Biblical Studies at Union Theological Seminary, New York, spoke to the standing committee on 10 October 1975 on the nature and function of canon.[29] A good deal of investigation and new discoveries such as those at Qumran have raised real questions about the traditional view or even the traditional view of critics on how the canon of the Hebrew Bible was shaped (at the Council of Jamnia, so-called, around 80 C.E.) and how the twenty-seven New Testament books were selected (commonly assumed to be on the basis of apostolic authorship, common usage, kerygmatic congruity, and episcopal agreement, by the fourth century). Morton Smith, for example, has stressed the political factors that went into selection of the Old Testament books.[30] A. C. Sundberg, Jr., warns against viewing Jamnia like a medieval Christian church council and feels key steps in canon making were taken later than most Christians assume.[31] Sanders himself had earlier directed attention to the beginning of the canonizing process rather than to its end result of "what's in, what's out,"[32] and in a recent article he had argued that the whole law-gospel relationship ought to be looked at from a different viewpoint.[33] He suggests that the term *torah* always encompassed *mythos* and *ethos* ("story" and "ethics"), giving identity and life-style, and that what Paul and early Christianity did was add a new chapter to the Torah "story" while no longer holding the Torah legal codes as absolutely valid for all time.

Sanders's presentation to the Lutheran group stressed canon as the community's "identity story" that issues in *ethos*, a Torah story which must continue to speak by being adaptable for life. Traditions in the community thus alternate between stability (fixity) and adaptability (to meet new needs), and hermeneutics is the mid-term in the axis between those two poles. Judaism adapted its Torah by adding oral laws or by principles of interpretation that might bypass the plain meaning so as to address new situations (Hillel's seven rules). Other Jewish groups stressed the haggadic side, new ways of telling the old story. Paul grew up seeing Torah as halakah, but came to see it, upon conversion, as a new Haggadah culminating in Christ.

This lead for rethinking law and gospel was not developed in ensuing conferences, nor was Sanders's emphasis on the varying shape of the emerging canon over the centuries. (It makes a difference whether one tells the epic story with David and Jerusalem as climax, or Joshua and the conquest, or Sinai and the giving of the law! The J and E accounts presumably thus differed from the present pentateuchal shape of the canon.) Sanders also made clear, however, that his interest in the tradition and its development did not mean he was not interested in historical, underlying events. It was a regret to all that some of the issues opened up here were never further explored later.

A second paper to the standing committee on 11 October introduced the subject of the lectionary. Victor R. Gold, Professor of Old Testament at the Pacific Lutheran Theological Seminary, Berkeley, California, had been a member of the subcommittee on the lectionary of the Inter-Lutheran Commission on Worship (ILCW). Teaching assignments on the use of the newly appointed lessons have often taken him among parish clergy in the West. His unpublished remarks to the theological forum of the Division of Theological Studies emphasized as context for canon the worshiping community—which is where the lectionary puts Scripture again. Alongside this are the modern concerns of the three-year cycle of readings: (1) It is ecumenical, used by Catholics, Episcopalians, Lutherans, and others. (2) The Old Testament has been belatedly emphasized, with its covenant and *social*-ethical themes. (3) Theologically, creation receives new emphasis and apocalyptic is employed at the end of the church year to show deliverance aspects.

Gold applauded reading of the Gospels so that Matthew, Mark, and Luke are used one each year. This enables people to see that there was variety and development after A.D. 30 in the way the story of Jesus was told. Likewise with the reading of the Passion in separate accounts rather than in a conflated "history." The Epistle choices, read in sequence from a letter, preserve their integrity, but commentators, even in the Fortress Press series "Proclamation: Aids for Interpreting the Lessons of the Church Year," unfortunately try to line them up with the Gospel for the Day, as in past approaches. The integrity of the Old Testament, however, is violated by being used as a support structure for the weekly Gospel selections.[34] While they are an improvement, the Old Testament lessons have a long way to go. There are unfortunate omissions, such as Amos 3:1–8, and the Apocrypha should have been used by Lutherans.[35]

The lectionary is thus a denominational "canon within the canon," this one chosen basically by Rome on the principle of getting before the people more Scripture from all parts of the Bible.[36] (To this extent it conforms to the wishes of those who want all parts of the canonical books read periodically.) Yet the calendar with holy days interferes with the planned sequence[37] in a Christocentric church year (rather than a Trinitarian one). Those revising worship forms among Lutherans have been prejudiced in favor of the three-year system, yet some regret that the tradition of a one-year lectionary and commonality with European Lutherans and the Church of England are thereby given up. Gold said that if as an Old Testament scholar he could make his own choices he would lay more stress on God/man/world interrelationships, covenant theology, and salvation history, and not opt for a continuous reading of the Old Testament.

THE FIRST NATIONAL LUTHERAN HERMENEUTICS CONFERENCE

This discussion and other publications[38] set the stage for the first LC/USA hermeneutics conference at Des Plaines, Illinois, 2–3 June, 1976. Twenty-eight persons were present,[39] and three major papers were heard.

"The Church Year as a Context for Exegesis" may seem a surprising topic to some, but the fact is that in liturgical churches the reading of a passage of Scripture on a certain festival automatically provides a specific setting in which it is heard. Carl L. Bornmann, at that time pastor of Saint Philip Lutheran Church (LCMS), Detroit, an inner-city, interracial congregation, addressed this initial theme. (1) He endorsed the church year in its specificity, even though some liturgical experts such as Pius Parsch have regarded it as "an abstraction of seasons and cycles."[40] (2) Lectionaries, he went on, should "serve the preacher who follows the church year, but not restrict him." The preacher asks the theme of a

Sunday in the church year and then considers the pericopes assigned in light of that theme from God's Word. One had the impression here of a hermeneutical circle, with the church year influencing interpretation of Scripture but also Scripture (especially the chronology of events in Luke-Acts) determining the church year. It is the church year, however, and its themes which emerge as guide for approaching Scripture. Furthermore, in Bornmann's judgment the new three-year lectionary plays down Jesus' birth, circumcision, and the coming of the wise men in favor of the baptism of our Lord; it eliminates "pre-Lent" (the "-gesima Sundays"), no longer emphasizes repentance in Lent, and minimizes the historicity and importance of the ascension.

The longest section of the Bornmann paper dealt with (3) exegesis for the church year context. Here use was made of the suggestions developed by Reginald H. Fuller in "Preparing the Homily,"[41] namely: understanding the rationale of the church year; text, translation, literary criticism, key words, your own paraphrase; then *Predigtmeditation.* Bornmann found that the three levels, or strata, in a Gospel text which modern scholarship so customarily seeks—the theology of the evangelist, the tradition, and authentic Jesus-material (so Fuller, and the *Jerome Biblical Commentary*)—were not in harmony with the context of the church year, for the church year "assumes that God's grace to people in the past is truthfully and reliably brought to us through the text of sacred Scripture. It does not allow for levels of authenticity or degrees of truth." Just as the church year protects the congregation from "the personal whims and pet peeves" of an individual preacher, so a parish must be protected from "the whims and peeves . . . of the commentators and their theories." Examples offered on the lessons for Holy Innocents Day[42] and Easter made clear a determination to allow "no human speculation" to "pass judgment on the textual truth," though the church year "would urge" the pastor "to harmonize the various accounts wherever the text is not done an injustice." This paper has been published with minor revisions in *Concordia Journal* 4 (November 1978): 246–51.

One seldom hears so firm a statement favoring "one Christ, one faith, one church year" (even in the Free Church tradition, of course, there may be formative, interpretative effects from the Fourth of July or Mother's Day on the use of texts) or using the church year to exclude biblical criticism, lest it distort and make things uncertain. Most participants were unconvinced, however, that the church year is so high and holy a thing that we can use it to block out the plain intention of a text.

Stanley D. Schneider, who spoke next, taught homiletics at Evangelical

Lutheran Seminary, Columbus, Ohio, at the time he served on the ILCW lectionary subcommittee. Little had he dreamed at the time, he said, that he would by his own choice be "using the lectionary as a parish pastor rather than as a source for classroom assignments."[43] His paper "The Lectionary as a Context for Exegesis" reflected that transition. Schneider began with (1) the purpose of a lectionary ("to provide an orderly series of readings which give good coverage to the whole of Scripture and which provide a basis out of which the proclamation in the form of the sermon grows") and the need for exegesis, even for properly reading the lessons. But what kind of exegesis?

The Schneider paper went on to (2) the principles employed with lectionary pericopes. The traditional historic Western lectionary seemingly had a dogmatic principle of fitting Scripture to the church year, often by fourfold (allegorical) interpretation. The text was not heard in its own voice. All too often, even in modern times, there has been no similarity between what is preached and what the text itself says. One result has been "topical" preaching, and another has been biblical illiteracy. In the new lectionary there is less of the thematic, dogmatic emphasis (e.g., of the church year) because there is more semicontinuous reading of Scripture, especially in the nonfestival half of the year. The latter influence was attributed in part to the influence of redaction-criticism in study of the Gospels. A good trade, Schneider felt, had been to give up a weekly theme in favor of the integrity of scriptural continuity! (3) Praxis or use of the lectionary by the parish pastor was described in very practical terms, including the limited resources (compared with a seminary campus) and the need for study teams among the clergy, even ecumenically, each week. The Epistle lessons might be a vehicle for parish teaching ministries.

The remark which perhaps stirred the most discussion was a passing observation in the paper that the fundamentalist and certain New Testament scholars—those scholars who seek to strip off accretions by the evangelists, to work back through the tradition, and to arrive at the historical-Jesus level—are really akin. Both assume "that the only way to communicate the truth is by factual data. What isn't factual isn't valid." Both assume that the "historical Jesus" and his utterances are somehow more inspired and authoritative than redacted verses. (Perhaps some of Joachim Jeremias's efforts after the *ipsissima vox Jesu,* "the very voice of Jesus," would illustrate what is meant.) Schneider's point was that the emphasis of redaction criticism on "the text as it is" has changed all that. But the remark was occasion for some to emphasize that "facts" mean that "the New Testament accounts happened as described" and for others to wonder about the metaphysics and definition of "fact" in such a stance or about specific cases such as whether Abraham had domesticated camels (Gen. 12:16) or whether there were Philistines in his day (Gen. 21:32).

The final paper at the conference, "Hermeneutical Tendencies in the Three-Year Lectionary," included in this volume, was given by Arland J. Hultgren, then Associate Professor of Religious Studies at Wagner College, Staten Island, New York. Some of his earlier publications on the lectionary have already been noted (see n. 38). His observations on the three-year pericope system and his discussion of tendencies in lectionary and current biblical scholarship reflected his wide reading and personal involvement in workshops on the subject. The questions Hultgren posed are worthy of further consideration.

At the close of the conference the custom was begun of having the subcommittee chairman attempt a summary. I did it somewhat along the lines sketched above, but I also used the occasion to sharpen questions and propose ideas. (1) It was obvious that we had already gotten into confessional themes (like law and gospel) and matters of (historical) method. (2) There were objections raised to the new lectionary in principle and in details. Was the old one-year system still not desirable for continuity with past centuries and uniformity with European churches? According to a recent poll, Lutheran pastors electing the three-year lectionary based on the Catholic *Ordo* selected it *not* for ecumenical reasons (because it "is used by churches in addition to Lutheran"—only 7 percent checked that) but because of its wide use of Scripture (51 percent) or because it "brings together main emphasis of the lessons for each Sunday in the best way" (20 percent—a doubtful assumption, however!). Old Testament choices were its weakest point; more use of narrative and of the prophets was desired. At times, traditionalist Roman Catholic views shine through.[44] And the calendar disrupts the scheme.

More important were the questions of exegetical method. The emphasis in *Ordo* Gospel selections on "the book as it stands" and "the final text," rather than any quest for sources or the underlying "historical," authentic facts, should fit directly with the "Stance Statement" on Scripture of the Missouri Synod.[45] But does it? Already the assumption had been voiced that the redacted text is identical with what happened and that no blessings can come by exploring differences or dissonances in

JOHN REUMANN

different accounts. Hence someone asked whether Scripture is "a data bank or proclamation." It had become clear that the calendar and the lectionary are a framework for hermeneutic, if not already hermeneutic in themselves. They are two lenses through which the average preacher examines and employs Scripture, and the means by which most parishioners have regular contact with the Bible.

CONFESSION AS HERMENEUTIC

It was our intention from the outset to face quite honestly the place the eight types of documents in the Lutheran Confessions[46] have in biblical interpretation. Questions on this matter had already begun to appear in the round on lectionary. There also existed a literature on the symbolical books and biblical exegesis.[47] We were particularly interested in Lutheran "propria," or characteristic doctrines[48] and their effects on biblical study.

Such a confessional impact on use of the Bible is by no means confined to Lutherans. All who accept the Apostles' Creed or any traditional statement think they have at hand a development and an interpretation of certain biblical themes,[49] which may influence how the Bible is understood among them. Some denominations place strong emphasis on "the church says," or "the traditions of the fathers," or "the consensus of the faithful," and these statements, traditions, and consensuses must be recorded somewhere in accessible form if they are to have any effect on transmitting the faith of the past and shaping the faith of the future. To one degree or another, Reformed churches make use of the Westminster Confession, the Anglicans have the Thirty-nine Articles, and Roman Catholics look to the decrees of the Council of Trent, Vatican I and II, and papal pronouncements. Some Protestants also have modern statements of faith such as the Presbyterian "Confession of 1967."[50] All these provide clues, guidelines, or expected tracks for biblical exegesis. Even in churches and groups that minimize creeds or say "No creed but Christ" there are nonetheless attitudes, understandings, shared experiences, statements of commitment, or a profile of faith, which serve as a framework for interpreting Scripture.[51] Needless to say, even theologians who fit no one denominational or confessional mold have tendencies, faith commitments, or actual statements that color their uses of Scripture.[52]

The LC/USA hermeneutics project sought in particular to take up the following topics under the heading "Confessions":

16

(1) What are the confessional themes or Lutheran propria (identifying marks or, others would say, peculiarities) that have shaped and/or should shape exegesis?

(2) What is the reciprocal relationship between these propria and Scripture itself? To illustrate: "Justification by grace through faith" is assumed by the Lutheran tradition to be a key to interpreting not only Paul's writings but also the whole New Testament and the rest of Scripture. But is the description of justification in the Confessions or Luther's writings or the later Lutheran fathers true to Paul, let alone to the rest of the New Testament? One need only recall the lively debate among New Testament scholars since Albert Schweitzer about the proper sense(s) of *dikaiosynē tou theou* (the righteousness of God or justification) in Paul—let alone its relation to the sense(s) of the same term in the Confessions—to know that the matter is disputed by (Lutheran) exegetes.[53]

(3) What is the proper hermeneutics of the Confessions? Like Scripture, the creeds and symbolical books are historical documents; how does the historical-critical method apply here?

(4) There was awareness that some attention would have to be paid to subsequent understandings by Lutherans since the Confessions in quasi-confessional doctrinal assertions about Scripture, for example, the Missouri Synod's "A Statement of Scriptural and Confessional Principles."[54]

To plunge into these matters the standing committee of the council's Division of Theological Studies spent an entire day, 19 March 1976, discussing three papers, and part of an additional theological forum on 22 October on a fourth presentation in this area. Two of the four appear in this volume. The other two, which sparked the greater controversy, are summarized here in more detail.

The paper of Horace D. Hummel of Concordia Seminary, Saint Louis, entitled "The Influence of Confessional Themes on Biblical Exegesis," is included in this volume. An appended note calls attention to some of his earlier relevant publications in the area. As Hummel himself says, the applications are drawn especially from his own discipline, Old Testament studies, and as others can attest, the paper reflects the odyssey of one who began his academic career in the Missouri Synod, venturing the views of critical scholarship on, for example, Second Isaiah, and who then taught in ALC and LCA seminaries and Notre Dame University before returning to the Saint Louis faculty. The paper falls into two parts: confessional themes and (Old Testament) applications. For this reason we have placed it in this volume after two more-general treatments that give principles for confessional use of the Bible and before an essay (different in approach) on confessional propria and the Old Testament.

Readers will find in the Hummel paper a good many of the classic Lutheran theological terms, which for those whose Latin is not keen may seem obscure. Hummel argued that "confessional" must mean "having content," the faith which is believed (*fides quae*) and not simply subjective faith by which one believes (*fides qua*). The content can be stated in the form of propositions. We deal with inerrant facts and inspiration of actual words. Because (*quia*)—and not simply "insofar as" (*quatenus*)—the Confessions agree with the Bible, they can serve as norm, though normed by Scripture in turn (*norma normata*, "the norm which is normed by something else"). Theology is to proceed in analogy to "the faith" and not simply be "correlated" to it. The exegete therefore works within limits set by the Confessions, and to step outside these limits is to become no longer Lutheran or confessional. The faith can condemn false doctrine as wrong and damned. (The Augsburg Confession says not only "we hold and teach" but also "our churches condemn. . . .")

Perhaps the most discussion came over the question of whether it is a Lutheran position seemingly to prohibit the Scriptures from norming the Confessions, for in this position the symbolical books seem to dominate exegesis. But, it was replied, the exegete still must examine and check out the "normed norm" of the Confessions by the Bible. Readers will find the paper saying yes and no on a canon within the canon and, from Hummel's Old Testament background, agreeing with Sanders that "Torah" is closer to "gospel" than to "law." The Old Testament is also seen as providing a "third use of the law," as it is put in that inner-Lutheran debate where one use is for civil life, to run political affairs; another is to convince me of my sinfulness; and a third is to guide the redeemed Christian. Hummel thus drew on Old Testament law to exclude ordination of women.[55]

The second paper the standing committee heard was entitled "Influence of the Doctrine of Justification by Faith on Pauline Exegesis" and given by Edwin D. Freed of the Gettysburg College Religion Department, Gettysburg, Pennsylvania. Freed stirred up a hornet's nest by arguing that the doctrine of justification by faith, "if not in error, is at least inadequate" for understanding Paul. We have already noted above the sort of debate among Pauline scholars upon which such a stance builds, but Freed's particular development of the evidence struck some as a misreading characteristic of the liberal theology a generation ago.

Freed began with Joachim Jeremias's well-known book *The Central Message of the New Testament*.[56] That central message, in Jeremias's analysis, turned out to be "justified by God's grace through faith," according to both Jesus and Paul. Freed preferred "several central messages" in the New Testament, and particularly in Paul the proper summary should be that "the convert's initial justification is a gift of God by his grace but that his ultimate salvation depends on his right moral and ethical life." "Good works . . . for ultimate salvation" is seen as the more central message in Paul, and Freed thus agreed with others who have thought Paul's greatest contribution lay in ethics and "moral probity."[57] If Jeremias stresses Romans 3:28 (and supports Luther's addition of *allein*, "justified by faith *alone*"), Freed countered with Romans 2:5-13, especially 2:6, God "will render to every man according to his works." If Ernst Käsemann and Bornkamm bring the gospel of justification to the fore, Freed argued in company with Stendahl, Schweitzer, and Wrede, who saw it as "a subsidiary crater."[58] If some stress the indicative about what God has done for us in Christ, Freed is struck by the imperatives about what we are to do. A moral change in our existence is seen as Paul's chief concern. "The righteousness of God becomes the righteousness of man as well." It is "partial exegesis" to ignore the apostle's moral and ethical teaching.

Those unaccustomed to such a reading of the evidence will be comforted to know that the standing committee minutes record that while "critical attention was given to each paper presented," members "took exception to certain emphases in Dr. Freed's interpretation of justification." It will not do, of course, just to object, for exegetical matters must be settled exegetically. The ethical *is* a major component in Paul's thought. One recent major study of the apostle has concluded that he and Palestinian Judaism of his day agreed that "salvation is by grace but judgment is according to works; works are the condition of remaining 'in,' but they do not earn salvation," though it is added that there is a "change of 'entire systems' " between Paul and the Judaism of Palestine.[59] But I doubt that up until the time he wrote Galatians "the moral and ethical lives of the new converts was Paul's main concern," for there are too many christological, kerygmatic formulas to assume that soteriology was not a concern in Thessalonica or Corinth. The relation of "indicative" and "imperative" is a famous subject for debate, and many of us are more convinced by Bultmann's one-two sequence than by Windisch's imperative emphasis.[60] To argue that in Romans 8:11–13 ultimate salvation is conditional, dependent on our good works, on the basis of the "if" clause ("if the Spirit . . . dwells in you . . ., if by the Spirit you put to death the deeds of the body") is precarious in view of Paul's emphasis of the power of the Spirit in the believer's life since baptism. But the Achilles' heel in the argument, as was recognized in discussion, was probably a verse that the paper quoted to illustrate the present-future contrast for the believer, Romans 5:9: ". . . now justified by his blood, much more shall we be saved *by him*. . . ." The last two words make ultimate salvation as much dependent on Christ as the present stage.

An ethical reading of Paul did not commend itself. But examination of the full scope of the apostle's thought makes us ponder whether many traditional interpretations are adequate.

Warren A. Quanbeck's paper, the third one presented to the standing committee in March 1976, is included in this volume as the lead essay in Part II, "Confessional Propria as Hermeneutic." This is in part because his analysis, "The Confessions and Their Influence upon Biblical Interpretation," may be said to repeat the position of so many Lutherans, especially those in the ALC and LCA. It is also placed first because for many readers it will provide a most helpful introduction to the history of the Reformation Confessions and their influence. For this task Quanbeck is admirably suited. Though teaching at Luther Theological Seminary, Saint Paul, in the area of systematic theology, his doctoral work, under Otto. A. Piper at Princeton Seminary, was in the area of the history of biblical interpretation and entitled "The Hermeneutical Principles of Luther's Early Exegesis."[61] He has long been involved in inter-Lutheran and ecumenical discussions, particularly Reformed and Roman Catholic dialogues.[62]

To be underscored from the essay are the three functions of Confessions in the church as doxology, as hermeneutic, and for purposes of self-identification by the group. Quanbeck suggests which documents in the Book of Concord exemplify each function and how the three thrusts have worked out among Lutherans since the sixteenth century. In opting to focus upon "the broader, systematic aspects of hermeneutics," rather than the work of commentators, Quanbeck provides a complement to the examination of specific exegetes set forth by Froehlich. His own analysis points out both the high Lutheran emphasis on Scripture and the "misuse" of "the doctrine of inspiration to transcend the historical relativity of the Scriptures," and also the misuse of the Confessions (as if verbally inspired) and of Luther's writings, as if here were *the* true exposition" and a "perennial theology." Modern historical-critical study can, for example, help us more rightly value apocalyptic and the Book of Revelation, which Luther put on the margin of his New Testament canon (Hummel agrees that apocalyptic need not be treated "with consummate horror," but *his* bête-noire is "liberal exegesis.") Though Luther was no systematician, Quanbeck agrees that there are certain Lutheran "propria" ("ethos" and "economy" are his terms), and beginning with Melanchthon and Calvin he sketches attempts to carry out the theological program of Luther. Ecumenically he observes the importance of seeing that the Bible does not have just one uniform theology and that "exegesis is no longer branded with denominational markings," even though there may be a Lutheran perspective and Lutheran themes.

Actually, the standing committee discussed all these papers prior to the first national conference, "Lectionary as Hermeneutic." It also heard two other papers prior to the second national conference, one of which concerned Confession as hermeneutic and the other of which will be summarized in Part III below.

On 22 October 1976 Robert H. Fischer, of the Lutheran School of Theology, Chicago, presented a carefully written paper entitled "Hermeneutics of the Lutheran Confessions." Fischer had been one of the collaborators in the 1959 Tappert edition of the Book of Concord, and as a scholar in American church history he edited a volume about the president of his church, Franklin Clark Fry.[63] His paper also revealed its author as a thoughtful student of hermeneutics,[64] both sixteenth-century and modern. He had decided to treat together "the principles by which one approaches the Lutheran Confessions" and "the principles which the Confessions themselves offer for approaching the scriptural message which they claim to serve."

At the outset Fischer sought to show what is at stake by citing some theses drawn up by Jaroslav Pelikan in 1957 in a paper entitled "Theology and the Confessions":[65]

(1) Exegetically, (a) "the Confessions authorize the exercise of *exegetical theology*" to test what they say, but (b) acceptance of the Confessions "may preclude certain exegetical conclusions."

(2) Historically, by the Augsburg Confession's definition of the church

as where the gospel is proclaimed and the sacraments rightly administered (Art. VII), the Confessions (c) "make the task of *historical theology* an ecumenical one" but (d) may turn it "into a disguised polemic."

(3) Systematically, the confessional principle of law and gospel (e) permits creativity and freedom in *systematic theology* but (f) may also stifle these.

(4) Practically, the Confessions (g) give new status to *practical theology* (e.g., homiletics and liturgics) but (h) by lack of contact between church life and the Confessions, depreciation results.

After quoting C. F. W. Walther, the famed Missouri theologian, as saying that "the strictest Lutherans" may depart most from "true Lutheranism" and that the teacher who "stands more in the way of the so-called 'strict churchly Lutherans'" than anyone is Luther(!),[66] Fischer focused on the current identity crisis brought on by "A Statement of Scriptural and Confessional Principles" and its adoption as a hermeneutical guide in the Lutheran Church—Missouri Synod.[67]

As a historian, Fischer set up the principle that "no phenomenon in the historical realm is exempt from critical historical investigation." Granted that there are "noisy claims to impartial methods," and the historian's "best ambition" must be "the highest attainable degree of probability," there is still "no alternative" to making one's "historical method" as "critically honest as possible." In this process the historian must also be a logician.

With "A Statement . . ." such a historian therefore has disagreements on four levels:

(1) *Textual details.* To state, as the LCMS document does (IV.E), that only "the *canonical* Word" is "authoritative" for the church today and that "we *therefore* [emphasis mine] reject" the view that "the meaning a canonical text has now may differ from the meaning it had when it was first written" is a non sequitur, "assuming its own authoritative interpretation of what 'authoritative' means"—especially since "Lutheranism has stedfastly declined to define the canon of scripture." "A Statement . . ." too easily assumes "*the* Lutheran view of Scripture" to be that held by the authors of that statement.[68]

(2) *Historical judgments.* "A Statement . . ." and the LCMS tradition too easily identify "true Lutheranism" as homogeneously stemming from the "apostolic purity" of the Augsburg Confession and two hundred years of subsequent documents, including Lutheran orthodoxy. "Selective and romanticized history," Fischer commented.

(3) *Motives and motivations.* When "A Statement . . ." says (IV.G) that "the same doctrine of the Gospel, in all its articles, is presented throughout the entire Scripture," and that without this principle it is "impossible for the church to have and confess a unified theological position," such a concept of church unity is "not self-evidently 'the Lutheran' view." The section in "A Statement . . ." on the infallibility of Scripture (IV.F) reflects not "original Lutheranism" but the seventeenth-century orthodoxy in reaction to the Catholicism that developed after the Council of Trent, with its emphasis on authority. (Missouri theologians, in response, pointed to how the Confessions regard Scripture as different from all other writings.[69]) The Concordia Seminary faculty members who had left the Saint Louis institution to form Seminex had spoken against a view of scriptural inerrancy as "a priori truth which guarantees the truth of the Gospel. . . . The Gospel gives the Scriptures their normative character, not vice versa."[70] Missouri Synod representatives assured the standing committee that it is not taught that inerrancy guarantees the gospel, however.

(4) *Church polity and practice.* Fischer asked whether the church now has "the authority to elevate non-scriptural, non-confessional, simply traditional opinions to confessional, binding status." This of course raises the question of the status of "A Statement . . ." for Missouri Synod Lutherans.[71]

A hermeneutic of and for the Confessions includes presuppositions, findings, and convictions or principles (see the Bohlmann paper, below, on this score for one reading of its principles), but it does not eliminate testing all three features. It tells us not "what we shall find when we look, but how we shall go about looking." Fischer thus advocated "a constant reexamination of our forms of doctrine, yes, of the doctrine itself." The Confessions are "majestically normative," but to say that "the Scriptures must be interpreted according to the Symbols, not vice versa" is "misleading and by no means a self-evident principle for faithful Lutheranism." Walther himself said a person is fit to be ordained only if he can "test the whole Book of Concord according to the Word of God," and this process scarcely ceases with ordination.

Fischer's hard-hitting remarks also included some positive suggestions. We must distinguish between what can be investigated without personal convictions and what is an affirmation of Christian faith. Law-gospel, the principle that God comes to us through his "external Word," and the distinction between "the teachings of God" and "the teachings of men" are characteristic Lutheran emphases. Precisely the latter distinction ought to make us wary of exalting traditional opinions to confessional status. Indeed, the existing Confessions even need to be tested for "errors," for study of Scripture could convince us that *torah* means "more than law as Luther understood it"[72] or that "substance" language may not be the best way to talk about the Lord's Supper or "that there is more to the Hebrew concept of sacrifice than Lutherans have traditionally allowed." Errors? "How you answer depends on what your conception of error, truth, and authority is." (See the essay below by Harold H. Ditmanson.)

THE SECOND NATIONAL LUTHERAN
HERMENEUTICS CONFERENCE

All three papers that were presented at the second national conference, 10–11 December 1976, on the use of the Confessions in biblical exegesis are included in this volume. Twenty-eight persons were in attendance at that conference.[73] We note especially points in the papers that were important for the closing summation.

"Confessional Biblical Interpretation: Some Basic Principles," by Ralph A. Bohlmann, was presented as a series of eight theses on a single sheet of paper and amplified by exposition that drew frequently on his 1968 book, *Principles of Biblical Interpretation in the Lutheran Confessions*.[74] Bohlmann's closeness to "A Statement of Scriptural and Confessional Principles" as executive secretary of the Commission on Theology and Church Relations at the time the study edition of "A Statement . . ." was developed, and his familiarity with issues at Concordia Seminary, Saint Louis, as a faculty member there (on leave with the CTCR part of the time) and, after Martin H. Scharlemann's acting presidency, as its president, as well as his familiarity with the topic,[75] made him an ideal choice to present this important matter from the Missouri Synod perspective. We have placed his essay in this volume after the Quanbeck essay since it is obviously a less general introduction, being rather an assertion of what the Confessions, on a high view of them, demand for proper use of the Scriptures. The Hummel essay reflects a similar confessional understanding on the part of an exegete.

Bohlmann's theses move from (1) the Confessions' view of Holy Scripture (to be derived, since it is not explicitly stated in them), with (2) Scripture as "qualitatively different" and God the "author of their every word," to (3) a brief account of how the Scriptures "must be read as historical literary documents." (4) As far as content is concerned, law-

24

gospel, "Christ alone," and soteriological purpose (justification) stand out. (5) Scripture is the "only source and norm" for doctrine, God's way to see that what we preach and administer is from God. Although "A Statement . . ." strongly emphasizes inerrancy in Scripture, it was noted that the intention was not to make "acceptance of the Scriptures" the basis for "saving faith."[76] "A Statement . . ." specifically rejects as a distortion the notion that "acceptance of the Bible as such, rather than the Gospel, is . . . the way to eternal salvation."[77] Moreover (6), one needs the Holy Spirit to understand Scripture's message. (7) The Scriptures present an organic unity of doctrine. (8) On unity, "the law-gospel distinction and the doctrine of justification" are exegetical presuppositions but do not determine or impose meaning on biblical passages.[78]

Discussion brought agreement that the "canon within the canon" of Luther is not in the Confessions but properly understood is necessary for our understanding. In thesis 3 Bohlmann seemed to accentuate "literary exegesis" without "historical setting." He suggested that the Confessions deal more with literary factors but that "historical exegesis is a necessity." The meaning lies, however, in the literary, not in any history of the functioning of the text. His concern always is to be "under the Word." Theses 6 (the Holy Spirit) and 3 (careful literary exegesis) must happen together, not as two stages (3, then 6).

"A Statement . . ." provides grist for some specific questions. Is acceptance of the historicity of Jonah or of Adam and Eve (IV.F) necessary for one to be counted "Lutheran"? (The Missouri Synod has affirmed both these things in conventions.[79]) If "the inerrant original" is not recoverable, is it enough to recognize "*apparent* contradictions . . . because of uncertainty over the original text"?[80] (We will touch more on text criticism later.)

The essays by Foster R. McCurley and Joseph A. Burgess show how non-Missouri Lutherans go about the task of applying the Confessions to the Old Testament and the New, respectively. McCurley, of the LCA, teaches at the Lutheran Theological Seminary at Philadelphia; Burgess, of the ALC, was then teaching at the LCA Lutheran Theological Seminary at Gettysburg. In a 1974 work McCurley dealt extensively with methods for treating Old Testament passages for preaching, following the lectionary and taking into consideration the stages in historical development of a text.[81] Burgess did his doctoral dissertation on the same passage with which Froehlich dealt, but he covered the history of exegesis of Matthew 16:17–19 from the rise of critical scholarship until Vatican II.[82]

McCurley's paper, "Confessional Propria as Hermeneutic—Old Testament," dealt especially with Luther as an Old Testament scholar. That raised discussion, in plenary and small groups, of the hermeneutical question within the Confessions of whether one confines oneself to the Book of Concord as guide or looks at the exegesis (and preaching) of those who wrote its documents. We have already seen that some would exclude a "canon within the canon" because it is in Luther (as his opinion) but not in the Confessions (and therefore not binding). But others point to the principle that we understand a work by any author better in the light of his other writings and also to the fact that the Formula of Concord itself appeals "to further extensive statements" in Luther's "doctrinal and polemical writings."[83] Besides exploring Luther, McCurley goes into three main issues: (1) the Word as *spoken* Word (especially in contrast to theophanies); (2) wisdom (where his analysis of it as empirical, anthropocentric reason, "good for what it's good for," found Hummel parting company with a view that did not stress its inspiredness; Hummel views it as "an alternate expression of genuine covenant ethics"); and (3) covenant, where Hummel found unacceptable McCurley's distinction between the Mosaic covenant, with its stipulations, and the Abrahamic covenant of grace and promise. Hummel, as Old Testament scholar and Lutheran exegete, insisted on the latter type of covenant including judgment and thus "the third use of the law." Some, including those who object to form-critical analysis, also raised the question about McCurley's emphasis on the word *therefore* in "announcements of judgment" or of "salvation."

"Confessional Propria in Relation to New Testament Texts," by Joseph A. Burgess, takes up (1) the characteristic Lutheran theme of "Scripture alone." *Sola scriptura* is not, however, an assertion that all parts of the Bible are equally valid, for by "content criticism" (*Sachkritik*)—judging parts of the Bible by whether or not they "bring Christ to us"—a canon within the canon is created. (In discussion Bohlmann preferred to say that "the Bible is in all its parts equally valid, but does not all 'preach Christ.'") Burgess also discusses (2) the question of a "center" for the New Testament (*solus Christus*, the gospel), and (3) the question of whether any one facet of a diamond with so many facets can be "the center." (4) The event of "justification," he suggests, is, however, really the canon within the canon for Lutherans.

Among the other propria considered in the Burgess essay are (5) law-gospel, based upon the *theologia crucis*—with *sub contrario* and *simul* as further possible themes (the Christian life exists "under contrary facts," the believer being "simultaneously justified yet sinner"); and (6) faith, which means "certainty" (from God and the Spirit) not "security." The

26

essay recognizes finally that the confessional preacher sometimes needs to preach "against" a given text, reinterpreting or even omitting it—yet without "triumphalism" or arrogance.

Discussion added to the list of propria original sin (Augsburg Confession, Art. II) and the fact that exegesis is communal, in the church's ministry, and not just a matter for individual scholars (Art. V). It is interesting that several voices, including one from the Missouri Synod, acknowledged the legitimacy of or need to hear the ethical emphasis in Paul, perhaps as part of "sanctification," stressed in the earlier paper by Edwin Freed. Some wished for more attention to Gospel sources. And there was sentiment, in face of the real questions that exist about theological use of Scripture, for those interested to pursue these matters in the light of their acceptance of modern biblical studies and ecumenical concerns today.

What can be said by way of summary about the second conference? "Confessional Propria as Hermeneutic" was an unclear title for some. One participant wrote afterward that he had come expecting to discuss "how the Confessions could furnish us with insights, examples, methods, and tools in order to interpret the Scriptures . . . for our ministries and witness." By and large, he felt, more remained to be done than had been accomplished. Nonetheless there had been an impressive list of characteristic Lutheran themes in approaching Scripture:

a Word theology
solus Christus, sola gratia
sola fide
sola scriptura and "canon within the canon"
"promise"
law-gospel
analogia fidei
simul justus et peccator
the clarity of Scripture (*perspicuitas*)
the finite is capable of the infinite

These and more were named, even if varying interpretations and emphases exist.

There were differences among the Lutherans involved in this discussion, but "we may be closer than we think," the chairman suggested. Much in Bohlmann's theses could be accepted by all, for example, in thesis 1, on the nature and interpretation of Scripture. But then a fundamentalist leader like Carl McIntire probably could accept it too. What matters is what is done with a thesis. Not everyone who accepts this first thesis would draw out of it what a fundamentalist might (and not everyone who employs historical-critical methods opposes being "under the Word"). So what we have is really a crisis of trust or attitudes among Lutherans (and toward others).

Again, all three papers were outlined. With regard to Bohlmann's thesis about using literary exegesis, with seemingly less rigorous emphasis on the historical and none on a "critical" approach (to avoid standing over the Bible, judging), I am doubtful that such a distinction can be carried out. For judgments are necessary even in literary and textual matters, and in Roman Catholic acceptance of modern biblical-study methods it has been precisely the allowing of genre research, a *literary* factor, which has been the significant step.[84]

As to the propria issue, the question was raised about the need to look more at the historical contexts of the Confessions themselves. My remarks then, and written comments by others later, suggest that we need to look even more at the praxis in the Confessions exegetically, the hierarchy within the Book of Concord among documents, and Luther's further writings.[85] One must ask whether the Confessions and Lutheran fathers drew the full implications of what the Reformer intended. One participant suggested that the hermeneutical function of the three creeds (which do *not* mention justification) in Part I of the Book of Concord needs elaboration. Likewise for the Catechisms.

A passing observation suggested how much Lutheran emphases have become part and parcel of critical biblical studies. When Gerhard von Rad emphasizes Israel's ancient "credo," is that a Reformation predilection for creed as formative?[86] Or when scholars salute Mark's achievement as the imposing of a theology of the cross on disparate traditions about Jesus, is that a Lutheran reading of the scene?[87] And when Käsemann speaks of *Schwärmer* in the early church, are there not sixteenth-century overtones? Or is it that the Lutheran Reformation was itself shaped by biblical themes?

The burning issues in our sessions seem to me to be:

(1) Is justification *the* proprium of propria, *the* canon? Or are there many other acceptable expressions of the gospel, in the rich variety of the Bible, as the Burgess essay also seems to argue?

(2) As a pointer to our final conference, *the* issue is use of the "historical method." Involved also is the value of *pre*canonical forms but likewise that of *post*canonical developments. Modern methods help us trace out for most texts something of the following stages: (a) the original event; (b) oral accounts thereof; (c) possible written accounts which

serve as source for (d) the biblical writer's version which we possess. But there is also (e) a further development of how these books coalesced into our canon; (f) subsequent interpretation of a passage, including any distillate from it or use of it in the Confessions; and (g) lectionary combinations and church calendar as setting for the preacher's use today.

Sometimes there may be two or more versions of "the original" in Scripture (e.g., the Lord's Prayer or the words of institution). If it is an Old Testament event and text there may be a further history of interpretation of it in the New Testament. I for one would be willing to see the Spirit's work *throughout* this process. But when is the text "Word of God"? Only at the fourth stage (d)?[88]

We had begun that "fraternal exchange" which Edmund Schlink had called for, between the Confessions and exegesis, the results of which might establish the scripturalness of the confessional statements, or make clear they are not complete expositions of Scripture or that some confessional declarations are contrary to Scripture.[89] In particular, we had thus far explored questions about lectionary (g) and Confessions (f) as hermeneutic, with some attention to canon (e). Now we were ready to tackle the biblical text and its previous development.

THE HISTORICAL(-CRITICAL) METHOD(S) OF INTERPRETING AS HERMENEUTIC

Just what the methods of historical criticism include and how they work when applied to texts were the concerns of nine papers commissioned by the Division of Theological Studies in its hermeneutics study. Three of these were presented at meetings of the standing committee (one of which is included in this volume), and the rest were presented at the third and final national conference (five of which are included here). Again we shall describe in more detail the papers not found in this volume, and in all cases what is pertinent for our conclusions.

Some seminary teachers like to use the device of showing how a method works by applying it first to a secular text, where there is less emotional investment than with a biblical text. Thus it can be helpful in a first-year class of theology students to demonstrate how, by literary-historical analysis, one of the Psalms of Solomon, for example, can be shown to contain two different views evidently flourishing among Pharisees in the first century B.C. about the restoration of the kingdom: the son of David will do it, according to 17:23ff., but according to 17:1ff., 38, God himself will be the king. Or the historical-critical method could be applied to some modern composition, ferreting out its sources and allusions and literary structure, as one standing-committee member did with T. S. Eliot's "Ash Wednesday."

On 22 October 1976 the standing committee heard a paper by George W. E. Nickelsburg, Jr., a Lutheran teaching in the School of Religion of the University of Iowa, entitled "Methods of Interpreting a Non-Canonical Text." He dealt with "The Assumption of Moses," a brief document in the Old Testament Pseudepigrapha.[90] We hoped to be able to grasp more fully how a biblical scholar works with an ancient text methodologically and to see implications for study of canonical documents, especially as regards literary genre and the "canon question," recognizing the contention of many that for scientific biblical studies one cannot confine the effort only to the sixty-six books in the Protestant canon.

The Assumption of Moses is a happy choice for such a probe. It consists of twelve short chapters—less than three hundred lines—of Latin text preserved in a deficient fifth- or sixth-century A.D. palimpsest manuscript. Presumably it is based on a Greek version, translated from an original in Hebrew or Aramaic. The contents consist of a long address to Joshua by Moses, near the close of his life, predicting what will happen to Israel—conquest, captivity, return from exile of two tribes, evil foreign kings (the Seleucids), apostasy by some of their own priests, priest-kings who work inquity (the Hasmoneans), and "an insolent king . . . not . . . of the race of priests" (taken to be Herod the Great) who will reign for thirty-four years, until "a powerful king of the west" shall come (perhaps the governor of Syria, Varus, who put down a revolt in 4 B.C.). From then on it becomes harder to identify what is meant, since the author is forced to predict a future that has not yet occurred instead of recapitulating a history that has already taken place. After a series of chaotic events and impious rulers when "the times shall be ended" and "a second visitation and wrath" come (including crucifixion for those who "confess their circumcision"), there shall arise "a man of the tribe of Levi" named Taxo, who with his seven sons retreats into a cave to fast and die rather than transgress God's commands. A poetic, apocalyptic chapter (10) follows, predicting that God will arise, punish the Gentiles, and exalt Israel. A date is given for this advent (A.D. 75–107, according to some commentators). The account ends with Joshua grieving and Moses comforting him.

Twice it is mentioned in the text that Moses will "sleep" with his fathers, and 10:12 refers to his "death." After the word *death* in 10:12, however, there also occurs in our single Latin manuscript the word *assumption,* which modern editors think is an addition by a first-century redactor. Ancient lists of writings about Moses refer not only to a "Testament" (which is what the extant contents outlined above really is) but also to an "assumption of Moses," an event not described in Scripture but developed in Jewish tradition (perhaps as a parallel to stories about Enoch [Gen. 5:24] and Elijah [2 Kings 2:11–12, 16–18]) in light of the statement at Deuteronomy 34:6 that "no man knows the place" of Moses' burial. In any case the New Testament Book of Jude reflects this tradition when it gives a quote about the archangel Michael disputing with the devil over the body of Moses (v. 9), and R. H. Charles thought that verse 16 and the references to the "ungodly" (v. 4) also reflect our pseudepigraphical writing. Charles felt that the "Testament of Moses" was written between A.D. 7 and 30 (i.e., during Jesus' lifetime) and a contemporary "Assumption of Moses" about the same time, with only part of the "Testament" being preserved and referred to (unfortunately) as "The Assumption of Moses."[91] It is thus an excellent document on which to practice any methodology that will make its obscure contents more clear.

Nickelsburg is well trained for working in writings like this between the Old and New Testaments, and his publications have concentrated on pseudepigraphal literature.[92] His paper carefully outlined appropriate methodology according to the canons of historical criticism, dealt with the Testament of Moses as we have it and the likely situation in which it arose, and explored connections with similar writings in the canon. For the progress of *Testamentum/Assumptio-Mosis* studies his paper was a significant step in its careful arguments about underlying sources and allusions and the likelihood of an earlier dating for sections of it than R. H. Charles (and most scholars who have been influenced by him) postulated.[93] It is a matter of regret that this fine piece of exegesis could not be included in our volume, but specialists will want to examine it when it is published elsewhere.

For the Lutheran hermeneutics process Nickelsburg's paper was important in establishing the following points. (1) "Historical criticism" includes not only the who, when, and why about a document but also its comparison with similar, related documents and an attitude toward the document being studied, including criticism of what others have said about it. (2) It is permissible, in the Missouri Synod view, to employ historical criticism on *non*canonical documents, but the canon is a different matter. As one LCMS standing-committee member argued, it is "irrelevant" to apply such methods to Scripture, for that would be an attempt to analyze divine actions, not human aspects, and these are not the same ("my ways are higher than your ways," says the Lord, Isa. 55:9; his ways are "inscrutable," Rom. 11:33). It is Nestorian to try to separate the two.

(3) Any attempt to draw implications for a canonical book (like Daniel or Revelation) from a noncanonical one like The Assumption of Moses met with rejection by those who drew a canonical/noncanonical line with regard to the historical-critical method. To see the Assumption of Moses text and the Book of Daniel even phenomenologically on the same level, as showing what apocalyptic is, was not acceptable. Involved therefore are the questions in what sense noncanonical history-of-religions material can be employed to elucidate the sense of a biblical text and in what sense parallels have value. A well-known warning by a Jewish scholar against "parallelomania" was invoked,[94] as well as what was called (Martin) "Franzmann's 'Third Law,'" that three "maybes" and two "probablys" do not make a "therefore." The call was heard to apply "logical canons," and it was also said that "unquestionable conclusions are unlikely with a single document" (i.e., apparently where we have just one manuscript). But would such a stance prevent the reaching of a conclusion that Moses did *not* write this "Testament" or application of the principle that an apocalyptist betrays the date when he is writing at the point where he passes from accurate summary to hazy inaccuracy in what his "ancient worthy" is "predicting"? If we apply the principle to Moses here, why not to Daniel or John the seer?

(4) Finally, Jesus. It was asked if for Nickelsburg it would have made a difference in his conclusions had Jesus referred in the canonical Gospels to the "Testament of Moses" as the work of Moses. "Not really," he replied. But that is precisely the issue for some for whom authorship issues are settled for all time in scholarship by what Jesus said, in spite of the *kenosis*.[95]

The papers by Nickelsburg and by Robert Fischer, discussed by the standing committee on the same day, shared a perspective on how revelation works in history—which an ALC member, among others, pointedly endorsed. The LCMS position insisted on the qualitative difference between Scripture and other writings to the degree that comparison between canonical and noncanonical apocalypses was seemingly excluded.[96]

On 18 March 1977 the final exegetical papers were presented to the standing committee—analyses of Old and New Testament texts, employing "critical" historical methods. Ronald M. Hals, Professor of Old Testament at the Lutheran Theological Seminary (ALC), Columbus, read the first paper to the theological forum, and Walter A. Maier, Professor of New Testament at Concordia Theological Seminary (LCMS), Fort Wayne, read the second. Each essayist had been invited to select his texts, treat them exegetically, and reflect on methodology.

The Hals paper is included in this volume as the first one in the section "Methods of Interpretation—The Historical-Critical Method as Hermeneutic?" and the only one by an Old Testament scholar in that section. It must be remembered, however, that two earlier papers, by Hummel and McCurley in the "Confessional Propria" section, dealt primarily with the Hebrew Scriptures. Hals, as a scholar, has concerned himself especially with form criticism and, reflecting his graduate program at Hebrew Union College, Cincinnati, with Christian-Jewish conversation.[97] For his essay, "Methods of Interpretation," he selected as his passage Ezekiel 18, a "word of the Lord" that the prophet speaks during the exile about how the proverb is no longer true, "The fathers have eaten sour grapes, and the children's teeth are set on edge" (vv. 1–4); about what a person must do ethically to live and not die (vv. 5–24); and about Yahweh's call to repent, though Israel says God's way is not just. But there is also attention to 36:26ff. and 11:19ff., where the demand to "get yourselves a new heart and a new spirit" becomes a promise, "a new heart I will give you, and a new spirit. . . ." The final passage treated is Ezekiel 33, where verses 1–9 are like chapters 1–3, with Ezekiel as watchman to warn the wicked to repent, and 33:10–20 like chapter 18, as the preaching of judgment.

What fascinates Hals in particular is how Ezekiel's message varies with the situation: before the fall of Jerusalem in 587 it was judgment and repentance, after 587 the promise of "a new gracious act of God." Hence he is willing to see repentance as either a command (18:31) or gift (11:19; 36:26). Hals illustrated it in an aside with the way the words "Come to my house" can be a command, but if one adds the words "and I'll give you dinner," it becomes a promise! That reopens the question of law and gospel (see his n. 12). Related is an interest in the ongoing history of the text. (Hals quotes Brevard Childs that "the study of the prehistory has its proper function within exegesis only in illuminating the final text," a sentiment akin to that in the LCMS Stance Statement that the investigation of "precanonical sources, forms, or traditions" may be "useful . . . for a clearer understanding of what the canonical text intends to say," but the latter is the authoritative word.[98]) Hals has in mind not merely future use in Israel of the text but also the New Testament continuity and discontinuity with Ezekiel 18 (which he goes into, though the New Testament never quotes Ezek. 18); his plea is for "canon criticism" in that sense.

Methodologically Hals finds the procedures used exegetically—even his strong insistence that one must start with form criticism, not literary criticism—to be "essentially neutral and their results open to revision," the text itself as starting point suggesting what is pertinent. The essay thus is an excellent example of attention to what was handed down in Israel (*traditum*) and how it was handed on (*traditio*), including changes in the use of forms when historical situations shifted. So it was what had been a "liturgy of entry" at the temple gate involving a priest became now in the templeless exile a vehicle of pastoral concern spoken by the priest-prophet. Hals thus seeks to make the tradition-history approach fruitful for us to understand the meaning of the text, in its own right and in the church.

"Form and Redaction Critical Analysis of the Gospel Accounts of the Feeding of the Five Thousand" was the title of the paper by Walter A. Maier. We have already quoted him speaking negatively on the use of historical-critical methodology as "blasphemous," and a recent book of his spells out objections to form criticism.[99] "Himself a representative practitioner of the Historical Grammatical Method" (as defined in a CTCR statement of the Missouri Synod),[100] he concluded in his paper for the Division of Theological Studies' theological forum that "it is not possible successfully to wed 'Lutheran presuppositions' to *genuine* form and redactional critical methodology," for "there is no room for the use of these extreme investigative methodologies in a church which regards the whole Bible as the Word and truth of God and which seeks to proclaim and believe nothing but its teachings."

Maier's approach sought to show how practitioners of the historical-critical method proceed with the feeding miracle recorded at Mark 6:32–44—parallels Matthew 14:13–21, Luke 9:10*b*–17, and John 16:1–15 (his sequence of references)—while suggesting that "the views of those who employ historical grammatical methodology . . . could also be noted." For purposes of time, only form and redaction criticism were treated. The paper first sketched "form critical analysis of the four feeding narratives," following Bultmann in his *History of the Synoptic Tradition* (with the assumptions that the aim was "to determine what was factual information regarding Jesus' life and teaching and what was fabrication"[101] and that for "Bultmann and form critics like him . . . there are no miracles," the tradition is "an invention of the church"). At the end of the section "the substance of the primitive tradition" was sketched: the historical Jesus once hosted a meal with bountiful food from a friend, or kept the people so interested they "forgot about meals."

Maier then presented a critique of the Bultmannian procedure: (1) The references to time and place were already in the sources (so E. Basil Redlich[102]), and Matthew and John would have been eyewitnesses. (2) The "form" is that of "miracle story," but only an "antisupernaturalism" can reject the "traditional, Lutheran, and Christian hermeneutics, that such miracles . . . did in fact occur." (3) The *Sitz im Leben* is to be found not in the community but in the life situation of Jesus himself. (4) Bultmann's "laws of popular narrative formulation" are to be rejected, as they are questioned by many scholars (Franzmann, Redlich, Vincent Taylor, E. P. Sanders); apostles and eyewitnesses would have prevented the developments supposed. In sum, the assumptions and procedures are not valid; "far better . . . to assume that everything reported as history is to be taken as factual . . . insured by . . . divine inspiration." Each account should be considered separately, but "it is unworthy and profitless to pit differing details of the stories against each other."

The second part of Maier's paper tackled redaction criticism. A brief history of the rise of the subdiscipline was sketched, and a book or two was discussed to exemplify *Redaktionsgeschichte* in each Gospel.[103] Unfortunately Marxsen's book on Mark does not treat this pericope. H. J. Held had far more to say on "Matthew as Interpreter of the Miracle Stories." Conzelmann on the passage in Luke is noted, and R. H. Lightfoot and J. Louis Martyn on John (as well as the treatment in Marxsen's *Introduction*). Maier allowed that each Gospel has its own "emphases and characteristics" and that "some observations" of the redaction critics "are illuminating and useful." But there are objections: (1) Redaction criticism presupposes form criticism—and is subject to all the strictures against the latter. (2) The reconstruction of the situation in the church which an evangelist reflects is "in many cases . . . speculative and incredible."[104] (3) There is "excessive subtlety," for example, Held's emphasis on the *disciples'* greater participation in the feeding, according to Matthew.[105]

Maier's conclusion has already been noted: there can be no accommodation of "the traditional, distinctively Lutheran technique of Bible interpretation" to "the radical . . . tenets of form and redaction criticism, and none should be tried." The paper clearly states what the "Missouri position" rejects and why.

Committee discussion made clear several points:

(1) In failing to cite any of the rich commentary, monograph, and periodical literature on the passage, the presentation was extremely restricted in seeing how redaction and form criticism really operate.

(2) The paper offers no exegesis of its own other than "it happened"

as the four narratives describe. It is not clear whether a Markan priority is assumed (though Matthew and John are suggested as eyewitnesses). It is unclear whether sources are assumed and whether the evangelists are to be credited with any work on the passage. The speaker indicated that one "cannot determine the interconnections of the Gospels," and, for all emphases on four accounts, allowed a tendency to harmonize. The question of "eucharistic overtones," pointed out by many commentators in the similarity of language to what takes place in the upper room, was dismissed as tending "toward allegory" or "homiletical," not based on the text. One is left wondering what "historical-grammatical" exegesis amounts to.

(3) Efforts to pursue methodology on other Gospel pericopes brought no clear solutions. To the question of the call of Peter, which in Mark is described as happening at the very start of Jesus' ministry (1:16–18) and in Luke much further along in the story (5:1–11) motivated by a miraculous catch of fish and by the healing of Peter's mother-in-law (4:38–39; in Mark *after* Peter's call, at 1:30–31), it was suggested there could be *two* such stories. (This is to say nothing of John 1:41–42, where Simon is originally called not by Jesus but by Andrew.) The same explanation was advanced for two temple cleansings, one early in the ministry (John 2:13–17) and the other late (Matt. 21:12–13); but there is the additional problem of Mark (11:15–17), where it occurs late in the ministry but a day *after* Matthew's dating.

(4) Nonetheless, there was certain agreement in that both the Hals and Maier papers assumed an authority of Scripture as normative and causative with power to produce conviction. How much closer, given a few more examples in exegesis, might those come who share a conviction about scriptural authority but differ over specific exegetical methodologies?

THE THIRD NATIONAL LUTHERAN
HERMENEUTICS CONFERENCE

Six papers attempted to provide some answers at the final national conference, 3–5 May 1977. Thirty-two persons were present, twelve new at this meeting.[106] The design for the three days, longer than previous conferences in order to accommodate twice as many papers, called for twin presentations on methods of interpretation by an exegete and a systematic theologian from The American Lutheran Church and then two more by a similar pair from the Lutheran Church—Missouri Synod. The final set

36

of papers called for a New Testament scholar from the LCA and another from the LCMS to treat the same passage using appropriate historical methods.[107] Ample time was given for plenary and small-group discussion, and provision was made for a written report at the conference from each discussion section. There was no conference statement, but the chairman again made a concluding summary.

David L. Tiede, who presented the first paper, is an Associate Professor at Luther Theological Seminary, Saint Paul. His Harvard doctoral dissertation dealt with sources in the biblical and pagan worlds on the so-called *theios anēr* ("divine wonder-worker") debated in recent scholarship as a prototype for early Christian depictions of Jesus christologically in the miracle stories.[108] His paper, "Methods of Historical Inquiry and the Faithful Interpretation of the Christian Scriptures," included in this volume, was an admirable one to start the conference, since it recognized the profound disunity existing among U.S. Lutherans on the hermeneutics issue but voiced a hope that, with admission of inadequacies by us all, the matter of scriptural interpretation might unite as well.

Tiede's "litany of questions" suggests that (1) text and translation are not the simple objective matters once supposed; note the comment from Gerhard Maier that infallibility means "authorization and fulfillment by God" not "anthropological inerrancy." (2) Source analysis need not serve positivistic historiography but can aid "explication of the full meaning of the biblical text" (Terence E. Fretheim). (3) Since an exegete must accurately describe what texts say, a diversity of biblical theologies inevitably results. Redaction criticism helps us see what a whole book says, and though our reconstructions of that situation which the book addressed may be tentative, they help the preacher relate to new times and situations. (4) Even form criticism can help us connect message, situation, and medium in the past and for today. Hence these methods of inquiry assist us to listen to the texts.

The Tiede paper concentrated on methods, not individual passages. Not surprisingly, discussion of the paper centered around specific pericopes: the facticity of Lazarus's being raised ("it was more relevant for Easter preaching, in the church fathers and Luther, *before* the critical methods arose"); the parable of the sower (to say it is "by the evangelist" as well as "by Jesus" violates what the Holy Spirit says and does "tear at the fabric of Lutheran unity"); the words of institution for the Lord's Supper ("confessionally we must hold our Lord historically instituted it 'on the night in which he was betrayed' "[109]); Jesus' resurrection (there can be no "bones, hair, skin, or teeth" left in the tomb on Easter Day). Each example was in part at least discussed. It emerged that some of the LCMS representatives would not regard Lutheran unity on Scripture as a *summum bonum* and that for others their "doctrine of and trust in the Holy Spirit" was "higher" than that of those who use critical methods on Holy Scripture. (But using the Holy Spirit as a hermeneutical principle raised real questions for still others.) About criteria for discerning when "the Word of the Lord breaks into our inquiry" and "the living Lord speaks," Tiede answered in terms of "preaching the gospel," "means of grace," and sacraments. Critics of the paper insisted that "what Scripture says took place, happened." Tiede responded that a stance on pericopes such as those suggested opens anew the issues of sequence in the Synoptics and John, and of sources, to which it was replied that for each difficulty there are explanations. Or, a non-Missouri voice: "You have a belief there is a satisfactory explanation."

James W. Voelz, who spoke next, entitled his paper "The Historical-Critical Method: An Analysis." He teaches at Concordia Theological Seminary, Fort Wayne, and has done his doctoral work at Cambridge University.[110] At the outset Voelz assumed that linguistic studies and textual criticism "would cause little, if any, furor, in even the most conservative circles," but that form, redaction, and content criticism (*Sachkritik*) are "the point of the whole discussion."[111] As a basic definition he proposed:

> The historical-critical method is essentially a way of approaching the texts of the New and Old Testaments, designed to *get behind those texts*, in order to reconstruct the events described therein and to analyze the reports of those events, for the specific purpose of determining how those reports were formed and/or shaped by the needs and concerns of various communities and individuals.

He contended therefore "that historical-criticism errs in the *way* it desires to get behind a text and . . . in its *reasons for desiring* to get behind that text."

As to the way "the criticisms" go behind the text in actual practice, form criticism (e.g., Martin Dibelius) errs in its "astonishing" assumptions about the early Christian community. For example, Dibelius said, "Preaching was the only activity of the early Christian community," but the Book of Acts (2:42) says that teaching was much earlier than Dibelius imagined.[112] Further, form criticism works in a circle (B. Gerhardsson), drawing conclusions from forms of literary traditions about communal life and also using communal life to understand the forms. The test then becomes "coherence" or consistency, Voelz said, but what is coherent may still be fictitious, and history "knows little of logic and comprehensiveness." The paper offered as an example Edgar Allan Poe's "The Murders in the Rue Morgue," where coherent logical solutions are disrupted by the fact that the killer turns out to be a rampaging orangutan! Redaction criticism is "even more . . . dubious" than form criticism, the way critics reconstruct the genesis of a book or fail to follow logically "even the simplest canons of common sense." "Surely it is just as logical *and much more natural* for an author or a community to *preserve* a story as it is for it to *invent* such a story because of its spiritual needs and desires." To argue that Mark 1:2–4 is redactoral (so Marxsen) "does not allow God to act *organically* with symbolism and type" and makes the redactor "more *deeply theological* than the Lord God of the universe himself."

The wrong reasons that the historical-critical method has for seeking to go behind the biblical text are tied up with its view of history. The failing here is that, as Troeltsch articulated it, modern historians operate by analogy—our present experiences and occurrences today are made the criterion of probability for what happened in the past. This led, in the case of miracles, to denial of them, in the name of a "closed universe" (though "Einstein and high-energy physics" have opened up the possibility of "intervention by the supernatural").[113] But analogy cannot be employed with the Bible because Scripture "deals with *unique* events," singular (not merely particular) and unparalleled. The historian must therefore not "philosophize on their probability" but examine "the sources, . . . the biblical records, to see if they are truly trustworthy." Parallels between New Testament literature and tales concerning pagan deities are ruled out because the Gospel writers (1) claim they are writing history (Luke 1:1–4) and (2) disavow myth (2 Pet. 1:15–16), and (3) the Gospel accounts are qualitatively different from extracanonical accounts (the Gospel of Peter was cited on the resurrection). The historical-critical approach is thus wrong because it does not take seriously God's activity in history, about which we must know through "recital theology" in the Bible, which is grounded in facts.

Perhaps the most interesting portion of Voelz's paper for generating discussion was the appeal to Kenneth Ewing Bailey and his book *Poet and Peasant*[114] to argue against the "development" of tradition in the early church and thus against distortion, invention, or any elements of myth coming into the tradition that stems from Jesus. In our discussions this book was also invoked as providing an alternative to form criticism.

Bailey, a missionary and teacher for over twenty years in the Middle East, argued for "a literary critical approach" and applied it in his doctoral dissertation at Concordia Seminary, Saint Louis, to four parables in Luke.[115] His emphasis is on "oriental exegesis," a blend of insights from peasant culture today, oriental versions of the Bible (Syriac, Arabic, etc.), and the ancient literature read against this background.[116] Bailey is also strong on discovering literary structure, especially that of a chiastic nature, in a passage. In treatments of Luke 16:1–13, 11:5–13, and chapter 15, within the outline of what he calls the "Jerusalem Document" (9:51— 19:48), Bailey concludes each time for a poem going back to Jesus rather than a gradual collection of materials by the early church. Q.E.D., no form criticism.

The matter is not quite so simple, for Bailey limits himself to a few examples in Luke, most of which are unique to that Gospel. Moreover, he does posit a written source by "a pre-Lukan Jewish-Christian theologian" (p. 83), and at times separate blocks of material are identifiable within a passage (p. 134). In addition, a few verses in his Jerusalem Document also occur in Matthew (see Luke 16:13; 11:9–13), so there is a source problem that Bailey never takes up. Finally, Bailey on occasion allows that Luke has rearranged the order of his Jerusalem Document— for example, 16:9–15 has been moved ahead of 16:16 as a corrective, so Greek readers would not misunderstand 16:8. Hence we have source and redaction, if not form, criticism, and Bailey does advocate using "the standard critical tools of Western scholarship" along with his "oriental exegesis."[117]

Voelz cited not only Bailey's book but also Bailey from personal conversations on "oral tradition and reliability," reflecting modern cases in village life. Significant events are told (1) solidified in set form, (2) with a core in set phrases, and (3) "when the story is retold, other elements may be added as it suits the interest of the teller, but . . . the essential core is always retained." The retelling of a village shooting five days afterward varied in details by tellers, but "eyewitnesses" controlled the tradition; so, Voelz concluded, "the case of the historical critics . . . is once again totally without foundation or support." Not so, said several who heard the paper. "Elements . . . added as it suits the teller" is precisely what is involved in form history and development. Besides, Bailey's whole case is an argument from modern analogy, so despised in the paper! Some saw, though, in the paper a cautious opening for reliable, not invented, oral tradition, in the manner of Vincent Taylor or C. F. D.

Moule, as when Paul cites an oral tradition in 1 Corinthians 11:23–25 or 15:3b–5, or when Jeremias treats the Lord's Prayer. In the last analysis the paper left the impression of forbidding use of any methodology that asked about what happened with the Gospels, for example, between Jesus and our existing texts—yet even Bailey was modestly into that subject.

Exegetes need systematicians to keep them honest methodologically, it is said, just as Scripture scholars are needed to keep dogmatics fair and square with the sources. The next two papers were offered by systematic theologians, the one, paired with Voelz's presentation, by a colleague at the same seminary, that in tandem with Tiede's by a professor from the same church body. Duane A. Priebe, of Wartburg Theological Seminary (ALC), Dubuque, Iowa, who spoke first, had done his graduate study in New Testament and hermeneutics and since has worked in systematic theology also; he presented a paper in the first LC/USA conferences on hermeneutics in 1968.[118] Kurt E. Marquart, of Concordia Theological Seminary, Fort Wayne, an American who once served in the Lutheran Church in Australia, has already been cited as an outspoken proponent of the "official Missouri" confessional position.[119] Both are familiar with the issues, Priebe also having been a participant in the LC/USA study "The Function of Doctrine and Theology."

Priebe's "Theology and Hermeneutics," included in this volume, can be termed as clear and simple a statement as is available on behalf of those who employ, though not uncritically, the tradition-history approach to biblical texts they treasure, as a hermeneutic to understand what the language of the Bible means. The essay takes up, in his own words, (1) "the necessity of hermeneutics in the relation between Scripture and theology," (2) "the polarity of distance and participation that belongs to understanding the hermeneutical task," (3) "the significance of historicity for understanding the hermeneutical circle," and (4) "the evocative power of the text to interpret the present and create new dimensions of meaning."

Priebe pictures a dialogue between Christian theology and God's activity in Israel and in Jesus Christ which is witnessed to in "the writtenness of Scripture." But already in the Hebrew Scriptures, he shows, there is a hermeneutical process of interpretation, which in a way has been going on ever since. For many people today, Priebe added, it will not do simply to repeat formulations of the Reformation or even of the Bible, for to do so in new situations alters their meaning. If anything, the historical-critical method, by taking seriously the situations of the biblical writers, heightens the distance of Scripture from us and often from the dogmatic

JOHN REUMANN

tradition of the church. Yet participation is still needed to let the power of Scripture dissolve the distance and create new understandings for us. Barth, Bultmann, and others have shown the inadequacy of the historical-critical method alone to accomplish this. What to do?

Employing the idea of "hermeneutics as a process of fusion of horizons" (Gadamer), Priebe argued for letting the historical-critical method show "the strange horizon of the text" in all its distance from the modern interpreter. But he also argued for letting a "new common understanding" emerge in "the hermeneutical circle" when the horizon of the text interacts with that of the interpreter, for texts have power evocatively to interpret us and our situation and to create new dimensions of meaning in today's scene, especially when set in the context of "the history of Israel culminating in Jesus" or "the inherent meaning of Jesus' history within . . . the history of Israel's traditions" (Pannenberg). Thus a text may have a "multiplicity of meanings" already in its history within the canon, let alone beyond. Yet the normative sense for the living word—for all its power to "provoke new meaning" and dynamically open our history into God's future (and Priebe insists "the future of an event belongs to the meaning of that event in history")—the normative and "authoritative Word" remains "the historicity of Scripture in its literal grammatical-historical sense."

While perhaps a majority of participants readily identified with such a hermeneutic, others objected. "No dogma is possible after a paper like this!" To be told one can no longer preserve a past theology by simply repeating its formulations was distressing to others; what of reciting the Apostles' Creed? Distressing also was the comment in the paper that when we read the Bible in the context of our dogmatic traditions, "we almost automatically find in [it] what our presuppositions lead us to expect, and we fail to notice the oddities that stand in tension with our expectations." (Priebe had illustrated with Stendahl's comments on guilt and forgiveness in Paul.) One voice was heard: "If I found something different exegetically from the confessional subscription I made [upon being ordained], I'd resign [from the office of the ministry]." Priebe's reference to the "multiplicity of meanings" in a text also called forth requests for examples and applications. Romans 10:4, "Christ is the end of the law" (in the sense of goal or climax? as the one who puts an end to law?), was one verse discussed, with Paul's meaning as a first stage in a process of interpreting that continues to today.

In contrast, in a paper clear in its outline and aggressive in its arguments (included in this volume), Kurt E. Marquart claimed that there

42

is "incompatibility between historical-critical theology and the Lutheran Confessions" for three reasons. Theologizing that accepts the historical-critical method as valid, necessary, or permissible is out, he says, because it "(1) subjects Scripture to reason, (2) introduces a deeply antiincarnational split between history and theology, and (3) relativizes all dogma into doubtful human opinions"—which will not permit the certainty necessary for theology proper.

Marquart will not identify the historical-critical method just with this technique or that, for most techniques, he admits "(e.g., literary criticism, redaction criticism) can be used up to a point, also by anticritical scholars." No, the historical-critical method, as a child of the Enlightenment, is instead marked by commitment to the sovereignty of human reason, so that the critic becomes the judge of the biblical documents. Inerrancy goes by the board; analogy and correlation to *my* experiences are in. This holds true for the "wider critical principle" and for the "narrow" one. The latter, according to Marquart, accepts "human intelligence as arbiter of truth," so that the Bible is read like any other book (it characterizes Anglo-Saxon scholarship), while the former goes further and rules out miracles as well (it "predominates among German scholarship"). The "wider" principle is incompatible with "bona fide subscription to the Lutheran Confessions." Is the "narrow" principle possible?

Marquart's answer ultimately is that use of the historical-critical method, with its appeal to reason, is allowable in the stage prior to faith, for apologetics, when one may by the scriptural evidence (e.g., in J. N. D. Anderson's "legal brief" on the New Testament) be moved to say, "This is most likely true," but it is "insufficient and sub-Christian" after faith, in the realm of theology proper, where one must say, "This is most certainly true." The path to this conclusion about a strictly limited role for the historical-critical method runs through two further points in the paper.

The critical approach, Marquart insists, has always sought to drive a wedge between "the divine and the human" in Scripture, the heavenly and the historical, the vertical and the horizontal. But "any retreat from facts and history" is "a retreat from the incarnation," where the divine and human were not divorced. Dividing up the temporal and eternal is termed docetic, Nestorian, or Calvinistic (the *extra Calvinisticum* was a doctrine, rejected by Lutherans, that *logos* did not cease, after uniting with the human nature of Christ, but continued also "outside"—*extra*—him). This christological appeal made by the essay is reflected in examples cited as unsatisfactory christologizing under the influence of historical criticism (by J. S. Setzer, Roy Harrisville). The final area has to do with the certainty needed, according to the essay, for proper theology. Historical criticism, even in its narrow form, allows only "probable judgments," but "*some* facts" must be "a priori certain and settled, namely, by divine authority and revelation," that is, in Scripture. Hence "either *sola scriptura*" as judge "or else critical human reason and scholarship. . . . The issue is nonnegotiable." And this means that amid a "crisis" or "breakdown" about the Bible, inspiration and inerrancy must be defended.

Appreciation was expressed for the way the paper clarified issues. But objections came on many points. The final paragraph, using anti-Zwinglian language about the sacrament with regard to the Bible, was said to have no organic connection with the rest of the paper. The principle in citing articles exemplifying the historical-critical method, such as that by Setzer (with which no one present would necessarily agree), seems to have been: "Some cases establish all examples as bad; would the essayist associate himself with *all* fundamentalists in the world?" The heart of the paper was seen by someone else to lie in its emphasis on "certainty." But the connection forged between certainty and "truth" is too tight. "Certainty" can be used in various ways, but if New Testament Christianity walks "by faith, not sight," it is faith in a Person, needing knowledge and confidence, but not "certainty." There was also a feeling that the approach must show exactly what techniques of scholarship can be legitimately used in Marquart's view, to what point or degree, and when (only before one comes to faith?).

The incarnational-sacramental unity and analogy between Scripture and the Lord's Supper invoked in the essay, as well as a reference to the Arnoldshain agreement, sparked a particularly striking discussion. This modern German theological statement was also raised elsewhere in the course of discussions by LCMS representatives. Marquart sees historical criticism as incompatible with confessional doctrine in that the theses developed at Arnoldshain by Reformed and Lutheran theologians in Germany from conversations between 1947 and 1957 seem to regard it as "no longer possible to connect" the institution of the Lord's Supper with "the night in which Jesus was betrayed."[120] Actually, Thesis I.1 says simply, "The Lord's Supper which we celebrate is based on the institution and command of Jesus Christ, who has given himself for us in death and who is our risen lord."[121] Presumably what is meant is the commentary on this thesis by Helmut Gollwitzer, who explained that the phraseology was deliberate.[122] We can scarcely equate the Lord's Supper that we celebrate today, Gollwitzer explained, directly with a naive understanding of the New Testament accounts of its institution as historical reports of Jesus' last supper. This is the "historical Jesus" question. Though some would plead for historical reliability,[123] the New Testament accounts as they stand stem from the early (Hellenistic) church (so form criticism), and the exact words of Jesus in the upper room remain in dispute.[124] Confessional assertions must be kept free from this dispute, Gollwitzer concluded, for "if they speak of an 'institution by Christ,' they are not making a historical judgment but . . . express the certainty that the commission and promise of the church's Lord, in his unity as earthly and exalted One, we perceive in the New Testament's testimony to Christ through the testimony of the community." Such a position, brought on by modern biblical studies, represents a new problem, unknown to the sixteenth century.[125] Marquart's answer is that what the Confessions say obligate us to hold dogmatically to the words of institution as having been spoken on Holy Thursday night in the upper room. But *which* words are to be used as efficacious today—Matthew's, Mark's, Luke's, or Paul's? (In actuality, most liturgical forms are composites of these.) It was answered: all are true; to say one or the other wasn't so is out. Someone else holding a conservative view said he would object if any form went beyond the four versions in the New Testament. Yet problems remain precisely with these four accounts and what presumably Jesus uniquely said that night in Jerusalem. One side sees it as difficult to know exactly what he said and reckons with churchly development, admittedly under the Spirit, within the New Testament; the other holds to four scriptural accounts and equates them historically with the upper room, unwilling to probe seeming differences.

At last on 4 May came examination of two methods for historical exegesis on the same passage, by Martin H. Scharlemann and Donald H. Juel. Scharlemann, widely known as a pioneer in New Testament studies among Missouri Synod Lutherans and for his role in recent debates, has been professor for many years at Concordia Seminary, Saint Louis and has published widely.[126] Juel, a younger scholar from the ALC, ordained by the LCA, has recently published his dissertation and coauthored an introduction to the New Testament.[127] He was teaching at the time at Princeton Seminary.

The two exegetical studies, which should be read side by side (Scharlemann's was presented first), deal with parables:

| Mustard Seed | Matthew 13:31–32 | Mark 4:30–32 | Luke 13:18–19 |
| Leaven | 13:33 | — | 13:20–21 |

As already noted, Juel focuses on just the first, but both essays go into context (Luke's differing from Matthew's and Mark's) and both reflect or use aspects of source, form, and redaction study, along with text and philological matters. Juel's paper has been somewhat more revised for publication. Scharlemann's deliberately approximates more a seminary-classroom setting; therefore he gives us sermonic outlines. Discussion focused far more on the Scharlemann paper.

Scharlemann chose to operate with a method he calls "radical ortho-doxy." This was explained to mean that it respects orthodox Lutheran theology but goes to the roots (*radix*) of things. His five emphases for "the art of interpretation" are spelled out at the start: the exegete, as theologian not just historian, is to uncover God's truth in the canonical text, "*not* some point in the trajectory behind it," for the Gospels "offer us the words of the exalted Christ standing in continuity with the earthly Jesus." Against form criticism it is insisted that communities cannot pro-duce anything of consequence. In practice this means that Jesus, as "the greatest, most creative, and most effective teacher who ever lived or ever will live" (as Scharlemann put it in a discussion group), likely told para-bles more than once; hence, the different settings. Form criticism is thus overleaped by Scharlemann, and even source criticism, for Q and redac-tion need not enter in. "The variety may well go back to Jesus himself." Very little except a phrase such as "saying to them" in Matthew 13:31 need be credited to the evangelist. Yet Luke 13:30 is adjudged nearer to the very words of Jesus (*ipsissima verba*), while the parallel at Matthew 13:33 was termed his very voice (*ipsissima vox*), though even here it was suggested it could have been put that way by Jesus on another occasion. (See Scharlemann's n. 10 for his understanding of these crucial Latin terms.)

Scharlemann's homiletical suggestions readily draw in passages from elsewhere in Scripture, for reasons not always indicated. There is a strong tendency to expand the text to theological language about "Word and sacrament." It was objected by one listener that even Käsemann could use a formula such as "the exalted Christ in continuity with the historical Jesus"; Scharlemann insisted that "whatever is given in the Gospels roots in some verbum of the earthly [his term for 'historical'] Jesus"—even the highest statements in the Fourth Gospel have a "point of attachment."[128] His view that Mark *chose* to omit the parable of the leaven was not accepted by all; there could be other explanations, one conservative thought. To specific questions Scharlemann answered that if there is Q material it is inspired only in the part taken into the canonical text, and the difficult saying about the purpose of parables in Mark 4:12 (contrast Matt. 13:21, "because" instead of "in order that") he would attribute in *both* forms to the historical Jesus *and* the risen Christ.

The Juel essay on the parable of the mustard seed presents much more the tradition-historical approach. Source criticism is not merely saluted but used. Redaction criticism is taken seriously enough that while Juel finds a continuity in what each Gospel has in reporting Jesus' parable, he tries to describe the nuance in each. The presentation begins with a series of observations about the passage. It eschews several lines of possible study in order to concentrate on the parable's meaning in Mark and then more briefly in the other Synoptics, then last of all on the historical-Jesus level. As it turns out, the passage is a poor one with which to do much form-critically or to make a lot of source usage, for most critical scholars are willing to trace it back to Jesus, and the high percentage of agreement in wording in all Gospel versions excludes much in the way of redaction or consideration of earlier shades of meaning. Juel too adds some homiletical comments.

One discussion group observed that both exegetical papers seemed to use the same method, although LCMS representatives "would probably not call it the historical-critical method." Another exegete felt "considerable agreement is shown when we get down to texts, without dragging in names of methods." Marquart stated that the Scharlemann paper was congenial to what he had enunciated in his paper and shows how an authority principle need not lead to a flat meaning.

The small-group discussions[129] were important for bringing out issues and agreements. One group, for example, said that if, as they found, there is general agreement that "Scripture is totally reliable and totally adequate" as authority but authority is to be seen not in "doctrinal extrapolations" but in the texts themselves, then it is crucial to discover how much commonality there can be in historical methods for getting at the texts themselves. Yet "it was argued that when differences of hermeneutical method lead to different results (e.g., the practice of ordaining women, . . . abortion), then these differences do in fact divide." That same group agreed "that Jesus in his life, ministry, death, and resurrection must be seen as the heart of the Christian faith," but was in disagreement over whether the historical-critical method, in dealing with Jesus, is "a *theology* which creates faith or . . . a *method* used by those in faith to open up the dimensions of the witnesses." Out of their discussions of inspiration came such questions as, Does an interpreter have access to the

Holy Spirit only through the text and the exegetical method or through a prior, speculative insight regarding the functioning of the Holy Spirit apart from the texts themselves, an insight which itself then becomes a hermeneutical principle, to which all Scripture must be subordinated? I might ask, If the latter, what is the relation to charismatic approaches?

Or again, what is the relation of the Spirit to the writers of Scripture (inspiration?) and to contemporary preachers (illumination?)? Would many hold, with Scharlemann, "that inspiration by the Spirit is in the 'final pen'" and does not occur in sources unless quoted by that pen which "set down the inspired text," and on the other hand that Jesus was "the greatest . . . teacher . . . ever" because of, among other reasons, the *communicatio idiomatum*?[130] Some felt that Scharlemann looked at Jesus in a nineteenth-century romanticist way, stressing "creative geniuses,"[131] and that he underemphasized the New Testament community's self-understanding of the Spirit at work in its corporate midst. Yet he did allow that the evangelists reworked material on the basis of their theological perspectives[132]—a point on which almost all agree.

One could not help but observe several times that discussion of actual exegesis continued to revolve around the topic of an earlier conference—confessional propria, especially classical Christology. If Marquart charged that historical-critical theology has Nestorian tendencies, a patristics scholar present added that critics of the method "veered in the direction of Eutychianism, that is, of the confusing of the two natures" of Christ (and of the "two natures" of the Scriptures). Constant concern was exhibited by such critics of the *intention* of those using historical-critical methodology—it was feared that they are out to destroy faith or deny the scriptural basis of doctrine (the term *dogma* was used interchangeably). Yet there was agreement, even by critics of the method, that "we cannot 'un-Lutheran' a person for explicating the diversity present in the Bible, with the proviso that the interpreter does not attempt to make authoritative an item which is not in the canonical text or which he claims to be in that text but which is not clearly discernible there." (But "discernible" to whom, by what methods? Does that include sources and forms found "in the text" by tradition criticism?)

One group agreed also on the following: (1) No one here has defended the view that the locus of revelation is in the historical Jesus alone (see Jeremias[133]), or in some Hellenistic community or *Gemeindetheologie* alone. (2) The options discussed for the locus of revelation appear to be: (a) the enfleshed Logos; (b) the "inscripturated word," the Bible (Mar-

48

quart and Scharlemann preferred this); or (c) Jesus in the flesh *and* canonical texts *and* the Spirit-filled community and individuals—though these three factors may be given different emphases by different theologians today.

An Attempt at Summary: Narrowing the Gap?

As at the close of the other national conferences the chairman again undertook to provide a summary of papers and discussions, organized around the themes in Table 1. The concerns for method, hermeneutics, and the Lutheran Confessions were shared by all participants. Depending on their background, people spoke of their method as "historical-critical" or "historical-grammatical," or of "historical-critical *theology*" and "radical orthodoxy." Opponents of the style that has grown up under the aegis of the historical-critical method stressed the method's origins in the En-

TABLE 1

Who Shall Be the Judge?

The Historical Method?	and/or	Confessional Fidelity?
	"Hermeneutics" as an attempt to decide	
presuppositions		canon biblical unity inerrancy
"wider critical principle"		"narrow critical principle"— "before faith" (allowable) "after faith" (??)

lightenment and presuppositions such as magisterial use of reason, secularized methods, use of comparative religion, and the principles of analogy and correlation. They also stressed the unity of what is in the canon, as a "seamless robe," absolutely necessary in order to have any dogma, and hence they champion biblical inerrancy. Proponents felt it useless to pretend that the seventeenth century (Lutheran orthodoxy) had not been followed by the eighteenth, and while they admitted that the roots of all historical methods (even prior to the Enlightenment, including those from the Renaissance employed by the Reformers) lie in human reason, they felt that they employed techniques (which even conservatives recognize) with appropriate limits and selectivity so as to enhance our understanding of biblical texts. One can scarcely be more unified or inerrant than the texts themselves without imposing a priori, oversimplified principles from outside, ignoring what Scripture in its rich variety does say.

As to Marquart's two types of "critical principles" and his contention that even the "narrow" one is allowable only *before* faith—so that Scripture, never human reason, is judge—there had been doubts expressed about his view at almost every point. Is what has been done by exegetes at this conference (Voelz, Scharlemann, Tiede, Juel) merely apologetics, not in the realm of gospel dogma, or simply under "law" and "the kingdom on the left," to use classic Lutheran terms? Those here who use the historical-critical method regularly invoke also the gospel or "promise" as judge over the texts. Moreover, Marquart's paper had quoted approvingly a 1972 statement from the Lutheran Church of Australia that once reason is *under* and not *over* Scripture "we affirm the fullest use of reason, with all its scholarly tools, as a servant, to understand and make clear what the sacred text says and means." In group discussion he also seemed to make use of a principle from outside the Bible, in order to distinguish between doubtless inspired texts and other documents, that is, "homologoumena" and "antilegomena."[134]

Given such a picture, can we narrow what seems to be a gap between two approaches? Comments made several times during the three days suggested that there was more agreement than there appeared to be. See Table 2. While the Missouri Synod statements put the emphasis (as others do) on "the *canonical* Word" ("A Statement . . .") or what the

TABLE 2

Can We Go Behind a Text (e.g., a statement of Jesus in the Gospels)?

Historical or earthly Jesus (died A.D. 30)	At Easter he becomes risen Christ and Lord			
	→Oral reports (?) transmit Jesus' statement	→Written sources (?)	→Final New Testament text results	→New Testament books collected, "canon" developed

Involvement of New Testament communities and evangelists and of early church

Seat of authority (?)

"final pen" set down (Scharlemann)[135] as authoritative, others seek to go behind the text to earlier forms. Is the error in attempting that at all, or in the *reconstructing* of a history of precanonical development or of a history *different* from that (which according to traditional views is presupposed) in Acts or in the Gospels? Or is the error in supposing that God was at work in these earlier stages? What of the relationship or "trajectory" of three or four *canonical* Gospel accounts of the same saying or incident? I for one had expected the supporters of a Missouri Synod approach to make much more of a one-to-one equation between the earthly Jesus and the canonical texts. I am uncertain about what their understanding(s) of this relationship is (are).

The real issue, of course, is form criticism. Yet even here one sensed at times a partial endorsement of what form criticism seeks to do as a discipline. (No one present would endorse merely Dibelius's approach to it, or Bultmann's full package of assumptions; in fact, some would agree with even certain German form critics that the whole methodology needs redoing.[136]) The Voelz presentation held that form criticism errs in practice and in its view of history, above all by insisting on analogy to *our* experiences (e.g., regarding miracles). (Does that mean one needs to be a neo-pentecostal or charismatic to appreciate such texts?[137]) Yet the approach by Bailey depends on analogy to the modern Middle East. And even if *Poet and Peasant* was endorsed as being anti-form-criticism, its breakthrough is said to lie in showing how Christians used stylistic phrases to fix material. It does seek, as in Voelz's example, to move from "event" to "essential core, solidified in set phrases" to final version after other elements have been added. Particularly when "recital theology" (like 1 Cor. 11:23–25?) is endorsed, we seem close to some sort of concern for what *Formgeschichte* has sought to get at.

The Scharlemann essay shows awareness of all the "criticisms," even though in this case form and source could be pretty well bypassed. For all the emphasis on the text as seat of authority to be "uncovered" by the exegete-theologian, and the contention that the early Christian community could have produced virtually nothing that went into Scripture (1 Cor. 11:23–25?), I found implied a line of development that runs something like this:

Jesus Christ		Development into Our Gospels	
earthly Jesus	who is also after Easter the "Lord Jesus"	*ipsissima verba* (e.g., Luke 13:20)	*ipsissima vox* (e.g., Matt. 13:33)

51

Continuity is stressed, and final text. So is the historical Jesus. Granted, Jesus may have told a parable twice, and hence we have two slightly differing canonical accounts; but that works better with sayings than with incidents like the temple cleansing or words of institution in the upper room. And though Q is rejected, can sources always be? (Recall Bailey's Jerusalem Document.) How does one describe the transmission of what is in our Gospels between the lifetime of Jesus on earth and the inspired writing of an evangelist? In any case, Scharlemann allows some discernible work by the evangelists (redaction), and so I think the gap in theory is narrowed again a bit in practice and would be more narrow as further texts are examined.

What about the methods, techniques, and subdisciplines of historical criticism? Frank discussion seemed to have established two things. (1) It is not so much the method itself which is objectionable but (a) some of its presuppositions and (b) the intention with which it is used. (2) A distinction is possible among methods, between those spoken against by conservatives (*antilegomena*) and those regarded favorably at least in the initial stages of exegesis (*prolegomena*, in the sense of "used beforehand" and "spoken in favor of"). According to essayists from the Missouri Synod we therefore have:

Permissible Methods: textual studies, linguistic studies (philology, word studies; see Voelz); literary techniques (see, e.g., Bohlmann);

Methods Opposed: form and redaction criticism (goes behind the text); *Sachkritik* (measuring content of one part of Scripture by content in another part); literary criticism, in the modern sense (Voelz).

But will such a distinction work for the exegete? Are the differentiations true? The assumption seems to be that a method is allowable when it "serves Scripture," is "objective" (not dependent on subjective decisions), and has no detrimental theological effects upon doctrine. Text criticism (note the latter noun!) is assumed by almost all conservatives to fit here.[138] Yet does it work in the ways assumed, without making judgments about the text? Nowadays almost everyone would accept as the proper reading at 1 Timothy 3:16 the word *hos* in Greek, "who," or as the Revised Standard Version renders it, "*He* was manifested in the flesh," referring to Jesus Christ. Yet two hundred and fifty years ago J. J. Wetstein was hounded by the orthodox because he claimed that this was the preferred reading rather than "*God* was manifest . . . ," which had been taken as a proof-text for the incarnation of God.[139] At Luke 24:34 a decision between *legontas* and *legontes*, and thus whether it is the eleven who report "The Lord . . . has appeared to Simon" or the pair on the Emmaus road (one of whom may have then been Simon), can be made not by weighing the number of manuscripts on each side but only by judgments about Luke 24:12 (and whether it is a "Western noninterpolation" or not) and Peter's whole role as a witness to the resurrection (see 1 Cor. 15:5). As someone objected, the point is not that all methods are subject to misuse but rather that text criticism does involve some subjective decisions about Bible content.

Much the same thing can be said about the word-study method used by all the exegetical essays (see Scharlemann's on "leaven"). Almost all exegetes, conservative and liberal, will allow that the word studies in the Kittel *Theological Dictionary of the New Testament* do show tendencies of varying sorts, in favor of "salvation history" or "existential interpretation" or "tradition criticism." The more recent *New International Dictionary of New Testament Theology*, avowedly more conservative (but often reflecting insights from form and redaction criticism), likewise shows biases and not just objectivity. There *is* truth to the statement quoted by Voelz that even a Greek dictionary "presupposes the historical-critical method." What is the alternative in dealing with documents of the past? And anyone who thinks he can do literary criticism or even apply literary techniques without getting into decision-making about the text has not faced the issues in practice. Bailey's extensive use of chiastic literary structure involves judgments not only about the work of fellow scholars but also on the text as the evangelist has given it to us.[140] Literary criticism is the harvest of observations on which much of redaction and form criticism rest.[141]

SOURCE AND FORM CRITICISM OF "A STATEMENT . . ."

In concluding his analysis of the study process, the chairman turned to what had been one of the significant documents in this Lutheran discussion about the legitimacy or illegitimacy of "going behind the text of the Bible," namely, "A Statement of Scriptural and Confessional Principles" of the Missouri Synod (1972–73). Part IV, Holy Scripture, Section E, "The Canonical Text of Scripture," reads:

We believe, teach, and confess that the authoritative Word for the church today is the *canonical* Word, not precanonical sources, forms, or traditions—however useful the investigation of these possibilities may on occasion be for a clearer understanding of what the canonical text intends to say.

We therefore reject the following views:

1. That there are various "meanings" of a Biblical text or pericope to be discovered at various stages of its precanonical history, or that the meaning a canonical text has now may differ from the meaning it had when it was first written.

Six other "rejected views" follow. Quite apart from the ambiguity of the last phrase, "the meaning it had when it was first written,"[142] we are faced with a statement of quasi-confessional status on the part of the Lutheran Church—Missouri Synod which is probably unparalleled in Christianity, as a bit of source analysis will suggest.

"We believe, teach, and confess" is a majestic phrase, occurring throughout "A Statement . . ." in combination with "We therefore reject the following. . . ." This formulation for what a confessing church believes and what it rejects occurs in fact as the basic structure for virtually every part of the document, varied slightly only here and there, as in IV.B (simply "we believe") or IV.H, I ("we affirm"). It is of course a formula going back at least to the Lutheran Confessions of the sixteenth century, in the Augsburg Confession ("We unanimously hold and teach") and more particularly in the Epitome of the Formula of Concord (1580), which regularly expounds each article of theology, "We believe, teach, and confess," followed after the affirmative theses by antitheses introduced with the words "Accordingly we reject and condemn" such and such teachings or errors (the Latin for the latter verb is *damnamus*). We have here a form with antecedents already in the biblical "anathema," as developed in the Middle Ages.[143] It is a sign of our age that "we condemn" has been omitted in favor of a simple statement of rejection.

The object or content of what "we believe, teach, and confess" varies in "A Statement. . . ." It may include material from the Confessions, as in Parts I or II, or a biblical phrase plus a modern composition, as in Part III on mission ("to make disciples of every nation" is combined with stress on "verbalizing the Gospel" and on "ministering to men's physical needs" as something necessary but secondary). In the case of IV.E we can pinpoint precisely the source of the statement about "the *canonical* Word."

In the 1960s the Committee on Theology and Church Relations (CTCR) of the Missouri Synod developed a Lutheran "Stance Statement" on "contemporary biblical studies." After outlining Lutheran presuppositions and "basic and legitimate elements of the so-called historical-critical method,"[144] this earlier statement went on to list some "necessary controls." The first read:

> The authoritative Word for the church today is the canonical Word, not precanonical sources, forms, or traditions—however useful the investigation of these possibilities may on occasion be for a clearer understanding of what the canonical text intends to say.

As can be seen at a glance, "A Statement . . ." has simply taken this wording over as the object of what "we believe, teach, and confess," making a change only in italicizing "canonical," to fit the topic heading for the section.

What has been achieved by this combination of confessional form and CTCR statement? I offered the reaction that the Lutheran Church—Missouri Synod had thereby become the only body I know which, as at least quasi-confessional teaching, calls *for* source, form, and redaction criticism on the part of exegetes as "useful . . . for a clearer understanding of what the canonical text intends to say." One may be delighted as a supporter of the fruitfulness of the tradition-history approach to see "the criticisms" thus enjoined, but at the same time one must be dismayed; to make it a matter of churchly confession is too much!

It was replied that this, of course, was not the intention of "A Statement . . ." (I agree, but it is thereby shown how difficult it sometimes is to discern intentions from what a text literally says) and that the subtheses (what is rejected) do not enjoin that. One must decide after looking for oneself at the full text, including subtheses. The first has been quoted above. Presumably it means that what the canonical text says is what it always meant and what it always will mean. On the one hand, precanonically, that seems to preclude even discussion of historicity—Matthew's version must be as true as Luke's, and we ought not to probe what "actually was said," for it was said twice (so Scharlemann); yet the Scharlemann essay itself ventures judgments as to which canonical version is ipsissima *verba* and which ipsissima *vox*. Postcanonically, assuming that a passage takes on no new dimensions when placed within the canonical collection, we are evidently locked into the view that "the *meaning* a canonical text has *now*" is "the meaning it had when it was *first* written" (emphasis mine); contrast Priebe's emphasis on "evoking new meanings," and even the influence of the Confessions and a lectionary as hermeneutic. I have great sympathy for what the LCMS statement is trying to do for the normative value of the scriptural text we possess, but it too rigidly ties up meaning and the power of Scripture to speak afresh. My concern as historian and theologian may be seen in quoting one other subthesis that is closely related. "A Statement . . ." rejects the view "that the essential theological data of Biblical theology is to be found in the precanonical history of the Biblical text." I would hope that some "essential theological data" *are* found prior to "the final pen" and what the amanuensis records, for example, that 1 Corinthians 11:23–25 or 15:3–5 are reliable traditions or that Q-sayings or the testimonies which Luke alone records but could not personally have been involved in during Jesus' ministry do give us "essential theological data."

The trouble with "A Statement . . ." at this point is that it too easily combined sources without considering original context and has endorsed and rejected things without carefully and fully working through the problems latent in the biblical texts. It is difficult to assess rightly always what "A Statement . . ." rejects, for some rejected views are said to be not actual opinions held by anyone in the Concordia, Saint Louis, faculty prior to 1972 but to have been included to allow them to deny what were *not* their views! Such an approach implies a high familiarity with the issues involved. Unfortunately the thrust and aim of the original CTCR Stance Statement was very different; it sought to allow use of historical-critical methods with "necessary controls." In "A Statement . . ." the control has become the norm to be confessed; yet the methods are included in what "we believe, teach, and confess," although the results are already confessionally predetermined here.

For all this debate I remain convinced—and the closing remarks on 5 May 1977 reiterated it—that in many areas of exegetical methods and techniques, as exhibited in actual practice, Lutherans involved in these discussions are closer than might have been thought. Where there is honest disagreement over methodology we need to reassure each other of our intentions. I did not hear those who practice the historical-critical method desiring to undermine Scripture; they want to employ every means at their disposal to let it speak more clearly. Nor did I hear those who are opposed to (aspects of) the historical-critical method desiring to ignore history or to return to allegory; to bring out the historical reality of what is in the Bible is precisely what they seek to do. Yet there remains a terrific fear on the one side that the distinctive emphases of Lutheran confessional theology will be undermined or set aside, and on the other that confessionalism will blind Lutherans to what Scripture itself says. I for one regard my church's Confessions as pointing me constantly to test my confessional heritage by going back to the Scriptures. That involves use of all appropriate methodologies, with theological awareness. But my theology or even that of my church dares not predetermine all that the scriptural text can say. I must constantly ask whether Lutherans cannot live with other expressions of the gospel in the Bible, such as the "kingdom of God" (Mark 1:15), without too readily transmuting it into "justification by grace." One must be alert to what "word of God" means in the New Testament[145] without immediately making it into some later understanding of "Word and sacrament."

Finally, in this study Lutherans of all stripes became aware of the need for further investigation of a good many topics, not least of which involves, beyond a philosophy of Scripture and refinement of how exegetical techniques should be used (which for the health of the church always ought to be under discussion, in principle and in specific applications), how we today understand "revelation" and the work of the Holy Spirit:

(1) What is (are) the "locus (places) of revelation":
in historical events,
in transmission of witness about these,
in the final form in a canonical document,
in the canonical collection,
in the history of subsequent use,
in the Confessions of the church,
in our lectionary and calendrical settings,
and in proclamation today?

(2) How shall we speak of the work of the Holy Spirit in this process? Where ought we to refer to inspiration, illumination or enlightenment or providence, fruitful hearing or reception, in the several stages from a text and what preceded it to us today?

A PERSONAL POSTSCRIPT

The above pages attempt to describe, with some objectivity, a study process. Especially in the chairman's summaries of each conference there is included a point of view that is reflective of the Lutheran Church in America historically and today and of the writer personally.[146] The whole is written with a certain optimism that the discussion is one from which all can learn. I appreciate the fidelity with which Missouri Synod voices call us ever to the sovereignty of Scripture and a confessional stance. There *are* excesses to the historical-critical method which in some practitioners are simply wrong. I hear no participant in this dialogue endorsing the wild extremes on either side. Lutherans are not inclined to burn Bible translations with which they disagree, close their eyes to ancient historical contexts, or ignore literary insights. The question is to what extent source, form, and redaction criticism help us use Scripture rightly. The Missouri Synod position is more fully set forth below (see the chapter by Samuel H. Nafzger). Throughout our deliberations, I suggest, differing views of authority do run and run deep. But to the historical-critical approach, in 1978 and the decades following, the alternative cannot be an unhistorical or uncritical methodology. My church's explicit statements and example, the Confessions themselves, and Holy Scripture[147] call me to as careful an exegesis as possible of every and any text, under God, revealed in Jesus Christ and his gospel, precisely because within the hermeneutical process it is in the Scriptures, ever beckoning to be better understood and enrich our existence, that I can expect to know of God, Christ, and the good news normatively as they can nowhere else be encountered. But the penultimate, Scripture, points to these ultimates beyond.

Perhaps part of our problem stems from a question James Barr faced in his recent inaugural lecture at Oxford,[148] "Does biblical study still belong to theology?" Yes, he said, it does, for theology and biblical study are the poorer when separated, and "theological study of the Bible does take place in the context of the church." But no, there is also the context of the "wider academic community," and there are "modes of study and interpretation, valid within that community, over which theology as theology cannot pronounce." (The "community of biblical scholarship," Barr thinks, is "more clearly manifest in the sphere of the Old Testament than in that of the New.") The Lutherans in this volume of hermeneutical essays would all agree on the fruitfulness of relating biblical study and theology in the context of the church. Not all would agree on the propriety of modes of study from the academic community within the church, but some have experienced more than others the insights of this "wider academic community," knowing the insights as well as the hazards such scholarship brings.

The closest parallel to this Lutheran Council study is, I think, the collection of some eighteen essays on principles and methods of New Testament interpretation by conservative evangelicals, edited by I. Howard Marshall.[149] Source, form, and redaction criticism, tradition history, demythologizing, semantics, and much more are assessed, constructively and critically, and applied. Given the caricature many have held of conservative evangelicals, there can only be surprise at the way such methods are often now accepted and employed. "Levels of meaning," "the historical critical method" as a "safeguard" against reading the New Testament through our "own doctrinal spectacles," a willingness to ask whether the conservative scholar ought not "adopt an approach of methodological scepticism" toward the text, and the allowance that some statements in the Gospels (such as Matt. 18:17) are "unlikely . . . authentic," that is, from the historical Jesus, all appear. Yet these conservative evangelical authors, the editor says, "share the same general outlook" of "high regard for the authority of Holy Scripture" and "belief that we are called to study it with the full use of our minds."[150] One may at times get the impression that the "expositor" has, and will have, a difficult time keeping up with the exegete![151] Yet "plurality of opinions is not surprising, and is not necessarily a bad thing," for "conservative evangelicals in particular have been slow to work out the implications of their view of Scripture for the task of interpretation and vice-versa."[152] So have others as well.

Lutherans, through the essays that follow, are sharing in the common task of biblical interpretation, testing implications for their view of Scripture, and their views of Scripture and authority by actual wrestling with texts. Luther is a paradigm for "beating importunately" upon a text and "ardently desiring to know" what it means. He found the meaning of "God's righteousness" by philology and grammar, analogy, and the mercy of God.[153] By what methods today?

NOTES

1. See James E. Adams, *Preus of Missouri and the Great Lutheran Civil War* (New York: Harper & Row, 1977); Frederick W. Danker, assisted by Jan Schambach, *No Room in the Brotherhood: The Preus-Otten Purge of Missouri* (St. Louis: Clayton Publishing House, 1977), a "moderate" viewpoint by a New Testament professor at Concordia who left to become a part of Seminex; *Exodus from Concordia: A Report on the 1974 Walkout*, by the Board of Control (St. Louis: Concordia Seminary, 1977), the "official" Missouri Synod version; Kurt E. Marquart, *Anatomy of an Explosion: Missouri in Lutheran Perspective*, Concordia Seminary Monograph Series 3 (Ft. Wayne: Concordia Theological Seminary Press, 1977), a theological-ideological analysis from the "official" Missouri standpoint by a faculty member at the synod's other seminary (formerly in Springfield, Ill.) against "the new doctrines which split the Synod" (p. v), above all about "the critical contagion," as he terms historical criticism.
2. Friend and foe of the approach agree that Edgar Krentz's *The Historical-Critical Method* (Philadelphia: Fortress Press, 1975) is a standard chronicle of the rise of the methodology and of its assumptions and characteristics. Krentz, who left Concordia, St. Louis, for Christ Seminary–Seminex, did the paper on this topic in the LC/USA study of hermeneutics in 1968 (see above, Preface, n. 4).

3. Walter Wink, *The Bible in Human Transformation: Toward a New Paradigm for Biblical Study* (Philadelphia: Fortress Press, 1973).

4. Ibid., pp. 1, 2.

5. Ibid., pp. 53, 60, 85, e.g. For some of the judgments expressed above, see my review "Bible Study 'Under New Management,'" *Interpretation* 29 (1975): 305–8. The "new management" for the old historical-critical tools that Wink proposes, namely, one which seeks to interpret Scripture so as to "enable personal and social transformation," has long been stock-in-trade of Pietism and Liberalism and will certainly not satisfy the attack on the historical-critical method being made in the Lutheran discussion.

6. Oswald T. Allis, *The Proposed Confession of 1967* (Philadelphia: Presbyterian and Reformed Publishing Company, n.d.), p. 1. The Confession of 1967 speaks of the Bible as "the word of God written" but holds that the church "has an obligation to approach the Scriptures with literary and historical understanding" (pars. 27 and 29); see Edward A. Dowey, Jr., *A Commentary on the Confession of 1967 and an Introduction to "The Book of Confessions"* (Philadelphia: Westminster Press, 1968).

7. Harold Lindsell, *The Battle for the Bible* (Grand Rapids: Zondervan Publishing House, 1976). For his treatment of the Briggs affair, see pp. 185–99; Southern Baptists, pp. 89–105; Fuller Seminary, pp. 106–21; North Park, Chicago, pp. 123–28. See also Richard J. Coleman, "Biblical Inerrancy: Are We Going Anywhere?" *Theology Today* 31 (January 1975): 295–303; and Richard Quebedeaux, *The Worldly Evangelicals* (New York: Harper & Row, 1978). A counterpart study in Britain to U.S. conservative Protestant debate is *New Testament Interpretation: Essays on Principles and Methods*, ed. I. Howard Marshall (Grand Rapids: Eerdmans, 1977), described at the end of this essay.

8. Lindsell, *Battle for the Bible*, pp. 72–88. The Maier quotation is from a conservative Missouri Synod polemical journal, *Affirm*, June A, 1971, p. 9; see also Walter A. Maier, "The Historical Critical Method as Employed in the Study of the New Testament," *The Springfielder* 35 (1971): 26–40.

9. Raymond E. Brown, "Our New Approach to the Bible," *New Testament Essays* (Garden City, N.Y.: Doubleday Image Books, 1968), pp. 21–35. The reaction came, ironically, under Pope John XXIII, regarded by many Protestants as a liberating hero who opened the windows of the Vatican.

10. *The Jerome Biblical Commentary*, ed. Raymond E. Brown, Joseph A. Fitzmyer, and Roland E. Murphy (Englewood Cliffs, N.J.: Prentice-Hall, 1968), p. xvii. Section 71 gives an account of Catholic hermeneutics; see 72:20–23 on Pius XII's "liberating encyclical" and 72:34–35 on "warnings" about the use of biblical criticism with regard to the Gospels and other sensitive areas. Especially significant in legitimating the use of form criticism were two articles by Augustine Cardinal Bea and the 1964 Instruction of the Biblical Commission, presented in English as *The Study of the Synoptic Gospels: New Approaches and Outlooks*, ed. Joseph A. Fitzmyer (New York: Harper & Row, 1965).

11. *The Birth of the Messiah: A Commentary on the Infancy Narratives in Matthew and Luke* (Garden City, N.Y.: Doubleday & Company, 1977), p. 7.

12. E.g., Ferdinand Hahn, "Exegese, Theologie und Kirche," *Zeitschrift für Theologie und Kirche* 74 (1977): 25–37; O. C. Edwards, Jr., "Historical-Critical Method's Failure of Nerve and a Prescription for a Tonic: A Review of Some Recent Literature," *Anglican Theological Review* 59 (1977): 115–34.

13. Peter Stuhlmacher, "Erwägungen zur Einheit der biblischen Theologie," *Zeitschrift für Theologie und Kirche* 67 (1970): 417–36; "Thesen zur Meth-

odologie gegenwärtiger Exegese," *Zeitschrift für die neutestamentliche Wissenschaft* 63 (1972): 18–26. For an earlier 1950 statement see Gerhard Ebeling, "The Significance of the Critical Historical Method for Church and Theology in Protestantism," in his *Word and Faith*, trans. James W. Leitch (Philadelphia: Fortress Press, 1963), pp. 17–61.

14. *Das Ende der historisch-kritischen Methode* (Wuppertal: Theologischer Verlag Rolf Brockhaus, 1974); English translation, *The End of the Historical-Critical Method*, trans. Edwin W. Leverenz and Rudolph F. Norden, with a foreword by Eugene F. Klug (St. Louis: Concordia Publishing House, 1977).

15. *The End of the Historical-Critical Method*, p. 9.

16. Ibid., pp. 80–92. The comment of Martin H. Scharlemann in "Der Stand der neutestamentlichen Forschung/The Status of New Testament Studies," in *Evangelium—"Euaggelion"—Gospel* (Bimonthly for Lutheran Theology and Church, Berlin) 4 (August 1977): 97, is worth quoting: "It is my prediction that most of the persons who purchase this book will be greatly disappointed, [i]f for no other reason than that anyone who hopes to get something out of the book must be quite familiar with the nuances of hermeneutical discussions. Moreover, Maier ends his book with a rather detailed description of what he calls 'Die historisch-biblische Methode,' covering about twelve pages out of a total of 95. What is there is useful but it is not done in depth, partly because of the theological strictures put on its author by the German publisher. [Footnote by Scharlemann: 'The R. Brockhaus Verlag, like some other publishing concerns, will not permit any specifically Lutheran accents to appear in its publications.'] Perhaps we ourselves can find some general guidance there and put his suggestions to a more thorough use." The LC/USA hermeneutics project allows precisely for that possibility.

On Luther's "canon within the canon," see *Jerome Biblical Commentary* 67:86 or Werner G. Kümmel, *Introduction to the New Testament*, trans. Howard Clark Kee, rev. ed. (Nashville: Abingdon Press, 1975), pp. 505–6. J. Theodore Mueller, "Luther's 'Canon within the Canon,'" *Christianity Today*, 27 October 1961, pp. 8–10 [72–74], reflects conservative opposition when he calls it "a myth, . . . an invented tale." At issue is the elevating of certain books to the center of the New Testament because they "preach Christ" most clearly and the demoting of others to the periphery of the canon versus a view where all books are regarded as equally inspired, equally authoritative, and therefore with themes and content on a par with each other. For modern development of the principle of "Christ" or "gospel" over canon, see Ernst Käsemann, "The Canon of the New Testament and the Unity of the Church," in his *Essays on New Testament Themes*, trans. W. J. Montague, Studies in Biblical Theology 41 (London: SCM Press, 1964), pp. 95–107; e.g., p. 106, "the canon . . . is only the Word of God in so far as it is and becomes the Gospel." This essay and those by Strathmann, Kümmel, and others are the particular targets of Gerhard Maier, who, after summarizing several of them in *The End of the Historical-Critical Method* (pp. 27–40), rejects all efforts to make something central in the canon, even the experience of justification by grace! "In short, whosoever makes justification of the ungodly his focal point on which all theology should be based . . . banishes important lines and basic thoughts of Scripture into powerless darkness" (p. 40). Further, Inge Lønning, *"Kanon im Kanon": Zum dogmatischen Grundlagenproblem des neutestamentlichen Kanons*, Forschungen zur Geschichte und Lehre des Protestantismus 43 (Munich: Chr. Kaiser Verlag 1972).

17. Peter Stuhlmacher, *Historical Criticism and Theological Interpretation of Scripture: Toward a Hermeneutics of Consent*, trans. with introduction by Roy A. Harrisville (Philadelphia: Fortress Press, 1977), pp. 66–71. Stuhlmacher sees "three fronts" which offer alternatives to the historical-critical method that Protestant theology "has long recognized . . . and practices with noteworthy success": first, Fundamentalism and Pietism, which mistrust the method; second, "a socio-critical political hermeneutic," "contemporary, empirical, service-oriented"; and third, those who adapt it to their scientific and theological needs ("kerygma neo-orthodoxy," "theological pietism," a stress on *Heilsgeschichte*). He classifies himself "as moving along the boundaries between kerygmatic theology, Pietism, and biblically-oriented Lutheranism" (pp. 19–21).

18. Ibid., p. 70; see Maier, *End of the Historical-Critical Method*, p. 84.

19. See H. Lindner, "Widerspruch oder Vermittlung? Zum Gespräch mit G. Maier und P. Stuhlmacher über eine biblische Hermeneutik," *Theologische Beiträge* (Wuppertal) 7 (1976): 185–97. Peter Stuhlmacher, "Biblische Theologie und kritische Exegese," *Theologische Beiträge* 8 (1977): 88–90.

20. "A Statement . . ." and "A Comparative Study . . ." are available from the Commission on Theology and Church Relations, Lutheran Church–Missouri Synod, 500 North Broadway, St. Louis, Mo. 63102. While commonly credited to President J. A. O. Preus, "A Statement . . ." is described in the study edition as drawn up "in consultation with the synodical Vice-Presidents." The LC/USA hermeneutics project was fortunate in having present at its sessions as members of its DTS standing committee the executive secretary of the CTCR at the time "A Statement . . ." appeared, Ralph A. Bohlmann, and his successor, Samuel H. Nafzger.

21. Paul G. Bretscher, *After the Purifying*, Thirty-Second Yearbook (River Forest, Ill.: Lutheran Educational Association, 1975).

22. In 1973 the Lutheran Church in America had engaged in its "Affirmations" study; see William H. Lazareth, *Exploration in Faith: Congregational Inquiries for the Study of Affirmations of Faith* (Philadelphia: Lutheran Church Press, 1973). The purpose was "to convey the meaning of the Lutheran Confessions to persons today." While hermeneutics was not an issue, the approach was committed to a view of the Word of God centered in Jesus Christ rather than a book (Leader's Guide, pp. 20–21). An analysis of "concrete, burning issues" in U.S. churches in 1973, compiled by representatives of the LCA and ALC for the Lutheran World Federation, refused to "elevate the Missouri Synod controversy over the historical-critical study of Scripture into a major issue for the rest of U.S. Lutheranism"; *The Church Emerging: A U.S. Lutheran Case Study*, ed. John Reumann (Philadelphia: Fortress Press, 1977), p. 24.

23. Karlfried Froehlich, *Formen der Auslegung von Matthäus 16, 13–18 im lateinischen Mittelalter* (Tübingen: Präzis, 1963).

24. H. C. Kee, F. W. Young, and K. Froehlich, *Understanding the New Testament* (Englewood Cliffs, N.J.: Prentice-Hall, 2d ed., 1965; 3d. 1973).

25. See *Peter in the New Testament: A Collaborative Assessment by Protestant and Roman Catholic Scholars*, ed. Raymond E. Brown, Karl P. Donfried, and John Reumann (Minneapolis: Augsburg Publishing House; New York: Paulist Press, 1973), pp. 83–101. Froehlich participated in this study team.

26. Names and dates for each conference are given below.

27. Rome: Typis Polyglottis Vaticanus, 1969. ILCW version: *The Church*

Year: Calendar and Lectionary, Contemporary Worship 6 (Minneapolis: Augsburg Publishing House; Philadelphia: LCA Board of Publication; St. Louis: Concordia Publishing House, 1973). An ILCW survey in early 1976 reported that 92% of LCA pastors were using the three-year lectionary in worship, and 90% and 87% of pastors in the ALC and LCMS respectively.

28. E.g., N. A. Dahl, "The Lutheran Exegete and the Confessions of His Church," *Lutheran World* 6 (1959): 2–10; Edward H. Schroeder, "Is There a Lutheran Hermeneutics?" in *The Lively Function of the Gospel: Essays in Honor of Richard R. Caemmerer,* ed. Robert W. Bertram (St. Louis: Concordia Publishing House, 1966), pp. 81–98; Amos N. Wilder, "Reconciliation—New Testament Scholarship and Confessional Differences," *Interpretation* 19 (1965): 203–16, 312–27; James M. Robinson, "A Critical Inquiry into the Scriptural Bases of Confessional Hermeneutics," *Journal of Ecumenical Studies* 3 (1966): 36–56.

29. Published as "Adaptable for Life: The Nature and Function of Canon," in *Magnalia Dei, The Mighty Acts of God: Essays on the Bible and Archaeology in Memory of G. Ernest Wright,* ed. F. M. Cross, W. E. Lemke, and P. D. Miller, Jr. (Garden City, N.Y.: Doubleday & Company, 1976), pp. 531–60.

30. Morton Smith, *Palestinian Parties and Politics That Shaped the Old Testament* (New York: Columbia University Press, 1971).

31. A. C. Sundberg, Jr., *The Old Testament of the Early Church,* Harvard Theological Studies 20 (Cambridge: Harvard University Press, 1964); idem, "The Making of the New Testament Canon," in *The Interpreter's One-Volume Commentary on the Bible,* ed. Charles M. Laymon (Nashville: Abingdon Press, 1971), pp. 1216–24; idem, "The Bible Canon and the Christian Doctrine of Inspiration," *Interpretation* 29 (1975): 352–71.

32. James A. Sanders, *Torah and Canon* (Philadelphia: Fortress Press, 1972).

33. James A. Sanders, "Torah and Christ," *Interpretation* 29 (1975): 372–90.

34. Mic. 6:6–8 as the first lesson for the Common of Saints was cited as a choice that misses the point of the passage.

35. The Roman *Ordo* and its Protestant Episcopal version include some first lessons from those books which Protestants regard as noncanonical but which many Bibles, including Luther's, place between the two Testaments. See *The Church Year* (cited above, n. 27), p. 23. The ILCW pericopes committee and liturgical texts committee included some eight passages from the Apocrypha, though always with a canonical alternative, but they were eliminated by the ILCW out of concern for reactions, particularly within the Missouri Synod. On the issue of past Lutheran practice, see Arthur Carl Piepkorn, "Theological Observer," *Concordia Theological Monthly* 43 (1972): 449–53.

36. See "Constitution on the Sacred Liturgy," chap. 2, sec. 51, *The Documents of Vatican II,* ed. Walter M. Abbott (New York: Association Press, 1966), p. 155.

37. E.g., the planned sequence for three Sundays in Year A—Pentecost 16, Matt. 18:15–20, on discipline and prayer; Pentecost 17, Matt. 18:21–35, on forgiveness (the unmerciful servant); and Pentecost 18, Matt. 20:1–16, the generosity of God (laborers in the vineyard)—was disrupted in September 1975 by the fact that the lessons for the last two Sundays were usurped by those of Holy Cross and St. Matthew's Day. This happens frequently enough to disrupt the lectionary's flow.

38. See Arland J. Hultgren, "Anticipating the 'Gospel of the Year' for 1975: A Preface to Preaching on Matthew," *Lutheran Forum* 8, no. 4 (November 1974): 20–22; "Thoughts on the 'Gospel of the Year' for 1976: Preaching Prospects with Mark," ibid. 9, no. 4 (November 1975): 21–27. Also, John Reumann, "Les sélections du lectionnaire dans la tradition luthérienne," *Concilium* 102 (1975): 57–67 (French, German, Italian, Dutch versions, but never published in English). An issue of *Interpretation* devoted entirely to lectionaries appeared later (31, no. 2 [April 1977]: John Reumann, "A History of Lectionaries: From the Synagogue at Nazareth to Post-Vatican II," pp. 116–30); Gerard S. Sloyan, "The Lectionary as a Context for Interpretation," pp. 131–38; Lloyd R. Bailey, "The Lectionary in Critical Perspective," pp. 139–53; Elizabeth Achtemeier, "Aids and Resources for the Interpretation of Lectionary Texts," pp. 154–64; and a treatment of the three lessons for the Tenth Sunday after Pentecost, cycle C, by Roy A. Harrisville, pp. 165–78. See also the "expository articles" (between exegesis and the sermon) which began in the January 1975 issue of *Interpretation* (vol. 29) and the issues devoted to a single Gospel with an eye to the lectionary preacher—Matt.: 29, no. 1 (January 1975); Mark: 32, no. 4 (October 1978); Luke: 30, no. 4 (October 1976), and John: 31, no. 4 (October 1977).

39. In addition to the standing committee, staff, and essayists, the participants included George M. Bass, St. Paul; John R. Brokhoff, Atlanta; Jerrold A. Eickmann, St. Louis; Victor R. Gold, Berkeley; John V. Halvorson, Aberdeen, S.D.; Brian L. Helge, East Chicago, Ind.; George W. Hoyer, St. Louis; Marshall Johnson, Waverly, Iowa; Jack D. Kingsbury, St. Paul; Kurt E. Marquart, Springfield, Ill.; Foster R. McCurley, Philadelphia; William A. Poovey, Dubuque, Iowa; Warren G. Rubel, Valparaiso, Ind.; and Martin R. Taddey, Palo Alto, Calif.

40. Pius Parsch, *Das Jahr des Heils*, 13th ed. (Klosterneuburg: Volksliturgisches Apostolat, 1947), pp. 5–11; English trans.: *The Church's Year of Grace*, vol. 1 (Collegeville: Minn.: Liturgical Press, 1957), pp. 7ff. See Adrian Nocent, *The Liturgical Year* (Collegeville, Minn.: Liturgical Press, 1977).

41. Reginald H. Fuller, "Preparing the Homily," in *Preaching the New Lectionary: The Word of God for the Church Today* (Collegeville, Minn.: Liturgical Press, 1974), pp. xvii–xxxii.

42. See Hultgren's article on Matthew (cited above, n. 38) and his hope that use of the dubiously historical account in Matt. 2:13–23 for Holy Innocents (28 December) might "be removed from the liturgical calendar" (p. 22). An editorial in the same issue (p. 5) sought "to defend the integrity of the church year in the light of its centuries-long development through the church's interaction with Scripture." Discussion followed between Paul L. Maier, who supported "historicity," and Hultgren in *Lutheran Forum* 9, no. 2 (May 1975): 10–13; 9, no. 3 (September 1975): 22; and 9, no. 4 (November 1975): 31. Bornmann wished to add to the Jewish babies at Bethlehem and the list of "innocents of all ages" suggested for remembering in the ILCW commentary on the day (Wounded Knee, S.D.; Guernica; Lidice and Auschwitz; Hiroshima; *The Church Year: Calendar and Lectionary*, Contemporary Worship 6 [Minneapolis: Augsburg Publishing House; Philadelphia: Board of Publication, LCA; St. Louis: Concordia Publishing House, 1973], p. 126) another category—"the millions of infants in the womb, murdered under the processes of abortion." He also assumed that the infants at Bethlehem must have been "saved," yet pointed to the confessional statement that "we cannot assume the salvation of children

who die without Baptism (unless God specifically says so) (Augsburg Confession, IX, 3, Latin version)."

43. Another ALC participant who worked on the lectionary subcommittee, John V. Halvorson, had in the interim moved from a seminary faculty, at Luther, St. Paul, to a parish.

44. E.g., on the Fourth Sunday after Pentecost, cycle A, the Gospel section from Matt. 9:35—10:7 (or 8), about the mission of the twelve, seems to be coupled with Exod. 19:2–6 (or 8), about "a kingdom of priests," because traditional Catholic thought saw the twelve as "the ordained ministry" and this combination of texts enables "ministry" to be construed as "priesthood." But ironically, modern understanding of the Exodus passage would stress its collective side, concerning the whole people of God, and even then of "a collective understanding of the Gospel reading." See Schuyler Brown, "The Sunday Lessons," *Worship* 49 (1975): 236–38.

45. "A Lutheran Stance Toward Contemporary Biblical Studies," issued by the Lutheran Church—Missouri Synod, Commission on Theology and Church Relations, in 1966, stated that "the authoritative Word for the church today is the canonical Word, not precanonical sources, forms, or traditions." This position has been reaffirmed in "A Statement . . ." (cited above, n. 20). See further, above, pp. 54–57.

46. *The Book of Concord: The Confessions of the Evangelical Lutheran Church*, trans. and ed. Theodore G. Tappert (Philadelphia: Fortress Press, 1959), contains, after a Preface from 1580: (I) The Three Chief Symbols (the Apostles', Nicene, and Athanasian creeds); (II) The Augsburg Confession (1530), and (III) Apology of the Augsburg Confession (1531); (IV) The Smalcald Articles (1537); (V) Treatise on the Power and Primacy of the Pope (1537); (VI, VII) Luther's Small and Large Catechisms (1529); and (VIII) Formula of Concord (1577). It should be remarked that while some German Lutherans accept all eight items, others, and especially some Scandinavians, accept only I, II, and VI. Such distinctions have carried over into the American Lutheran scene, and even the constitutions of churches like the LCA which accept all eight may arrange the documents in a hierarchically descending list of authorities, subordinate in turn to Christ, the gospel, and Scripture (in that order).

47. See above, n. 28, for representative Lutheran and ecumenical samplings. Further, see Edmund Schlink, *Theology of the Lutheran Confessions*, trans. P. F. Koehneke and H. J. A. Bouman (Philadelphia: Fortress Press, 1961), pp. 1–36 and esp. 297–317, on questions that exegesis of the Scriptures raises for the Confessions; Wilhelm C. Linss, "Biblical Interpretation in the Formula of Concord," in *The Symposium on Seventeenth Century Lutheranism* (St. Louis: Symposium on Seventeenth Century Lutheranism, 1962), 1:118–35; Ralph A. Bohlmann, *Principles of Biblical Interpretation in the Lutheran Confessions* (St. Louis: Concordia Publishing House, 1968); *The Confession-Making Process*, "Studies" series (New York: Lutheran Council in the U.S.A., 1975).

48. E.g., justification, the concept of the Word, law and gospel, the theology of the cross, *simul justus et peccator*, "the finite is capable of the infinite." For recent treatments, see Eric W. Gritsch and Robert W. Jenson, *Lutheranism: The Theological Movement and Its Confessional Writings* (Philadelphia: Fortress Press, 1977), or *Lutheran Identity* (Strasbourg: Institute for Ecumenical Research, 1977).

49. E.g., O. Sydney Barr, *From the Apostles' Faith to the Apostles' Creed* (New York: Oxford University Press, 1964).

50. See above, n. 6. Par. 29 sets forth "two types of principle for interpretation": in light of "God's work of reconciliation in Christ" and "sensitivity to the historical and cultural forms in which the message of reconciliation is communicated" (see par. 49, and Dowey, *Commentary*, pp. 106–8, 144–47). These two foci, without giving much attention to the centuries between the first and our own, may be influenced by "Karl Barth's remark that the Christian should have the Bible in one hand and the newspaper in the other" (ibid., p. 145), but that that is oversimplification is shown by the way in which the Westminster Confession and the Barmen Declaration, among other older statements, are reckoned with (e.g., ibid., pp. 103, 107) and by the fact that this new document is part of the Book of Confessions for Presbyterians.

51. An example would be the Fuller Seminary "statement on faith" on Scripture, to be signed each year by faculty "without mental reservation," discussed in Lindsell, *Battle for the Bible* (cited above, n. 7), pp. 107ff.

52. See the exemplary study by David H. Kelsey, *The Uses of Scripture in Recent Theology* (Philadelphia.: Fortress Press, 1975), covering the work of Barth, H. W. Bartsch, Bultmann, L. S. Thornton, B. B. Warfield, and G. Ernest Wright.

53. Out of the extensive literature one may cite simply Krister Stendahl's 1961 essay "The Apostle Paul and the Introspective Conscience of the West," published most recently in his *Paul among Jews and Gentiles and Other Essays* (Philadelphia: Fortress Press, 1976), pp. 78–96 (but cf. pp. 23–40), and the work of Ernst Käsemann, notably his 1965–66 lecture "Justification and Salvation History in the Epistle to the Romans," in his *Perspectives on Paul* (Philadelphia: Fortress Press, 1971), pp. 60–78.

54. Most Lutheran bodies in this country have historic "operating statements" on Scripture, notably the "Baltimore Declaration on the Word of God and the Scriptures" of the United Lutheran Church in America (1938), the "Pittsburgh Agreement" of that body with the American Lutheran Church (1940), and the "Brief Statement of the Doctrinal Position of the Missouri Synod" (1932). The texts are conveniently available in *Documents of Lutheran Unity in America*, ed. R. C. Wolf (Philadelphia: Fortress Press, 1966), nos. 150, 157, and 158. The three above range from more "liberal" (ULCA) to more "conservative" (LCMS), the Brief Statement insisting on "infallible truth, also in those parts [of Scripture] which treat of historical, geographical, and other secular matters." For "A Statement . . . ," see above, n. 20.

55. See Hummel's effort to derive a Christian doctrine of the ordained ministry from the Old Testament, "The Holy Ministry from Biblical Perspective," *Lutheran Quarterly* 18 (1966): 104–19.

56. Joachim Jeremias, *The Central Message of the New Testament* (New York: Charles Scribner's Sons, 1965).

57. See Morton Scott Enslin, *The Ethics of Paul* (Nashville: Abingdon Press, Apex Books, 1962), pp. 309–10; idem, *Reapproaching Paul* (Philadelphia: Westminster Press, 1972), pp. 136, 142.

58. The phrase was Schweitzer's, comparing justification to *The Mysticism of Paul the Apostle* (New York: Henry Holt & Company, 1911), p. 225.

59. E. P. Sanders, *Paul and Palestinian Judaism: A Comparison of Patterns of Religion* (Philadelphia: Fortress Press, 1977), pp. 543, 550.

60. For references and discussion, see Victor Paul Furnish, *Theology and Ethics in Paul* (Nashville: Abingdon Press, 1968), pp. 224–27, 264–65.

61. Quanbeck's dissertation is summarized in *Catalogue of Doctoral Dissertations, Princeton Theological Seminary 1944–1960* (Princeton, 1962), pp. 26–27; see Warren A. Quanbeck, "Theological Reorientation: The Thought of the Epistle to the Romans," *Interpretation* 14 (1960): 259–72.

62. E.g., in *Marburg Revisited: A Reexamination of Lutheran and Reformed Traditions*, ed. Paul C. Empie and James I. McCord (Minneapolis: Augsburg Publishing House, 1966), pp. 1–24 ("Gospel, Confession and Scripture") and pp. 184–90 ("Confessional Integrity and Ecumenical Dialogue").

63. *Franklin Clark Fry: A Palette for a Portrait*, Supplementary number of the *Lutheran Quarterly* 24 (1972).

64. Fischer took hermeneutics for sacred literature to be "not basically different" from the approach to secular literature. It involves how we listen to a body of writing. The Confessions *are* a hermeneutic of the Scriptures in that they help people listen to God's offer "to make out of 'No-People' his own cherished people."

65. To an international conference of Lutheran theological professors, prior to the Lutheran World Federation meeting in Minneapolis (reproduced in the paper by Pelikan's permission).

66. In *Der Lutheraner* 13 (1856–57): 58*b*; trans. E. Lueker, "Walther and the Free Lutheran Conferences of 1856–1859," *Concordia Theological Monthly* 15 (1944): 537–38.

67. LCMS representatives called attention to the two prefaces to the CTCR study edition of "A Statement . . ." concerning the status of the document. Drawn up as "a tool to identify theological and doctrinal issues," "A Statement . . ." could be, according to the 1972 preface, either "the Synod's Scriptural and confessional stance on a number of important topics" or "a personal theology . . . un-Lutheran, unbiblical, unconfessional, and unevangelical." Seemingly this either/or was answered by adoption at the 1973 LCMS convention, which declared "A Statement . . ." "in all its parts, to be Scriptural and in accord with the Lutheran Confessions" and a document which expresses the synod's position on current doctrinal issues" and the "more formal and comprehensive statement of belief" for which the 1971 convention had called. But is it a confession to which one subscribes at ordination? Is it a standard by which teachers and pastors are to be measured? No, according to Article II in the LCMS Constitution, but opinions have varied. There had been similar uncertainty within Missouri circles over whether the Brief Statement of 1932 had or had not been added to the church's confessional basis; a convention resolution in 1959, until declared unconstitutional in 1962, declared that it had been.

68. Fischer cited and made use of articles in *The Cresset* (Valparaiso, Ind.: Valparaiso University), "A Review Essay of 'A Statement of Scriptural and Confessional Principles,'" by Walter F. Keller, Kenneth F. Korby, Robert C. Schultz, and David G. Truemper, 36, no. 7 (May 1973): 6–20, and 36, no. 10 (October 1973): 21–38.

69. See Formula of Concord, Epitome 2 and 7, in *Book of Concord*, pp. 464–65; Solid Declaration 1–3, 9, pp. 503, 505. On the tendency to read Scripture in light of the Confessions, the Confessions in light of the Formula, and indeed all this in the light of Lutheran orthodoxy, see Robert D. Preus, *The Theology of Post-Reformation Lutheranism: A Study of Theological Prolegomena* (St. Louis: Concordia Publishing House, 1970), esp. pp. 405–13, for Preus sees in orthodoxy not only a "monolithic" unity to be accepted or rejected by later Lutheranism and a position where "the latitudinarianism of

unionism" is "a threat as dangerous as straight-out heresy" (hence one "will often be quite intolerant toward those who do not share one's convictions"), but also a continuation in orthodoxy of the Confessions themselves. That this is so as regards inerrancy and related matters, R. D. Preus argued in *The Inspiration of Scripture* (Edinburgh: Oliver & Boyd, 1957). "That the bibliology of later Lutheran orthodoxy resembles at every point that of the Lutheran Confessions is made clear," he says (p. 413, n. 3), by Bohlmann's *Principles* (cited above, n. 47).

70. *Faithful to Our Calling, Faithful to Our Lord* (St. Louis: Concordia Seminary, 1972–73), Pt. I, p. 21.

71. See above, n. 67.

72. See Sanders, above, pp. 10–11, and Hummel, above, pp. 17–18.

73. In addition to committee and staff, the following were present from the previous national conference and standing committee forums (see above and n. 39): Bornmann, Fischer, Freed, Hultgren, Hummel, McCurley, Quanbeck, and Schneider. Attending for the first time were: Charles M. Cooper, Berkeley; Ronald M. Hals, Columbus; Frederick R. Harm, Huntley, Ill.; Delmar L. Jacobson, Northfield, Minn.; Leigh D. Jordahl, Gettysburg, Pa.; Gerhard Krodel, Philadelphia; Wilhelm C. Linss, Chicago; Walter A. Maier, Ft. Wayne; Gerhard C. Michael, Jr., Merrill, Wisc.; Norman E. Nagel, Valparaiso, Ind.; and Walter H. Wagner, Warren, N.J.

74. Cited above, n. 47.

75. The book represents Bohlmann's doctoral-dissertation area at Yale. See also his contribution "Is Writing Confessions Possible Only Where Scripture Speaks?" in the LC/USA-DTS "Studies" report *The Confession-Making Process* (cited above, n. 47), pp. 19–24.

76. As it was said had been done by the Concordia Seminary faculty statement, *Faithful to Our Calling* (cited above, n. 70), and Bretscher's *After the Purifying* (cited above, n. 21), p. 74.

77. IV.C.1 (study edition, p. 23).

78. Bohlmann, *Principles* (cited above, n. 47), p. 115, should be consulted to follow his example of how "James *teaches*—he is not *made* to teach—justification by grace."

79. 1965 *Resolution* 2-27:5, 9, and 2-19:9, respectively; cited in "A Statement . . . ," study edition, p. 33.

80. Even defenders of "A Statement . . ." recognize that the wording is open to misunderstanding here; see "Report on Dissent from 'A Statement . . .'" (St. Louis: LCMS-CTCR, 1974), pp. 20–21. At issue is not only facticity of biblical characters but also the fact that Jesus spoke of Jonah (Matt. 12:38–42; par. Luke 11:29–32). There had been an earlier CTCR report entitled "The Witness of Jesus and Old Testament Authorship." Parallels exist in the history of Roman Catholic biblical scholarship. See the decisions of the pontifical biblical commission on Gen. 1–3 (1909) or Davidic authorship of psalms cited in his name such as Pss. 2, 15, 17 in the New Testament (1910), or the Monitum of the Holy Office to Biblical Scholars (1961); the texts are conveniently assembled in *Rome and the Study of Scripture*, 7th ed. (St. Meinrad, Ind.: Grail Publications, 1962), pp. 122–26, 174. See for the fuller context and later situation the *Jerome Biblical Commentary* 72:25–35.

81. Foster R. McCurley, *Proclaiming the Promise: Christian Preaching from the Old Testament* (Philadelphia: Fortress Press, 1974).

82. Dissertation, Basel, 1966 (O. Cullmann, B. Reicke). Published as *A His-*

tory of the Exegesis of Matthew 16:17–19 from 1781 to 1965 (Ann Arbor: Edwards Brothers, 1976).

83. Formula of Concord, Solid Declaration, Rule and Norm 8 and 9 (also 1); Book of Concord, pp. 505, 503.

84. See Jerome Biblical Commentary 72:34–35; Bea, Study of the Synoptic Gospels (cited above, n. 10), esp. pp. 29ff.

85. For the Formula (which some felt had not received enough attention), see Linss, "Biblical Interpretation in the Formula of Concord" (cited above, n. 47). As to "hierarchy," it is widely assumed that the Augsburg Confession and the Catechisms of Luther attract wider assent and therefore are more "authoritative" than other later documents in the Book of Concord. This is borne out by the fact that some Lutheran churches do not accept these later documents as part of their confessional basis or by the way they list the items in their constitutions (see above, n. 46). The significance of the Augsburg Confession is suggested also by recent proposals that the Roman Catholic church recognize it as a valid ecumenical statement of faith. The McCurley and Burgess papers did, of course, explore Luther's own writings.

86. E.g., Gerhard von Rad, Old Testament Theology, trans. D. M. G. Stalker, 2 vols. (New York: Harper & Row, 1962–65), 1: 105–28. Deut. 26:5–9 is "the Credo" preeminent.

87. E.g., H.-D. Knigge, "The Meaning of Mark: The Exegesis of the Second Gospel," Interpretation 22 (1968): 53–70; Theodore J. Weeden, Mark—Traditions in Conflict (Philadelphia: Fortress Press, 1971). The way in which Weeden stresses Mark's achievement as imposing a theologia crucis upon the "theology of glory" held by Peter and the Twelve has made some Roman Catholic readers feel that the author is a Reformation polemicist engaged in antipapal propaganda, rather than a Baptist seminary professor who did a dissertation at Claremont Graduate School.

88. In an address during the Festival of Biblical Studies at Seminex (St. Louis) on 27 October 1976 I had explored some of the questions in such an overall approach to the Bible; see "Exegetes, Honesty and the Faith: Biblical Scholarship in Church School Theology [for "Theology," read "Teaching and Pericopes"]," Currents in Theology and Mission 5 (1978): 16–32.

89. Schlink, Theology of the Lutheran Confessions (cited above, n. 47), p. 315.

90. Trans. with introduction by R. H. Charles, The Assumption of Moses (1897), and in The Apocrypha and Pseudepigrapha of the Old Testament in English (Oxford: Clarendon Press, 1913), 2: 407–24. For a brief description, see M. Rist, "Moses, Assumption of," in The Interpreter's Dictionary of the Bible (Nashville: Abingdon Press, 1962), 3: 450–51.

91. Apocrypha and Pseudepigrapha 2: 407, 411.

92. See the revision of Nickelsburg's 1967 Harvard Divinity School dissertation, Resurrection, Immortality, and Eternal Life in Intertestamental Judaism, Harvard Theological Studies 26 (Cambridge: Harvard University Press, 1972); and the seminar studies which he edited and to which he contributed, Studies on the Testament of Moses, Septuagint and Cognate Studies 4 (Cambridge: Society of Biblical Literature, 1973); and Studies on the Testament of Joseph, Septuagint and Cognate Studies 5 (Missoula, Mont.: Scholars Press, 1975), and 6, Studies on the Testament of Abraham (Missoula, Mont.: Scholars Press, 1976).

93. Nickelsburg, following J. Licht, opted for a date just prior to the apoca-

lyptic portions of Daniel in his *Resurrection* . . . , and in "An Antiochan Date for the Testament of Moses," in *Studies on the Testament of Moses,* pp. 33–37 (both cited above, n. 92).

94. Samuel Sandmel, "Parallelomania," *Journal of Biblical Literature* 81 (1962): 1–13. It was scarcely the intention of this article to prevent comparison of canonical with noncanonical literature, merely the wild extremes.

95. An earlier study document of the LCMS Commission on Theology and Church Relations entitled "The Witness of Jesus and Old Testament Authorship" concluded that, in spite of his *kenosis* (emptying himself of divine attributes and knowledge in the incarnation), Jesus "used the designations of authorship employed by His people," e.g., David for the Psalms, Moses for the Pentateuch, and Daniel, but "indication of the authorship of the passages in question is never the main thrust of Jesus' utterances." "A Statement . . . ," however, rejects the view "that statements of Jesus and the New Testament writers concerning the human authorship of portions of the Old Testament on the historicity of certain Old Testament persons and events need not be regarded as true" (IV.F). The authorship and dating of Daniel does not seem to be mentioned in the study edition of "A Statement . . . ," but Lindsell, *Battle for the Bible* (cited above, n. 7), several times notes the point as a benchmark of inerrancy (pp. 99–100, 156–57)—it was written by Daniel, before the Maccabean age, as Jesus attests!

96. Contrast Gerhard Maier: "It would be a gross misunderstanding if one were to look upon historicoreligious endeavors as only condemnatory apologetics . . . it should not scare us if similarities to Biblical statements emerge out of the history of religion" *End of the Historical-Critical Method* (cited above, n. 14), p. 83.

97. See Ronald M. Hals, "The Promise and the Land," in *Speaking of God Today: Jews and Lutherans in Conversation,* ed. Paul D. Opsahl and Marc H. Tanenbaum (Philadelphia: Fortress Press, 1974), pp. 57–72. Hals has also published *The Theology of the Book of Ruth,* Facet Books 23 (Philadelphia: Fortress Press, 1969).

98. See Hals chapter, below, n. 13; for the Stance Statement, see above, n. 45.

99. See above, n. 8, and Walter A. Maier, *Form Criticism Reexamined* (St. Louis: Concordia Publishing House, 1973). The writer is a son of Walter A. Maier, longtime preacher on "The Lutheran Hour."

100. See above, n. 20. The CTCR "Comparative Study" often fails to offer real comparisons. The "Historical-Grammatical (Traditional)" column never mentions form or redaction criticism but allows "certain general principles of interpretation" since the Bible is "a human book"; these include "recognition of the literary forms employed" (hymn, parable, treaty, etc.), the *original* situation and *particular* historical context, and "the gains of New Testament scholarship which broaden and deepen our understanding of apostolic writings." Under "The Historical-Critical View" there is no reference to form or redaction under "The Mediating Position" but only the following under "The Radical Position": "the interpreter who applies historical reasoning to the Bible is at the same time a literary, form, redaction, and content critic—that is, he makes decisions about the meaning of the text [based] entirely on the way he relates the text to the history from which it emerged. The text is not interpreted as though by some supernatural activity it represents more than the result of historically conditioned human reflection and thought" (pp. 11–12). How that comparison works out can be seen only from the work of individual exegetes.

101. *History of the Synoptic Tradition*, trans. John Marsh (New York: Harper & Row, 1963). But does Maier's either/or really reflect Bultmann accurately? Compare Schneider's remark (see above, p. 14) that fundamentalists and some New Testament scholars share a quest for "the factual."

102. *Form Criticism: Its Value and Limitations* (London: Duckworth, 1939). Other secondary works cited below by Maier are: M. Franzmann, *The Word of the Lord Grows* (St. Louis: Concordia Publishing House, 1961); V. Taylor, *The Formation of the Gospel Tradition* (London: Macmillan Company, 1935); and E. P. Sanders, *The Tendencies of the Synoptic Tradition* (Cambridge University Press, 1969). But all those writers, including Franzmann, pp. 216–17, see more legitimate emphases to form criticism than Maier does.

103. Maier treats Willi Marxsen, *Mark the Evangelist*, trans. Roy A. Harrisville et al. (Nashville: Abingdon Press, 1969); G. Bornkamm, G. Barth, and H. J. Held, *Tradition and Interpretation in Matthew*, trans. P. Scott (London: SCM Press, 1963); Hans Conzelmann, *The Theology of St. Luke*, trans. G. Buswell (London: Faber & Faber, 1960); R. H. Lightfoot, *St. John's Gospel* (London: Clarendon Press, 1956); and J. Louis Martyn, *History and Theology in the Fourth Gospel* (New York: Harper & Row, 1968); and, in addition, Willi Marxsen, *Introduction to the New Testament*, trans. G. Buswell (Philadelphia: Fortress Press, 1968).

104. Maier's examples include the supposed imminence of the Parousia in Mark and its delay in Luke. He quotes Joachim Rohde, *Rediscovering the Teaching of the Evangelists*, trans. Dorothea M. Barton (Philadelphia: Westminster Press, 1968), in rejecting each (but Rohde basically does work redaction-critically). Maier regards Marxsen's sketch of three stages of development in John (sources, the evangelist's own work, and church redaction) as "pure conjecture and fantasy."

105. Held (see above, n. 103) pointed out that Matthew omits the disciples' question at Mark 6:37 ("Shall we go and buy two hundred denarii worth of bread, and give it to them to eat?") so that the disciples thus show better comprehension of Jesus' command, "You give them something to eat"; further, only in Matthew does the statement occur that Jesus told the disciples to bring the loaves and fish they have (14:18); and finally that Matthew 14:19 phrases it, Jesus "gave the loaves to the disciples, *and the disciples gave them to the crowds*" (in place of Mark's, "he gave them to the disciples to set before the people"). Maier says, "Most of Held's presentation is imaginative and lacks textual warrant." But what he makes of Matthew's changes of Mark (or Mark's changes of the "eyewitness" Matthew) we were not told.

106. In addition to committee and staff the following were present from previous national conferences and standing-committee forums (see above, nn. 39, 73): Bornmann, Fischer, Freed, Hals, Hultgren, Hummel, Krodel, Marquart, McCurley, Nickelsburg, Quanbeck, Schneider, and Wagner. Attending for the first time were: Edgar M. Carlson, Minneapolis; Terence E. Fretheim, St. Paul; Donald H. Juel, Princeton; James G. Manz, Chicago; Albert M. Marcis, Parma, Ohio; Dean L. Moe, Minneapolis; Duane A. Priebe, Dubuque, Iowa; Martin H. Scharlemann, St. Louis; Charles P. Sigel, Philadelphia; David L. Tiede, St. Paul; James W. Voelz, Ft. Wayne; and Paul A. Zimmermann, River Forest, Ill. Among previous study participants unable to attend were Jack D. Kingsbury, St. Paul; and Walter A. Maier.

107. Martin Scharlemann of St. Louis and Gerhard Krodel of Philadelphia, who originally accepted the assignment, agreed to do the parable of the leaven.

When the latter had to withdraw from preparing a paper upon being elected dean at Gettysburg Seminary, Donald Juel agreed to undertake the assignment. Because of the brevity of the parable it was suggested that the parable of the mustard seed be added. The two papers at the conference covered both parables. In the authors' revisions for publication, that by Juel concentrates solely on the parable of the mustard seed.

108. David L. Tiede, *The Charismatic Figure as Wonder Worker*, Dissertation Series 1 (Missoula, Mont.: Society of Biblical Literature, 1972).

109. The foil here was said to be the "Arnoldshain Theses" concerning the Lord's Supper where Lutheran and Reformed theologians in Europe came to agreements, especially in the exegetical area, on the biblical *Verba* and their development. Indeed, the words of institution were suggested as a topic for the final pair of exegetical papers at the conference but were deemed too complicated to handle in the time available. The fact is that the wordings in Matt. 26:26–28 (pars. Mark 14:22–24, Luke 22:17–20) and 1 Cor. 11:23–25 do not agree. One can scarcely say it happened several times (so that all wordings are historically correct), and the effort of Jeremias to trace back the wording to an Aramaic original is problematic. There are difficulties on any reading of the evidence, but will it do to insist on "historical event" with three or four varying New Testament accounts, without some explanation of development and variety?

110. His dissertation, under Geoffrey W. H. Lampe, was entitled *The Use of the Present and Aorist Imperatives and Prohibitions in the New Testament*.

111. In a later paragraph Voelz specified the first category as including "lexicographical work, word and concordance studies, lower criticism, even isagogics," though he cited a quotation from the LCMS *Lutheran Witness* (Oklahoma District), 9 November 1975—"anytime anyone uses the Greek New Testament or a Greek dictionary, it presupposes the historical-critical method"—as "half-true." The second category was said also to include "literary criticism (in the modern sense)."

112. To be accurate, Dibelius did put primary emphasis on preaching as the means for spreading abroad the missionary message of Christianity, but he also allowed some room for teachers and other "interests of the life of the Church"; see his *From Tradition to Gospel*, trans. B. L. Woolf (New York: Charles Scribner's Sons, 1935), pp. 13, 31. But when E. Fascher said, with some justice, that Dibelius's "foundation thesis" was "In the beginning was the sermon," we have not just a play on John 1:1 but also a reflection of German Evangelical-Lutheran church life! It was Bultmann's achievement to describe other perennial situations in early church life affecting materials in the Jesus tradition, but the Voelz paper discusses only Dibelius here.

113. On the historian as "historicist," Voelz did note a seminary faculty colleague who said "that as a historian he could not assert that Bartimaeus had been healed, only that people thought that he had been healed."

114. Kenneth Ewing Bailey, *Poet and Peasant: A Literary Cultural Approach to the Parables in Luke* (Grand Rapids: Eerdmans Publishing Company, 1976).

115. Martin Scharlemann was the thesis adviser. See also Bailey's *The Cross and the Prodigal* (St. Louis: Concordia Publishing House, 1973).

116. Bailey calls for a view not from the study window, even in Palestine (Dalmann, E. F. F. Bishop), but from the bench outside a peasant's house, with careful controls over the native resource people. His book never men-

tions, however, the translations and commentaries by George M. Lamsa, who claimed to have been born into the Middle Eastern background here stressed. One wonders if there is a parallel to the "Arabist" phase of Old Testament studies when Arab folk customs and etymologies were used to explain the Hebrew Scriptures.

117. *Poet and Peasant* (cited above, n. 114), p. 30; see p. 94, n. 35, for one of the few direct references to form criticism. On the Jerusalem Document (the chiastic structure of which owes much to M. D. Goulder), see ibid., pp. 79–82. Charles H. Talbert finds a different chiastic pattern in 10:21–18:30; see his *Literary Patterns, Theological Themes, and the Genre of Luke-Acts,* SBL Monograph Series 20 (Missoula, Mont.: Scholars Press, 1974), pp. 51–56. On Bailey's work as a whole, see the review by John Dominic Crossan in *Journal of Biblical Literature* 96 (1977): 606–608; he concludes that "the book rushes from hypothetical parallelism to historical Jesus and virtually ignores the necessary passage through source, form, and redaction criticism"; it is "as if the parables never managed to challenge his theology but only to reflect it and confirm it."

118. See above, Preface, n. 4. Priebe was a translator for Wolfhart Pannenberg, *Jesus, God and Man* (Philadelphia: Westminster Press, 1968).

119. See above, n. 1.

120. See below, p. 330. The secondary source Marquart quotes gives no specific references. The Arnoldshain report is published as *Zur Lehre vom Heiligen Abendmahl: Bericht über das Abendmahlsgespräch der Evangelischen Kirche in Deutschland 1947–1957 und Erläuterungen seines Ergebnisses,* ed. G. Niemeier et al. (Munich: Chr. Kaiser Verlag, 1959).

121. Eng. trans. Eugene M. Skibbe in "Discussion of Intercommunion in German Protestantism," *Lutheran Quarterly* 11 (1959): 109, from the text in *Evangelische Theologie* 17 (1958): 425–27. See also Skibbe's *Protestant Agreement on the Lord's Supper* (Minneapolis: Augsburg Publishing House, 1960).

122. What follows is summarized from *Zur Lehre vom Heiligen Abendmahl* (cited above, n. 120), pp. 23–24.

123. As did Albrecht Oepke, a member of the commission, in "Kann die Auslegung der Abendmahlstexte des Neuen Testaments für das Abendmahlsgespräch der Kirchen hilfreich sein?" in *Theologische Literaturzeitung* 80 (1955): cols. 130–42.

124. See the encyclopedia article "Abendmahl in NT" in *Die Religion in Geschichte und Gegenwart* (1956), by Eduard Schweizer, one of the participants in the German discussion; Eng. trans. James M. Davis, *The Lord's Supper according to the New Testament,* Facet Books 18 (Philadelphia: Fortress Press, 1967). Reflective of interconfessional debate is Schweizer's famous judgment that in the early church "if the question had been posed concerning the nature of the elements . . ., then the Palestinian would have given a 'Reformed' answer, 'the bread signifies the body,' and the Hellenist, a 'Lutheran' answer, 'the bread *is* the body.' "

125. So Lienhardt's context, for the quote cited in Marquart.

126. For references to his role in recent Missouri Synod history, see Danker, *No Room in the Brotherhood,* and *Exodus from Concordia* (both cited above, n. 1). Scharlemann's dissertation at Union Seminary, New York, for a second doctoral degree was published in a Roman Catholic series, *Stephen: A Singular Saint,* Analecta Biblica 34 (Rome: Pontifical Biblical Institute, 1968). See also

his *Proclaiming the Parables* (St. Louis: Concordia Publishing House, 1963) and numerous published articles in *Concordia Theological Monthly, Journal of Biblical Literature*, and elsewhere.

127. Donald H. Juel, *Messiah and Temple: The Trial of Jesus in the Gospel of Mark*, SBL Dissertation Series (Missoula, Mont.: Scholars Press, 1977); and idem, with James S. Ackerman and Thayer S. Warshaw, *An Introduction to New Testament Literature* (Nashville: Abingdon Press, 1978).

128. This was taken by Scharlemann to include such verses in John as 14:25–26, 16:12–13, and the "I am" statements. See also below, n. 130.

129. Charles P. Sigel and Walter H. Wagner, as recorders, produced extremely accurate and helpful summaries.

130. "The communication of properties of the two natures of Christ, divine and human, within the one person, Jesus Christ." On this view the divine properties, except where limited by his *kenosis*, or self-emptying, were at work during the earthly ministry of Jesus. After Pentecost, Scharlemann added, the exalted Lord spoke through the Holy Spirit to remind the first Christians of what he said. Hence sayings can be attributed to both the historical Jesus and the risen Christ.

131. See below, p. 336. In a discussion group Scharlemann listed among the assumptions for his paper not only those quoted above on Jesus as the greatest teacher and the canonical text of the "final pen" as the inspired one, but also this: "Communities are themselves not creative geniuses, i.e., communities by themselves produce nothing creative, only individuals do."

132. "In dealing with the various accounts of Jesus' cleansing of the Temple, Prof. Scharlemann agreed that the evangelists, under the inspiration of the Holy Spirit, may move events around, except when a particular evangelist deliberately emphasizes the necessity of the event occurring at a particular time" (Group III discussion, p. 4). But see John 2:13; Matt. 21:1, 12, 17; and Mark 11:1, 11, 12, 15.

133. Joachim Jeremias, *The Problem of the Historical Jesus*, Facet Books 13 (Philadelphia: Fortress Press, 1964), pp. 23–24.

134. In discussing inspiration, Marquart noted that the *text*, not persons, is the primary object of inspiration (2 Tim. 3:16, "every *writing* . . . inspired by God"). But, it was asked, what of 2 Pet. 1:20–21, "*men* moved by the Holy Spirit spoke from God"? Answer: 2 Peter is among the "disputed" books in the canon, traditionally not used to establish doctrine. Response: but this seems to create a "canon within the canon" for doctrinal authority, on the patristic basis of books as *antilegomena* ("spoken against") in contrast to those accepted *(homologoumena)*; see Kümmel, *Introduction* (cited above, n. 16), pp. 495–96, and thus does judge what Scripture is by an external historical-theological standard. Marquart commented that he would allow the "narrow critical principle" to act not on or within Scripture but only on statements about canon or the merits of biblical manuscripts. Reason can have a "ministerial" role, to establish and elucidate what the text says, but not a "magisterial" role, disagreeing with or correcting "the proper and intended sense of biblical assertations."

135. This can raise questions about differences between what the inspired evangelist or apostle wrote and what we later have as canonical text, e.g., the woman taken in adultery (John 7:53–8:11) or the endings after 16:8 to the Gospel of Mark. Discussions stressed that such matters do not affect church doctrines (but for a long time 1 John 5:7–8 did) or that text criticism is allowable.

136. See E. Güttgemanns, *Offene Frage zur Formgeschichte des Evangeliums: Eine methodologische Skizze der Grundlagenproblematik der Form- und Redaktionsgeschichte* (Munich: Chr. Kaiser Verlag, 1970). More basic is a book that queries certain practices and findings in text as well as form criticism: Humphrey Palmer, *The Logic of Gospel Criticism: An Account of the Methods and Arguments Used by Textual, Documentary, Source, and Form Critics of the New Testament* (London: Macmillan Company, 1968).

137. Traditional Lutheranism has been severe on all forms of *Schwärmerei*, and Missouri Synod seminaries in particular have taken a stance against charismatics. On the topic generally, see the LC/USA study essays published as *The Holy Spirit in the Life of the Church, from Biblical Times to the Present*, ed. Paul D. Opsahl (Minneapolis: Augsburg Publishing House, 1978). It is worth recalling major views about the New Testament miracles: (1) they are an essential part of biblical Christianity and we should expect them today; (2) we moderns can/must deny that such things happen today and thus there are other explanations for what is reported as having happened then; and (3) miracles were unique to the apostolic period, to "launch" the church more successfully in the world. Analogy—to which experience and view of ours?

138. No one I know of in Lutheran circles, certainly none of those present at the LC/USA conferences, would argue for the *Textus Receptus* of the New Testament or repristinating the 1883 defense of it by John W. Burgon, *The Revision Revised* (reprinted by Paradise, Pa.: Conservative Classics, 1978) as some conservative extremists have done.

139. The United Bible Societies' Greek New Testament gives *hos* a B level of certainty on an A (virtually certain) to D scale, with *ho* ("which") as chief rival; "God" does not appear in manuscripts until the eighth or ninth century. See Bruce Manning Metzger, *A Textual Companion on the Greek New Testament* (New York: United Bible Societies, 1971), p. 641. On Wetstein, see John Reumann, *The Romance of Bible Scripts and Scholars* (Englewood Cliffs, N.J.: Prentice-Hall, 1965), pp. 117–18.

140. *Poet and Peasant* (cited above, n. 114), pp. 44–75. See above, pp. 39–41, on modest use of source and redaction by Bailey.

141. In the Fortress Press Guides to Biblical Scholarship Series see Norman C. Habel, *Literary Criticism of the Old Testament* (Philadelphia: Fortress Press, 1971), esp. pp. iii–ix, 1–2; and William A. Beardslee, *Literary Criticism of the New Testament* (Philadelphia: Fortress Press, 1970), pp. iii–iv, 1–13.

142. Does that mean "first written down" in a source? Presumably not. (But then the redactor's meaning really prevails!) In the case of an Epistle, "first written down" could mean what the amanuensis recorded, what Paul intended, or, less likely, what the audience of a letter heard when what was written was read to it. In the case of Jeremiah (chap. 36), would it be what was written first as 36:10 records (which the king destroyed, v. 23), or what Jeremiah dictated and Baruch wrote as final and expanded version (vv. 27, 32)? The phrase in "A Statement . . ." is not clear.

143. See Hans-Werner Gensichen, *We Condemn: How Luther and 16th-Century Lutheranism Condemned False Doctrine* (1955), trans. Herbert J. A. Bouman (St. Louis: Concordia Publishing House, 1967). Gensichen did not, however, intend his negative-sounding title to prejudge requirements for church fellowship today; rather, he hoped for "a modest positive contribution to a better understanding among churches" to come from his historical study (p. iv).

144. The steps accepted in the Stance Statement include: (1) establishing the text; (2) ascertaining the literary form of the passage; (3) determining the

historical situation; (4) apprehending the meaning that the words had for the original author and hearer or reader; (5) understanding the passage in the light of its total context and of the background out of which it emerged. As the Stance Statement itself notes, the five come directly out of the Oxford Report of a conference held at Wadham College under the Study Department of the World Council of Churches in 1949 to seek "Guiding Principles for the Interpretation of the Bible" in social and political questions; see *Biblical Authority for Today*, ed. Alan Richardson and Wolfgang Schweitzer (Philadelphia: Westminster Press, 1951). The CTCR version removes such terms as *Sitz im Leben.*

145. For an individual attempt, see my address to Canadian pastors in 1977, published as "The New Testament Concept of the Word," in *Consensus: A Canadian Lutheran Journal of Theology* 4 (July 1978): 15–24.

146. It has been claimed that my seminary in Philadelphia and particularly Professor C. M. Jacobs (1875–1938) were responsible for introducing historical criticism into American Lutheranism and for distinguishing the Word of God from a flat equation with Scripture. See Marquart, *Anatomy of an Explosion* (cited above, n. 1), pp. 101–3. The "honor" is probably somewhat overstated.

147. The scriptural events claim to have happened in a world of time and space; that makes them the object of historical investigation. The Confessions point us back to Scripture to test what they say. The LCA sees a clear hierarchy of authorities—God, Christ, and the gospel—norming the Bible (see LCA Constitution, Art. II). Theologians of the Lutheran Church—Missouri Synod, on the other hand, seem intent on writing new confessional statements to safeguard the Bible from any question about its contents. "The approach of higher criticism is likely to result in questioning, again and again, the evangelical doctrine which is drawn from the right reading of the Sacred Scriptures," Robert D. Preus writes, in *Getting into The Theology of Concord: A Study of the Book of Concord* (St. Louis: Concordia Publishing House, 1977), pp. 21–22. Therefore David P. Scaer asserts in a companion book that "a definitive confessional answer" is needed to "the false assertion that the Biblical accounts do not report historical occurrences," and "our generation will write its own history about her strength to provide such an answer" (*Getting into The Story of Concord: A History of the Book of Concord*, p. 96). But what "evangelical doctrine" has been questioned in the LC/USA discussions? Perhaps the notion of *torah* as "law" in the seventeenth-century sense, or "biblical inerrancy." But are these *confessional* doctrines?

148. *Does Biblical Study Still Belong to Theology?* Inaugural lecture as Oriel Professor of the Interpretation of Holy Scripture, 26 May 1977 (Oxford: Clarendon Press, 1978). The quotations that follow are from pp. 16–17.

149. Cited above, n. 7.

150. The points are made respectively in ibid., on pp. 15 (I. Howard Marshall), 68 (Graham N. Stanton), 134 (Marshall), 168 (David R. Catchpole), and 8 (Marshall).

151. Compare R. T. France's exegesis of Matt. 8:5–13 and 2 Pet. 3:18–22 (ibid., pp. 252–81) with John Goldingay's expounding of the passages (ibid., pp. 351–65).

152. Ibid., p. 9.

153. *D. Martin Luthers Werke*, Kritische Gesamtausgabe (Weimar, 1883–), 54: 186. Eng. trans. in *Luther's Works* (American Edition), Vol. 34, *Career of the Reformer IV*, ed. Lewis W. Spitz (Philadelphia: Muhlenberg Press, 1960), p. 337, "1545 Preface to the Complete Edition of Luther's Latin Writings."

Perspectives on the Hermeneutics Debate

HAROLD H. DITMANSON

Professor of Religion
Saint Olaf College
Northfield, Minnesota

The essays contained in this volume were solicited by the Division of Theological Studies of the Lutheran Council in the U.S.A. as a part of its continuing effort "to seek to achieve theological consensus . . . on the basis of Scripture and the witness of the Lutheran Confessions." The Preface explains the circumstances that led the Division to select hermeneutics as the subject of study for a series of conferences held between 1975 and 1977. The proper understanding of the nature and interpretation of the Bible has been a central concern of Lutheranism throughout its history. The peculiar blend of agreements and disagreements associated with this topic and the importance of its implications for church unity make it a tantalizing yet frustrating candidate for periodic reexamination.

Whether it can be said that Lutherans in the past have agreed or disagreed on hermeneutics depends very much on what one means by "agreement." Some think that a sufficient agreement has been reached on a topic that will always resist clear and final formulation. Others hold that any broad statement which allows for diversity in the understanding and use of Scripture is harmful to the existence and mission of the church. It is clear that the present study is like previous studies in that no common statement which all participants would be content to regard as a consensus has emerged. Paul Opsahl, in his Preface, acknowledges this fact and expresses the hope that the discussion will help Lutherans "take seriously one another's commitment to Scripture and the witness of the Confessions."

HAROLD H. DITMANSON

AGREEMENTS

A serious commitment to Scripture and to the Lutheran Confessions is of course a significant area of agreement, and without it the churches participating in the Lutheran Council would not be engaged in common work and conversation. But it is my belief that the mutually acknowledged commitment actually embraces many important points of agreement. Some of these points pertain to the uniqueness of the Bible, others to the centrality of the Bible in the life of the church, and still others to the indispensable role of the Confessions.

The unique status of the Bible as the Word of God is expressed in every essay. "Scripture must be seen as the bearer of the divine self-disclosure" (Quanbeck). "In, with, and under the rich diversity of voices in the Scripture, the living Lord speaks to us, to our times and condition" (Tiede). "God addresses man in law and gospel throughout Scripture in order to lead him to salvation through faith in Jesus Christ" (Bohlmann). It is acknowledged by all that the unique combination of the historical and divine dimensions in Scripture means that as a book it is qualitatively different from all other books (Bohlmann, Quanbeck). The exact nature of the qualitative difference can be variously stated in relation to the doctrine of biblical inspiration, but there is unanimity with respect to the Bible's christological content and soteriological purpose (Hummel, Bohlmann, Hultgren, Burgess, McCurley, Priebe). The grace of God in Jesus Christ for the justification of the unrighteous (Hultgren, Burgess, McCurley, Hummel) is the heart and center of Scripture, and Scripture has in fact been effective in its proclamation of the saving gospel (Priebe).

The primacy of Scripture as "the only source and norm for all doctrine" is clearly asserted (Bohlmann). "Commitment to the gospel and to the Scriptures has informed Lutheran theology and behavior throughout the history of the Lutheran church" (Quanbeck). Theology then must take the form of "a dialogue with Scripture" (Priebe). In view of the unique nature and status of the Bible, the interpreter's fundamental attitude is one of listening (Hultgren, Priebe, Tiede, Hals). Hermeneutics "presupposes that understanding is not something we already possess but something we seek with the help of the text. . . . We listen for a Word from God in which the text that once was God's Word to people in a different time and place might again become God's Word for us" (Priebe). The massive soteriological content and purpose of Scripture gives it a unity which dictates that in the act of listening the reader will respect the principle that Scripture interprets Scripture (Bohlmann, Hummel, Hult-

78

gren, Tiede, Scharlemann). The Word of God will not be heard if alien categories are imposed on the text. On the other hand, the understanding of the text and certainty concerning the authority of Scripture cannot be the product merely of philological work or of exegetical techniques. Such understanding and confidence are the work of the Holy Spirit, the *testimonium spiritus sancti internum* (Hummel, Quanbeck). Although the church listens to the text with the help of the Holy Spirit, it does not do so on the assumption that an empty mind provides the most appropriate receptacle for the Spirit's guidance. On the contrary, "careful literary exegesis" is required as the means of "gaining access to the historical context and meaning of biblical material" (Bohlmann, Priebe). While scholarly methodologies are necessary, it is to be expected that as rational constructions they will share in the inadequacies of all human thought. The historical-critical method is acknowledged by all participants to be fallible. Beyond that it is said that in some forms the historical-critical method has the effect of concealing or silencing the claims of the biblical text upon the reader. It would be misleading to suggest any substantial agreement about the nature and use of historical and critical methodologies. Yet it is noteworthy that the dangers implicit in critical procedures are recognized by warnings against rationalism (Marquart), allegorism (Hummel), hermeneutical reductionism (Hultgren), positivistic historiography (Tiede), and religious irrelevance (Priebe).

Loyalty to the church as the place within which responsible listening to the text of Scripture takes place is clearly affirmed. The Lutheran Confessions are frequently cited as normative testimonies to the revelation of God in Christ. The Confessions are said to serve as declarations of praise, as standards and guides to the interpretation of the Bible in the church, and as the means of identifying the characteristic features of the Lutheran tradition of churchmanship (Quanbeck).

DISAGREEMENTS

It is my impression that the convergences of opinion noted above are not merely verbal or superficial and that Paul Opsahl has good reason to hope that the essays in this volume will help Lutherans "take seriously one another's commitment to Scripture and the witness of the Confessions." But the essays also make it clear why the areas of agreement do not warrant a statement of consensus at this time. Earlier studies of the hermeneutical issue, especially the extensive discussion conducted by the committee that reported on the topic "The Function of Doctrine and

Theology in Light of the Unity of the Church," have reflected differences among Lutherans in the United States, with respect to the legitimacy of the historical-critical method of biblical interpretation. The division among Lutherans ran along two rather than three lines. Representatives of the Lutheran Church in America (LCA) and The American Lutheran Church (ALC) have approved of the historical-critical method, and representatives of the Lutheran Church—Missouri Synod (LCMS) have rejected it.[1]

The broad division between these two attitudes and groups is also quite evident in this volume. The agreements are real, yet there are wide differences among Lutherans regarding the interpretation of these agreements. While the historical-critical method tends to set Lutherans into opposing theological camps, the argumentation surrounding that issue brings to light a whole range of characteristically different conceptual and attitudinal factors. As I seek to identify and evaluate the disagreements that are to be found in this volume, I cannot pretend to occupy the role of an impartial judge. It is my intention to comment on the hermeneutical problem among Lutherans in the United States as a representative of the ALC. My immersion in and allegiance to the tradition of the ALC will be quite evident, even though I wish to be fair to those with whom I disagree.

The Bible as the bearer of God's self-revelation is seen from two different perspectives. That the nature and will of God are uniquely disclosed in Scripture is common ground. The ALC and LCA essays, however, speak of revelation in terms of divine activity. The God of Israel is known by what he does in history, as in the deliverance of Israel from Egypt. The New Testament is written around the life and death and resurrection of Jesus Christ, events that are interpreted as acts of God. In these events and others associated with them God brings about actual changes in the course and quality of the lives of persons and groups, and God is "known" as the one who effects the changes. Thus the redemption is itself the revelation. Later generations are in touch with the revelatory activity through the documents that describe and interpret the saving events (Priebe). A rationale of this sort seems to lie behind Hultgren's reference to "the history of God's saving acts to which the whole Bible gives primary witness" and his assertion that "the Bible contains a history of proclamation of the divine activity." The understanding of revelation as divine redemptive activity is also conveyed by Quanbeck's description of Luther's theology as "the exposition of this self-disclosure of God in the man Jesus Christ, who dies on the cross and by God's power manifest in the resurrection is declared Son of God."

The LCMS essays speak of revelation primarily in terms of God's authorship of Holy Scripture (Bohlmann). The subject of Scripture is, of course, the saving activity of God in the historical events recorded in the Old and New Testaments. But the LCMS explication of the relation between revelation and Scripture does not typically include the distinction made in the ALC and LCA essays between the revelatory happenings and testimony to those happenings. It is not clear to me whether the LCMS emphasis on Scripture as such is seen as a full doctrine of revelation or whether it is a corrective move made in response to the threat of "gospel reductionism" found in some "liberal" theologies (Hummel). But the thrust of the LCMS language is quite clear. "Holy Scripture is the product of the unique and miraculous action of God the Holy Spirit upon his chosen prophets and apostles whereby he spoke his Word in their words, so that he is the true author of their every word" (Bohlmann). The Bible is "identifiable" with the Word of God. "God has revealed his truth in the Scriptures, in its noetic and propositional aspects as well as in its existential sense. He reveals there not only himself, but also facts, history, and doctrine about himself" (Hummel).

Since revelation must be understood as "propositional," it follows that such terms as *factual inerrancy* and *verbal inspiration* are required to express the truth that Scripture shares in the perfection of its divine author (Hummel). "Because the Scriptures were authored by God they address man as God's own infallible, powerful, and authoritative speech" (Bohlmann). The unity of Scripture, "the assumption that ultimately it has only one theology because it has only one Author," consists not in its uniformity of expression but in its harmony with the mind of God (Hummel).

The way in which the LCMS essays describe the relation between revelation and the Bible does not deny or ignore the human and historical dimension, but it is said that in the case of this one book in the history of the world the miraculous divine action "used" the humanity of its historical authors in such a way that the frailties and limitations of human nature played no part in the composition of the documents. It is as though the authority of the Bible depends upon its perfection and it is endowed with perfection by making it less and less human until God is credited with full responsibility for everything in it.

The ALC and LCA essays emphasize the human and historical means through which God has chosen to reveal himself, but they do not maintain that in the composition of Scripture God overrides the limitations of the human authors in such a way as to confer upon Scripture a finite perfection which corresponds to the perfection of his own being or purpose. Quanbeck contends that no doctrine of inspiration should attempt "to transcend the historical relativity of the Scriptures." In speaking of the critical method, Tiede affirms that "out of a long living history of the people of God preserving, cherishing, perverting, and transmitting these Scriptures, an amazingly coherent textual tradition can be recovered." It can be said that all the ALC and LCA essays contain an implicit or explicit rejection of the "propositional" conception of revelation. Priebe's discussion of the history of traditions, for example, is far removed from the view that God reveals information about himself and that our response consists in learning the information correctly. The ALC-LCA picture of the way in which God "used" the humanity of the writers leads Tiede to reject any notion of a "transubstantiated text" and to affirm the "earthen vessels" that were used for the transmission of the treasure. The ALC writers warn against the Platonism or Docetism implicit in any failure to affirm the honorable, effective, and indispensable character of the "earthen vessels" in all their human and historical specificity.

The ALC essays speak of the authority of the Bible in relation to its character as a means of grace. "Its authority is the authority of the God who speaks in and through" it. Scripture therefore has an instrumental function (Quanbeck). Its effectiveness as a means of grace is not dependent upon its factual inerrancy. The ALC writers incorporate the notions of inerrancy and infallibility within their perspective, but not in the sense of the formal perfection of the text of Scripture. The Constitution and the "United Testimony on Faith and Life" of the ALC use the terms *inerrant* and *infallible*.[2] It is generally agreed within the ALC that the term *inerrant* means "truthful" and the term *infallible* means "reliable." The terms refer to the message and power of Scripture, not to its text.[3]

This view of inerrancy and infallibility is consistent with the position that the Bible is a means to the end of bringing sinners into a saving relationship with God. It is in this sense that Scripture is instrumental. In its gospel-bearing function Scripture has not failed. It is infallible. The ALC and LCA representatives will point out that, unlike the Calvinistic Confessions, the Lutheran symbols contain no dogmatic theory of inspiration, nor do they contain a list of the books that are received as canonical. The remarkably casual references to the Scriptures in the earlier confessions indicate that the authority of the Bible was not in dispute at that time. A formal statement on the subject was not offered until 1577. But even the Formula of Concord does not spell out a view of verbal inerrancy and infallibility comparable to that found in later Lutheran dogmaticians. In fact, when the Confessions do make explicit references to the infallibility of Scripture, it is in contexts that are associated specifically with the gospel to which the Bible points in a completely truthful and reliable way.

This is, of course, not the view of the LCMS essays. Hummel points out that inerrancy is not to be confused with literalism or with a denial of the "historical conditionedness" of the various parts of Scripture. But inerrancy does rule out the "allegorism" that in keeping with secular and skeptical presuppositions denies the historicity and unity of Scripture. Marquart challenges what he perceives as a distinction between revelation and witness to revelation by saying that "the 'rule' for interpretation is not some abstract gospel floating above, beyond, or behind the text but the 'sure and clear passages of Scripture,' in other words, concrete biblical texts [Apology of the Augsburg Confession XXVII.60]." Gospel is inseparable from the specific text, and if historicity or factuality is questioned, then the gospel is questioned. Marquart writes: "If the sacred text is subject to error, and therefore to human correction, then it is no longer the standard, rule, and norm of truth but is itself in need of such a standard." He refers to "the hopeless self-contradiction involved in the affirmation of the Bible's authority and the simultaneous denial of its inerrancy."

The ALC and LCA representatives clearly work with a different understanding of the relation between language and reality. Priebe, for example, uses the example of the incarnation to argue that just as "the transcendent mystery of God" was redemptively present and accessible "in Jesus, whose human and historical origins were known," so "God's word of address" in Scripture is given to us in and through the human and earthly medium of language. The transcendent is expressed within the limits of the finite without requiring of either Jesus or the Bible an exemption from the limitations that are inherent in the very notion of the finite. The ALC and LCA writers affirm that since the books of the Bible were written by human beings they have the character of historical documents. Yet God has chosen to use them as they are, and their human character does not impair their divine effectiveness any more than the authentic humanness of Jesus obstructed the transcendent grace of God (Tiede). If one can affirm this, one has no need of linguistically related notions of inerrancy because one already has a firm and sufficient basis for knowledge of and confidence in the gospel. Thus theories about verbal perfection become well-meaning but unnecessary speculations.

In his defense of inerrancy Marquart claims that scholars who use the historical-critical method have driven "a wedge . . . between that which is divine and that which is human in Scripture." Once the "human side" has been isolated, rationalistic criticism reduces it to myth and symbol, thus evacuating Scripture of factual-historical content and directing faith to "an ever more vague 'divine side.'" He sees this approach as "a retreat from facts and history as such" and therefore "a retreat from the incarnation." Accordingly, Lutheran scholars such as Edgar Krentz and Roy Harrisville, who attack "the idolatry that confuses the temporal and the eternal," are said to be involved in "a docetic theologizing that no longer regards the historical facts . . . as very important or relevant to 'faith'"

An ALC representative must respond to this view by pointing out that the essays in this volume, as well as the official documents of the ALC, do not in any way advocate an antiincarnational retreat from facts and history. They do in fact express the reality and relevance of history in such a full Chalcedonian sense that Marquart's position seems to them to be too close to Apollinarianism and/or Eutychianism for comfort. It would appear that Marquart's effort to guard against a "Nestorian" attempt to separate the divine and the human leads him to an identification of the temporal and the eternal in the case of Jesus Christ, Mary, and the Bible. He would surely not endorse the confusion of the temporal and the eternal to which Krentz objects, but he does come close to the view of Apollinaris that the human nature in Christ was transmuted into the divine nature, so that the very body of our Lord was no longer of the same essence as ours, but was a divine body. Flavian's synod at Constantinople in 448 saw that this view was really Docetism appearing in a new guise, and that the distinction between the divine and human natures in Christ must be preserved if a real incarnation was to be maintained.

When Tiede urges Lutherans to admit "the inadequacy and brokenness of all human attempts to state the truth," or to "confess before each other and the world that there are some questions with which we struggle," his words reflect an acceptance of the historical relativity implicit in an authentic incarnation or indeed in any transaction between the Creator and the creature. He urges us to be humble with respect to our knowledge of the truth, yet confident with respect to the abiding presence of the Holy Spirit. Such a combination of humility and confidence is consistent with the Pauline principle that "we walk by faith, not by sight" (2 Cor. 5:7). Proof, in the sense of demonstration, is not something that belongs to the sphere of religious belief. It is of the essence of Christian assurance that it springs from faith, and it is of the essence of Christian faith that it cannot guarantee itself or be verified by anything that belongs to the sphere of "knowledge" in contrast to faith. When the Christian faith rejected the docetic heresy by insisting that the Word was made *flesh,* with all its frailties and limitations, it accepted the attendant risk that God incarnate might not be acknowledged as such. Since God chose not to make himself obvious, the risk was a real one, and the Word was indeed rejected by many. Christian belief is as vulnerable as was Christ himself. Yet the risk and the relativity have not made the message of God's atoning action inscrutable or impotent, for the preaching of the cross has had its effect even without rational proofs or objectively verifiable records.

Claims for verbal inerrancy or propositional infallibility are associated by Marquart with faith's need for "certainty." "Faith cannot live on empirical probabilities." Therefore the factual "correctness of the gospel's historical framework" is indispensable to genuine faith and cannot be subjected to critical questioning. An ALC response to this line of thought would point out that faith does in fact live in the presence of empirical probabilities and a failure to acknowledge the personal faith and churchly loyalty of those who endorse the critical method must be traced to a rather doctrinaire epistemological theory rather than to the intrinsic impossibility of personal certitude in the face of objective uncertainty. But it is a serious error to describe these Lutherans who do not endorse theories of inerrancy and infallibility as being skeptical or indifferent with respect to history. The ALC and LCA essays in this volume clearly affirm that although the details of a critical study of the New Testament may vary, it is nonetheless possible to map out a hard historical nucleus of reliable data about the life of Jesus (Hultgren). This conviction is not a deliverance of faith but the result of careful study. Far from being docetic or Gnostic with respect to history, the ALC and LCA essayists actually insist that faith is based on history and that history gives rise to faith. There is more danger of a Gnostic flight from history in the position of those who, like Bultmann, wish to protect the independence of Christian faith by refusing to concede its vulnerability to the ambiguities and particularities of historical investigation. The flight from history can take the form either of saying, as Bultmann does, that Christian faith has no need of any historical scaffolding, or of going to the other extreme and saying that Christian faith cannot exist without an inerrant and infallible record of its historical scaffolding.

Characteristic differences between two theological perspectives emerge once again when we turn from the theme of revelation and the Bible to the topic of biblical interpretation. All participants agree that the elementary task of exegesis is the precise reading of what is written. All consideration of philological, literary, and historical questions is a means to the end of arriving at an understanding of the gospel attested to in the Scriptures in its significance for the total life of the church and the world. But the ALC and LCA essays, without exception, endorse and use the historical-critical method as the most effective means of understanding the biblical message. Quanbeck declares that "new techniques of study, form, tradition, and redaction criticism . . . have given an ampler understanding of the way the Scriptures have come into being, and it would be foolish to deny ourselves the benefits made available in this way."

Historical scholarship, according to Burgess, "forces us to read what the text really said." Hals and Tiede, in commenting on redaction criticism and source criticism, state that such procedures represent "an attempt to take the obligation to listen to the text with fullest seriousness." The procedures of textual criticism, source analysis, redaction history, and form criticism are defined and illustrated by Tiede, Hals, Burgess, Hultgren, McCurley, and Juel. They are in agreement that critical methods have made it possible to attempt a restoration of the earliest possible text, to distinguish earlier strands of tradition, to trace the history of theological interpretation contained in these traditions, and to determine that the center of Scripture is the gospel of the crucified and risen Lord Jesus Christ and the salvation offered in his name. These methods do not challenge the authority of the Bible (Hals), nor do they allow the Bible to dissolve into a kaleidoscope of various literary forms, theological teachings, and types of religious life. These scholars aim at "a faithful interpretation of Scripture" that will assist the preacher in his task of heralding the Word of God (Tiede, Hultgren).

Priebe claims that "in our day the historical-critical method provides us with a set of interpretive tools [that help us] understand the literal historical sense of Scripture in terms of what it meant for the author and for the people to whom it was originally written as God's Word. In this way the historical-critical method functions positively in carrying out the Reformation's concern for the literal grammatical-historical sense of the text as its authoritative meaning." At this point sharp differences arise. Hummel sees the historical-critical method, especially in its presuppositions and motivations, as an abandonment rather than a continuation of "the Reformation's *sola scriptura*." Marquart explains that the historical-critical method is the product of the Enlightenment and could not function apart from its dependence upon such characteristic dogmas of the Enlightenment as the autonomy of human reason and an exhaustively immanentist causality. A theology that embraces such ingredients will assume that the Bible is on the defensive in the presence of "magisterial human reason." It will de-historicize the gospel through its "brash reductionism" and produce an antiincarnational theology that can give believers not "a Spirit-given certainty of faith" but only doubts and uncertainties. "The whole point of the method has been and is emancipation from all theological authorities or controls." Scriptural and confessional subscription is in "irreconcilable conflict with the historical-critical method." One will have one or the other, "but not both." Although Scharlemann in his exegetical papers does not dwell upon the dangers of the historical-critical method, he does explain that the presuppositions of his study "constitute a conscious rejection of major ingredients found in much of contemporary New Testament interpretation."

In contrast to the LCMS position, the ALC-LCA representatives deny that the historical-critical method is a direct transcript of the secularistic ideology of the Enlightenment. Hals writes: "I find all the various methods of interpretation employed and discussed here to be essentially neutral and their results open to revision." Quanbeck refers to the interconfessional character of present-day biblical scholarship. The methodological objectivity of exegesis requires that one's findings and arguments be verifiable by other scholars as independently as possible of the exegete's own particular convictions. Thus the value of one's work will rest upon one's competence as a scholar. Current exegesis is therefore a cooperative venture and "is no longer branded with denominational markings."

But while the methods of scholarship are neutral, the interpreter cannot be neutral. He will respect the integrity of a descriptive enterprise even as he brings to his work deep convictions about listening to the Word of God (Hals). A way must be found between objectivity and commitment, and the success of one's efforts can be judged by other scholars only on the basis of the validity of one's arguments. By maintaining a certain detachment between the interpreter and the materials and tools of knowledge, it is possible to hold that any kind of knowledge, whatever its origins or implications, can be used in the light of criteria supplied by a particular faith-stance. Augustine used Neoplatonism, Luther used Occamism, and Gerhard used Aristotelianism without becoming captives to the basic principles of those philosophical systems. The ALC and LCA essayists reflect an openness toward "contemporary scholarship" (Hultgren) or to the "new perspectives and insights" of "the last four hundred years" (Quanbeck). They do so in the belief that the God of Scripture is also the God of all truth. Therefore they can urge that the historical-critical method is one of God's gifts to his church in modern times. It is not something to be rejected or opposed, nor is it to be seen as infallible. It is a method or approach, and many Lutheran scholars see it as a necessity of modern biblical study. As a method it is subject to correction. Tiede writes: "Historical criticism, like all other human enterprises, has been required to learn to serve the subject matter of the text rather than dominate it, and needless to say, that process continues. In some sense, finally the interpreter is interpreted, and the process of careful historical inquiry becomes the occasion for hearing as well as asking."

Different understandings of the unity of the Bible follow quite consistently from opposing attitudes toward the historical-critical method. The LCMS essays speak of the unity of the Bible as a necessary implicate of the unity of its divine authorship. Since Scripture expresses the mind of God in an inerrant and infallible manner, it contains "only one theology," "an organic unity of doctrine both within and between the Old and New Testaments" (Hummel, Bohlmann). Hummel acknowledges more than once the "many obvious differences in formulation and degrees of clarity" in Scripture and affirms the value of "external evidence, such as that richly provided by archaeology, and even history of religions, for fuller understanding of vocabulary, metaphors, secondary symbolism." But the Lutheran exegete should not conclude from such differences that the Bible contains errors or theological dissonances, or that it is not equally valid in all its parts. The differences in the Bible are unified by the use of certain hermeneutical principles. "Scripture interprets Scripture" and the "law-gospel distinction," or the doctrine of justification, serve as controls or presuppositions for all biblical interpretation.

The ALC and LCA essays also speak of the unity of the Bible, agree that the exegete must let the Bible speak for itself without imposing alien categories that might silence or distort its message, and affirm the material principle of the Reformation as the correct theological reading of the gospel. But the distinction the ALC-LCA writers make between revelation and testimony to revelation leads them to locate the unity of the Bible not in its "organic unity of doctrine" but in the consistency of its "proclamation of the divine activity" (Hultgren) or the centrality of its witness to "the redemptive purpose of God" (Quanbeck). Tiede argues that form criticism demonstrates the clear intention of the New Testament writers to assure the predominance of "the cross-resurrection shape of Christian preaching" over "a variety of other ways of telling the story of Jesus." After observing that Scripture contains differences in emphasis and perspective, Priebe concludes that the biblical writers represented "the richness of the meaning of God's action in Christ" in terms of "its many facets" rather than in the form of "a single, homogeneous picture." "The unity of Scripture" would then have somewhat of a "mosaic character" and would best be represented as a "dynamic dialogue of the parts, in which Scripture as a whole is taken into account."

Since this view of the unity of the Bible rests upon its proclamatory effectiveness rather than upon the reflection of its divine authorship in its textual inerrancy, those who hold it are under no constraint to reject the notion of theological pluralism. The fact of theological pluralism is affirmed as consistently by the ALC and LCA writers as it is denied by the LCMS essayists. Quanbeck argues that "the realization that the Scriptures present not just one theological interpretation of the work of God in Christ also affords new enrichment to the church. The work of salvation is proclaimed in several complementary presentations—Lukan, Pauline, Johannine, and so on—not in contradiction to each other but not to be reduced to a single pattern." Priebe finds that "there are more or less diverse, if not contradictory, theologies in the Bible itself." Hultgren announces that the accent on "the diversity of theological affirmations within the New Testament" is one of the results of the use of the historical-critical method in the twentieth century. He states that awareness of the pluralism of the New Testament is to be seen in Luther's evaluation of the books of the New Testament as well as in the Inter-Lutheran Commission on Worship lectionary, which accepts the fact of pluralism in its principle of "canonical catholicity."

The essay by Burgess presents a detailed examination of the difficulties encountered when the Lutheran interpreter goes to the actual biblical text with the *sola scriptura* principle. He argues that it was because Luther "took Scripture seriously, and in its literal sense," that he found "problem passages" which he dealt with by means of "content criticism." The determination of a canon within the canon is simply unavoidable, but the discernment of the "center" of the New Testament presents many complexities. Burgess describes the efforts to locate the "center" in *solus Christus*, the gospel, justification by grace alone, law and gospel, the cross, and faith alone. In no case does the actual text present a fully harmonious account unless, of course, the interpreter postulates an organically unified textual witness by using a hermeneutical principle derived from the theological tradition of the church. In Burgess's essay one can see the tension between the objective historical scholarship that helps to keep "content criticism" honest and the element of Christian commitment that leads him in the long run to find the "center" of the New Testament in "justification by grace through faith in the cross of Jesus Christ." It is very puzzling indeed to consider on what grounds anyone can say that historical-critical scholarship as practiced by Burgess, Hals, McCurley, Juel, and Hultgren is marked by rationalism, dogmatic immanentism, brash reductionism, existentialism, mysticism, destructive christological theologizing, or willful emancipation from all theological controls.

The role of the Lutheran Confessions is a third point at which characteristic differences of opinion become apparent. An awareness of the differences begins with the observation that the ALC and LCA essays in this volume rarely contain citations from the Confessions. This is true in a general sense of the literature produced by these church bodies. The LCMS essays, however, frequently cite the Confessions in order to indicate the authoritative criteria in terms of which a theological statement can be said to be correct or incorrect. This practice characterizes LCMS statements in general.

This difference in style reflects a difference in attitude toward the Confessions which operates despite agreement among the three church bodies as to what is authoritative in faith and life. The Bible is acknowledged as the only rule and norm for the faith and life of the church. The ecumenical creeds and the Lutheran confessional writings contained in the Book of Concord are affirmed as true and faithful expositions of the gospel and the Scriptures. Yet the differences we have noted with respect to the nature and interpretation of the Bible make their presence felt once again in relation to the role of the Confessions.

Unlike the LCMS, the LCA and ALC divide the Lutheran confessional writings into two groups. The ALC Constitution stipulates that subscription to the ecumenical creeds, the Augsburg Confession, and Luther's Small Catechism shall be required of all its members. The other documents in the Book of Concord are recognized as further elaborations of the first group of Confessions, but subscription to the second group is not required. They are regarded as "normative" for theology. Historical reasons can be given for this distinction in the case of the ALC. When the Book of Concord appeared in 1580 the Scandinavian churches were unwilling to become involved in the fierce theological debates that troubled Lutherans in Germany during the half-century prior to the publication of the Formula of Concord.

Quanbeck's essay provides a theological rationale for the ALC position. His exposition is consistent with, but not dependent on, the historical circumstance mentioned above. He asserts that the Confessions serve a threefold function in the church: (1) The doxological function is confession in the primary biblical sense of the word, the expression of praise and thanksgiving to God for his saving work in Jesus Christ; this element predominates in the Augsburg Confession, which shows the church of the Reformation affirming its continuity with the true Catholic heritage and its fidelity to the Word of God. (2) The hermeneutical function is to provide guidance for the interpretation of Scripture, especially with reference to controverted theological topics; this element predominates in the Apology and plays an important role in the Formula's extensive discussion of conflicting doctrines. (3) The element of identification defines the convictions that constitute the sense of self-awareness and unity of a particular tradition of churchmanship; this element is most prominent in the Formula of Concord and comes to the fore whenever Lutherans feel themselves under pressure to emphasize their own distinctive teachings as over against unacceptable theologies.

Quanbeck points out that all three functions are served by the Augsburg Confession, although in that document and in the Catechisms the doxological element prevails. It would follow, then, that because of its primary commitment to the ecumenical creeds, the Augsburg Confession, and the Small Catechism, the ALC in its use of the Confessions will give major emphasis to the elements of praise and thanksgiving, fidelity to the scriptural presentation of God's saving act in Jesus Christ, and continuity with the pre-Reformation church. The ALC form of subscription perceives the Confessions as assuming a positive rather than a negative position with respect to the development of Christian thought and life, rejecting only what had "been erroneously accepted by the corruption of the times." Luther maintained that the true church continued to exist even under the papacy.

If the Lutheran Confessions are differentiated into two groups, and if their functions are described as threefold, and if it is the case that the emphasis shifted from doxology to hermeneutics to identification as the increasing pressure of controversy through several decades led to a markedly defensive posture, then it is understandable that the ALC's commitment to what it considers the primary Confessions reflects its judgment that the doxological element will always be absolutely central, that the hermeneutical element, while still important, has been modified by the fact that exegesis has become significantly interconfessional, and that the element of identification, which remains important, has also been modified by the discovery that many other churches have theological concerns very similar to our own.

All Lutherans agree that Scripture is the sole authority in the church, both as the source and the norm of the church's message. They agree further that the doctrinal statements of the Confessions have their authority not in themselves but only as a correct interpretation of Scripture. The starting point of this interpretation, for Luther as for the Confessions, was Jesus Christ. At the heart and center of the Bible the Confessions saw Jesus Christ, the gospel, reconcilation with God in Christ, justification by faith. All the teachings that revolve around this center as expanding concentric circles must be judged by Scripture as "the sole rule and standard." Thus Luther and the tradition of the pre-Reformation church were reduced to secondary status, and along with them the Confessions themselves. "Other symbols and other writings are not judges like Holy Scripture, but merely witnesses and expositions of the faith."[4] It is evident that the writers of the Confessions were aware of the occasional and historically conditioned situation in which they were giving concrete answers to concrete questions. The Formula of Concord expressly states that the Augsburg Confession is "the symbol of our time."[5] To take the historical nature of the Confessions seriously means that we cannot close our eyes to the temporary and accidental character of their terminology or of the framework into which they were cast.

The ALC scholars are simply unable to find that the Confessions describe themselves as logically infallible, exegetically perfect, and historically final systems of doctrine. Quanbeck argues that "while the Confessions have indeed a certain confessionally qualified paradigmatic function, to assert this function in an unqualified way is in effect to deny that the Holy Spirit has granted any illumination to the church since the sixteenth century." Therefore the ALC representatives maintain that dissent is possible from confessional positions that do not deal directly with the gospel itself. Theology should not take the form of an exegesis of the Confessions. It is compatible with the ALC position to hold that the Confessions contain *a* true exposition of the Bible, but not *the* true exposition (Quanbeck). Since Lutheranism began as a protest against the magisterial authority claimed for the doctrinal tradition of the Roman Catholic church, it must not claim a similar magisterial authority for the content of its own Confessions. Lutheranism can hardly object to the dominance of tradition over Scripture in the Roman Catholic church if it claims that its own Confessions contain the true and irreformable interpretation of Scripture. The Lutheran church has a legitimate existence only as it gives biblical research its freedom. On the basis of the gospel given in Scripture it should be ready to give an account of whether its own teaching is scriptural.

If we are to allow the possibility of difference between Scripture and the dogmatic tradition of the church, then we must ask the question, Does the interpretation of Scripture in the Confessions have an independent authority and significance in relation to scholarly exegesis? The LCMS answer appears to be an affirmative one: "Subscription to the Lutheran Confessions includes acceptance of the confessional position on the nature and interpretation of Holy Scripture." An explanation is added that while "the law-gospel distinction and the doctrine of justification . . . are basic presuppositions for the interpretation of all Scripture," they do not provide "general criteria for the correctness or legitimacy of particular exegetical considerations" (Bohlmann). On the face of it this statement seems to permit a distinction between exegesis and dogmatic tradition by acknowledging that the confessional articulation of the law-gospel distinction and the doctrine of justification does not determine the correctness of "particular exegetical considerations." But it would probably be a mistake to interpret this statement as an endorsement of the degree of exegetical freedom insisted upon by the ALC and LCA representatives. The LCMS understanding of the "pure preaching" or "teaching of the gospel" includes all the articles of faith set forth in all the Lutheran Confessions. This view is consistent with the belief that Scripture in all its parts presents "an organic unity of doctrine." The LCMS position can grant that there are secondary teachings and materials of temporary significance in Scripture, that the Confessions contain nonfundamental articles, and that there are open questions in theology. But rigid restrictions are placed on the identification and use of such items, with the result that the theological structure of the LCMS is at once homogeneous and inclusive. There is to be no subjective selectiveness with regard to Scripture or the Confessions. The Confessions indicate the major direction and themes that Lutheran exegetes will pursue, and set the perimeters beyond which one is no longer "confessional." There is freedom within the confessional perimeters, but it is that of "the exegete who internally agrees with what the Confessions confess" (Hummel). Marquart goes as far as to say that "any theology which cannot or will not subserve the faithful proclamation and celebration of Christ's life-giving gospel and sacraments in the churches, in the sense of the Lutheran Confessions, has thereby declared itself insolvent."

The ALC-LCA theologian responds to the LCMS conception of confessional authority by concluding that the Confessions do in fact control exegesis. Quanbeck warns that as long as the view prevails that the language of Scripture is uniform, and that the Bible presents only one theology, most exegetes will tend to show, perhaps unconsciously, the agreement of the Scriptures with the doctrinal position of their own church. In contrast to Hummel's warning against "the divorce of exegesis and systematics in theological curricula," Hultgren insists that exegesis cannot be "enclosed within frontiers fixed by systematic theology" and dogmatics cannot be "simply a summary of biblical teaching." In commenting on "the power of tradition to shape our understanding," Priebe contends that we read Scripture "in the context of traditions that provide us with powerful presuppositions about the message of Scripture, and without a great deal of care we almost automatically find in it what we already expect it to say and fail to notice the oddities that stand in tension with our expectations." When this happens, "even our Lutheran tradition . . . can easily slip back into a pre-Reformation dominance of Scripture by the interpretive power of tradition." According to Tiede it is precisely by confronting us with the "oddities," the nontraditional items to be found in Scripture, that "the methods of historical inquiry are leading us into direct conversation with the theological issues and struggles of the first-century church."

The ALC and LCA representatives insist that exegesis cannot be bound by the Confessions in the sense that its results are already fixed in advance by the doctrinal affirmations of the Confessions. The Confessions can be given that sort of authority only on the assumption that they present an infallibly and exhaustively correct interpretation of Scripture. But if that assumption is operative, then Scripture can say nothing new and the doctrinal tradition cannot be challenged at any point. The ALC-LCA representatives fear, however, that if we cannot hear from Scripture something more than we already know, the church is not really listening to God's Word but is imprisoned within an ecclesiastical monologue.

THE MEANING AND ROLE OF AUTHORITY
IN THEOLOGY

Each essay in this volume deals in some way with the problem of authority. The question about authority can be asked in two ways, and it appears that many of the theological disagreements between American Lutherans can be traced back to different reasons for being interested in authority.

The question of authority must inevitably be raised within the sphere of theological activity. The church must decide between the theological alternatives that are presented to it by the historical setting in which it finds itself. Thus the question arises, By what authority is one theological statement preferred over another? Whenever it is assumed that one theological doctrine is true and another false, or that one is more nearly true than another, a critical tool or principle of theological authority has been employed. The representatives of the LCMS seem to be concerned chiefly about authority in this sense. They are asking, On what authority, in the last resort, do we base our claim that this or that doctrine is part of the gospel and therefore true?

A second way of asking the question of authority is more characteristic of the ALC and LCA essayists. It is related not so much to the internal necessities of systematic theology as to concerns that are associated with an acknowledgment of the vulnerability of Christianity within its historical setting. This, at least, is the impression the essays make upon me, and in the following pages I will try to describe a view of authority that is consistent with the ALC and LCA contributions to this volume.

The second approach to the question begins by affirming that the ultimate authority under which human life is lived is the authority of God. The God with whom we have to do is the God who made himself known in redeeming us from sin and death in Jesus Christ. The revelation of God in Christ was no mere substitute for God but God's actual self-disclosure. Therefore loyalty to that revelation is synonymous with loyalty to God. This was the import of the ecumenical decisions of the fourth and fifth centuries.

Jesus Christ, however, was a historical figure. Thus from the first century the problem of authority was made inescapable by virtue of the fact that the church exists within history, a flow of unique and unrepeatable events. As time goes on, the Originative Event recedes into the past and the anxiety of the church expresses itself in the question, In what way does the work of Christ 100, 500, 1,000, 2,000 years ago affect our life and action today? How can distant events be actualized for us here and now? The same question can be given another form: How can we be sure that the church of the twentieth century is the same church as that which the Holy Spirit called into being in the first century? We know that historical entities are subject to change and that institutions are notoriously liable to diverge from the intentions of their founders. How do we know that the church of Jesus Christ still exists? Where can it be found? Framed in this manner the question of authority is thrust upon us by the facts of historical distance and change, and the center of interest lies in continuity. These concerns play a large part in the essays by Priebe, Quanbeck, and Tiede. The two ways in which the question of authority is raised are not unrelated, since that which bridges the gap between God's advent in the world two thousand years ago and our Christian existence today will also be that which determines true doctrine.

If we are to put the best construction on what our neighbors say and do, we must surely see that it is this concern for continuity and authenticity, not a mere lust for power and glory or a craving to win arguments or a will to isolation, that stands behind the grim insistence with which church bodies cling to their distinctive doctrines. Each is concerned in its own way with the reality of continuity.

Lutherans give the classically Protestant answer to the question. The Bible fills the gap between Jesus Christ and any subsequent century. Protestant churches treasure, more or less, the liturgy, theology, and traditions of Christendom, but they believe that the reality of God's presence in Christ is mediated through Scripture as it is read, expounded, and responded to within the church.

Catholic bodies bridge the historical distance between Jesus Christ and the contemporary believer by the authority of the church as it speaks through its tradition. We can know that what the church says is true because it possesses in Holy Scripture an infallible source of knowledge about Jesus Christ. But the infallible message about Jesus Christ has had to be handed down from one generation to another by the living voice of preachers and teachers. Since the fullness of the Christian faith is not explicitly developed in the Bible, the Holy Spirit has been active in every stage of the church's history, enabling the church to develop what is only implicit in Scripture. Whereas Scripture is fixed in its written form, tradition is fluid and dynamic. The task of the church is to see that the gospel is handed down without being corrupted. In his mercy God has endowed the bishops of the church with power to act as guardians of the tradition, and the chief bishop of the church can speak infallibly and irreformably on faith and morals. God protects his church from error by giving the Vicar of Christ the capability of saying things that are as true as if Christ himself had said them. Therefore we know that what the church says is true and we are saved from ignorance, confusion, and reliance upon mere probabilities. Scripture, tradition, and the church belong together and to each other, but the relationships are not identical. Christ is the head of the church, and through the Scriptures the church is both taught and judged by him. Tradition serves the church by interpreting the Scriptures to which it is subordinate. Thus episcopal succession bridges the gap, whether through teaching authority or liturgical authority, and guarantees the continuity of the true church.

There is a third way of closing the gap between Jesus Christ and believers in any succeeding epoch. Mystics, Pietists, and theologians of religious experience have claimed that the Holy Spirit mediates between past and present, heaven and earth, the eternal and the temporal, by his impact upon the interior life, the sphere of personal experience. The overwhelming and exalting character of Christian experience guarantees that the claims of Jesus Christ are true and that the Holy Spirit is present with his gifts. Thus there is no need for an infallible book or an infallible church. No external means can serve as authoritative, for that which is external, whether the text of Scripture or the dogmatic tradition, is impotent and almost irrelevant until it becomes internalized. Objective reality, however sacred or true, is simply "out there" unless it is subjectively and personally appropriated. Revelation requires a receiver, knowledge a knower, and belief a believer. The very words of Scripture are lifeless until the Holy Spirit makes them alive, contemporary, and personal in the believer's experience. Thus the Holy Spirit does not move along the horizontal plane of history, through book or church, but descends vertically to create and re-create the true church in every moment of time.

Much can be said both in support and in criticism of the three classic ways in which Christians have dealt with the problem of continuity. But it is sufficient to make the point that all but a very few Christian churches have in fact worked with a triadic notion of authority, whether it be described as Scripture, Tradition, and Sound Learning; or Bible, Church, and Conscience; or Bible, Church Tradition, and Christian Experience. It is obvious that any recognizable version of Christian faith has involved biblical, traditional, and experiential elements. It is also obvious that these elements have never achieved a perfect balance. One or another element has tended to predominate in a given setting, with the result that the subordinated elements have been unable to enhance or challenge the life of a particular church. Thus we are accustomed to speak in negative terms of traditionalism, biblicism, or subjectivism.

Is there a way of recovering these elements from the extremist forms in which they tend to point to themselves and thus, in their isolation, silence the voice of Scripture or ignore the need for a constant reformulation of the Christian message or make of Christian teaching a set of intellectual abstractions rather remote from personal experience? The first step is to recognize that the element of authority does indeed reside in Scripture, in the historically fashioned tradition of the church, and in the evangelical content of personal experience. Each confronts us with that which is other than ourselves and which constrains us to respond with assent and allegiance.

The second step is to recognize that each of these authorities is relative in the sense that it is the channel of a more ultimate authority. The final authority is precisely that gospel of grace to which Bible, church, and experience bear witness. Few Lutherans would question the primacy of grace, the fact that the Christian faith begins, and must be seen theologically to begin, with the movement of God to man, not with a movement of man to God. Surely grace is unassailably primary. Yet the concept of authority is usually developed in terms of the constituents of the witnesses rather than in terms of that to which they witness. Grace itself *is* the authority, since it designates God himself in his goodwill toward persons. The Christian recognizes in the reality of God's gracious self-giving that to which his life must be subject, that by which his life must be regulated, that against which he has no complaints, that which is the source of his joy and striving and the end of all his loving.

If the grace of God manifest in Jesus Christ is the ultimate authority, then Christians should not speak of an infallible book, an infallible church, or an infallible experience. Rather, they should say that the authority of the Bible is relative to its power to convey the gospel of grace, the authority of the church is relative to the degree to which it proclaims the gospel of grace, and the authority of experience is relative to the sense in which the gospel of grace confronts persons and gives them comfort and hope.

When we affirm the relative character of Scripture, tradition, and experience by seeing in them witnesses to the ultimate authority, we are on the way to developing a theology of "the earthen vessels," as Tiede suggests in his essay. The earthenness of the vessels follows inescapably from the First Commandment, which points to the Creator of all being, the Lord who is alone absolute. When the sovereign God acted decisively for human salvation, he chose to send his Son in the incognito of the carpenter-rabbi of Nazareth. The Holy Spirit chose to create faith in him through the medium of the "foolishness of preaching." The experience of direct access to the Father of Jesus Christ was mediated historically through proclamation, Scripture, church tradition, and liturgy.

It is evidently difficult for Christians to acknowledge the earthenness or relative character of these media through which the sovereign God comes to us in the form of a servant. Surely as Christian people we ought to desire to live under the authority of God, and under the authority of persons or things only as they mediate to us the authority of God. But it is a sign of our imperfection that we cannot restrain ourselves from seeking an ultimate source of authority somewhere within the created order. When we pursue any infallibility short of the infallibility of God himself, we are hankering after a kind of security that God has not seen fit to give us.

Protestants like to use the phrase "the Reformation must continue." But we cannot mean what we say unless we follow the Reformers in applying the First Commandment to the existence of the church within history. This involves rejecting every human claim to finality. Every religious institution, every creed, every pattern of worship, every systematic theology shares in the limitations of this life. There should be nothing in Christian faith which points to itself, only that which points to a divine reality that transcends and redeems it.

Such an approach to the concept of authority obviously involves the very element of risk from which many religious people hope "authority" will deliver them. But the risk is there and it must be there even though many cling to the belief that somewhere within space and time there is a substratum of divinely given truth or presence which is indubitable and invulnerable. But we cannot have it both ways. We cannot both proclaim the good news of what God has done in Christ in the history of this world and also claim that our perception and account of his doings is immune to criticism. We must be content with the kind of finality God has seen fit to give us, and that is not the finality of a sign from heaven or of a system with all the answers. It is a finality of real incarnation, of real submission to God in the conditions of this world. It is therefore a finality in which nothing is finished. It remains hidden, just as hidden, yet real, as is the reality of the church, the body and blood in the bread and wine, the life with Christ in God.

Does this approach to the question of authority leave the church wide open to a flood of subjectivism? What check do we have on individualistic and possibly eccentric interpretations of the Christian faith? Where shall we turn in our quest for whatever objectivity there may be? The case is not hopeless. First, as the foundation of everything, we turn to our faith in God who is faithful and true and who wills us to grow in knowledge of himself. Second, we look to the contribution of theological scholarship, accepted as a gift and task from God. As reverent and careful scholarship looks back over God's dealings with his people, it will try to distinguish at each stage of the process genuine insights from wild speculations and misconceptions caused by personal and cultural circumstances. As serious scholars study the total data yielded by the life of the church, publish their findings, and argue with one another, there is built up as near an approach to objective judgment as we have any right to expect. It is the particular responsibility of systematic theology to probe the presuppositions of all who speak for the church. It must test these by the criteria of Christian truth which are implied by the central act of God in Christ and which are present in the entire range of statements that must be made in order to tell the evangelical story in its fullness. The systematic theologian ought to lay bare assumptions that have been unrecognized. The systematician asks his colleagues, "Is *this* what you consciously assume and is *this* the direction in which a genuinely Christian faith compels you to go?" It is in this spirit that one may raise questions about the traditional formulations of the doctrine of authority.

When systematic theology declares that Scripture, tradition, and experience are relative authorities, it goes on to observe that they are relative, that is, related, to something or someone. No matter how muted or misused they may have been, seen from a larger perspective they clearly point beyond themselves and in the same direction. They all bear witness to the grace of God in Jesus Christ. The agreement of the three primary witnesses is very important. It does not, of course, prove that Christ is the true authority over life in the sense that anyone who can respond to evidence will readily believe that claim. But the agreement makes it clear that it *is* the grace of God in Jesus Christ to which these witnesses point. In a secondary sense this convergence of testimony carries great moral, spiritual, and intellectual weight. It carries the weight that a consensus carries, and what other sort of weight can there be in a world in which we must "walk by faith, not by sight"?

Associated with the convergence of these authorities on a single center is the fact of their interlocking character. Scripture, tradition, and experience can be isolated only for the sake of analysis. In practice they interlock because each exercises some interpretive control over the others. It is through the response of personal faith to the truth in Christ that it becomes one's own truth. But apart from Scripture and the corroborative testimony of ecclesiastical experience, the truth about God's act in Christ could not have been mediated to anyone. All Christians regard the Bible as the Word of God, but it would remain a dead letter apart from the response of faith and unknown apart from the church that has preserved it. All Christians acknowledge the authority of the church, but it is Scripture which tells them that this social institution is the Body of Christ and apart from the evangelical experience church membership is merely nominal.

The interdependence of Bible, tradition, and experience ought to caution us against ascribing finality to any single witness and it should remind Lutherans in particular that the problem of biblical authority cannot be cleared up in isolation. The authority of the Bible is intertwined with other authorities—church, liturgy, conscience, reason. Yet it is a distinctively Lutheran and Protestant move to insist that among these relative and interdependent witnesses one has priority. Despite our recognition that we never have bare Scripture but always Scripture-in-the-church, we will continue to say that Scripture, as the account of the apostolic faith, is always normative, and the church, as the extended effort to reflect upon and to hand on the apostolic faith, is always derivative.

Thus it is necessary to understand the priority of the Bible in such a way that it is seen to be prior and normative within a constellation of media that includes conscience, reason, decision, consensus, and tradition. A rationale for this insistence upon the primacy of Scripture would begin with the observation that Christian faith is faith in Jesus Christ. Our knowledge of Jesus Christ is derived from the Bible. But no one is ever initiated into the mystery of faith by the *whole* Bible. In fact, no one ever reads the Bible as a whole. One reads the Bible page by page and brings to each separate bit of it a perspective that is abstracted from the parts. That perspective or "center" we call the "gospel." The Bible engenders faith only when a person grasps the significance of Jesus Christ for his own life within the people of God. That significance comes home to one when the whole ministry of Christ is seen as the decisive and compelling exhibition of God's kindness. Thus it is the "gospel" about Jesus that gives its authority to the many documents in the Bible, and apart from this "gospel" they would be unable to bring home to one the offer of salvation even though they were regarded as absolutely reliable historical documents. It was because of the efficacious divine message or *kerygma* present in our Gospels that the early church placed them in the canon.

All the biblical books can be read in a purely historical way, and as such their content does not lead us to grasp the divine significance of Jesus' ministry. But God can use all the biblical books to proclaim his gospel from various angles. Thus the whole Bible is a means of grace, but only when the whole is seen in relation to the gospel that brings the redemptive power of God directly into the reader's grasp. From this perspective the Bible can be seen to be a unity. The books with their various dates of composition, their different literary forms, their multiplicity of historical data, and their diverse sets of theological categories and metaphors are unified by the single divine purpose to which they witness.

When we look at the Bible we see a people living under the authority

101

of God. We also see some people not living under the authority of God, but that is the negative counterpoint to the positive and obvious thrust of Scripture. Thus in our attempt to understand biblical authority we must start from the reality of believing people. To say that we must begin with the believers' experience is not to land in wild subjectivism. This experience is not simple raw experience but an experience of Christ. Luther and Calvin were at one in basing their belief in the religious or redemptive power of the Bible not upon any theories of revelation or inspiration but rather upon personal experience. The Bible is more than an historical record. The Holy Spirit uses it to "capture," "call," "enlighten," or, as John Wesley put it, "strangely warm" the believer's heart. How the Bible does this is a mystery, although we come close to the heart of the matter when we say that what captures us in the biblical message is its quality of *truthfulness*.

To apprehend the truthfulness of the Bible is of course a very personal and subjective determination. It happens in the interiority of one's own mind and spirit. The testimony of other people or of Christian literature may impress or encourage, but there is no direct transfer of faith from one person to another, nor is there any appeal beyond one's apprehension to any form of confirmatory evidence. It should not be overlooked that the acquisition of all vital truth proceeds in this manner. Whenever we move beyond the barest skeleton of logic or of perceptual awareness and undertake to form significant judgments, we are forced to introduce some degree of subjective determination. Empirical science is based upon the acceptance of sensory experience, and rational analysis is based upon the discernment of logical relationships. But no appeal to logical axioms can validate the reliability of sensory experience, nor can an appeal to sensory experience verify the acceptance of logical criteria. In each case the form of the certitude that is possible and desirable permits no appeal beyond itself.

Subjectivity is thus an elemental and inexpugnable ingredient of all knowledge. It is there to stay. Theology cannot hope to escape from the subjective. Its statements are of the nature of invocations or possibilities and are not subject to sensory or logical confirmation, nor should we want them to be. They are either grasped in the passion of inwardness or they are not grasped at all. They are subject only to the kind of validation that is appropriate to a decision to trust a person or to reorient one's life about a gift, a loyalty, a hope.

Subjectivity goes wrong only when people refuse to test the truthfulness of their convictions by subsequent experience or are incapable of assimilating their intuitions to the other ideas of their consciousness or are utterly unable to explain what they mean by the words they use. It must be emphasized that the experiential ground of theology does not absolve it from the demand that its formulations be subject to the tests of consistency and order. Now we move from the experience of believers to the function of reason because religious people think as well as have experiences. If it were not for the operation of thought, they could neither interpret their experiences for themselves nor communicate them to others. Thus theology must by the use of reason indicate the inferences that may be drawn from the convictions thrown up by experience. If these inferences are to be grasped, they must be presented in propositional form. In the formulation of such inferences theology must utilize the same principles of logical and grammatical procedure that are used in other areas of thought.

Reason, then, is inseparably related to Christian experience in that the believer seeks to assimilate intuitive apprehensions to the other contents of his mind and spirit. But this assimilation does not mean that the new truth must be understood as the logical outcome of what one already knows. To the contrary, the effect of the Bible is to convince one that something new has entered his experience. The content of the Bible compels us to organize all our knowledge and behavior around the person and work of Christ as the center of reality. This may be what Paul meant when he said, "We take every thought captive to obey Christ" (2 Cor. 10:5).

The experience that is created by the gospel and is formulated and tested by reason is given to the individual within the listening and witnessing community. We move at this point from experience to reason to consensus. Consensus is the extension of private experience. Or, more accurately, consensus is the agreement of those who realize that the private experience of each participates in some shareable quality that corresponds to the transcendent ground of the experience. Because God created for himself a people, Christian experience is a joint experience, a joint listening, a joint response. Personal religious experience occurs within a corporate context, a web or network of grace.

Since many persons experience the same grace of the same Lord, they can come to similar conclusions about the implications of the common experience and common faith. If we allow that the guidance of the Holy Spirit does not cancel out the real humanity of those who are guided, we can say that all the decisions of the church represent a consensus, no more and no less, and consensus has, in principle, the same kind of authority that personal experience carries. We know that the elevation of twenty-seven books to canonical status took place in a largely informal and unofficial manner. There came a point when the church had to decide which books contained true Christian teaching, but behind the official recognition, which was in itself a consensus, there lay a gradual recognition of worthy writings in the life of the worshiping congregations. Consensus produced the ecumenical creeds and the denominational confessions.

If consensus is shared experience, we can say that tradition is codified and transmitted consensus. Tradition would have, in principle, the same kind of authority as that possessed by personal experience, save that it would carry the greater weight of a consensus or general agreement. As group testimony to the experienced and formulated biblical gospel about Jesus Christ, tradition represents the church's collective understanding of Scripture. Since the Holy Spirit never ceases to guide the church, this collective understanding of Scripture develops and is not to be thought of as confined to any one age or area of the church. It is truly ecumenical in space and time. Its purpose is to lead Christians quickly and accurately into the meaning of Scripture. In fact, we all receive our understanding of the Bible through the teaching of the church as well as through our direct study of it.

Protestants have been quite unself-conscious in their possession of tradition and quite unrealistic in their disavowal of it. It seems clear that the principle of *sola scriptura* has never actually worked. Most of the early Reformation theologians were unable to free exegesis from the systematic theology of medieval Scholasticism, and since that time biblical theology has been affected to a high degree by dogmatics. Even though biblical theology itself appears to be a part of the ongoing tradition of the church, however, *sola scriptura* is still an important principle, since there have clearly been times when Scripture has judged tradition and found it inadequate. Perhaps we must say that the Bible is both immanent and transcendent in relation to the church.

We have seen that the gospel in Scripture stands in a unique originative relation to experience, reason, consensus, and tradition. Since experience can be eccentric, reason fragile, consensus mistaken, and tradition self-serving, we want to say that the whole cluster of authorities should be subject to correction by constant recourse to the Bible. Sinful and ignorant men can manipulate each of the authorities, including the Bible, for their own muddled or unregenerate purposes. But the fixed text of canonical Scripture gives the corrective power of the gospel the best chance to assert itself. The text of the Bible can exercise its power to maintain and renew the life of Christian people if we recognize a distinction between Scripture and the dogmatic tradition of the church and if we allow biblical exegesis the freedom that scholarship requires.

Faith is the correlate of God's manner of self-disclosure. Revelation should be understood not in terms of sheer immanence or of sheer transcendence but in terms of what John Chrysostom called the *sunkatabasis* of God, the condescension of God to the measure of his creation. If God has come to us in condescension and lowliness, then that image must control all our thinking about revelation, inspiration, and authority. The test of our faith in him is our willingness to walk by the kind of light he has seen fit to give us. God has given us faith through the authority of the gospel. Why should we ask for more?

NOTES

1. "The Function of Doctrine and Theology in Light of the Unity of the Church," in *Studies* (New York: Lutheran Council in the U.S.A., 1978).
2. *Handbook of the American Lutheran Church*, 1977, pp. 45, 147.
3. See E. Clifford Nelson, *Lutheranism in North America 1914–1970* (Minneapolis: Augsburg Publishing House, 1972), pp. 179, 195.
4. Formula of Concord, Epitome, Rule and Norm 8, in *The Book of Concord*, ed. Theodore G. Tappert (Philadelphia: Fortress Press, 1959), p. 465.
5. Ibid. 4, p. 465.

Scripture and Word of God

SAMUEL H. NAFZGER

Executive Secretary of the
Commission on Theology and Church Relations
Lutheran Church—Missouri Synod
Saint Louis, Missouri

The summary report of a consultation involving representatives from the three major North American Lutheran denominations on "The Function of Doctrine and Theology in the Light of the Unity of the Church" has recently been published by the Lutheran Council's Division of Theological Studies. First there was some good news to report:

> All of our church bodies see the gospel as the fulfillment of the Old Testament and as the central point, the focus, of the whole Bible, without which it is clouded and not properly understood. The Scriptures, therefore, are the means by which God conveys this "good news" to humanity. They are the written record of God's promises and mighty acts in history.[1]

But there were also disagreements:

> Differences within American Lutheranism on the nature, function, and legitimacy of the historical-critical methods of Biblical interpretation were reflected in this consultation. Representatives of the ALC and LCA generally affirm the appropriateness of this method and have employed it in their presentations, arguing that it affords insight into the development of the biblical testimony to Jesus and that it gives solid rooting to that testimony within human history. . . . Representatives of the LCMS, while affirming that the Scriptures are to be read as historical documents and that the best scholarly tools should be employed, reject the legitimacy of the historical-critical method, arguing that any effort to read the Scriptures precisely like other ancient literature not only diminishes their revelatory character as the Word of God, but frequently results in conclusions that challenge the authority, truthfulness, and unity of the Scriptures. These

divergent approaches to the methodology of Biblical interpretation have resulted in widely different conclusions about the legitimacy of affirming the existence of discrepancies, contradictions, mistaken notions, or diverse theologies within the Scriptures. Because of the importance of this issue for all theological activity carried out under the norm of Holy Scriptures, Lutheran theologians will need to continue their strenuous efforts to resolve such differences.[2]

I rejoice over the areas of agreement which this consultation reports. At the same time, I heartily endorse the need for Lutheran theologians "to continue their strenuous efforts to resolve" their differences on the doctrine of Scripture, and I regard the publication of this volume of essays as a part of this process. It is therefore my sincere desire that this introductory essay contribute toward the understanding of the nature of these differences so that they may be removed as obstacles to Lutheran unity in the United States.

The essays included in this volume provide abundant documentation, in my opinion, in support of the accuracy of the conclusions presented in the "Function of Doctrine and Theology" (FODT) report. No progress is to be made, it seems to me, by using this essay to point out that all essayists are in agreement that "the focus of the Christian faith is upon Jesus Christ, crucified and risen, not on the Bible itself" (Hultgren), for example, or that ALC and LCA essayists disagree with the claim that "historical-critical theology . . . introduces a deeply antiincarnational split between history and theology" (Marquart).

What is particularly helpful about these essays is not merely that they demonstrate and substantiate the fact that critical differences do exist between North American Lutherans on the doctrine of Scripture, but also that they provide documentation for taking a significant step beyond the FODT report. The FODT report states that "the widely different conclusions about the legitimacy of affirming the existence of discrepancies, contradictions, mistaken notions, or diverse theologies within the Scriptures" result from "divergent approaches to the methodology of Biblical interpretation."[3] While this is undoubtedly true, it leaves unanswered the important question of *what accounts for* these divergent approaches. The essays presented in this volume suggest the answer that one of the fundamental factors influencing the approach to biblical interpretation is the interpreter's conception of the relationship that exists between Scripture and Word of God.[4]

In order to develop this point, I shall first refer to Karl Barth's influential treatment of the relationship that exists between Scripture and the Word of God. Next I shall examine briefly two recent books by Gerhard

Maier and Peter Stuhlmacher. Then I shall review the essays included in this volume. In all cases I will illustrate at least in a preliminary way how the interpreter's view of the relationship between Scripture and Word of God affects his attitude regarding the appropriateness of using the historical-critical method in the study of Scripture. In conclusion I shall offer a syllogism that I hope will stimulate further discussion on this issue.

KARL BARTH

"The root of the evil [in theology] is the interchangeable use of the terms 'Scripture' and 'Word of God.' "[5] Karl Barth was undoubtedly familiar with this contention of Johann Salomo Semler, the eighteenth-century professor of theology at the University of Halle who is sometimes called the father of historical-critical theology.[6] Barth's voluminous writings on the theology of the Word indicate that he was certainly sympathic to Semler's concern.[7] He made this clear already with the 1919 publication of his widely read and highly acclaimed *The Epistle to the Romans*. He addresses himself directly to this question in the opening lines of the preface to the first edition of this work:

> The historical-critical method of Bible investigation has its rightful place: it is concerned with the preparation of the intelligence—and this can never be superfluous. But, were I driven to choose between it and the venerable doctrine of inspiration, I should without hesitation adopt the latter, which has a broader, deeper, more important justification. The doctrine of inspiration is concerned with the labour of apprehending, without which no technical equipment, however complete, is of any use whatever. Fortunately I am not compelled to choose.[8]

Although it may not have been obvious at the time, Barth had already cast his lot with Semler's call for the distinction between Scripture and the Word of God. That this was so becomes clear just as soon as one notes that Barth adds that "the venerable doctrine of inspiration" has to do with "the labour of apprehending."[9]

Just how far Barth had departed from the traditional identification of Scripture and Word of God soon became clear with the publication of the first two volumes of his monumental *Church Dogmatics*. Protesting against what he regarded as the humanization of theology in nineteenth-century liberalism, Barth, having rediscovered the meaning of revelation, strove valiantly to lay bare the exclusive nature of God's self-revelation in his Word.

According to Barth, the Word of God comes to man in three forms:

the Word of God in preaching, the Word of God in Scripture, and Jesus Christ as the Word of God.[10] The most important of these forms is the Word of God in Jesus Christ. He is the Word of God in the strictest sense of the term: "Revelation in fact does not differ from the Person of Jesus Christ, and again does not differ from the reconciliation that took place in Him."[11] First and foremost the Word of God is a person, the person of Jesus Christ, according to Barth. In the true and strict and original sense of the term, only Jesus Christ is the Word of God, and he alone can be called revelation. This Word of God comes to people today in proclamation, the second form of the Word of God. Connecting the Word of God in Jesus Christ with the proclamation of the Word today and serving as its norm is the witness of the prophets and apostles in the Scriptures.

Barth takes up the specific discussion of the relationship between Scripture and Word of God in part two of the first volume of *Church Dogmatics* in two sections under the headings: "Scripture as a Witness to Divine Revelation" and "Scripture as the Word of God." The order of discussion is significant, for it highlights the fundamental distinction that Barth consistently draws between Scripture and the Word of God. Although Barth from time to time does speak of Scripture as the Word of God, such statements must always be understood in the light of his primary emphasis that the Bible is not the Word of God without qualification. Properly speaking, Scripture is the witness to revelation, and "a witness is not absolutely identical with that to which it witnesses."[12] Therefore, "the men whom we hear as witnesses speak as fallible, erring men like ourselves. What they say, and what we read as their word, can of itself lay claim to be the Word of God, but never sustain that claim."[13] Nor do the human failings of these witnesses to revelation extend only to history and other secular affairs, for according to Barth, "the vulnerability of the Bible, i.e., its capacity for error, extends to religious or theological content. . . . Not only in part, but all that they [the biblical writers] say is historically related and conditioned." Barth continues: "Like all ancient literature the Old and New Testaments know nothing of the distinction of fact and value which is so important to us, between history, on the one hand, and saga and legend on the other."[14]

Barth reasons that just as the understanding of a human word presupposes that the attempt to speak and hear has succeeded, so also revelation is something dynamic and not something static. Therefore the Bible could never be directly identified with Word of God, says Barth. The Bible becomes the Word of God when and where it actually functions as the word of a witness in an event. Barth puts it this way:

> Such direct identification of revelation and the Bible . . . is not one to be pre-supposed or anticipated by us. It takes place as an event, when and where the word of the Bible becomes God's Word. . . . But for that very reason we should realize that and how far they are also always not one, how far their unity is really an event. . . . But in the Bible we are invariably concerned with human attempts to repeat and reproduce, in human thoughts and expressions, this Word of God in definite human situations. . . . In the one case *Deus dixit,* in the other *Paulus dixit.* These are two different things."[15]

So the Scripture is not itself Word of God or revelation for Barth, but it is the occasion for the Word of God to take place.

Barth's discussion of inspiration further elucidates what he had in mind when in the preface to *The Epistle to the Romans* he spoke of "the venerable doctrine of inspiration." He points out to begin with that *theopneutos* is not a quality inherent in the text of Scripture itself. Like revelation, inspiration has to be understood as a dynamic concept. Says Barth: "The Biblical concept of *theopneustia* points us to the present, to the event which occurs for us."[16] He continues: "The *theopneustia* is the act of revelation in which the prophets and the apostles in their humanity became what they were, and in which alone, in their humanity they can become to us what they are."[17]

Lest he be misunderstood regarding the inspiration of Scripture, Barth notes that already in the early church there was a tendency to theorize about the operation of the Holy Spirit on the biblical writers in a way which resulted finally in what he refers to as the orthodox doctrine of "verbal inspiredness."[18] According to Barth this theory must be rejected. He writes:

> Therefore we have to resist and reject the seventeenth-century doctrine of inspiration as false doctrine. The development and systematization of the traditional statements concerning the divine authority of the Bible meant an actualising of the Word of God by eliminating the perception that its actualisation can only be its own decision and act, that our part in it can consist only in the recollection and expectation of its eternal presence.[19]

It is only in this sense, therefore, that Barth can say that Scripture is the Word of God: "If we say: The Bible . . . is the Word of God, we must first replace . . . the 'is' by a 'was' and 'will be.' It is only as expounded

111

in this way that the two words correspond to what we can actually know and say."[20]

In view of this brief exposition of what Barth meant by "the venerable doctrine of inspiration" it should no longer be surprising that he was able to say he was not compelled to choose between it and the historical-critical method. He had already rejected the identification of Scripture as Word of God and the traditional understanding of the term *inspiration* in favor of his *own* "venerable doctrine of inspiration." Since according to this theory Scripture was not Word of God but the fallible human witness to revelation, there was no reason for him to reject the historical-critical method. Therefore Barth concludes: "We can read and try to assess their word as a purely human word. It can be subjected to all kinds of immanent criticism, not only in respect of its philosophically historical and ethical content, but even of its religious and theological. We can establish lacunae, inconsistencies and over-emphases."[21] Given Barth's understanding of the relationship between Scripture and Word of God, his position is consistent. Had he maintained that Scripture was in fact Word of God, without qualification, the application of historical criticism to it would have been quite out of the question for him. In that case he would not have been able to avoid making a choice between the historical-critical method and "the venerable doctrine of inspiration." But as he says, he did not have to make that choice, for he did not consider Scripture to be without qualification Word of God.

TWO CONTEMPORARY EXAMPLES

If we can assume general agreement with the conclusion of the FODT report that the reason for "widely different conclusions about the legitimacy of affirming the existence of discrepancies, contradictions, mistaken notions, or diverse theologies within the Scriptures" can be traced to "divergent approaches to the methodology of Biblical interpretation," then it becomes important to know why some theologians reject certain methods of interpretation and why others do not. We have already shown how Karl Barth could affirm the historical-critical method only by giving up the identification of Scripture and Word of God. Let us now examine the recent books of Gerhard Maier and Peter Stuhlmacher to see how their understanding of the relationship between Scripture and Word of God affects their attitudes toward the historical-critical method.

In 1974 Gerhard Maier, whose doctoral studies were carried out at Eberhard-Karls-Universität in Tübingen where he is presently leader of studies at the Albrecht Bengel House, published a book entitled *The End of the Historical-Critical Method*. In this book Maier reviews the fifteen essays written during the period 1941–70 included in *Das Neue Testament als Kanon* [The New Testament as Canon] edited by Ernst Käsemann, which he believes constitutes "a representative cross section of contemporary German exegesis and systematics."[22] This collection of essays by practitioners of the historical-critical method, says Maier, should be viewed against the background of two centuries of development and can be regarded as "a balance sheet that demands an accounting."[23] What Maier finds in his accounting is not good: the exegetes regard the New Testament no longer as a unit but merely as a collection of often contradicting testimonies; the formal canon is not to be equated with the Word of God; the search for a "canon in the canon" has failed; and the net result of all this is that "uncontrolled subjectivity has the last word concerning what should have divine authority."[24] "The use of the higher-critical method," says Maier, "has put us into a monstrous hole." He continues by saying that "the subtle net woven by the higher-critical method" has resulted in "a new Babylonian captivity of the church."[25] What is to blame for this sorry state of affairs? Maier answers: "It would be a big mistake to blame this development of things on the incompetence of the *methodizers*. Rather, it is the fault of the *method* they have selected."[26] According to Maier the very "concept and development of the higher-critical method present an inner impossibility to the extent that one holds to the position that the witness of divine revelation is presented in the canonical Scriptures." Since the historical-critical method cannot "do without preconceived ideas of what 'genuine faith' and 'the Word of God' is," it can never deliver a "canon in the canon."[27] The historical-critical method, concludes Maier, "has arrived at the end of a blind alley." There is no choice but to reject the historical-critical method and to face up to the "responsibility of finding a different method of Biblical inquiry and scholarly study—one better suited to its subject."[28]

One of those who has reacted to Maier's book is Peter Stuhlmacher, his former teacher and the successor to Ernst Käsemann in the chair of New Testament at Tübingen. In his 1975 book *Historical Criticism and Theological Interpretation of Scripture* Stuhlmacher presents his own critique of the historical-critical method. He begins by declaring the continued relevance of Gerhard Ebeling's 1950 statement: "The question of the critical-historical method is far from being a formal, technical problem of methodology: it is a question which, from the historical and factual point of view, touches on the deepest foundations and the most difficult interconnections of theological thinking and of the church situation."[29] He notes that contemporary Protestant theology is "still hounded and harried by the fundamental problems of historical criticism"[30] and he refers to "the problem-area of New Testament exegesis, which has made of the biblical canon such a ruinous heap of hypothetical possibilities."[31] He warns against screening ourselves "from the negative consequences of radical Protestant Bible criticism" and rendering them "innocuous by an appeal to the effects of historical criticism as serving the true faith and freeing from illusion." He admits that the consequences of historical criticism are serious. He writes: "For colleagues in the discipline, for pastors performing their office, and for students, historical criticism is the agent of a repeated and growing rupture of vital contact between biblical tradition and our own time. We have seen that this problem is inherent in the structure of historical criticism."[32]

On the basis of these critical comments regarding historical criticism one might expect that Stuhlmacher would be somewhat sympathetic to his former student's declaration that the historical-critical method is at an end. Such an expectation, however, could be entertained only by someone who had yet to discover the fundamental difference in the way these two theologians view the relationship between Scripture and Word of God. Far from indicating agreement with Maier's analysis of the problem and his proposal for its solution, Stuhlmacher "reserves his most critical comments for Maier."[33] Declaring that "the thesis of Protestant Orthodoxy regarding the verbal inspiration of the Greek and Hebrew text is ruined beyond hope,"[34] Stuhlmacher gets right to the heart of the matter in the opening lines of his "Excursus: Gerhard Maier and the *End of the Historical-Critical Method.*" First noting that "theological inadequacies reflected in certain attempts to reassert the hermeneutical necessity of a doctrine of inspiration can best be illustrated by a review of the book by Gerhard Maier," Stuhlmacher then proceeds to offer this commentary on the key paragraph of Maier's analysis of the problem: "Maier would rather retreat behind the historical-scientific ranking of the biblical books with other ancient sources (made since Semler) and behind the distinction between the scriptural text and the word of God (in use since Semler) to an evaluation of the biblical canon as the inerrant source of revelation and the inspired word of God."[35] These words reveal as much about Stuhlmacher's conception of the relationship between Scripture and Word of God as they do about Maier's analysis of the problem.

In the light of these comments by Stuhlmacher it becomes readily apparent why he comes to a radically different solution to the admitted problems caused by the historical-critical method. Whereas Maier calls for the rejection of the historical-critical method in favor of one that surmounts "the philosophically based cleavage between Scripture and the Word of God introduced by Semler and his colleagues,"[36] Stuhlmacher stands with Semler in opposition to Maier's contention that "the Bible is a book *sui generis* (peculiar to itself)" which should be investigated only by "an exegetical method which is in accord with revelation in the form of the Holy Scripture."[37] Therefore, although Stuhlmacher can affirm the need for a "principle of inspiration," talk about "Scripture as witness to the revelation" which possesses an "independent power and efficacy," and even state that "theological interpretation can be carried on only within the horizon of a concept of truth which allows the historical contact or encounter of immanence with transcendence,"[38] he can also conclude that "there is no occasion to speak summarily of a collapse of historical criticism,"[39] assert that "any scientific alternative to this method is out of the question,"[40] hold that in view of the "ever-increasing abundance of insight concerning the origin and uniqueness of Holy Scripture" the decision to use the historical-critical method is "irrevocable,"[41] and argue for what he calls its "correction"[42] and its "solely instrumental use."[43] It seems clear that it is Maier's identification of Scripture with the Word of God which causes him to reject the historical-critical method in principle, while it seems just as clear that it is Stuhlmacher's rejection of this identification which allows him to advocate its continued use, albeit corrected, in the study of Scripture. So long as Maier and Stuhlmacher continue to disagree on the fundamental question "Is Scripture Word of God?" they are also going to continue to disagree on the appropriateness of the use of the historical-critical method in the study of the Holy Scriptures.

REVIEW OF THE ESSAYS

Our brief review of Karl Barth's doctrine of Scripture and the recent books by Maier and Stuhlmacher on historical criticism seems to indicate that there is a clear relationship between the understanding of the relationship which exists between Scripture and Word of God and the decision concerning the appropriateness of using the historical-critical method in the study of Scripture. Whereas both Barth and Stuhlmacher reject the identification of Scripture and Word of God and affirm the use of historical criticism, Maier expressly states that because Scripture is Word of God, the historical-critical method is not suited to deal with revelation in the form of Holy Scripture. It should be noted, however, that despite their repudiation of the identification of Scripture and Word of God, both Barth and Stuhlmacher continue to speak in a qualified way of the inspiration of Scripture and even occasionally refer to it as God's Word, although in a way carefully distinguished from the traditional use of these terms. Karl Barth, for example, after a prolonged discussion in which he sought to demonstrate that Scripture should not be identified with Word of God and in which he even called such "an actualising of the Word of God" false doctrine,[44] nevertheless entitled his second paragraph on the topic of Holy Scripture "Scripture as the Word of God," and began it with these words: "If what we hear in Holy Scripture is witness, a human expression of God's revelation . . . what we hear is revelation, and therefore the very Word of God."[45] Moreover, he insists that "the biblical texts must be investigated for their own sake to the extent that the revelation which they attest does not stand or occur, and is not to be sought, behind or above them but in them."[46] By the same token Stuhlmacher, despite his rejection of Maier's identification of Scripture and Word of God, expressly endorses the "hermeneutical significance of the idea of inspiration"[47] and speaks of "Scripture as witness to the revelation [which] possesses an independent power and efficacy"[48] and of "biblical propositions which speak of God's truth."[49] We must keep this in mind as we now look briefly at the essays included in this volume.

If the thesis set forth above is correct—namely, that there is a direct relationship between the interpreter's understanding of the relationship between Scripture and Word of God and his decision regarding the appropriateness of using the historical-critical method in the interpretation of Scripture—we should expect to find some confirmation of it in these essays on hermeneutics by theologians of the ALC, LCA, and LCMS. On the basis of the FODT report's finding that "representatives of the ALC and LCA generally affirm the appropriateness of this [historical-critical] method," we should expect to find that the ALC and LCA essayists would reject or at least qualify in some way the identification of Scripture and Word of God.[50] By the same token, we should anticipate that the LCMS essayists, on the basis of the FODT report's conclusion that "representatives of the LCMS . . . reject the legitimacy of the historical-critical method," would expressly affirm an unqualified acceptance of Scripture as Word of God.[51]

The question before us at this time, then, is whether or not such expectations can be sustained by an examination of the essays presented here. It is not possible within the limitations of this introductory essay to carry out the careful and detailed analysis of each essay which would be necessary to establish a conclusive answer to this question. A quick overview of these essays, however, seems to indicate that the ALC and LCA essayists do in fact have a tendency to qualify in some fashion the identification of Scripture and Word of God, while the LCMS essayists quite clearly and explicitly identify Scripture and Word of God. A few examples in support of this conclusion can be presented at this time.

The ALC and LCA Essays

Despite the fact that Arland J. Hultgren speaks on one occcasion of "the divinely inspired writings," his essay does not provide any indication as to what he meant by the word *inspired*. He does specifically state that "the theological unity of the Bible has become problematic, and one can say that there is no biblical theology today." He holds that the "unity of the Old Testament and Christian proclamation written into the New" can be seen "only in terms of historical dynamics in which God is himself the dynamo." Says Hultgren: "One cannot demonstrate that the Christian has followed God's tracks through the Old Testament correctly while the Jew has been sidetracked or become lost in the wilderness." Since "the biblical writers of both Testaments are a pluralistic lot," the interpreter "will have to enter into the precarious arena of canonical criticism." The interpreter will "have to ask how the text before him can be re-presented today . . . so that the word of the biblical narrator, prophet, sage, evangelist, or letter writer becomes address today." Hultgren continues: "The question has to be raised, How is that which these writers said to their readers able to become an address to our own times? Canonical and theological reflection enter the picture here, as must prayer, invocation of the Spirit, and meditation, so that one's own moment of proclamation takes up into itself all that was written in former times and transforms it into what we dare to call God's Word for our own time." Such a statement raises several questions. What is meant by the statement that one's moment of proclamation transforms all that was written in former times into what we dare to call God's Word for our time? Was that which "was written" God's Word for the former time but not for today? In what sense *was* it God's Word then? In what sense can this proclamation be called God's Word today? A later comment by Hultgren seems to indicate that that which distinguishes the witness of the present-day interpreter from the witness presented in the Scriptures is merely the fact that the latter is primary: "Not only does the text before him [the interpreter] by Amos, Paul, or Luke attest to a moment of witness, but so does he. His own reflection and proclamation, like those of the biblical writers themselves, are tethered to the history of God's saving acts to which the whole Bible gives primary witness."

117

Whatever relationship Hultgren envisions between the text of Scripture and the present proclamation, it is questionable whether he intends for either of them to be directly identified in any static way with Word of God.

Warren A. Quanbeck takes up the question of Scripture in his essay, "The Confessions and Their Influence upon Biblical Interpretation." He speaks of Scripture in a careful and yet ambiguous way. For example, he calls Scripture "the bearer of the divine self-disclosure." He refers to "the sense of the revelatory function of Scripture." He states that "in Scripture the very Word of God is encountered," and he talks about "the efficacy of the Word of God in the Scriptures." But even when he speaks of the uniqueness of Scripture he is careful to avoid any direct identification of Scripture with the Word of God: "The exposition of Scripture could never be seen on the same level as the literary study of the classics. It was seen as qualitatively different, *for it was concerned with matters essential to human destiny*" (emphasis mine). It is significant to note that for Quanbeck, according to this statement, the uniqueness of Scripture is to be found in its subject matter and not in what it is.[52]

Quanbeck also takes up the specific question of the use of the historical-critical method. He recognizes that "there are indeed exegetes and preachers whose exposition of the Scriptures is soteriologically inadequate," and he sympathizes with Christians who are disturbed when the Scriptures "are read as paradigms of historical-critical method." Nevertheless he criticizes what he considers to be the defensive actions of Lutheran dogmaticians who have attempted "to buttress" the church's "sense of the unique role of Scripture in the life of the church" by developing "incidental or supplementary aspects of the Scriptures" such as "its many literary excellences, its historical accuracy and candor, [and] its inner consistency" into indications of "infallibility and inerrancy." It is his contention that the dogmaticians of the seventeenth century, for example, "misuse the doctrine of inspiration to transcend the historical relativity of the Scriptures." It does not come as a surprise, therefore, when Quanbeck speaks of the "great contributions to the understanding of the biblical message" which "the historical-critical study of the Bible set in motion by the Renaissance and Reformation" has produced, nor that he expressly says that "it would be foolish to deny ourselves the benefits" of the "new techniques of study, form, tradition, and redaction criticism" which give "an ampler understanding of the way the Scriptures have come into being."

Quanbeck's attitude toward historical-critical methodology seems typical of the ALC and LCA essayists. It is not unusual to find in the ALC and

LCA essays references to its "inadequacy" (Priebe), "liabilities" (Hultgren, who speaks of "certain liabilities" of redaction criticism), and its "too willing service to the dogmas of historicism" (Tiede). But, like Stuhlmacher, these essayists indicate that the historical-critical method has not reached its end but continues to be an "inescapable necessity" (see Hals). As David Tiede puts it: "Historical criticism, like all other human enterprises, has been required to learn to serve the subject matter of the text rather than dominate it, and needless to say, that process continues" (see also Priebe and Burgess). Donald Juel does not hesitate to make use of the various techniques of historical criticism in his examination. Although he concludes that Mark's use of the parable of the mustard seed is probably quite similar to the way Jesus actually used it, he admits this would not necessarily have to be the case. He states that the awareness that the parables may have had an original setting "significantly different from the present literary setting of the parables *demands* that students of the parables attempt the reconstruction" (see McCurley, who says, "Matthew *puts* on the lips of Jesus the sayings of Wisdom"; emphasis mine).

None of the ALC or LCA essayists rejects the historical-critical method in principle. At the same time, one searches through these essays in vain for any direct identification of Scripture and Word of God. This is not to say that the essayists do not want to take the Bible seriously. They do. But they do not speak without qualification of Scripture as Word of God. Rather, as Duane Priebe puts it, the interpreter approaches the text expectantly, listening "for a Word from God in which the text that once was God's Word to people in a different time and place might again become God's Word for us."[53] While the intention of this essay has not been to demonstrate that the ALC and LCA essayists explicitly reject the identification of Scripture with Word of God and *say that this is the reason* they do not object in principle to the use of the historical-critical method, a preliminary overview of these essays seems to confirm the thesis that "one of the fundamental factors influencing the approach to biblical interpretation is the interpreter's conception of the relationship that exists between Scripture and Word of God."[54]

The LCMS Essays

The LCMS essayists make no attempt to hide the fact that they regard Scripture without qualification as Word of God. For example, while acknowledging that "the Confessions, like the Scriptures, indeed put quantitatively more accent on the functional or existential dimensions because God's Word is first of all something to be believed and proclaimed, not explored theoretically," Horace D. Hummel states categorically that "the symbols *do* identify the Bible with the Word of God."[55] Hummel writes: "God has revealed his truth in the Scriptures, in its noetic and propositional aspects as well as in its existential sense. He reveals there not only himself but also facts, history, and doctrine about himself." Likewise, Ralph A. Bohlmann holds that the Scriptures, authored by God, address men as "God's own infallible, powerful, and authoritative speech." He writes: "Holy Scripture is the product of the unique and miraculous action of God the Holy Spirit upon his chosen prophets and apostles whereby he spoke his Word in their words, so that he is the true author of their every word. Because of their divine authorship, the Scriptures are qualitatively different from every other form of human expression in every age." Kurt E. Marquart, pointing out that the Formula of Concord specifically distinguishes between "divine and human *writings* (*scripta*)," says: "The biblical text, as God's Word, stands over against all 'human beings' writings'—even if the latter are gospel-centered and gospel-permeated creeds, catechisms, and confessions!" Martin H. Scharlemann lists as one of the basic presuppositions with which the interpreter approaches the text of Scripture "that God's truth is *deposited there* by his Spirit to be uncovered rather than discovered" (emphasis mine).

Not only do the LCMS essayists identify Scripture with Word of God, but they also expressly state that this fact has certain direct consequences regarding the kinds of methods of interpretation with which Scripture may be approached. Scharlemann, for example, notes that his method of interpretation, which he calls "radical orthodoxy," constitutes "a conscious rejection of major ingredients found in much of contemporary New Testament interpretation." Hummel, after having argued that the adjective "propositional" is correctly placed before "revelation" and that this propositional revelation is canonical Scripture, states that "a whole host of traditional hermeneutical axioms then ensue." Included among these are the unity of Scripture, the qualitative difference between canonical and extracanonical tradition, and the principle that "*scriptura sui ipsius interpres est.*" Marquart states explicitly that the historical-critical method cannot be employed in the study of Scripture because it is God's Word. He writes: "Since it is self-contradictory to take issue with God's Word, but since the right to take issue with biblical statements is an inherent, constitutive necessity for the historical-critical method . . . it is clear that the application of criticism to Scripture cannot theoretically be justified so long as the biblical writings are regarded as inviolable, divinely inspired truth given in human language."

It should be pointed out, however, that the LCMS essayists are in no way opposed to the careful historical and literary study of Holy Scriptures. Having stated that they are opposed to the historical-critical method on the basis of the fact that Scripture is God's Word, the LCMS essayists unanimously call for a careful historical and literary study of the Holy Scriptures. Marquart notes that "most of the techniques (e.g., literary criticism, redaction criticism) can be used up to a point also by anti-critical scholars." Scharlemann's study on the parables of the leaven and the mustard seed illustrates how this is possible through his use of textual criticism, word studies, and literary and certain aspects of redaction criticism. It is important to note, however, that Scharlemann rejects as false "one of the cardinal presuppositions of form and redaction criticism"—that variations in the parallel accounts of the same parable "may be due to the treatment given a parable of Jesus during the time of the oral tradition." Bohlmann insists that "the Scriptures must be read as historical literary documents in order to discern God's intended meaning. . . . Careful literary exegesis is therefore not an option but a necessity for the Christian interpreter." Hummel, who calls for the use of external evidence such as archaeology and the history of religions for the fuller understanding of vocabulary, metaphors, and secondary symbolism, expresses the principle underlying the rejection of the historical-critical method and the use of those techniques that are consistent with the understanding of Scripture as Word of God when he says, "The question is whether external (historical) evidence may be used to test *whether* or not the Bible is true or whether its legitimate use is limited to helping us better understand *what* truth is revealed there." Because Scripture is Word of God, the former is excluded, while the latter is not only possible but necessary.

This review of the LCMS essays clearly shows that the essayists' understanding of the relationship between Scripture and Word of God is one of the fundamental factors that affect their approach to methods of biblical interpretation. As a direct result of their conviction that Scripture is Word of God, the LCMS essayists reject in principle the use of the historical-critical method.

CONCLUSION

If the thesis is correct that one of the fundamental factors influencing the approach to biblical interpretation is the interpreter's conception of the relationship existing between Scripture and Word of God, a number of conclusions should follow. While there appears to be general agreement

121

in these essays regarding the centrality of the gospel (the material principle of theology), the necessity of employing textual criticism in attempting to reconstruct as nearly as possible the original text of Scripture, the importance of literary criticism in order to discern God's intended meaning in the text, and the use of external evidence in order better to understand the truth presented in the text, the central problem that emerges seems to lie beyond mere questions of interpretation or even methods of interpretation. For if it is true that the factor which accounts for the divergence in the essayists' approaches to the methodology of biblical interpretation is the understanding of the relationship that exists between Scripture and Word of God, the problem dividing North American Lutherans is far more serious than merely a hermeneutical discussion about how this or that text is to be interpreted. Rather, the important questions become: What is this book that is to be interpreted? Is it the very Word of God in the words of men, or is it *only* the fallible witness of human beings to God's revelation of himself in history through which he somehow continues to speak? Is Scripture itself revelation, or is it *only* the occasion for revelation to take place once again? Is the root of the evil in theology the interchangeable use of the terms *Scripture* and *Word of God* (Semler), or is the root of the problem the wedge that has been drawn between them? Seen from this perspective, the differences between the ALC/LCA and the LCMS as listed in the FODT report and documented in the essays here presented take on the most serious proportions, for the fundamental problem is therefore not the fact that the ALC/LCA and the LCMS disagree regarding "the existence of discrepancies, contradictions, mistaken notions, [and] diverse theologies" (FODT report), nor is it even the use or nonuse of historical criticism. If the thesis of this essay is correct, then these differences must be seen as merely symptoms of a much more fundamental problem which opens up such important issues as the concept of authority,[56] the meaning of confessional subscription (since the Lutheran Confessions clearly identify Scripture and Word of God),[57] the continued viability of the Reformation *sola scriptura* principle,[58] and the very possibility of incarnational theology.[59] The seriousness of these issues is only obscured by those who set forth their personal acceptance of traditional positions on such key articles of faith as the virgin birth of Christ or his resurrection in defense of the use of historical criticism. To defend the use of historical criticism on the basis of the results achieved by certain of its practitioners is to fail to see the fundamental problem that its use in the study of Scripture necessarily raises.

But I would close this essay on a positive note. As one who shares the view of the LCMS essayists that Scripture is Word of God because it makes this claim for itself (e.g., 2 Tim. 3:15–17; 2 Pet. 1:21; 1 Cor. 2:13; 1 Thess. 2:13),[60] I believe that these essays are helpful in directing attention to a substantive issue troubling not only Lutherans in North America but all of Christendom today. It is refreshing to get beyond the discussion of such matters as the number of Philistines killed in this or that battle, the presence or absence of vocal cords in the serpent in Genesis 3, whether or not Jonah was really swallowed by a fish, or how many angels were at the tomb on the first Easter. It is progress, I believe, if the problems surrounding inerrancy, hermeneutical methods, and the interpretation of individual pericopes can be seen and discussed from the perspective of the underlying issue: Is Scripture without qualification Word of God?

As a stimulus for discussion and as a way of testing the thesis presented in this paper, I offer the following syllogism:

1. The historical-critical method is by definition inappropriate for application to Word of God.
2. Scripture is without qualification Word of God.
3. Therefore the historical-critical method is by definition inappropriate for application to Scripture.

Disagreement regarding the conclusion is the result, I believe, of disagreement regarding not the major premise but the minor one.

May God the Holy Spirit guide and direct our continuing study of the Holy Scriptures "so that we may with one voice glorify the God and Father of our Lord Jesus Christ" (Rom. 15:6).

NOTES

1. "The Function of Doctrine and Theology in Light of the Unity of the Church," in *Studies* (New York: Lutheran Council in the U.S.A., 1978), p. 9.
2. Ibid., pp. 11–12.
3. Ibid., p. 12.
4. The sequence Scripture and Word of God is important since the topic under consideration in this essay will be the relationship obtaining between *Scripture* and the Word of God. Not at issue in this essay are the various meanings of the term *Word of God*. While all essayists would agree, for example, that Word of God may properly be used to refer to the Second Person of the Trinity, gospel, the proclaimed Word, and so on, it is the contention of this essay that not all essayists in this volume agree that Scripture is without qualification Word of God.
5. Hermann Strathmann, "Die Krisis des Kanons der Kirche: Joh. Gerhards und Joh. Sal. Semlers Erbe," in *Das Neue Testament als Kanon,* ed. Ernst Käsemann (Göttingen: Vandenhoeck & Ruprecht, 1970), p. 52.
6. Edgar Krentz, *The Historical-Critical Method* (Philadelphia: Fortress Press, 1975), p. 19.

7. See Karl Barth, *Church Dogmatics* (Naperville, Ill.: Alec R. Allenson, 1960), vol. 1, pt. 2, pp. 457–740, esp. p. 522.

8. Karl Barth, *The Epistle to the Romans,* trans. Edwyn C. Hoskyns, 6th ed. (New York: Oxford University Press, 1968), p. 1.

9. Jérome Hamer, *Karl Barth,* trans. D. M. Maruca (Westminster, Md.: Newman Press, 1962), p. 17.

10. Barth, *Church Dogmatics,* vol. 1, pt. 1, pp. 98–140.

11. Ibid., p. 134.

12. Ibid., pt. 2, p. 463.

13. Ibid., p. 507.

14. Ibid., p. 509.

15. Ibid., pt. 1, p. 127.

16. Ibid., pt. 2, p. 506.

17. Ibid., pp. 507–8.

18. Ibid., p. 518.

19. Ibid., p. 525.

20. Ibid., p. 502.

21. Ibid., p. 507.

22. Gerhard Maier, *The End of the Historical-Critical Method,* trans. Edwin W. Leverenz and Rudolph F. Norden, with a foreword by Eugene F. Klug (St. Louis: Concordia Publishing House, 1977), p. 47.

23. Ibid., p. 26.

24. Ibid., p. 47.

25. Ibid., p. 48.

26. Ibid., p. 49.

27. Ibid., p. 25.

28. Ibid., p. 49.

29. Peter Stuhlmacher, *Historical Criticism and Theological Interpretation of Scripture: Toward a Hermeneutics of Consent,* trans. with an introduction by Roy A. Harrisville (Philadelphia: Fortress Press, 1977), p. 19.

30. Ibid., p. 21.

31. Ibid., pp. 74–75.

32. Ibid., p. 65.

33. Ibid., p. 10. So says Roy A. Harrisville in his introductory essay to Stuhlmacher's book.

34. Ibid., p. 66.

35. Ibid., pp. 66–67.

36. Maier, *End of the Historical-Critical Method,* p. 50.

37. Ibid., pp. 50–51.

38. Stuhlmacher, *Historical Criticism and Theological Interpretation,* p. 60.

39. Ibid.

40. Ibid., p. 20.

41. Ibid., p. 59.

42. Ibid., p. 65.

43. Ibid., p. 59.

44. Barth, *Church Dogmatics,* vol. 1, pt. 2, p. 525.

45. Ibid., p. 473.

46. Ibid., p. 494.

47. Stuhlmacher, *Historical Criticism and Theological Interpretation,* p. 60.

48. Ibid.

49. Ibid., p. 89.

50. This assumes that the ALC and LCA essayists are in agreement with

the position of the ALC and LCA representatives to the FODT discussions. One of the essayists, Warren Quanbeck, was also an ALC representative to the FODT consultation.

51. Once again this expectation assumes that the LCMS essayists are in agreement with the position of the LCMS representatives to the FODT discussions. One of the LCMS essayists, Ralph Bohlmann, was also an LCMS representative to the FODT consultation.

52. The contrast between Quanbeck's understanding of "qualitatively different" and that of the LCMS's Commission on Theology and Church Relations (CTCR) in 1967 is striking. For the CTCR the Holy Scriptures are "the product of the Spirit who produces in history that which is not of this world," and for this reason "there is a qualitative difference between the inspired witness of Holy Scripture in all its parts and words and the witness, explicit or implicit, of every other form of human expression." "A Lutheran Stance Toward Contemporary Biblical Studies," Report of the CTCR, 1967, p. 10.

53. Tiede speaks in a similar fashion when he says: "But as we ask and listen, as we attend carefully to what a given author intended to say and ponder the relevance of that message for our times and situations, the Word of the Lord breaks into our inquiry. Through, in the midst of, or in, with, and under the rich diversity of voices in the Scripture, the living Lord speaks to us, to our times and condition."

54. See above, p. 109.

55. Hummel states that "the importance of the material principle as a major, positive hermeneutical guide can scarcely be overstated."

56. David Kelsey, in his fascinating study on the uses of Scripture in recent theology, notes that "one basic distinction to be made among different notions of 'authority' is the distinction between understanding authority functionally and understanding it as an intrinsic property of canonical writings" (David H. Kelsey, *The Use of Scripture in Recent Theology* [Philadelphia: Fortress Press, 1975], p. 30). E. C. Blackman says that the conflict between historical criticism and the authority of Scripture "may indeed be reckoned the most serious test the church has had to face through nineteen centuries (with the possible exception of the division between East and West in the tenth century)" (E. C. Blackman, *Biblical Interpretation* [Philadelphia: Westminster Press, 1957], p. 16). Krentz, *Historical-Critical Method*, p. 4, indicates his agreement with this assessment.

57. Herbert J. A. Bouman reports in an unpublished study entitled "Source Material on 'The Word of God in the Lutheran Confessions' " that the phrase "Word of God" is equated with Scripture at least seventy-seven times in the Lutheran confessional documents.

58. For example, Ted Peters has recently written: "Since the Reformation a significant proportion of the Protestant tradition sought to reduce the sources for theology to one, the Bible. Reacting against the allegedly illegitimate authority of ecclesiastical tradition and dogma, the Reformers sought to make Scripture the sole normative authority for Christian faith and theological reflection: *Sola Scriptura*. But history played a dirty trick on this scripture principle. No sooner had confidence in scriptural authority become accepted than the Western World became modern. Modernity brought a view of nature as a big machine with little or no need of a divine being even to push the buttons. It brought humanism, pluralism, relativism, secularism, and historical criticism. Relativized and historicized, the Bible began to lose its stature as authority" (p. 268). Peters continues: "Given the alternatives, 'Scripture

SAMUEL H. NAFZGER

alone' or 'Scripture and tradition,' the Roman Catholic Church undoubtedly has the better position; for whoever admits *Sola Scriptura*, in the sense of holding that the canonical New Testament is the sole norm, rule, and standard, goes the way of the Roman Catholic—only not as consistently" (p. 275) (Ted Peters, "Sola Scriptura and the Second Naiveté," *Dialog* 16 [Fall 1977]: 268–80).

59. For an excellent discussion of the implications of "the revolution in consciousness" (p. 4) which historical criticism involves for the relationship between faith and history, see Van A. Harvey's *The Historian and the Believer* (New York: Macmillan Company, 1969).

Norman Perrin states: "Redaction criticism . . . raises above all the question as to whether the view of the historical Jesus as the locus of revelation and the central concern of Christian faith is in fact justifiable, and it raises this question because it shows how truly foreign such a view is to the New Testament itself" (Norman Perrin, *What Is Redaction Criticism?* [Philadelphia: Fortress Press, 1969], p. 72).

60. His recent writings notwithstanding, James Barr's comment is to the point: "God can speak specific verbal messages, when he wills, to the men of his choice. But for this, if we follow the way in which the Old Testament represents the incidents, there would have been no call for Abraham, no Exodus, no prophecy. Direct communication from God to man has fully as much claim to be called the core of the tradition as has revelation through events in history. If we persist in saying that this direct, specific communication must be subsumed under revelation through events in history and taken as subsidiary interpretation of the latter, I shall say that we are abandoning the Bible's own representation of the matter." (James Barr, "The Interpretation of Scripture," *Interpretation* 17 [April 1963], 201–2.)

Problems of Lutheran Hermeneutics

KARLFRIED FROEHLICH

Professor of Church History
Princeton Theological Seminary
Princeton, New Jersey

It is well known that the Middle Ages used a fourfold sense in interpreting Scripture: the literal, allegorical, tropological, and anagogical. This traditional quadriga is easily misunderstood. It was not a rigid scheme into which each biblical text could be pressed. Other senses were acknowledged, and an exegete would rarely feel compelled to explain a text according to all four senses. Basically, the interpreters worked with two of them, the literal and the spiritual sense, of which allegory, tropology, and anagogy were but subcategories. Moreover, no either/or was intended. The literal sense did not exclude the spiritual, or vice versa. Rather, the two were related in a dialectical movement from one to the other. Thomas Aquinas reestablished the older Augustinian principle that all exegesis must start with the literal sense but must move on from there dynamically to the spiritual level toward which all God's revelation is leading. At the same time Aquinas made clear that a spiritual understanding of Scripture is of no use in theological argument and therefore must be grounded in the literal sense in order to attain its persuasive power.

One could, of course, collapse these two basic senses further into a single sense. Critics of medieval scholasticism, Luther among them, already talked about the one and only sense of Scripture in a polemical and almost propagandistic fashion. Yet, if one seriously pursued this option, the dialectic would vanish. If exegesis is to remain part of a dynamic movement from text to life situation, letter to spirit, and back, any postulated single sense would have to assume the functions of both poles and thus would not differ much from the structure of the double sense under-lying the fourfold sense of the Scholastics. Luther was aware of this logic. Along with his insistence on the one, clear, simple, literal sense of all Scripture we find him saying that Scripture is everywhere about Christ, even in the Old Testament, and that this "literal sense" is the essence of the true spiritual understanding of Scripture.[1] Insistence on the unity of scriptural senses did not mean neglect of the tension between the literal and spiritual components.

The history of biblical hermeneutics itself presents a parallel picture. A survey such as that offered by R. M. Grant[2] distinguishes numerous stages: allegorism, authoritative exegesis, medieval literalism, Reformation principles, rationalistic exegesis, historical criticism. But again the scheme cannot be pressed. The stages overlap, there are anticipations, reorienta-tions, and conflations. One could easily reduce the entire development to two stages characterized by two basic emphases: the emphasis on the divine author of the Bible in the era before the seventeenth and eigh-teenth centuries, and the emphasis on the human author(s) in the modern age since then. Again, these emphases do not suggest a clear-cut either/ or. Consideration of the divine author never excluded interest in the human element of biblical language and biblical content, and concentra-tion on the human author of a scriptural text does not imply that the divine element of the Word of God in Scripture is of no concern. One could collapse the two emphases further. The entire history of biblical interpretation could be considered as one age determined by the assump-tion of one authorship only, divine or human. But then the dialectic of these two elements would get lost—to the detriment of theological dis-course, which is dependent upon it. There are examples of such an at-tempted collapse. Origen of Alexandria drew from his strict inspirational theory the consequence that even the human faults of the biblical text, including scribal errors, have been put there on purpose by the divine author. For him all passages of Scripture have a spiritual sense but not all have also a literal sense. On the other hand, biblical critics since J. S. Semler have often advocated an understanding of biblical texts simply as part of human literature. Such scholars pursued their efforts as a special-ization of the general history of religions bracketing out the question of the Word of God in Scripture. In both cases it is difficult to see their biblical exegesis as a dynamic process of faith that links the scriptural witness to Christian life and takes seriously the dialectic of human and divine elements. One of the two poles is too easily swallowed up and exegesis becomes a one-way road too readily. The church has resisted this trend and has tried to keep the dialectic movement. Historically the insistence on the unity of scriptural authorship, human or divine, in the church was not meant to do away with the tension between human and divine aspects of Scripture, however much the one author might be stressed.

Lutheran exegesis starts with the affirmation that Scripture is the only norm for Christian doctrine and life. The *sola* principle gave the fathers of the Lutheran Reformation the criterion by which they saw themselves distinguished from the Romanists as soon as they had to face up to their independent existence. Even today, the rhetoric of *sola fide, sola gratia, sola scriptura* is regarded as a distinctive mark of the Lutheran theological stance. In light of our previous deliberations a certain suspicion may arise in face of this rhetoric of unity, singularity, and exclusivity of the norm. Could it be that the *sola scriptura* principle itself is the result of a process of collapsing, for the sake of emphasis, two distinct poles of a total picture without the intention of losing the dialectic and thus one's fundamental openness toward the dynamic movement between text and tradition within the scriptural norm itself?

The problem appears in sharp profile when we ask *how* the scriptural norm can be applied, either with regard to a specific issue in the life of the church or with regard to a particular text. *Sola scriptura*—does this imply the application of one single method of interpretation as a condition of a proper functioning of Scripture as norm? If so, what does "method" mean in this context? The question seems further complicated by the Lutheran confessional stance. Most Lutheran churches specify in their constitutions that the Confessions of the sixteenth century serve for them as the normative guide to the interpretation of Scripture because (or, in another reading, insofar as) they express the truth of the scriptural norm in purity.

Some Lutherans like to read this stance as implying that one norm indeed must mean one method. Norm for them refers to a tool necessary for testing, verifying, and deciding the yes or no of a judicial process in which the Lutheran character of a specific interpretation is in question. The normative role of the Confessions must then be seen as providing a bridge to the one method, because the Bible itself gives little help in identifying one single method of its interpretation. *Sola* becomes in a very real sense a *particula exclusiva.* The one norm, Scripture, interpreted by one method which must be linked to the normative Confessions, allows the interpreter to identify what is Lutheran and to detect and reject what is false doctrine. Still, the question of what "method" means would not be answered. Modern enemies of the historical-critical method sometimes try to show that the Confessions advocate a different method.[3] But their argument must proceed by implication. The simple fact is that the Confessions have no article on method in the sense of exegetical procedure and never spell out normative principles in this area. Norm for them is a theological concept, and Lutherans will have to be content with the procedural ambiguity that this entails. At any rate, to read the logic of the *sola* rhetoric as implying that one norm and one method must lead to one interpretation would be an unwarranted restriction.

There are other ways of reading the Lutheran confessional stance. If a normative text needs "normative guidance" for its interpretation, the dilemma of a close link between norm and method is evident. In fact, instead of narrowing the scope of the scriptural norm to one method, and ultimately one exegetical result, in any act of interpretation, the normative function of the Confessions may be seen as freeing the scriptural norm from a one-sided method precisely because the *sola scriptura* is meant to lead the interpreter *into* the dialectic of letter and spirit, human and divine author, not out of or beyond it. If the rhetoric of *sola scriptura* really presupposes a collapsing of two poles into one for the sake of theological emphasis, the confessional guidance could help to keep the goal of the dynamic process in focus without binding the norm to methodological uniformity. Biblical interpretation can become the place where the movement from letter to spirit and from spirit to letter is experienced in an authoritative, direction-giving encounter. *Sola scriptura* can become a *particula inclusiva*: not one norm, one method, one interpretation, but one norm, all kinds of methods, manifold expressions of the one theological emphasis. The logic of the *sola* rhetoric, properly understood, may lead Lutherans into the immense richness of lived Christian lives, nourished by a rich variety of biblical interpretation. And yet variety does not mean chaos. Within the Lutheran confessional stance the accents are clearly marked. Luther collapsed the manifold senses of Scripture into one in order to stress that *all* Scripture is about Christ and his benefits for us. If this gospel appears with power and clarity, the purpose of the process of scriptural interpretation in the church is fulfilled.

What this means is that even identical presuppositions in terms of methodological procedure can yield different interpretations. This had been Luther's own experience. These interpretations cannot be classified as right or wrong simply on the basis of their conformity to specific procedural canons. The difference is a theological one. Considered in their context, they are right inasmuch as they lead into the evangelical dialectic of text and life by grace; they are wrong inasmuch as they fail in this task. In the last analysis exegesis is not an arcane discipline practiced by specialists and judged by specialists only. It is a "life science," admittedly based on technical, time-bound, methodological principles, but aimed at the ongoing process of nourishing the faith of Christians in all ages. Oneness of aim, and therefore the *sola* principle, does not depend on uniformity of method or conformity of the individual interpretation.

How much room there is for disagreement within this oneness of aim can best be seen by looking at the exegetical history of a particular text. I have chosen a well-known, controversial verse that has been important throughout the centuries for Lutherans and Catholics alike—Matthew 16:18: "Thou art Peter, and upon this rock I will build my church, and the gates of hell will not prevail against it." We will look at Luther's interpretation as an example of the first period of our earlier classification, and then at four other attempts by Lutherans in more recent times.

"Thou art Peter, and upon this rock I will build my church." Luther saw the word not addressed to Peter alone.[4] Peter, according to Luther, stands for all believers as the parallels of Matthew 18:18 and John 20: 22–23 suggest. Peter is the confessor. His confession of Jesus as Messiah and Son of God (Matt. 16:17) is the presupposition of both name and honor. Thus Peter cannot be identical with the rock. On the one hand, Christ really is the rock (1 Cor. 10:4) and cornerstone (Eph. 2:20) of the church. On the other hand, the rock must be firm against the gates of hell, but Peter and the pope were not. It is true that Peter's name *derives* from Christ because Peter had confessed him. In this sense the confession, that is, Peter's proclamation in fact and as his "office," may be termed "rock" derivatively. The church that Jesus promised to build is not the Roman church but the church of those who believe in God's revelation. It includes the invisible church and in this sense successors to Peter—not in the singular but in the person of all believers of the future.

Adolf von Harnack's interpretation[5] presupposes a consensus of scholars in the late nineteenth century which was suspicious of the attribution of this word to Jesus. They were influenced by the absence of the saying from Mark and Luke, the rarity of the term *church* before Paul, the incongruity of the promise with Peter's actual role after Easter, and the recollection of his unstable character. For Harnack the fact that the church fathers of the second century did not quote verse 18 after verse 17 was a decisive clue. From an early variant in Tatian's *Diatessaron* he concluded that Jesus' original word said only, "Thou are Peter, and the gates of death will not overcome you." This would mean that the name was figuratively related to the idea of protection against death, and that a person, Peter, not the church, was promised here not to die. "And upon this rock I will build my church" was then a later symbolical substitution for the personal address to Peter in the interest of rendering the incorrect prediction understandable. Harnack thought that the "corrected" version of the verse was inserted into Matthew's Gospel in Rome at the end of the second century as a boost for Roman primacy claims.

Albert Schweitzer[6] did not join the consensus. For him the saying was authentic but (on the basis of a comparison with Mark) belonged in the setting of the revelatory speeches after Jesus' transfiguration. Jesus predicts an extraordinary authority that the disciple would enjoy in the coming end time when what he confessed on the basis of an anticipatory revelation would be plain and open. "Church" here refers not to the later organized institution with Peter as officeholder but to the preexistent heavenly *ekklesia*, ready to be revealed in the end time and identical with the inbreaking kingdom.

Ethelbert Stauffer[7] saw the key to the text in its absence from Mark, whom tradition claimed as Peter's personal interpreter. Since the word speaks in the future tense, yet (apart from the first appearance of the risen Jesus, Luke 24:34) remains unfulfilled in the early church, Stauffer interpreted it as coming from a Galilean appearance after Easter that Matthew restyled and retrojected into the earlier scene to counter Paul's claims to authority. In fact several pieces from tradition may be combined here, especially the post-Easter explanation of Peter's name and Jesus' charge to him. "Thou art Peter" is not a name-giving word but introduces the explanation of an unusual name in Old Testament style. The term *ekklesia* does reflect post-Easter Christianity but takes up an emphasis of a Jesus who must have thought about a "people" as belonging to the Son of Man, the Messiah. In the word about the gates of hell Stauffer saw an addition following the tradition of Luke 22:32, which promises Peter that his faith will not fail.

We conclude with a somewhat less formal but extensive commentary by a theologian of the Lutheran Church—Missouri Synod. Theodore Hoyer[8] saw the word as addressed to Peter and to no other person. But the distinction bestowed upon Peter rests solely on his confession, which in turn expresses the faith of all disciples. As a sinful man, he is Simon; as a confessor, a rock, standing on the rock, Christ. A building of the church on Peter is not intended because the gender of the words changes from *Petros* to *petra*. Also, the idea would be unparalleled. Mark and Luke do not have it, and other foundation passages speak of "apostles" in the plural (Eph. 2:20; Rev. 21:10ff.). Hoyer feels that such an argument from total silence is tantamount to proof, especially since neither the earliest church (Matt. 18:18; John 20:22–23) nor Peter himself (Acts 2, 4, 10; 1 Peter 5:1; 2 Peter 1:1) seem to have reckoned with a personal Petrine primacy. The real rock for the church's foundation was Christ. Many Old Testament and New Testament parallels point to this fact. Here alone and out of the blue sky Jesus should have designated Peter as the church's "rock"? Hoyer does recognize that the saying connects Peter figuratively with the rock, Christ. In this case the rock could be linked to Peter's confession—not to the *man*, to the *confessor!* But his sole advantage rests in a temporal priority of expressing the foundational confession to Christ first.

The broad variety of interpretations cannot obscure the fact that all these interpreters wrote from within and for the church, particularly the Lutheran church. Scripture for all of them was the norm of Christian teaching and living. They were churchmen, each of them in a characteristic and prominent way. But they shared more than this.

Luther came to his anti-Roman polemical exegesis on the basis of hermeneutical presuppositions similar to those of his contemporaries. He not only embraced the divine authorship emphasis that was characteristic of the age but he shared even more specific presuppositions of the late Middle Ages. I mention three of them:

(1) *Interest in the literal sense.* This had been a current phenomenon for quite some time. What was advocated was attention to the simple, natural sense of words as opposed to an unbridled, free-for-any-guess allegorism. Texts first of all have one ordinary, uncomplicated sense that everyone is able to grasp. This was not to say, however, that the meaning of these words according to the mind of the author, the Holy Spirit, was always simple. Many exegetes spoke of a "double literal sense" in the Bible, distinguishing mere words, a purely grammatical sense, the dead letter, from the true, ordinary, literal sense as the Spirit intended it, the *sensus litteralis theologicus*. Literal exegesis for Luther and his contemporaries excluded an unreflected pure literalism.

The tools for pursuing this interest consisted of increased knowledge of the original languages, including Hebrew, word study and comparison, and close attention to grammatical detail and rhetorical figuration, which since Aquinas was reckoned as part of the literal sense. For the exegete it was of utmost importance that God chose these and no other words to communicate what he wanted to be known. Luther used these tools in his interpretation of the Matthew text: The linguistic difference between *Petros* and *petra* became for him an important clue, as did his understanding of Peter as a "figure" of all believers. The context, focused in verse 17 and verse 23 rather than in verse 19, was crucial for his understanding. There can be no doubt that he regarded his interpretation as literal.

(2) *Interest in the clarity of Scripture.* Much of the justification for medieval allegorism was drawn from the conviction that the Bible was a "dark" book, full of riddles and obscurities. The notion of the true meaning of Scripture being like the kernel hidden under a rough bark stood behind the ecclesiastical insistence that only experts and officials such as bishops and later university professors should interpret Scripture authoritatively. With the ascendancy of the literal sense, however, the idea that Scripture says clearly what needs to be heard gained wide currency. It was particularly important for the late-medieval preacher whose moral appeals in an increasingly lax culture drew on the "clear and unambiguous" teachings of the Bible. Basically, the emphasis goes back to Augustine, who had declared that all Scripture teaches love of God and neighbor as its central scope. Whatever promotes love and charity expresses the clear intention of the divine author. Augustine already stressed the tools for attaining this clarity: the comparison of passages, harmonization, and especially the principle that what is not clear in one place is clarified in another, that is, that clear passages must be used to explain the unclear ones. Luther developed these tools, particularly the latter, to which he gave the classical form: "Holy Scripture is its own interpreter" (*scriptura sui ipsius interpres*). For him as for his contemporaries the *claritas* or *perspicuitas* of Scripture did not mean that everything in Scripture is found on the surface. With the entire Augustinian tradition he reckoned with an infinite depth of Scripture that discloses itself only to the patient, pious, and persistent efforts of the serious seeker. Luther even shared the self-assurance of the professional exegete. As a professor of Scripture he was qualified and entrusted with the task of dealing with the obscurities of Scripture. Utterly clear, however, is Scripture in all things that pertain to human salvation. About this point its message can be investigated and understood by everyone. If there are obscurities in the text of Matthew 16:18 they are illuminated for Luther by other clear passages. We saw how Luther used the weight of Matthew 18:18 and John 20:23, or the "clear" passages about Christ as rock and foundation of the church, in his interpretation. The clear message of the text concerned faith and the promise to all believers.

(3) *Interest in historical continuity.* Medieval exegesis was not interested in new interpretations. On the contrary, only what was in line with

well-established tradition could pass as correct and worthy of attention. To find new support in authoritative texts constituted an achievement, and increasingly so in the late Middle Ages. But in principle nobody could find in the Bible something really new. What was discovered there was the true meaning of the divine author, which had always been there and could be recognized as such when it coincided with the church's tradition. Again, the exegesis of late-medieval preachers drew much of its authority from the claim to theological continuity.

The tools to cultivate this interest were available in the literature of the fathers and their exegetical work. The *consensus patrum* was an important subject for investigation in the late Middle Ages, but not simply as a statistical fact. It meant the consensus of the *true* church—a term which could be understood either as referring to the original, the primitive church (and thus could lead to a humanist attempt to get "back to the sources") or to the authoritative church of the present, with its judicial structure and its magisterium. Luther shared this emphasis, especially in its humanist form, eagerly using the newly available editions of the fathers. Conformity to the earliest church remained a constant ideal for him and his friends, and it determined much of their exegetical interests. In the case of Matthew 16:18 Luther and Melanchthon challenged the Roman interpretation precisely at this point of its lack of conformity to the exegesis of the fathers. It must be admitted, however, that they drew on one line of the exegetical tradition only, the one represented mainly by Augustine, at the expense of others.

We noted earlier that the two basic stages in the history of biblical interpretation can be distinguished by the replacement of the earlier stress on the divine author through the stress on the human author(s) in more recent times. For the modern age this does not mean the automatic denial of the divine element in Scripture or the renunciation of the task of reading God's mind and proclaiming his will on the basis of Scripture. But since the authorship emphasis has been moved, exegesis now has its primary focus at the level of the concerns of those human authors. Interest is concentrated on the biblical books as literary documents or the diversity of standpoints expressed and the differentiation among writers and traditions. What emerges is a far more complicated picture of the Bible as the medium for a message. The same book that continues to be regarded as the norm for Christian life and doctrine now has to answer a range of questions very different from what had been asked of it before. The object of interpretation has not changed, but the context for its understanding has.

It is widely recognized today that the shift to the modern age with its new emphases coincided with the development of Protestantism. Thus it is no surprise in terms of the history of exegesis that the specific presuppositions which the Reformers shared with their contemporaries continued to play a role in the new framework mentioned above. In this way many of the characteristic tenets of late-medieval exegesis have remained surprisingly influential, even for modern exegetes who rarely reflect on this fact. This can be demonstrated by another quick glance at the three principles discussed above.

(1) Interest in the literal sense continues unbroken. In fact, it has become the hallmark of all respectable professional exegesis. To listen carefully to "what the text says" is regarded as the main, if not the exclusive, task of the interpreter. It still expresses itself by detailed attention to original language, word study, grammar, and context. But it also includes a number of prior questions. One of them is *what text*? Textual criticism, the weighing of variants and rival textual traditions, has become a major concern of the interpreters. Another question is *what author*? With the shift to the human author this question now demands careful differentiations. In the Gospel materials, for example, account has to be taken of several levels: Jesus as the original speaker, the earliest church (source criticism, form criticism, tradition history), the Gospel writers, and perhaps later redactors (redaction criticism). The question of literal sense applies to all these levels, the differentiation of which, while complicating the process, has become necessary for any exact understanding of what a text really says. The tools in this area have been considerably sharpened: biblical philology, and textual, literary, and historical criticism have developed into extremely sophisticated specialties of theological scholarship. But the hermeneutical emphasis on the literal sense itself has remained the same.

(2) Interest in the clarity of Scripture is still a major factor, especially in the pastoral application of biblical texts. On the one hand, the notion has retained the central soteriological thrust of the Reformers: *claritas scripturae* means first of all that the Bible teaches clearly all that is necessary for salvation. On the other hand, clarity of Scripture no longer means one thing only. With the stress on the human author(s) it must also be related to their thought and its structure. Differences, even contradictions between different authors, can be pointed out precisely because they are, for the modern exegete, part of what is clear in Scripture. There is no need for artificial harmonization if the profile of an individual author or text is at stake. The principle of *scriptura sui ipsius interpres*, however, maintains its firm place both in the process of pursuing the

theological message of a text and in approaching the intention of the human author. Literary criticism in its many forms is the method for investigating the latter. Yet here too prior questions now have to be included and they complicate the picture. The parallels on which one draws to illuminate a human author's work must reach out into the total world within which he wrote; archaeology, history of religion, and cultural and political history—all are part of the framework needed so that the clarity of Scripture on this level may appear. The nineteenth century tended to believe in an almost unlimited potential of such parallels from outside when it came to explaining a text. Exegetes today are far less optimistic. The canon itself is again the main resource for parallels.

(3) The interest in historical continuity remains an ongoing concern, particularly with Lutheran exegetes—not necessarily as a proof-text method, which collects supporting authorities, but as a sensitivity for theological identity and the historical place of one's own interpretation. Studies in the exegetical history of particular texts are much in vogue today and often form part of the total endeavor of understanding a text. With the emphasis on the human author(s) of Scripture, continuity is no longer sought in terms of church fathers and ecclesiastical consensus. Rather, the exegete sees himself in relation to a scholarly consensus, explaining and defending his own interpretation with reference to the work of others. Interpretation of Scripture cannot be done today without participation in this dialogue. Interpretation is performed and judged in terms of one's perception of the present state of scholarship. There is room for the fathers in this picture. But the historical continuity in which exegetes are interested today is more adequately expressed in the surveys of the recent history of interpretation, which precedes almost any extensive treatment of a biblical text. A thorough command of the commentary literature serves as the tool here. It has become almost indispensable in modern times. The interpretation of Scripture still does not claim to find totally new things in the Bible; it discovers for our time what is already there. But it can shed fresh light on the meaning of Scripture on the level of its human authors when it is done in the context of the historical situation to which all its peers contribute.

Returning to our examples of interpretations of Matthew 16:18, we can easily see that these presuppositions and their tools are everywhere present. Interest in the literal sense appears in the linguistic considerations about *Petros* and *petra* and in the discussions over the background of the word *church*, but also in the attempts to reconstruct the earliest text or to distinguish levels of authorship. Interest in the clarity of Scripture is evident in the ever more ingenious use of scriptural parallels from

137

Matthew 18:18 to the Old Testament "rock" passages or Moses/Abraham typologies, but also in the efforts to find an original context for the word that would allow its point to emerge with greater clarity. Interest in historical continuity stands behind the decisive use of patristic exegesis, for example, in Harnack, but it expresses itself also in the dialogue with exegetical peers: Harnack, Schweitzer, Stauffer—they all develop their interpretations in careful reaction to their colleagues and predecessors.

The use of these presuppositions has no doubt led to a better understanding of the text. We can say today, for instance, that the Aramaic pun underlying the *Petros/petra* phrase militates against making a difference between the person of Peter and the "rock" of the church here. We can also say that a different original context for the whole word is very likely, or that the "church" here does not have an unambiguous referent in the institution of later centuries. But this common use has not led to a single interpretation. The differences are considerable and extend to all the details. Modern interpreters do not hide them because they do not pretend that theirs is the last word in an ever-changing theater of the history of interpretation. But they *are* interested in the divine component, in the Word of God for their time, and in the dialectic movement from the text as they have interpreted it to the Christian life. Thus, they often build the interpretation into their wider understanding of the message communicated by the scriptural norm. Harnack saw Matthew 16:18 as unrelated to the central thrust of Jesus' simple gospel and could therefore speak with conviction of the "later" origin of the word in its present form. Schweitzer connected it with the fervent eschatological hope which he saw in Jesus and which for him was the basis of an interim ethics for the church today. He could in this context interpret the future character of the word as related to the immediacy of the inbreaking kingdom. Stauffer challenged the church to take seriously the double origin of its guidance in the earthly life of the Lord and in the authority of the Risen One. He consequently interpreted the word without difficulty in a post-Easter setting. All these interpretations of one passage lead into a more comprehensive context, not only historically but also in their theological intention of proclaiming Word of God for their time. They cannot be read in isolation. But precisely because of this double interest they remain tentative, aware of their incompleteness and open-endedness. They challenge the reader not just to accept them or to contradict but to enter on his own into the dialectic of the interpretive circle in which all interpretations, on whatever presuppositions they rest, are moving as partners in one and the same search.

The one exegesis that was not so tentative and did not seem to be in need of a wider context was that by Theodore Hoyer. It was openly polemical. Since this is a characteristic of other interpretations of Matthew 16:18 in the Lutheran tradition, it may be helpful to look at it once more.

Hoyer does share the methodological presuppositions of which we spoke earlier. The interest in the literal sense, that is, reading the text literally as it is, is even his avowed purpose. He understands this intention as the most efficient weapon in the anti-Roman argument which he develops. He works with the Greek terms, investigates the grammatical structure, and acknowledges the presence of figurative language. The use of parallels from all parts of Scripture is prolific and shows the author's interest in the principle of *scriptura sui ipsius interpres,* and thus in the clarity of Scripture. Historical continuity is also a concern, particularly in terms of the *consensus patrum Lutheranorum* and their patristic arsenal. But with all these interests Hoyer's interpretation does not take advantage of the chance to understand the text better by placing himself in the context of modern exegesis. None of the prior questions about author, authenticity, redaction, and original place are being asked. Hoyer simply disregards them and indicates that he does not take them seriously. In this way he is not talking to the concerns of other exegetes. They are either deliberately kept out or the author wants to keep himself aloof from their company. In either case the tendency is toward an unnecessary sectarianism. If the interest in historical continuity is just with the normative past, that is, the Lutheran fathers and their ancestry, and does not take account of the delicate balance of present-day biblical scholarship, it is in danger of isolation. Hoyer and others like him want to take the divine authorship of the Bible seriously. There is nothing wrong with this intention. But does it imply a method of interpretation that must exclude the questions of scholars who look at the divine authorship in a dialectical relationship with their primary consideration of the human authors? Does the exegete really face an alternative: either to regard Scripture merely as the words of men written at different times and to be interpreted by methods commonly used for any piece of literature, or to regard it as God's own Word so that "one's interpretive technique will reflect this unique factor"? Even if one accepts the alternative and opts for the latter, the questions would remain, *How* can this factor be reflected? Is Hoyer's interpretation a satisfactory example of such a technique when it looks more like an abridged and unsophisticated version of a methodology used elsewhere with texts of human authorship? Can the emphasis on God's Word in Scripture justify a simplistic reduction of the questions to be addressed in modern exegesis?

We said earlier that the principle of one scriptural norm does not mean one method, much less one resulting interpretation. Common belief in the inspired Scriptures and a shared emphasis on the divine author did not prevent dissension and disagreement over scriptural interpretation. Luther came to results in Matthew 16:18 which were quite different from those of his Roman contemporaries, although he shared their presuppositions. In fact, the shared emphasis deepened the rift and intensified the controversy because both sides saw their fight as nothing less than a fight for God's truth and honor. Hoyer's interpretation still reflects this polemical pathos.

The modern shift to the human authors may have helped to liberate exegesis from this kind of pathos. It has made exegetes humbler in approaching their task of leading Christians into the dynamic movement between human and divine elements in Scripture. If one has to be in dialogue with the questions and arguments of so many other attempts at understanding the text, one's own contribution cannot pretend to be the final word either. Scholarly consensus about the *sola scriptura* does not need one method and one result. It is much more tentative, open, and vulnerable when it comes to a particular text. This is its strength in a given historical situation because there always will be more such situations.

What a consensus may look like today with regard to Matthew 16:18 may be seen in a recent, rather unusual book: *Peter in the New Testament.*[9] This volume represents the first ecumenical attempt by Protestant and Roman Catholic scholars to say about this and other Petrine texts in the New Testament what modern scholars from such widely different backgrounds are able to say together. It is astonishing that such a group can talk in common about sensitive exegetical problems at all. Even more amazing is the degree of consensus even in details that is documented here as the result of an intensive dialogue. While the scriptural principle does not *need* one method and one result, it does not exclude such a consensus either. Lutherans should welcome this signal of the potential of modern exegesis for the ecumenical situation today. It is a sign of hope.

NOTES

1. See Karl Holl's essay, still one of the best in the field, "Luthers Bedeutung für den Fortschritt der Auslegungskunst," in his *Gesammelte Aufsätze zur Kirchengeschichte* (Tübingen: J. C. B. Mohr, 1921), vol. 1, pp. 414–50.

2. Robert M. Grant, *A Short History of the Interpretation of the Bible* (New York: Macmillan Company, 1963).

3. See, e.g., Ralph A. Bohlmann, *Principles of Biblical Interpretation in the Lutheran Confessions* (St. Louis: Concordia Publishing House, 1968).

4. The following is based on Luther's comments on the passage collected in E. Mühlhaupt, *Luthers Evangelienauslegung* (Göttingen: Vandenhoeck & Ruprecht, 1963), vol. 2, pp. 522–63.

5. Based on Adolf von Harnack, "Der Spruch über Petrus als den Felsen der Kirche (Mt. 16, 17f.)," *Sitzungsberichte der Berliner Akademie der Wissenschaften* 1 (1918): 637–54.

6. Based on Albert Schweitzer, *Geschichte der Leben-Jesu Forschung*, 2d ed. (Tübingen: J. C. B. Mohr, 1913), pp. 416, 426ff.

7. Ethelbert Stauffer, "Zur Vor- und Frühgeschichte des Primatus Petri," *Zeitschrift für Kirchengeschichte*, 1943/44, pp. 23–25.

8. Theodore Hoyer, "The Papacy," in *The Abiding Word*, ed. T. F. K. Laetsch, Centennial Series 2 (St. Louis: Concordia Publishing House, 1947), pp. 728–39.

9. *Peter in the New Testament: A Collaborative Assessment by Protestant and Roman Catholic Scholars*, ed. Raymond E. Brown, Karl P. Donfried, John Reumann (Minneapolis: Augsburg Publishing House; and New York: Paulist Press, 1973).

PART I

Lectionary
as Hermeneutic

Hermeneutical Tendencies in the
Three-Year Lectionary

ARLAND J. HULTGREN

Associate Professor of New Testament
Luther Theological Seminary
Saint Paul, Minnesota

To discern and describe the hermeneutical tendencies in the three-year lectionary in use among Lutherans in North America is to do redaction-critical work on a recent document.[1] That is to say, our task is to look at what has been produced by persons who not only were concerned about providing the church with a rich fare of Scripture but also made conscious decisions in the formulation of a published document we call the lectionary, which is to be used in the present churchly setting. Our job here is to try to describe their theological motivations as these can be seen in the selection and arrangement of the materials.

Naturally there is a certain amount of guesswork in the procedure. Unless one has been a member of the lectionary committee of the Inter-Lutheran Commission on Worship (ILCW), it is difficult to say what motivations were operating in the selection of texts and the formation of the final product. Tendencies that appear to exist in certain cases, for example, may be due not to hermeneutical considerations at all but to other factors, such as the requirements of the church year (which of course might also be considered a hermeneutical tendency) or traditional associations between texts. Nevertheless, in spite of the fact that some guesswork is inevitable, some help can be found concerning the general principles of selection and arrangement. There is, first, a brief commentary on the Roman Catholic lectionary written in French by Father Gaston Fontaine,[2] who was secretary of the Roman Catholic international lectionary committee (Coetus XI, "De lectionibus in Missa," a committee of eighteen members that was appointed in 1964), and second, there is considerable information given in the introduction to *Contemporary Worship 6* (*CW-6*) itself.[3]

Our discussion falls into three parts. First, we shall make some observations about the hermeneutical tendencies that appear in the three-year lectionary, especially in its Lutheran form. Second, we shall discuss the relationship of certain lectionary tendencies to tendencies in biblical studies today. And third, we shall close with some critical questions.

OBSERVATIONS

A "Synoptic Fundamentalism"

The most striking thing about the three-year lectionary is so obvious that it could miss our consideration: it contains three series, each of which is based essentially on one of the synoptic Gospels. At the base of the whole structure, then, is a "synoptic fundamentalism."

The question should be raised why this is so. Why is the lectionary a three-year lectionary, and why is it based essentially on the synoptic Gospels? It was the intention of the Roman Catholic founders of the lectionary and of its Lutheran revisers that more Scripture be provided for worshipers than a one-year lectionary prescribes.[4] Certainly a three-year lectionary does that, but so would a four-year lectionary devoted in each year primarily to one of the four Gospels, or so would a two-year lectionary which could offer the historical pericopes one year and a second set, sometimes parallel in thought, for the second year; more radically revised, a two-year lectionary could incorporate new readings for both years from all four Gospels.

But the fact remains that we have a three-year lectionary, and the fact is that in each of the successive years (A, B, and C) there is primary use of the synoptic Gospels in their canonical order. The explanation given for a three-year cycle by Fontaine is that the committee considered it to be the most practical. Both two-year and four-year cycles had been considered. A two-year lectionary had been established and published in 1964 by Presbyterians in America.[5] Another was proposed in the mid-1960s in Great Britain, while the Roman Catholic work was being carried on, by the Joint Liturgical Group made up of representatives of the Anglican, Presbyterian, Methodist, Congregational, and Baptist churches, together with the Churches of Christ.[6] This was followed up specifically within the Church of England in 1968 when its Liturgical Commission proposed a two-year lectionary for experimental use in that communion, which was based on the earlier work of the Joint Liturgical Group.[7] The Roman Catholic committee, however, rejected the idea of a two-year lectionary on the ground that it would omit important texts from the Bible, especially from the Old Testament and the Epistles.[8] Likewise, a four-year lectionary was considered, but rejected because it would necessitate either the repetition of a good number of texts, especially from the Gospels and Epistles, or the inclusion of less significant texts.[9] A three-year lectionary was settled upon by the Roman Catholic committee for its practicality in fulfilling the mandate before the committee to provide more texts for worship. Precedents for three-year lectionaries had already been set in the Lutheran churches of Scandinavia since the 1920s and by the Reformed Church in France in 1963, and the Roman Catholic committee took these precedents—and their relative success—into account, as well as the writings of scholars in the liturgical field who had also proposed three-year lectionaries.[10]

But it should be stressed that a three-year lectionary, for all its practical benefits, does not in itself require that each year be devoted primarily to one of the *synoptic* Gospels. Other considerations are at work. One is the fact that lectionaries, at least in the Western churches, have always prescribed synoptic texts for most Sundays of the year—with Johannine texts having a privileged place in the Easter cycle and to some degree in Lent. But even having given tradition its due, there is implicit here a hermeneutical statement that should be brought to light. It is assumed that it is supremely in the synoptic Gospels that the gospel story of the deeds and teachings of Jesus Christ is made known. At least since Clement of Alexandria the Gospel of John has been considered the "spiritual Gospel,"[11] a Gospel that relates not so much the career of Jesus Christ as his significance for faith. And in the West we have traditionally been concerned in our worship and preaching largely with Jesus' deeds and his teachings, perhaps mainly for catechetical reasons, and it has been assumed that the Synoptics give us these for the ordinary believer. With the rise of form criticism and redaction criticism in modern times it has been realized more clearly than formerly that even the three Synoptics have their own tendencies in theology and spirituality. Nevertheless, the "synoptic fundamentalism" is still with us.

Most of us would probably not have it otherwise with the lectionary. But we should remind ourselves that the primary use of the synoptic Gospels which the lectionary provides does not necessarily, from a Lutheran perspective, offer more opportunities for the gospel to be heard. Martin Luther, it will be remembered, discerned that the gospel was proclaimed preeminently in the Gospel of John[12] and said that the Fourth Gospel is "the one, fine, true, and chief gospel."[13] Furthermore, comments are made now and then that there is a bit of synoptic "overexposure" in the three-year system, and that, given the requirements of a three-year span (171 Sundays; there are 57 Sundays per year, not 52, to which texts are assigned, because of the varying lengths of the seasons of Epiphany and Pentecost), some filling in of the gaps must have been done for each year since some texts are particularly difficult for preaching. More material is not necessarily better for preaching. In any case, the "synoptic fundamentalism" of the Western tradition is probably the most decisive factor in aiding and abetting a three-year lectionary, and it brings certain liabilities along with its much more positive benefits.

Salvation History

One of the express aims of the Roman Catholic committee was to assemble texts that set forth the history of salvation.[14] This is an explicit hermeneutical tendency, and it can be seen to be operative in the lectionary itself.

But it must be asked how this is worked out in practice, and a contrast will help us arrive at the answer. The lectionary proposed by the Liturgical Commission of the Church of England sets forth the history of salvation in each of two years in conjunction with a radical revision of the church year. The church year in its revised form begins nine Sundays before Christmas, and there is a controlling lesson—not necessarily or even usually the Gospel—for each Sunday throughout the year. During the nine Sundays before Christmas the controlling lessons are the Old Testament texts, which set forth in sequence the Creation, Fall, Noah, Abraham, and Moses, followed by readings from the prophets up to Christmas. Then from Christmas to Pentecost the Gospel for the Day is the controlling lesson. And during the Sundays after Pentecost the controlling lessons are from Acts and the Epistles.[15]

The Roman Catholic *Ordo* and the ILCW lectionary obviously do not set forth the history of salvation in such a continuous fashion. They do not call for a radical change in the church year. Moreover, the Gospel for the Day is still the controlling lesson for each Sunday, even though it need not be the text for preaching.[16] The Old Testament is read generally in light of its fulfillment in Jesus Christ, so that salvation history is portrayed, but it is set forth in a punctiliar way—with the Gospel letting parts of the Old Testament shine through selectively, rather than in a semicontinuous fashion in analogy to the semicontinuous reading of the Gospels and

Epistles. Salvation history is presented then through display of moments of promise and fulfillment determined by the Gospel for the Day—not a presentation of the epochs of salvation history in sequence.[17] If one insists that the epochs of salvation history are attended to in the sequence of Advent, Christmas, Easter, Pentecost, and so on, of course it has to be granted that this is not incorrect. But it is nevertheless quite different from the structure of the Anglican proposal.

Harmonization

A third hermeneutical tendency in the lectionary is the harmonization of texts between the Old Testament and the New. It is assumed that Scripture interprets Scripture[18] and that such a principle should be made explicit in a lectionary. The point was made by the Roman Catholic committee that it intended to avoid a rigid and artificial "thematization" but that a "harmonization" based on an internal cohesion of texts was considered appropriate.[19] This harmonization is called "cohesion" and "interlocking" of texts in *CW-6*.[20]

This harmonization of texts is the most evident working procedure in the lectionary. Old Testament readings are frequently presented as background for the Gospel readings. They illustrate the legal, cultic, haggadic, or cultural presuppositions of the Gospel, or they show that a particular act or teaching of Jesus has a precedent in Old Testament practices or teachings.[21] From the standpoint of hermeneutics this means that an essential unity of the Scriptures as witness to Christ is frequently affirmed in the lectionary.

At some points there appears to be dissonance (rather than consonance) too. There are instances in which the Gospel relates teachings of Jesus that are critical of certain Old Testament passages. For example, in Year A, Epiphany 7, the First Lesson (Deut. 19:15–21) contains the famous *lex talionis,* and the Gospel (Matt. 5:38–48) has Jesus rejecting that law and calling for nonresistance and perfection. And in Year B, Pentecost 2, the First Lesson (Deut. 5:12–15) sets forth Sabbath law in a very inclusive way, but in the Gospel (Mark 2:23–28) Jesus says that the Sabbath was made for man, not man for the Sabbath, and that the Son of man is lord over the Sabbath.

This dissonance, however, serves to illustrate the background of the Gospel for these days and thereby to disclose facets of Jesus' ministry itself, in which he was critical of applying certain texts to life without discerning the weightier matters of God's will.[22] The lectionary therefore reflects what one finds in the Gospels themselves. The dissonance between certain Gospel readings and the Old Testament in the lectionary shows that Jesus goes beyond what was written for former times to establish the will of God for the new age. Strictly speaking, "harmonization" may be the wrong term to use in these cases of dissonance ("interlocking of texts" is better), but the choice of the Old Testament texts is obvious in a lectionary that seeks to relate the Testaments.

Typological Correlations

A fourth hermeneutical tendency in the lectionary is the occasional use of typological correlations between the First Lesson and the Gospel. Typological thinking is found in the New Testament, and it asserts that there are events in the Old Testament which foreshadow or prefigure events in the career of Jesus or the saving events of the end time. Old Testament events are "types," "prototypes," or illustrations of what is to come, the so-called antitypes.[23] Typological correlations can be seen, for example, in Lent 4 of Year B, on which there is reference in the Gospel (John 3:14–21) to the lifting up of the serpent in the wilderness by Moses (Num. 21:9) as a "type" foreshadowing the crucifixion of the Son of man, and the Old Testament passage (Num. 21:4–9) to which the Gospel refers is the First Lesson of the day. Another example is found in Year C, Pentecost 12, on which the Second Lesson (Heb. 11:1–3, 8–16) refers to Abraham and his descendants who died in faith as aliens on the land and still desiring a better country, which has now been prepared by God (the heavenly "country," 11:16); and the First Lesson is a recitation of God's promise to Abraham (Gen. 15:1–6). Other examples can be found showing typological correlations.[24]

Johannine Criticism

A fifth apparent hermeneutical tendency in the lectionary concerns its use of the Gospel of John. In spite of what was said earlier about the "synoptic fundamentalism" of the lectionary, it has to be emphasized that the Gospel of John is used abundantly. Readings from John appear on fifty-three occasions over the three-year cycle,[25] and forty of these are on Sundays.

What is of interest, however, is the way John is used. Some of the readings are where we might expect them. For example, the traditional reading concerning Jesus and Thomas (20:19–31) is found all three years on the Second Sunday of Easter. Furthermore, the prologue (1:1–18) is read each year on the Second Sunday after Christmas. Aside from these two readings, each read three times, however, most readings fall into two categories. Seven are found in Year B in the season after Pentecost. Thirteen others are readings for Sundays of Easter all three years,[26] "making John the Gospel of the Easter season."[27] Beyond these, the readings from John are scattered over the three years with one generalization as an exception: there is a reading from John on Epiphany 2 of each year.

The use of John in the season after Pentecost of Year B and in the Easter season of all three years reflects critical discernment. Almost without exception those readings assigned in Year B for the season after Pentecost are taken from what has been called—even apart from source theories—the "Book of Signs" of the Gospel of John (chaps. 2–12), in which Jesus conducts his public ministry in sign and word to show himself as the revelation of the Father.[28] The only exception is the last Sunday of the church year, Christ the King, when the reading is from John 18:33–37 (Jesus' witness before Pilate concerning kingship).

For the Sundays of Easter in all three years a different picture emerges. In each year on Easter 4 there is a reading from chapter 10 (A, 10:1–10; B, 10:11–18; C, 10:22–30), so that that particular Sunday now becomes "Good Shepherd Sunday,"[29] which had traditionally been a week earlier.[30] These readings belong to the Book of Signs. But other readings (minus one exception—21:1–14 on Easter 3 of Year C) for the Sundays of Easter for all three years are selected from John between chapters 13 and 20, which Raymond E. Brown has called the "Book of Glory,"[31] in which Jesus shows his glory to believers by his return to the Father, but also in which his meaning for the believer is set forth in discourses and in which the promise of the Spirit is given and he prays for his own. Although these readings are located in the Johannine sequence prior to the events of Good Friday and Easter, their emphasis on Jesus' return to the Father (14:1–12 in A, Easter 5; 17:1–11 in A, Easter 7; and 14:23–29 in C, Easter 6), his glorification (17:1–11 in A, Easter 7; and 13:31–35 in C, Easter 5), and his prayer for the fidelity and unity of his own (Easter 7 of all three years: 17:1–11 for A; 17:11b–19 for B; 17:20–26 for C) makes them particularly appropriate for the Sundays of Easter. Naturally, the fact that John is the Gospel for the Easter season can be attributed partly to tradition.[32] But the perpetuation of this tradition and the location of the various Johannine texts in the lectionary conforms to a critical reading of the Johannine material in terms of contemporary scholarship. This is an instance of a fortuitous convergence of tradition and scholarship.

Canonical Critical Quest for the Doctrinal, Kerygmatic, and Evangelical

Finally, there is a sixth hermeneutical tendency in the lectionary, and it is here above all that canonical criticism—in the sense of discerning that which "preaches Christ and makes him real" (as Luther put it[33])—can be seen to have played a major role.[34] In *CW-6* it is said that the Second Lessons for the various Sundays confront the hearer with the "doctrinal" or "kerygmatic" as well as the ethical.[35] The point is made that former lectionaries often stressed only the latter. It is also said that lessons were chosen for their congruity with the gospel, the good news of God's redemption and reconciliation.[36] In sum, there has been a canonical-critical quest for the doctrinal, kerygmatic, and evangelical.

One result of the historical-critical method in the twentieth century has been that the diversity of theological affirmations within the New Testament has been accented. In the attempt to be descriptive—to find out what the text "meant" rather than what it "means" for today[37]—biblical scholars have exposed the pluralism of the New Testament. Sometimes this unleashing of the heavy artillery has resulted in overkill, but generally it must be granted that the pluralism seen in the New Testament is based on sound descriptive work. Such pluralism was seen in earlier times too, such as in Luther's own well-known evaluation of the various books of the New Testament, but it is much more obvious today.

Certain scholars have stated rather explicitly that canonical criticism cannot be avoided. But if there is a pluralism, the question has to be raised whether there is also some sort of unity to the Bible, or at least a central message of the New Testament. Kurt Aland has tried to champion a canonical catholicity. He has written that while there is a "formal" canon—the complete, officially recognized canon—there is in practice for each Christian confession or theological camp an "effective" canon, which is selective and based on the self-understanding of each confession or theological persuasion, and he calls for all Christians to come to terms again with the whole "formal" canon and thereby achieve unity of faith and church.[38] But Ernst Käsemann has claimed that in fact the canon has never been, and in principle cannot be, the foundation of unity of the church. The sole foundation of the church is not the canon, after all, but the gospel.[39] The canon must be used critically to serve the proclamation of the gospel, and its center is the message of justification of the ungodly.[40] Werner G. Kümmel finds the "heart" of the New Testament at virtually the same place: the divine condescension in which God, in Jesus Christ, comes to us with the offer of salvation, which is seen particularly in Jesus' own acts and in the writings of Paul and John.[41]

The ILCW lectionary, by intention, seeks to present a canonical catholicity,[42] which implies that pluralism is to have its place. Nevertheless, canonical criticism has been employed. There are readings from James,

Hebrews, and Revelation, but the Pauline and Deutero-Pauline letters have much wider and more frequent usage. Of the twenty-one Epistles in the New Testament, the Pauline and Deutero-Pauline make up about 66 percent of the total by verse count; the Catholic Epistles and Hebrews make up the remaining 34 percent. But in lectionary usage for the Second Lesson, 72.5 percent of the readings are from the Pauline and Deutero-Pauline Epistles, 20 percent are from the Catholic Epistles and Hebrews, with readings from Acts and Revelation making up the remaining 7.5 percent. Or, to see the contrast in another way, Hebrews and James together contain about as many verses as Romans.[43] But while these two Epistles are read on twenty Sundays in the lectionary, Romans is read on thirty-one Sundays.

There are probably no surprises here, nor is there anything here with which most would find fault. What is of interest, however, is that while canonical catholicity is aimed at, canonical criticism with a view toward the doctrinal (especially along Pauline lines), the kerygmatic, and the evangelical is a centripetal force of remarkable magnitude. On only one Sunday out of five are the Catholic Epistles and Hebrews read, while on nearly three out of four it is the voice of Paul or his school that is heard.

TENDENCIES IN THE LECTIONARY AND TENDENCIES IN BIBLICAL STUDIES TODAY

We have already indicated some ways in which tendencies observed in the lectionary correspond with certain tendencies in biblical studies and theology today (e.g., Johannine criticism and canonical criticism). But there are broader and more difficult questions to deal with. The lectionary demands that the preacher reexamine his own hermeneutical tendencies and sharpen his consciousness of what he does and can do with the texts assigned. So we shall ask here whether there are current tendencies in biblical studies that can be of help in dealing with tendencies in the lectionary. By the nature of the case this section will be partly prescriptive, not merely descriptive. There are three intersections to explore.

Lectionary Tendencies and the Unity and Diversity of the Bible

The first area of concern has to do with the unity and diversity of the Bible. In the present system of theological education, in which there is usually a rather clearly defined division of labor between Old Testament and New Testament studies and in which the atomizing effects of the

153

historical-critical approach accent the diverse and pluralistic, there is sufficient cause to wonder whether the seminary graduate is equipped to handle the question of the unity of the Bible in a critical and responsible way. He has been cautioned sufficiently that he should not read Second Isaiah as a handbook of prophecies concerning the historical Jesus and that he should not interpret Matthew through a theological grid fashioned out of a study of Paul.

The sheer number of texts assigned for a three-year period can exacerbate the difficulties. The polyphony of the biblical witnesses is there, and we might well be concerned lest it become a cacophony.

The theological unity of the Bible has become problematic, and one can say that there is no biblical theology today.[44] The older view that Protestant dogmatics is simply a summary of biblical teaching, at least by intention, is seen today to be obsolete. When exegesis was enclosed within frontiers fixed by systematic theology, that view had some currency. But today exegesis knows no frontiers, not even those of a methodological sort. Naturally the study of the biblical text goes on largely within a field of common concerns, but the boundaries are not fixed, as is shown in current trends in interdisciplinary studies, structural analysis, trajectory criticism, and the increasing attention to the intertestamental and paratestamental literatures.

Nevertheless the question of unity must be faced at least in theological reflection that seeks to serve the church and its proclamation.[45] In this quest there are two approaches that cannot finally work in light of present-day exegesis and reflection on the nature and function of the biblical writings. First, it is inappropriate to claim that the unity consists in an unfolding of a higher and higher spiritual capacity from the more limited to the more sublime.[46] Second, it is inappropriate to impose systematic conceptions upon all parts of the Bible, whether these be from traditional, but nevertheless postbiblical, systematic theology, or whether they happen to be concepts that have been coined abstractly out of apologetic motivations, such as covenant, redemptive history, law and gospel, prophecy and fulfillment, or even promise and fulfillment.[47] All such approaches fail to take seriously the function of the actually existing biblical books within their historical settings, and they prevent us from hearing what the various authors were trying to say in their own times and places.

Any attempt to discern the unity of the Bible in terms of its historical continuity, on the one hand, and its canonical breadth, on the other, must begin by acknowledging that the Bible contains a history of proclamation of the divine activity, always addressed to contemporaries of the proclaimers, and that its writers set forth also divinely given promises for the future which God will bring about. No single catch phrase can adequately describe what is there. But what one observes essentially is that again and again in the Bible there is a kerygmatic re-presentation of the acts of God for the sake of the present—and often a kerygmatic presentation of his promises for the future. The category of "promise and fulfillment," which has gained some favor recently,[48] does not deal with the material sufficiently, nor finally does the somewhat related view of Gerhard von Rad, who writes that the "Old Testament leads forward to the New."[49] According to von Rad, the Old Testament is a book of ever-increasing anticipations[50] and "Israel's history with God thrusts violently into the future."[51] And of course von Rad affirms that such anticipations in the Old Testament are fulfilled in Jesus as the Christ.[52] But such an approach bears the burden of demonstrating that the Old Testament writers themselves, as they composed their narratives, psalms, and prophetic oracles, saw their works as functioning in that way. As one examines the documents themselves, one finds that they function primarily to re-present the acts of God of the past for the present community so that the latter sees that all has been accomplished for its own day. To mark the contrast sharply, von Rad writes that in light of Israel's rising expectations God's debt to Israel was constantly being increased.[53] But that can hardly be left unchallenged. On the contrary, what one sees is that in the passage of time Israel's debt to God is constantly being increased, and that is what the writers of both Testaments want their contemporaries to see.

Some illustrations are necessary to clear things up. At the level of writing, the Yahwist of Solomon's time re-presents the acts of God of the past to show his contemporaries their indebtedness to the Lord, who has given Israel its land and national existence, and to proclaim at that moment implicitly that Israel has a future as well. The Yahwist, to be sure, asserts that the present circumstances are rooted in the promise of land and posterity given to Abraham (Gen. 12:1–3), so the promise and fulfillment schema is not lacking. But the question has to be raised concerning the function of this technique. It functions at the level of the Yahwist as kerygma "to secure the irrevocable validity of the gift bestowed by God."[54] The past is re-presented in the present so that the Yahwist's contemporaries see themselves as heirs and therefore indebted to the Lord, and it is on the basis of that understanding that the future is essentially bright,[55] since the Lord who has brought all these things about is ever faithful. But the process of kerygmatic re-presentation and promise does not end there. Sometime later, presumably in the eighth or seventh century, the

Deuteronomist re-presents the past kerygmatically to his own contemporaries. The land, the law, and peoplehood are again to be seen as God's gifts, gifts that can slip out of Israel's hands if she should forget and assume that all these things are due to her own success (8:11–20). The Deuteronomist insists that Israel is an elect people, but not because of its numerical strength or any such human standards of accomplishment (7:7–8; 9:4–5). Moreover, the present day is a time to realize that all that has been done in the past is for the present generation: "Not with our fathers did the Lord make this covenant, but with us, who are all of us here alive this day" (5:3); "the Lord has declared this day concerning you that you are a people for his own possession, as he has promised you, and that you are to keep all his commandments" (26:18). Yes, Israel is indebted to God. Israel comes once more under the sovereignty of the Lord in order to be claimed by him as his people—a "holy people" (7:6; 14:2, 21; 26:19; 28:9).[56] And the Deuteronomist envisions a day in the future on which this covenant people will be at rest (12:9; 25:19) on the land. Still later the Priestly writer re-presents the promise to the patriarchs in his own day, but he expands it to include not only land and posterity, already in the Yahwist's work, but also the declaration that God wills to be the God of Abraham and his posterity for ever (Gen. 17:6–8),[57] a promise which becomes even more significant in the time and place of the Priestly writer—and still more among generations to come that experience upheaval, dislocation, and a highly tenuous connection with the land, living as so many do in the Diaspora. The re-presentation of the past equips the covenant people to understand themselves even in the Diaspora no less than their ancestors on the land as debtors to the divine activity, and they can also expect a future with Yahweh as well, for he is ever faithful.

To take another illustration, the monarchy comes into being, and it is celebrated in the Royal Psalms (2, 18, 20, 21, 45, 72, 89, 110, and 132) in particular as a divinely given institution. Naturally, one finds in them references to the promise to David (18:15; 45:6; 89:3–4, 19–20, 29, 36–37; 132:10–11), but even these re-presentations of promise function to affirm that the present anointed one now has significance in the historical and even cosmic purposes of Yahweh.[58] Moreover, it is Yahweh, not the historical king himself, who occupies the decisive position as king;[59] the present king is his agent. It is certainly the case that these psalms were preserved in the exilic and postexilic communities, and that their superlatives concerning kingship both kindled and served messianic hopes.[60] But this does not mean that God's debt to Israel, which was paid off centuries later in the New Testament era, was being increased. These psalms were preserved in their old form and were presumably sung in worship to re-present the acts of God so that the contemporary generation could see that its own existence as a community, still intact and moving back to Zion and into the second temple, is dependent upon the Lord who has brought Israel into being and who is the true King of the universe and Lord of history, which these old psalms proclaim. Lest we press too hard the importance of the Davidic ideology as leaning toward the New Testament, we should recall that something even more important historically was going on in the exilic and postexilic periods even while these psalms were being preserved and sung. Judaism was coming into existence. The old religio-political state located in Palestine was in shambles; now a Torah-centric community preparing to live in the Diaspora emerged. It is now Moses, not David, who comes to the fore,[61] and the Torah becomes the formative constitution for the community and also the inspiration and basis of instruction for the individual Jew wherever he might live, who has to assume personal responsibility and carry the "Torah story" in his head.[62]

In the New Testament we see this history of kerygmatic re-presentation and kerygmatic promise continued. To be sure, one finds in the New Testament writings an amazing number of instances in which the prophecy and fulfillment schema is employed,[63] so that countless moments and events in Jesus' career are seen to be instances of fulfillment, as, for example, his triumphal entry (Matt. 21:1–11 as fulfillment of Zech. 9:9) or even such an incidental item as the casting of lots for his garments at the foot of the cross (John 19:23–24 as fulfillment of Ps. 22:18). But what one also encounters in the New Testament are instances in which the saving work in Christ is seen to have taken place according to the will and plan of God as a whole, who has done yet a new thing. Scripture is referred to in a general sense, and it is thought that the new saving event calls to mind the words and deeds of God in the past, recorded in the Scriptures, as anticipations of the end of the story, which has now taken place. This way of thinking appears to pre-date the typical proofs from Scripture that one finds in the prophecy/fulfillment schema.[64] According to the pre-Pauline formula (1 Cor. 15:3–4), Christ died for our sins "according to the Scriptures" and was raised on the third day "according to the Scriptures," but no specific texts are given. Elsewhere too in the New Testament there are references to the Scriptures in general in connection with Jesus' passion (Matt. 26:54, 56; Mark 14:49; Luke 18:31; Acts 3:18; 13:29), resurrection (John 2:22; 20:9), or saving significance and destiny

(Luke 24:27, 32, 44–47; John 5:39; 17:12; Acts 10:43; 17:2–3, 11; 18:24, 28; 26:22–23; Rom. 1:2–3; 16:26; Gal. 3:8). But again specific passages of Scripture are not called forth as witnesses; rather, Scripture is seen as a unity.[65] In such instances Isaiah 53 may well be presupposed in terms of the passion, and certain psalms (e.g., 16:8–11; 110:1; 118:16) in terms of the resurrection.[66] But the New Testament writers in these instances take for granted that the Scriptures in their entirety speak to the present no less than to the past, because the present is the moment of their denouement in Christ. So Paul can write that what was written formerly was written "for our instruction, upon whom the end of the ages has come" (1 Cor. 10:11; see 9:10; Rom. 15:4). The divinely inspired writings as a whole, even apart from particular proof-texts, speak to the present generation in light of Christ. It is Christ risen who opens the Scriptures, as Luke has it (24:32; see 24:27). Through the cross and resurrection of Jesus, God has done yet another saving act, and now one sees the law, the prophets, and the psalms in a new way.[67] The story, the oracles, and the songs of Israel must be re-presented and then reinterpreted in the church in light of what has happened, and they must be supplemented by a recitation of what God has done most recently in Christ, which itself conforms to the scriptural witness of the past for those who see it. The Christian is to understand himself, like those before him in ancient Israel, as one who is indebted to the inheritance of divine activity. And the kerygma also contains promise, of course. Those who have been reconciled to God in Christ and who are Christ's own shall also belong to Christ at his coming again and in the world to come.

All this has hermeneutical implications for today. The interpreter of Scripture, insofar as he is informed by contemporary exegesis and historical scholarship in general, should recognize that the unity of the Testaments is a theological affirmation made this side of the cross and resurrection. Even Luther began to think along these lines in his distinction within the "double perspicuity" of Scripture: on the one hand, a study of words and grammar must be carried on, but much may remain unclear concerning such externals—a stance which anticipates our own descriptive aims and results today; on the other hand, there is an internal clarity made known in Christ that is perceived by faith.[68] In our own times we must go even further. It cannot be demonstrated to the impartial observer that the Old Testament funnels directly into the New any more than it funnels into the Talmud.[69] Any alternative is to descandalize, deoffensify, and empty the cross of its power. The New Testament writers themselves do not see the Old Testament flowing directly into their own times, except through a new divine activity which is foolishness and a scandal to the unbelieving but which reveals the meaning of all past activities, oracles, and songs for those who believe. Both Testaments have similarities in that their various writings call forth the acts of God in prior times for the present generation. In so doing they try to communicate that the present generation is in God's debt. Precisely when the old traditions are re-presented, the believer in the temple, synagogue, and church is to see himself as standing under grace and to see that his life is to manifest the consequences of that grace: a walking by the Torah, as the Jew would put it; or a walking by the Spirit, as Paul has put it (Gal. 5:25).

The unity of the Old Testament and Christian proclamation written into the New must be seen today, then, in a way no different from what it was formerly, even back in the first century before the writing of the New Testament documents themselves. It is an assent of faith that Israel's traditions, re-presented and reinterpreted in Israel itself, must once again be re-presented and reinterpreted in light of the new situation brought about by God's activity in Christ. One cannot see the unity in static or dogmatic terms, nor by means of an apologetic which asserts that the Old Testament writers, redactors, or "canonizers" (if we can call them that) of the Torah and prophets lived in ever-increasing expectations of God, who is thereby obligated to pay off his debt with Jesus of Nazareth as the Christ. One can see the unity only in terms of historical dynamics in which God is himself the dynamo and his people those who try to keep up with him. But one cannot demonstrate that the Christian has followed God's tracks through the Old Testament correctly while the Jew has been sidetracked or become lost in the wilderness. The unity of the Testaments is an affirmation of faith, not science, by those who have been apprehended by God in Christ for his own saving purposes.

What has been said here does not deal with all the problems. Besides the problem of continuity there is also the problem of canonical breadth. The biblical writers of both Testaments are a pluralistic lot, and some of the writings lie further to the periphery of the canonical collections of synagogue and church than do others, and no amount of fanciful exegesis can cause one to believe otherwise. That means, then, that the interpreter will have to enter into the precarious arena of canonical criticism. As a Christian, he will ask the question of how a particular text before him functions in its original setting to proclaim God's saving activities and promises. That will often be more of a problem with Old Testament texts, but it may also be a problem with some in the New. Finally he will have to ask how the text before him can be re-presented today in light of the canonical core, God in Christ for the lost, and in light of the present moment, so that the word of the biblical narrator, prophet, sage, evangelist, or letter writer becomes address today. Such a stance takes seriously the axiom that the biblical documents are themselves located at particular moments in the history of proclamation, and its corollary that one's own proclamation is a moment in that same history.[70] Of course one's own proclamation must be faithful to that which has gone before, and it will be more or less so to the degree that it stands in continuity with the canonical core, the story of God's dealing with the world—particularly his reconciling work in the mission of Jesus to the lost and, above all, in Jesus' death and resurrection as saving event to justify the unrighteous.

This lengthy discussion must now be tied in with the question of hermeneutical tendencies in the lectionary. In actual use of so many texts over a three-year period, the interpreter will find all kinds of configurations. Sometimes there will be harmonization, sometimes dissonance, sometimes prophecy and fulfillment, sometimes typological correlations, and sometimes no obvious connections at all. The interpreter is advised to see that each text before him stands at a moment of proclamation. He should realize that the old texts are not addressed primarily to himself or to his congregation, or primarily to one and the same setting within antiquity. Speaking candidly, one must say that the connections between the Old Testament lessons and the Gospel pericopes run not from the past forward but from the first Christian century back. A case could therefore be made that in liturgical reading the Gospel should precede the Old Testament lesson. But no one would really want that, and the interpreter is on safe ground anyway if he realizes that the Gospel is the chief lesson of the day and that it takes up into itself that which was written in former times. Even there, however, we have proclamation addressed to first-century congregations, not to ourselves. The question has to be raised, How is that which these writers said to their readers able to become an address to our own times? Canonical and theological reflection enter the picture here, as must prayer, invocation of the Spirit, and meditation, so that one's own moment of proclamation takes up into itself all that was written in former times and transforms it into what we dare to call God's Word for our own time.[71]

Lectionary Tendencies and Redaction Criticism

There is a second area in which the lectionary and today's tendencies in biblical studies intersect. That is the intersection between the semicontinuous reading of a given Gospel for a year and redaction criticism, the attempt to describe a particular evangelist's perspectives on the story of Jesus Christ through study of his editorial techniques and emphases.[72]

A one-year lectionary does not require as much of the preacher as does a three-year lectionary. Earlier a preacher might have done redaction criticism to one extent or another, but now he is in the position where he actually has to, if he is going to do expository preaching. He lives with a particular Gospel for most of a year and he will want to know something about that Gospel's setting, and particularly about its themes, its fundamental teachings, and its emphases on aspects of Jesus' ministry.

A great benefit of this intersection is that it can revitalize the use of Scripture and cause a reassessment of its nature and function at the parish level. It is generally fair to say that most people still see the Gospels as stenographic accounts of the ministry of the historical Jesus, and that many accept theories of the origins of the Gospels which are not compatible with external and internal evidence. The three-year lectionary offers the opportunity for both the pastor and lay persons to study the Gospels intensively, and aids are being produced by various publishers both for the pastor[73] and for lay study groups.[74] Inevitably differences in the Gospel portraits of Jesus and his ministry will be brought to consciousness as never before. The possibility is there for persons, clergy and lay, to come to terms with the kerygmatic and didactic nature of the Gospels and to see that the focus of the Christian faith is upon Jesus Christ, crucified and risen, not on the Bible itself.

On the other hand, redaction criticism brings with it certain liabilities too. Handled in one way it can lead people into thinking that the four evangelists stand as roadblocks between us and Jesus Christ, or that the Gospels are merely humanistic portraits of the life of Christ, no less authoritative than modern historical novels about him. But having allowed for these liabilities, it is nevertheless the case that the evangelists are interpreters of the Jesus story, and the pastor or study leader should realize two points. First, while the evangelists do indeed interpret the Jesus story, they do not thereby falsify it.[75] There is a commonality to the portraits of how Jesus dealt with the outcasts of society, for example, and in his conduct and attitudes toward religious traditions, his essential ethical teachings, and in the story of his passion, death, and resurrection. Second, it should be stressed that although the evangelists are theologians working in historical-ecclesiastical settings, they are not humanists but collectors and arrangers of traditions who seek to witness to a divine activity upon earth in the ministry, death, and resurrection of Jesus of Nazareth. Because the Christian faith claims that it is founded upon such activities in history, it treasures and keeps going back ever and again to the old documents that witness to it. They are not the only or even necessarily the oldest documents that provide such witness, but they have been selected through a process of critical discernment in the ancient church as to what would constitute the standard over against possible distortions.[76]

Lectionary Tendencies and Tendencies in Hermeneutical Reflection

The third place in which lectionary tendencies and tendencies in biblical studies intersect is in the area of reflection upon the hermeneutical task itself.[77] The lectionary faces us with a vast amount of biblical material, selected with canonical catholicity as a centrifugal force but canonical criticism as a centripetal one. Likewise, in biblical studies and systematic theology there are forces pulling outward and inward on the question of hermeneutics.

Dialectical and existentialist theology have tended toward a hermeneutical reductionism, and its effects are still with us. The work of Rudolf Bultmann is taken easily as representative (or at least more thoroughgoing) of this tendency toward reductionism, in which biblical language and imagery are seen to be expressions of self-understanding and in which the hermeneutical task is taken to be existential. The proper question is, "How is man's existence understood in the Bible?" and thereby one can gain an understanding of the possibilities for one's own life.[78] It is assumed that the message of the New Testament is descriptive of a reality which is both meaningful and essential to man, including modern man. Existentialist hermeneutics is still with us and is seen particularly in the writings of various scholars who use the term *early catholicism* in a pejorative, not simply descriptive, sense and who go on to evaluate the books of the New Testament according to the degree that they lend themselves to an existentialist interpretation: Paul and John rate high; Luke-Acts and the Catholic Epistles rate lower.[79] This evaluation coincides with that of Luther, of course, but the center of gravity has nevertheless been shifted. For Luther the question was the degree to which a book preaches Christ and makes him real; for existentialist theology the question is the degree to which a book causes the reader to reflect on his own existence.

The so-called new hermeneutic came and went in the 1960s,[80] but it was very esoteric, using language and models of tortuous complexity,[81] and it hardly made any lasting effects on exegesis, theology, or preaching.

Alongside the existentialist and new hermeneutical programs have been heard the voices of those who call for breadth and careful listening to the biblical texts in all their difficulty and diversity. Here we shall simply itemize some of the concerns expressed by various persons without trying to develop a consensus or common statement. Krister Stendahl has written that the first task in biblical interpretation is the descriptive one, in which the various books are seen in all their complexity and diversity and in which one then moves on to the question of their meaning for today—not by an existential or nonhistorical reductionism but by conceiving human existence both then and now as a part of sacred history in which the acts of God both then and now are continually proclaimed and celebrated[82]—we would add—both then and now. Oscar Cullmann has taken to task existentialist hermeneutics most systematically. He writes that the paradox of New Testament faith is that "I gain my self-understanding when I am not observing my self-understanding."[83] Faith is turning away from self to beholding the events of salvation history and, seeing that this history includes myself, becoming aligned with it. The hermeneutical task involves the expression in modern language of the ideas expressed in the text,[84] and the interpreter, like the biblical writers themselves, is obliged constantly to reinterpret for the everchanging present that which has been written.[85] Wolfhart Pannenberg, drawing on the insights of Hans-Georg Gadamer, writes that the interpreter of the Bible must expand his intellectual horizon to the extent that it encompasses those in the text to be interpreted.[86] This involves establishing the differences between ourselves and the biblical texts and then annulling them, as the interpreter takes up questions of his own time in relation to what the biblical writers have attested in their own language and concepts. And finally, James M. Robinson has written that the anthropological hermeneutic, pioneered by Bultmann, will have to give way to one which takes on ever-broader concerns of human life, presenting alternatives for modern man in his social and political life, and which he can either reject angrily or accept happily.[87] In so many words, Robinson appears to be accusing the anthropological or existentialist approach of being too apologetic. The Christian message does not merely illuminate personal existence and offer authenticity; it challenges both personal existence and social reality in order to reshape them.

The breadth or canonical catholicity of the lectionary requires a hermeneutical stance that is open to the various accents of the Bible. Naturally, every interpreter comes to the biblical texts with certain presuppositions. But there is enough being said in contemporary reflection on hermeneutics that calls upon the interpreter to try his best to span the distance of time and culture between himself and the texts so that he becomes truly "bilingual," that is, familiar with the modes and patterns of biblical thought and those of today.[88] This does not mean that he will give an uncritical repetition of all that is there. Canonical and theological criticism will be employed. But that is after the job of hearing has been done and after the interpreter has realized that not only does the text before him by Amos, Paul, or Luke attest to a moment of witness, but so does he. His own reflection and proclamation, like those of the biblical writers themselves, are tethered to the history of God's saving acts to which the whole Bible gives primary witness.

CRITICAL QUESTIONS

Certain problems have been referred to all along in the discussion to this point. But there are two related to the stated purposes of the Roman Catholic and Lutheran committees that should be addressed. These are raised not as criticisms but as points for further discussion.

The Use of the Old Testament

First there is the question of how the Old Testament is used. A stated purpose in the formation of the lectionary, as spelled out by the Roman Catholic committee, was that it give witness to the continuity of salvation history.[89] This implies a priori that there will be readings from the Old Testament which declare the marvelous acts of God through the patriarchs, Moses and the Exodus, the wandering, the settlement of Palestine, the rise of the monarchy, the exile, the restoration, and so on. Moreover, we would expect that Old Testament readings would frequently consist of Haggadah (the edifying narratives of the Old Testament). In fact, however, Haggadah is not prominent. In the ILCW lectionary the Sunday readings from the narrative books of the Old Testament make up slightly more than 32 percent of the whole and only 23 percent in Year A,[90] and not all these readings consist of Haggadah; many would have to be classified as essentially halakic (giving legal prescriptions). Moreover, readings from the prophets amount to 48 percent of all the readings over three years.[91] Does this not mean, then, that the common assumptions of churchgoers get reinforced, that is, that the Old Testament has two basic features: first, that it contains essentially law, which certainly it does not;[92] and, second, that when it is not prescribing laws it is predicting the coming of Christ, which usually it is not? The reason for this state of affairs is that the Old Testament lessons have been harmonized with the Gospel for the Day. Perhaps this is as it should be. But we should also be aware, then, that a presentation in lectionary readings of the continuity of salvation history is not, and perhaps cannot, be achieved, and that the lectionary may not lead people into a better understanding of the sweep and edificatory nature of the Old Testament. These might be achieved by some semicontinuous reading of the Old Testament, perhaps in certain seasons, each year.[93] But such reading is reserved for the New Testament books.

Canonical Catholicity

Second, an express purpose of the lectionary subcommittee was to achieve "canonical catholicity."[94] But the question should be asked what is meant by "canonical catholicity." Study of the lectionary shows that there are two things it does not mean. It does not mean that all parts of the canon are used, and it does not mean that all forms of Israelite and Christian piety and teaching are given expression.

Perhaps at the expense of exaggeration, canonical catholicity appears to be worked out as follows: for the Gospels, a presentation of major narratives and teachings of Jesus; for the Second Lessons, a fairly broad spectrum of texts having to do with Christian doctrine and praxis; but for the First Lessons any apparent catholicity achieved is due to a harmonization between them and the Gospels, not to a selection of texts on their own merits apart from the New Testament texts. Canonical catholicity, in short, applies to the New Testament but not actually to the Old. Perhaps this is as it should be in a Christian lectionary. But the objection can be raised that there should be more, for example, from the ethical teachings of the prophets (and there is some) in passages which have nothing to do with an apparent harmonization with the Gospels. The lectionary serves to nurture Christians in the Lord's vineyard, but does it equip the church for its prophetic mission in society? Amos, for example, is heard on only three Sundays over the three years; Micah only once on a Sunday, and that is a messianic prediction used during Advent (Year C, Advent 4, 5:2–4). Isaiah is used a great deal, but the fact that its passages so frequently harmonize with the Gospel readings illustrates the point even more.[95]

These questions are not meant to detract from the marvelous achievement that the three-year lectionary represents. An explicit purpose of the Roman Catholic founders was to prepare a liturgical lectionary,[96] and that implies on the other hand that it is not intended to be an abridgment of the Bible. The lectionary goes a long way in prescribing texts that set forth the biblical witness to Jesus Christ as God's Word and revelation. Lutherans who have used the lectionary of the *Service Book and Hymnal* (1958) have been accustomed for years to hearing Old Testament lessons read in worship. We must remind ourselves that the use of the Old Testament in liturgical reading is relatively new in the Roman Catholic and Anglican-Episcopal churches. Nevertheless, it might be said with justification that in future work on the lectionary more help should be solicited from Old Testament scholars who are not beholden to pressures for harmonization, typology, and promise and fulfillment, so that the credos and edifying narratives of Israel, as well as ethical passages from the great prophets, are given a more prominent place. The lectionary cannot be an abridgment of the Bible, but precisely because it is for liturgical use, the recitation of the history of God's people before Christ, set forth in the works of Israel's faith-full historians and prophets, should be read in the faith-full assemblies of today.

NOTES

1. The lectionary is found in *The Church Year: Calendar and Lectionary*, Contemporary Worship 6 (Minneapolis: Augsburg Publishing House; Philadelphia: Board of Publication, LCA; St. Louis: Concordia Publishing House, 1973), pp. 48–119 (hereafter cited as CW-6).
2. Gaston Fontaine, *Commentarium ad Ordinem Lectionum Missae* (Vatican City: Typis Polyglottis Vaticanus, 1969).
3. CW-6, pp. 12–24.
4. Fontaine, *Commentarium*, p. 12; CW-6, p. 14. Impetus for this was initiated in the Constitution on the Sacred Liturgy from Vatican II (1963), which sets forth this goal: "The treasures of the Bible are to be opened up more lavishly." To this end, the Scriptures are to be read "over a set cycle of years." Quoted from *The Documents of Vatican II*, ed. Walter M. Abbott (New York: Association Press, 1966), p. 155.
5. *Services for the Lord's Day and Lectionary for the Church Year* (Philadelphia: Westminster Press, 1964), pp. 38–47. This is referred to by Fontaine, *Commentarium*, p. 12, as having been given attention.
6. *The Calendar and Lectionary: A Reconsideration by the Joint Liturgical Group*, ed. Ronald C. D. Jasper (London: Oxford University Press, 1967), pp. 15–29, 36–49. The work of the group took place between 1963 and 1966.
7. Published a year later in *The Calendar and Lessons for the Church's Year* (London: S.P.C.K., 1969).
8. Fontaine, *Commentarium*, p. 12.
9. Ibid.
10. Ibid., pp. 12–13.
11. "Last of all, aware that the physical facts had been recorded in the gospels, encouraged by his pupils and irresistibly moved by the Spirit, John wrote a spiritual gospel," wrote Clement of Alexandria, as reported by Eusebius *Ecclesiastical History* 6. 14. 7. Quoted from Eusebius, *The History of the Church*

from Christ to Constantine, trans. G. A. Williamson (Minneapolis: Augsburg Publishing House, 1975), pp. 254–55.

12. Martin Luther said: "John's Gospel and St. Paul's epistles, especially that to the Romans, and St. Peter's first epistle are the true kernel and marrow of all the books [of the New Testament]" ("Preface to the New Testament," trans. Charles M. Jacobs and rev. E. Theodore Bachmann, in *Luther's Works,* vol. 35, *Word and Sacrament* I, ed. E. Theodore Bachmann [Philadelphia: Fortress Press, 1960], pp. 361–62).

13. Ibid., p. 362.

14. Fontaine, *Commentarium,* p. 9.

15. Neville Clark, "The Lectionary," in *Calendar and Lectionary,* p. 18 and passim; *Calendar and Lessons,* pp. 8, 9, 11.

16. CW-6, p. 15.

17. Illustrations for the promise and fulfillment schema are as follows. In all three years on the Baptism of Our Lord (Epiphany 1) the First Lesson is Isa. 42:1–7, which speaks of the endowment of the Spirit upon the Lord's Servant. In Year A, Advent 4, the Immanuel sign of Isa. 7:10–14 is read as the First Lesson, to which the Gospel (Matt. 1:18–25) refers in the Matthean "formula quotation" (1:22–23); in the same year, Epiphany 3, a second formula quotation is read (4:14–16 within Matt. 4:12–23), and the First Lesson gives the Old Testament reference (Isa. 9:1–2 in the reading of 9:1–4). (Two other Matthean formula quotations are given in Year A, but the corresponding Old Testament texts are not read as First Lessons; these are the alternate from Advent 1, Matt. 21:5 within 21:1–11, and the Sunday of the Passion, Matt. 27:9–10 within 26:1–27:66.) In Year B, Epiphany 4, the First Lesson consists of the divine promise in Deuteronomy that the Lord will raise up a prophet like Moses who shall utter the Lord's words (Deut. 18:15–20), and the Gospel (Mark 1:21–28) portrays Jesus as the Holy One of God who utters a new teaching with authority. And in Year C, Epiphany 3, the First Lesson sets forth the words of the Lord's Servant in Isa. 61:1–6 that the Spirit of the Lord is upon him, which are repeated by Jesus in his inaugural sermon at Nazareth (Luke 4:14–21). Not all instances of promise and fulfillment correlations appearing in the lectionary are given here.

18. CW-6, p. 17.

19. Fontaine, *Commentarium,* p. 14.

20. CW-6, p. 17.

21. Many examples could be cited to illustrate the interlocking of lessons, but only one is given here for each year. In Year A, Pentecost 23, the commandment to love one's neighbor as oneself, given in Lev. 19:18, is read in the First Lesson (Lev. 19:1–8) and it is reported in the love commandment in the Gospel (Matt. 22:34–40). In Year B, Pentecost 21, the First Lesson is Prov. 3:13–20, in which it is affirmed that wisdom is better than wealth, and the Gospel (Mark 10:17–27) relates the story of the rich young man. And in Year C, Pentecost 19, the preaching of Amos against the rich who neglect the poor (Amos 6:1–7) coheres with the Gospel's story of the rich man and Lazarus (Luke 16:19–31).

22. For a collection of such passages, see Henry M. Shires, *Finding the Old Testament in the New* (Philadelphia: Westminster Press, 1974), pp. 90–95.

23. For a discussion of typology, see ibid., pp. 49–51. A more extensive study is found in Gerhard von Rad, "Typological Interpretation of the Old Testament," in *Essays on Old Testament Hermeneutics,* ed. Claus Westermann, English trans. ed. James Luther Mays (Richmond: John Knox Press, 1963),

pp. 17–39; and in his *Old Testament Theology*, trans. D. M. G. Stalker, 2 vols. (New York: Harper & Row, 1962–65), 2:319–429 (esp. pp. 329–35, 364–71).

24. Other examples of typological correlations between the First Lesson and the Gospel: Year A, Pentecost 14 (Exod. 6:2–8, Yahweh's name; Matt. 16:13–20, Peter's confession); Year B, Epiphany 6 (2 Kings 5:1–14, the healing of Naaman; Mark 1:40–45, the healing of a leper), Lent 1 (Gen. 22:1–14, the testing of Abraham; Mark 1:12–15, the temptation), and Pentecost 11 (Exod. 16:2–15, the manna; John 6:24–35, bread-of-life discourse); Year C, Pentecost 3 (1 Kings 17:17–24, Elijah's raising a widow's dead son; Luke 7:11–17, Jesus' raising the widow's son at Nain). Other typological correlations between the First Lesson and the Second: Year A, Lent 1 (Gen. 2:7–9, 15–17; 3:1–7, creation of Adam and Eve, the Fall; Rom. 5:12–19, Christ the new Adam), and Lent 2 (Gen. 12:1–8, call and promise to Abraham; Rom. 4:1–5, 13–17, Abraham's faith accepted as righteousness). Certain other typological correlations in the Bible do not appear in the lectionary; for example, Exod. 34:28 and the temptation (Mark 1:13 par.); the wandering in the wilderness and 1 Cor. 10:1–5; and Exod. 34:29–34 and 2 Cor. 3:12–18.

25. CW-6, p. 21, note.

26. If John 20:19–31 (Easter 2, Years A, B, and C) is counted for all three years, the total is sixteen.

27. CW-6, p. 20, n. 1.

28. The term *Book of Signs*—used without prejudice for or against source theories—is used by certain scholars, such as C. H. Dodd, *The Interpretation of the Fourth Gospel* (Cambridge: Cambridge University Press, 1963), p. 289 and passim; Raymond E. Brown, *The Gospel according to John, I-XII* Anchor Bible 29 (Garden City, N.Y.: Doubleday & Company, 1966), 1: cxxxviii; and D. George Vanderlip, *Christianity according to John* (Philadelphia: Westminster Press, 1975), pp. 31, 178. For a survey of recent discussions on whether John 2–12 is not only a Book of Signs (as a subsection of the Gospel) but also based on a "signs source," see James M. Robinson, "The Johannine Trajectory," in *Trajectories through Early Christianity* by James M. Robinson and Helmut Koester (Philadelphia: Fortress Press, 1971), pp. 235–38; and Robert Kysar, *The Fourth Evangelist and His Gospel* (Minneapolis: Augsburg Publishing House, 1975), pp. 10–37.

29. CW-6, p. 85.

30. I.e., the Second Sunday after Easter (also known as "Misericordia Domini"). See the *Service Book and Hymnal* (Philadelphia: Board of Publication, LCA et al., 1958), pp. 90–91.

31. Brown, *John*, 1:cxxxviii; also idem, *The Gospel according to John, XIII-XXI* Anchor Bible 29A (Garden City, N.Y.: Doubleday & Company, 1970), 2:541–42 and passim. Other terms have been used. Dodd, *Interpretation*, p. 289 and passim, refers to it as the "Book of the Passion."

32. Traditionally passages from John 14–16 have been used for the Easter season. See CW-6, p. 20.

33. *Luther's Works*, 35:396.

34. The term *canonical criticism* is not used here to encompass all that has been set forth in the "call to canonical criticism" by James A. Sanders, *Torah and Canon* (Philadelphia: Fortress Press, 1972), pp. ix–xx, i.e., giving attention to the origins and functions of canon. It is used in the more restricted sense of discerning the canon within the canon. The latter, however, is related to the more general interest insofar as that too must deal with the question, in determining both origins and function of canon, How did this particular book come

to be considered normative in the community in relationship to others which were undisputed (or less disputed)? Therein lies an implicit recognition of a protocanon within the process of canonization itself. The phrase "canon within the canon" implies not an exclusion of certain books but a critical discernment of what corresponds more or less to the underlying message concerning God's saving activities culminating in Christ. See Werner G. Kümmel, *Introduction to the New Testament*, trans. Howard Clark Kee, rev. ed. (Nashville: Abingdon Press, 1975), p. 510.

35. CW-6, p. 22; see also p. 18.

36. Ibid., p. 16.

37. The distinction has been made most notably by Krister Stendahl, "Biblical Theology, Contemporary," in *Interpreter's Dictionary of the Bible*, ed. George A. Buttrick (Nashville: Abingdon Press, 1962), 1:419 and passim, and in Stendahl's essay "Method in the Study of Biblical Theology," in *The Bible in Modern Scholarship*, ed. J. Philip Hyatt (Nashville: Abingdon Press, 1965), pp. 196–209.

38. Kurt Aland, *The Problem of the New Testament Canon* (London: A. R. Mowbray, 1962), pp. 28–33.

39. Ernst Käsemann, "The Canon of the New Testament and the Unity of the Church," in his *Essays on New Testament Themes*, trans. W. J. Montague, Studies in Biblical Theology 41 (Naperville, Ill.: Alec R. Allenson, 1964), pp. 95–107; Käsemann writes that "the New Testament canon does not, as such, constitute the foundation of the unity of the Church. On the contrary, as such . . . it provides the basis for the multiplicity of the confessions" (p. 103). Käsemann takes the same position in his essay "Thoughts on the Present Controversy about Scriptural Interpretation," in his *New Testament Questions of Today*, trans. W. J. Montague (Philadelphia: Fortress Press, 1969), p. 275. Rudolf Bultmann, *Theology of the New Testament*, trans. Kendrick Grobel (New York: Charles Scribner's Sons, 1951–55), 2:142, quotes Käsemann with approval.

40. Käsemann, "Thoughts on the Present Controversy about Scriptural Interpretation," p. 282. Essential agreement with Käsemann has been expressed by the systematic theologian Friedrich Mildenberger, "The Unity, Truth, and Validity of the Bible: Theological Problems in the Doctrine of Holy Scripture," *Interpretation* 29 (1975): 391–405.

41. Werner G. Kümmel, *The Theology of the New Testament*, trans. John E. Steely (Nashville: Abingdon Press, 1973), pp. 322–33; see also his *Introduction to the New Testament*, pp. 509–10.

42. CW-6, p. 17.

43. By verse count Hebrews (303 verses) and James (108 verses) total 411 verses, while Romans totals 433. The ratio is approximately 95 to 100.

44. See Gerhard Ebeling, "The Meaning of 'Biblical Theology,'" in his *Word and Faith*, trans. James W. Leitch (Philadelphia: Fortress Press, 1963), pp. 91–92; Wolfhart Pannenberg, "The Crisis of the Scripture Principle," in his *Basic Questions in Theology*, trans. George H. Kehm (Philadelphia: Fortress Press, 1970–71), 1:1–14; and Mildenberger, "The Unity, Truth, and Validity of the Bible," pp. 394–95.

45. The point is made especially by Mildenberger in "The Unity, Truth, and Validity of the Bible," p. 397.

46. This is essentially the view put forth by H. H. Rowley, *The Unity of the Bible* (Philadelphia: Westminster Press, 1953), pp. 1–29 (esp. p. 8).

47. See von Rad, *Old Testament Theology*, 1:121; 2:410–13; and Brevard S.

Childs, *Biblical Theology in Crisis* (Philadelphia: Westminster Press, 1970), pp. 201–2.

48. Walther Eichrodt, *Theology of the Old Testament*, trans. J. A. Baker (Philadelphia: Westminster Press, 1961), 1:501–11; Walther Zimmerli, "Promise and Fulfillment," in *Essays on Old Testament Hermeneutics*, ed. Westermann, pp. 89–122; Claus Westermann, "The Way of the Promise through the Old Testament," in *The Old Testament and Christian Faith: A Theological Discussion*, ed. Bernhard W. Anderson (New York: Harper & Row, 1963), pp. 200–224; and Claus Westermann, *The Old Testament and Jesus Christ*, trans. Omar Kaste (Minneapolis: Augsburg Publishing House, 1968), pp. 75–80.

49. Von Rad, *Old Testament Theology*, 2:322.

50. Ibid., p. 319.

51. Ibid., p. 332.

52. Ibid., p. 374. He writes: "No special hermeneutic method is necessary to see the whole diversified movement of the Old Testament saving events . . . as pointing to their future fulfillment in Jesus Christ. . . . The coming of Jesus Christ as a historical reality leaves the exegete no choice at all; he must interpret the Old Testament as pointing to Christ." See also pp. 333, 369–71, 382.

53. Ibid., p. 320.

54. Zimmerli, "Promise and Fulfillment," p. 95.

55. Sanders, *Torah and Canon*, pp. 23–24, writes that "the J collection . . . probably began with the account of creation in Genesis 2, emphasized the patriarchal and exodus-wanderings-conquest traditions, and reached its climax in the account of Solomon's accession to the throne in Jerusalem and the building of the First Temple (as recorded in I Kings up to chapter 8)."

56. Gerhard von Rad, "Deuteronomy," in *Interpreter's Dictionary of the Bible*, 1:837.

57. See Martin Noth, "The 'Re-presentation' of the Old Testament in Proclamation," in *Essays on Old Testament Hermeneutics*, ed. Westermann, pp. 82–83.

58. Zimmerli, "Promise and Fulfillment," p. 111.

59. Georg Fohrer, *Introduction to the Old Testament*, trans. David E. Green (Nashville: Abingdon Press, 1968), p. 270.

60. Zimmerli, "Promise and Fulfillment," pp. 111, 113.

61. See Sanders, *Torah and Canon*, pp. 25, 44–53.

62. The point is made especially by James A. Sanders, "Torah and Christ," *Interpretation* 29 (1975): 381, 383.

63. For a survey of such passages, see Shires, *Finding the Old Testament in the New*, pp. 43–49, 66–72, 183; and Foster R. McCurley, *Proclaiming the Promise: Christian Preaching from the Old Testament* (Philadelphia: Fortress Press, 1974), pp. 29–32.

64. See Hans von Campenhausen, *The Formation of the Christian Bible*, trans. J. A. Baker (Philadelphia: Fortress Press, 1972), p. 28.

65. See Gottlob Schrenk, "*Graphō*," in *Theological Dictionary of the New Testament*, ed. Gerhard Kittel, trans. and ed. Geoffrey W. Bromiley (Grand Rapids: Wm. B. Eerdmans, 1964), 1:752; and Hans Conzelmann, *A Commentary on the First Epistle to the Corinthians*, trans. James W. Leitch (Philadelphia: Fortress Press, 1975), p. 255.

66. See Barnabas Lindars, *New Testament Apologetic: The Doctrinal Significance of the Old Testament Quotations* (London: SCM Press, 1961), pp. 32–74. Lindars lists other passages in addition to those given above, but these are the most important.

67. C. F. D. Moule, *The Birth of the New Testament* (New York: Harper & Row, 1962), pp. 69–70, writes that for the early Christians "upon Jesus converged the whole history of Israel in the present" and that it was "the coherent organization of all this into a single inclusive personality that made a completely new thing of Old Testament exegesis." See also Childs, *Biblical Theology in Crisis*, p. 106. A survey of how various New Testament writers made use of the Old Testament is given by D. Moody Smith, Jr., "The Use of Old Testament in the New," in *The Use of the Old Testament in the New and Other Essays: Studies in Honor of William F. Stinespring*, ed. James M. Efird (Durham: Duke University Press, 1972), pp. 3–65. Sanders, "Torah and Christ," pp. 372–90, shows how the apostle Paul reappropriated the "Torah story" in light of Christ.

68. See Willem Jan Kooiman, *Luther and the Bible*, trans. John Schmidt (Philadelphia: Fortress Press, 1961), pp. 220–21, who cites the relevant texts in Luther.

69. Lest this sound too radical (or even heretical), a digression is in order. Our exegesis of the Old Testament must "come of age," and perhaps an illustration from the *New York Times*, 2 June 1976, is appropriate. Traditionally it has been thought that mathematics is the most exact of the sciences; it offers conclusions which are either correct or incorrect. But recently in one branch of mathematics two researchers came to different conclusions. They exchanged their proofs so that each might try to find an error in the work of the other. But neither succeeded. Other examples come to mind. In physics there are two theories concerning light—the wave theory and the particle theory—but neither falsifies the other. And in scientific cosmology (theories of the origins of the universe) there is the "Big Bang" theory and the "Steady State" theory, but neither falsifies the other. Regarding one's estimate of the Old Testament, Christian and Jew see its fulfillment in different ways. Is it not possible to have our exegesis "come of age" and acknowledge that the one position does not necessarily falsify the other? The view of von Rad (see n. 52) that the exegete must interpret the Old Testament as pointing to Christ is therefore not satisfactory. Christian *proclamation* in the church will make such a connection to Christ, but *exegesis* that tries to see what a text meant in its original, historical setting will not.

70. See von Rad, *Old Testament Theology*, 2:384–87; John Reumann, "Methods in Studying the Biblical Text Today," *Concordia Theological Monthly* 40 (1969): 655–81, (esp. pp. 659, 681); and Reginald H. Fuller, "Preparing the Homily," *Worship* 48 (1974): 442–57, (esp. p. 447).

71. Edmund A. Steimle, "Preaching and the Biblical Story of Good and Evil," *Union Seminary Quarterly Review* 31 (1976): 211, writes that biblical preaching today "will keep bringing us back to the Story in light of our stories and the stories of our times," and it will "prod our hopes in the faithfulness of God to his promises as that faithfulness comes to light in the biblical story."

72. A basic handbook on this discipline is by Norman Perrin, *What Is Redaction Criticism?* (Philadelphia: Fortress Press, 1969). An extensive treatment of the convergence between lectionary usage and redaction criticism has been written by John Reumann, "*Redaktionsgeschichte* and Roman *Ordo*: Some Principles and Problems in Lectionary Reform," in *Vita Laudanda: Essays in Memory of Ulrich S. Leupold*, ed. Erich R. W. Schultz (Waterloo, Ont.: Wilfrid Laurier University Press, 1976), pp. 25–58.

73. But these are of unequal quality. Four helps that take exegesis seriously are particularly worthy of mention. Reginald H. Fuller, *Preaching the New*

Lectionary: The Word of God for the Church Today (Collegeville, Minn.: Liturgical Press, 1974), has done exegesis of texts for all three years and has given suggestions for preaching. Gerard S. Sloyan, *Commentary on the New Lectionary* (New York: Paulist Press, 1975), has provided commentary for all three years; he does not suggest homiletical themes explicitly, but he does make a connection between exegesis and broader theological and historical questions. These works by Fuller and Sloyan are based on the Roman Catholic *Ordo*. The most in exegesis and sermon suggestion is given in *Proclamation: Aids for Interpreting the Lessons of the Church Year* (Philadelphia: Fortress Press, 1973ff.), written by several sets of co-authors for each year (eight slim volumes for each year) and based on the ILCW lectionary. Finally, Fortress Press has published a fine series of Proclamation Commentaries, edited by Gerhard Krodel. Those on the Gospels are *Mark* (by Paul J. Achtemeier, 1975), *Luke* (Frederick W. Danker, 1976), *John* (D. Moody Smith, 1976), and *Matthew* (Jack D. Kingsbury, 1977).

74. A Lectionary Bible Studies series is being published for lay study groups jointly by Augsburg Publishing House and Fortress Press. Written by various authors, the volumes are entitled *The Year of Matthew, The Year of Mark*, and *The Year of Luke*.

75. See Nils A. Dahl, "The Problem of the Historical Jesus," in *Kerygma and History*, ed. Carl E. Braaten and Roy A. Harrisville (Nashville: Abingdon Press, 1962), pp. 151–59 (esp. p. 153).

76. For recent discussions concerning the New Testament canon in terms of its historical development (and problems), see David L. Dungan, "The New Testament Canon in Recent Study," and Albert C. Sundberg, Jr., "The Bible Canon and the Christian Doctrine of Inspiration," *Interpretation* 29 (1975): 339–51, 352–71. Von Campenhausen, *Formation of the Christian Bible*, p. 261, writes that the truly "crucial factor" in selecting the New Testament canon (as reflected in the Muratorian Canon) was not authorship but "the usage and judgment of the one true church, spread throughout the world" (see also pp. 331–33).

77. A survey of trends in hermeneutics is given by Edgar Krentz, "A Survey of Trends and Problems in Biblical Interpretation," *Concordia Theological Monthly* 40, no. 5 (1969): 276–93.

78. Rudolf Bultmann, *Jesus Christ and Mythology* (New York: Charles Scribner's Sons, 1958), p. 53. See also his essay "The Problem of Hermeneutics," in his *Essays Philosophical and Theological*, trans. James C. G. Greig (New York: Macmillan Company, 1955), pp. 234–61, (esp. pp. 256–59); and idem, "New Testament and Mythology," in *Kerygma and Myth*, ed. Hans Werner Bartsch, trans. Reginald H. Fuller (London: S.P.C.K., 1957), 1:1–44. For a recent, brief exposition of Bultmann's hermeneutic, see David H. Kelsey, *The Uses of Scripture in Recent Theology* (Philadelphia: Fortress Press, 1975), pp. 74–83.

79. This tendency is seen, e.g., in Ernst Käsemann, "New Testament Questions of Today," in *New Testament Questions of Today*, pp. 21–22, 236–37, n. 1. Critical response to Käsemann and others has been expressed by Ulrich Wilckens, "Interpreting Luke-Acts in a Period of Existentialist Theology," in *Studies in Luke-Acts*, ed. Leander E. Keck and J. Louis Martyn (Nashville: Abingdon Press, 1966), pp. 60–83; and Werner G. Kümmel, "Current Theological Accusations against Luke," *Andover Newton Quarterly* 16 (1975): pp. 131–45.

80. Major essays on this project are gathered in *The New Hermeneutic*, ed. James M. Robinson and John B. Cobb, Jr. (New York: Harper & Row, 1964).

81. Among the critical assessments are Amos N. Wilder, "New Testament Hermeneutics Today," in *Current Issues in New Testament Interpretation*, ed. William Klassen and Graydon F. Snyder (New York: Harper & Brothers, 1962), pp. 38–52; James D. Smart, *The Interpretation of Scripture* (Philadelphia: Westminster Press, 1961), pp. 48–49; Carl E. Braaten, "How New Is the New Hermeneutic?" *Theology Today* 22 (1965/66): 218–35; Paul J. Achtemeier, "How Adequate Is the New Hermeneutic?" *Theology Today* 23 (1966/67): 101–19; and Childs, *Biblical Theology in Crisis*, pp. 80, 102.

82. Stendahl, "Biblical Theology, Contemporary," pp. 425–31. See also his essays "Implications of Form-Criticism and Tradition-Criticism for Biblical Interpretation," *Journal of Biblical Literature* 77 (1958): 38; and "Method in the Study of Biblical Theology," pp. 205–9.

83. Oscar Cullman, *Salvation in History*, trans. Sidney G. Sowers (New York: Harper & Row, 1967), p. 321.

84. Oscar Cullman, "The Necessity and Function of Higher Criticism," in his *The Early Church*, trans. S. Godmann (Philadelphia: Westminster Press, 1956), p. 4.

85. Cullmann, *Salvation in History*, pp. 326–27.

86. Pannenberg, "Crisis of the Scripture Principle," pp. 9–11.

87. James M. Robinson, "The Future of New Testament Theology," *Religious Studies Review* 2 (1976): 17–23.

88. So Stendahl, "Biblical Theology, Contemporary," pp. 430–31. See also G. Ernest Wright, *God Who Acts*, Studies in Biblical Theology 8 (London: SCM Press, 1952), p. 108; and Willi Marxsen, *Introduction to the New Testament*, trans. G. Buswell (Philadelphia: Fortress Press, 1968), p. 10.

89. Fontaine, *Commentarium*, p. 12.

90. Included as narrative books in the computation are the Torah, the Former Prophets (Joshua, Judges, 1 and 2 Kings, and 1 and 2 Samuel), and certain writings that are predominantly narratives where used in the lectionary (viz., Ruth and 1 Chronicles—both appointed in Year C).

91. In this computation are included books of the so-called Latter Prophets (Isaiah, Jeremiah, Ezekiel, and the twelve minor prophets).

92. Abraham J. Heschel, *God in Search of Man: A Philosophy of Judaism* (New York: Farrer, Straus, and Cudahy, 1955), pp. 320–35, has insisted that even the Torah (or Pentateuch) is largely Haggadah; only a portion of it is legalistic, and he deplores the "pan-halachistic" way of thinking attributed to Judaism in general and to the Torah in particular. Sanders, *Torah and Canon*, p. 4, writes, "The basic structure of the Pentateuch is not that of a law code but rather that of a narrative."

93. This would be not necessarily by books but by sections of the Old Testament (Torah, Deuteronomic history, and so on).

94. CW-6, p. 17.

95. With the exception of the Psalms, Isaiah is more often cited in the New Testament than any other Old Testament book. See Shires, *Finding the Old Testament in the New*, p. 75.

96. Fontaine, *Commentarium*, p. 31.

PART II

Confessional Propria
as Hermeneutic

The Confessions and Their Influence upon Biblical Interpretation

WARREN A. QUANBECK

Professor of Systematic Theology
Luther Theological Seminary
Saint Paul, Minnesota

The Lutheran Confessions serve a threefold function in the church: (1) *doxology*—they articulate the church's confession of praise and thanksgiving to God for his saving work in Jesus Christ; (2) *hermeneutic*—they serve as standards and guides to the interpretation of the Bible in the church, showing how the Bible has been understood at certain critical times, especially with regard to theological issues in controversy; and (3) *identification*—they serve the self-identification of the church, indicating what things matter most in the life of God's people and offering perspectives on the relationships of other concerns to those things that are seen as most important.

All three of these functions of the Confessions have influenced Lutherans in their interpretation of the Bible and continue to do so today. At various times one or another of these functions receives more emphasis in the life of the church and may even push the others into the background for a time. Thus, for example, all three functions are at work in the Augsburg Confession, but because of the ecclesiastical-political situation of the time, the doxological element is most strongly emphasized. The Reformers become true confessors as they stand before the emperor and the diet contending for the truth of the gospel. This element is also prominent in the Smalcald Articles and in the Small and Large Catechisms.

The hermeneutic element is most prominent in the Apology of the Augsburg Confession as Melanchthon speaks for the Reformers in reply to the Catholic Confutation. He finds it necessary to focus on problems of biblical interpretation and on the history of this interpretation in the life of the church. The element of identification is most prominent in the Formula of Concord. At a time when prospects for reuniting the churches seemed quite dim, Lutheran leaders strove to secure the unity of the churches of the Reformation. They provided language to enable contending groups within the family to speak together on issues that threatened to divide them. They also indicated the range of possibilities permissible within the Reformation understanding of Christian truth, marking sound doctrine off from ancient misunderstandings and heresies as well as from positions taken in their own day by theologians of different religious communities.

The ferocity of the ecclesiastical-theological struggles of the century following the indulgence controversy inevitably led to greater emphasis upon the element of identification. The doxological and to some extent the hermeneutical functions receded in the complex struggles—political, social, and theological—for the continued existence of the Lutheran churches. The same tendency appears in nineteenth-century American Lutheranism, where minority Lutheran groups contended against the dominant Puritan-Anabaptist religious and cultural synthesis. The confessionalism of C. P. Krauth, C. F. W. Walther, and others is more concerned to undergird Lutheran theological self-consciousness by stressing what is distinctively Lutheran than to explore the relationships of Lutherans to other Christians or to the *una sancta*. But even though in these times the element of identification is most prominent, the other elements are seldom absent and sometimes exert unexpected power.

We shall look at the influence of the Confessions upon the interpretation of Scripture, not by examination of commentaries but in the light of the broader, systematic aspects of hermeneutics. To focus solely upon the expositions of the exegetes may cause us to lose sight of some very important concerns of the Reformation and of the Confessions and perhaps also to adopt inadequate perspectives for the evaluation of exegesis.

DOXOLOGY

The doxological thrust of the Confessions has been important to the Lutheran tradition for maintaining a theocentric perspective. As the church sings God's praises for his goodness in creation and his mercy in Christ, it is constantly reminded that salvation is the work of God, that it is offered to humans apart from their deserving, and that it is accomplished in the work of Christ and mediated to sinners in forgiveness. God's justification of the ungodly remains an object of awe to Christians and of offense to the self-confident. It calls attention to the role of the church in God's plan of salvation and to the important functions exercised by the Christian ministry among the people of God. It is a deterrent to confidence in human enterprise, a reminder that Christians have standards and perspectives different from those held by the world, and an exaltation of the cross as the sign of God's strange love and of the Christian's call to conformity with Christ. Against all the tendencies within the church to domesticate the gospel and to manipulate God and his gifts, the Confessions assert the sovereignty of God, the priority of his will and purpose, and the astonishing character of his grace and love.

The doxological sense of the Confessions was especially strong in the earlier period of the Reformation. The Reformers were aware of their danger as they defied the authorities in both church and state to hear testimony to the gospel as they had encountered it in exposition of the Scriptures. They saw their situation as historically critical, perhaps even apocalyptic, and recognized that they might be called upon to seal their witness with their lives. Their leader had been excommunicated and outlawed, and he lived in constant danger but continued to witness to the gospel with courage. The sense of standing for God against human and demonic forces imbued their thinking with great earnestness and dedication. They had committed themselves to the Word and promise of God, to the Scriptures, and to a common confession, and they were not to be diverted by threats or bribes.

This commitment to the gospel and to the Scriptures has informed Lutheran theology and behavior throughout the history of the Lutheran church. It has nurtured the conviction that in Scripture the very Word of God is encountered. The Scriptures cannot therefore be dealt with simply as historical accounts of the development of religion in Israel or of the growth of the early Christian community. Scripture must be seen as the bearer of the divine self-disclosure, as the decisive revelation of God's will for his creatures. This exaltation of the Scriptures as the Word of God has been expressed through the centuries in the high estimation of public worship and of the proclamation of the Word and the celebration of the sacraments. It is seen also in the intense concern for the proper education of pastors, in the attention given to the original languages of Scripture, and in the seriousness with which the Bible has been studied. We take many of these concerns for granted today, and we need to be reminded how much toil and sacrifice our fathers endured in order to secure and defend them.

The sense of the revelatory function of Scripture helped Lutheran exegetes, and preachers, however immersed in linguistic, literary, or historical matters, seldom lost sight of the end served by these details. The exposition of Scripture could never be seen on the same level as the literary study of the classics. It was seen as qualitatively different, for it was concerned with matters essential to human destiny.

At times this sense of the uniqueness of the Scriptures could go out of focus because of polemical or apologetic problems. Lutheran dogmaticians have all known that certainty concerning the authority of Scripture is the work of the Holy Spirit, the *testimonium spiritus sancti internum.* Yet they have often delighted to assemble the evidences of the Bible's unique place in human history, to enumerate its many literary excellences, its historical accuracy and candor, its inner consistency, and so on. In times of intense polemics, or in the face of the results of critical studies, Lutheran theologians have become defensive. Then these incidental or supplementary aspects of the Scriptures have been assigned greater importance as indications of the infallibility and inerrancy of the Scriptures. These tendencies, so often ascribed to a less-than-evangelical quest for certainties, may also be seen as manifestations of the church's sense of the unique role of Scripture in the life of the church and as an attempt to buttress its position against attacks.

The Reformation sense of the instrumental function of Scripture can also be detected as a motif in the rejection or restriction of historical studies. While only the most anxious or irresponsible heirs of the Reformation completely reject the historical study of the Bible, many are moved to question or limit its role because it seems to treat the Scriptures on the same level as any other historical document, and thus they overlook its distinctive role in the mediation of the gospel. There are indeed exegetes and preachers whose exposition of the Scriptures is soteriologically inadequate. If they are read as paradigms of historical-critical method, one can understand why Christians are disturbed.

It is interesting to note that the dogmaticians of the seventeenth century, although underestimating the historical problems in biblical interpretation and giving improper focus to the Scriptures in their prolegomena, nevertheless preserve in the locus on the means of grace a more dialectical, dynamic, and functional understanding of the Scriptures. Their concern to establish the authority of the Bible leads them to misuse the doctrine of inspiration to transcend the historical relativity of the Scriptures. Some of them assert that the very vowel points of the Masoretic text have the guarantee of divine inspiration. Yet even amid such historically indefensible theological curiosities they remember their lessons when they discuss the means of grace. There they recognize that the authority of Scripture cannot be given some decisive external guarantee but that its authority is that of the God who speaks in and through the Scriptures and whose message is differentiated as law and gospel.

I do not suggest that this continuing awareness of the instrumental function of Scripture is solely the contribution of the Confessions. Worship, instruction, pastoral counseling, and many other factors have combined to keep this consciousness alive in the Lutheran church. But the Augsburg Confession and the two Catechisms have been an important part of the life of Lutheran congregations for centuries and have had great influence upon the formation of attitudes toward Scripture.

HERMENEUTIC

The second function of the Confessions is hermeneutical, to provide a guide to the proper interpretation of the Scriptures. The Confessions emphatically assert the primacy of Scripture in the church.

> Holy Scripture remains the only judge, rule, and norm according to which as the only touchstone all doctrines should and must be understood and judged as good or evil, right or wrong.
>
> Other symbols and other writings are not judges like Holy Scripture, but merely witnesses and expositions of the faith, setting forth how at times the Holy Scriptures were understood by contemporaries in the church of God with reference to controverted articles, and how contrary teachings were rejected and condemned.[1]

The Lutheran churches have joyfully accepted this commitment to Scripture. It must be acknowledged, however, that in certain respects the carrying out of this commitment has fallen short of the intentions of the Reformers.

Lutherans have sometimes elevated other writings to the same level as the Scriptures. They have not done so deliberately, but especially in the heat of controversy they have treated the Confessions or the writings of Luther as though they *were* Scripture. They have been known to speak of the verbal inspiration of the Confessions and to insist that the interpretation of Scripture in the Confessions is not only *a* true exposition of the Scriptures but *the* true exposition. They have also at times treated Luther's writings as this kind of exegetical authority, insisting that the Confessions or, lacking treatment of a passage in the Confessions, the writings of Luther, provide the ultimate authority for the interpretation of a biblical passage. This kind of hyper-Lutheranism should be recognized as a well-meant aberration, one which brings back into the church the very kind of magisterial authority that the Reformers rejected.

Lutherans have sometimes behaved as though the exegesis and theology of the Confessions or of the Reformers were paradigmatic, a new *theologia perennis*. While the Confessions have indeed a certain confessionally qualified paradigmatic function, to assert this function in an unqualified way is in effect to deny that the Holy Spirit has granted any illumination to the church since the sixteenth century. In view of the fact that there have been more studies in the Scriptures in the last four hundred years than in the previous fifteen hundred, it would seem unwise to limit study of the Scriptures to the problematics of the sixteenth century or to the insights of the Reformers. The historical-critical study of the Bible, set in motion by the Renaissance and the Reformation, has made great contributions to the understanding of the biblical message. It has underscored and reinforced the teaching of the Reformers at many points, but it has also added new perspectives and insights and, at some points, even corrected the Reformers' interpretations. For example, the Reformers did not know how to interpret apocalyptic literature, and Luther confesses that his spirit could not feel at home in the Book of Revelation. Modern studies have shown what apocalyptic literature is and how it is to be interpreted, so that while much remains obscure, the message of apocalyptic literature in the Scriptures is clear. New techniques of study, form, tradition, and redaction criticism, for example, have given an ampler understanding of the way the Scriptures have come into being, and it would be foolish to deny ourselves the benefits made available in this way. The realization that the Scriptures present not just one theological interpretation of the work of God in Christ also affords new enrichment to the church. The work of salvation is proclaimed in several complementary presentations—Lukan, Pauline, Johannine, and so on—not in contradiction to each other but not to be reduced to a single pattern.

Perhaps the most serious shortcoming in the Lutheran stewardship of confessional resources has been the failure to work out the systematic consequences of the doctrine of justification. Luther regarded himself as an expositor of Scripture—he held the appointment as professor *in biblia* at Wittenberg—and did not see dogmatics as his main responsibility. His unexpected vocation as Reformer nevertheless gave him occasion to draw out the systematic consequences of his exegetical studies, and he did so in a wide variety of treatises. The renaissance in Luther studies has shown how threadbare is the old apology "But Luther was not a systematic theologian." For all his dedication to the task of biblical exposition, Luther is the systematic theologian of his century, not a systematician in the traditional Scholastic pattern, as Lennart Pinomaa has shown, but in a new way of doing theology—paradoxical, dialectical, existential.[2] He was a ferocious opponent of the Scholasticism of his day, chiefly on the ground that it imposed Aristotelian categories upon Christian thought and thus obscured the biblical message beneath enormous heaps of pagan speculation and moralism.

Luther intended to end the dominance of Aristotle in Christian theology and to expound the biblical message in more appropriate categories. His training in the Occamist tradition with its insistence upon the independence of theological and philosophical truth enabled him to opt for theological truth and leave philosophical truth to philosophers. Accordingly he never worked out a methodology for theology based on the unity of all truth. But as the Heidelberg Theses, the Theses against Scholasticism, and numerous other writings show, Luther intended to reconstruct theology around Jesus Christ, God and man, crucified and risen, as center. In place of Scholasticism, which he characterized as a theology of glory, he proposed a theology of the cross, showing God's paradoxical way of dealing with his creatures. God shows his wisdom in the foolishness of preaching, his power in a man helpless in the hands of his enemies, his strength in weakness. The task of expounding the theology of the cross has occupied the best efforts of many scholars and it is not yet completed.

The shape of this theology can be discerned in Luther's doctrine of God. He rejects the Scholastic method of building upon natural theology and proceeding by way of eminence and negation to a doctrine of God based upon human insight and speculation but purified by the systematic application of reason. He denies the Thomistic assertion that the products of this process are theologically valid as far as they go and lack only the completion provided in the biblical revelation. He takes a quite different line: what we know about God from nature, history, and conscience is a knowledge of the God of wrath and can lead only to despair. The God of grace and love is known only in Jesus Christ. Therefore the Christian clings to Christ and his cross. Here alone he has the assurance of God's love to the fallen human race and most specifically to himself. Luther resists all suggestions to look elsewhere for the knowledge of God. He desires to know nothing other than the God revealed in Jesus Christ. His theology is the exposition of this self-disclosure of

God in the man Jesus Christ, who dies on the cross and by God's power manifest in the resurrection is declared Son of God.

Luther, in effect, rejects substantialist theology as the intrusion of an alien spirit into the house of God and turns instead to the exposition of the functional theology of the Scriptures. The knowledge of God comes not by speculation, moral discipline, or mystical techniques but through God's gift of himself in his address to his creatures, in his Word, whose climactic expression is Jesus Christ. The Scriptures must be read as a christological document, avoiding the errors of atomism, anachronism, literalism, and legalism.

In the sixteenth century two attempts were made to carry out Luther's theological program. The first is the *Loci Communes* of Philip Melanchthon, published in 1521. He abandons the traditional Scholastic approach and writes a simple exposition of the way a sinner is saved by God through the work of Christ. He deals with the human predicament in sin, the purpose and function of the law, the work of the gospel, the status of the believer in the grace of God through justification, and the life of the justified believer. Later editions of the *Loci* became more elaborate and unfortunately returned to Scholastic methods. The significance of the *Loci* of 1521 has not been appreciated by Lutherans. The reasons are probably two: the assumption that only Scholastic theology is truly systematic theology, and the suspicions that clung to Melanchthon because of his somewhat ambiguous role in attempts to reunite the separated churches.

The second of the attempts to carry out Luther's program is the *Institutes of the Christian Religion* of John Calvin. The renaissance in Calvin studies has rescued him from the domination of his seventeenth-century interpreters and shown that his intention, like Luther's, is to expound the scriptural message. John Leith[3] has compared the *Institutes* to a wheel without a rim: Calvin, he maintains, begins at the hub, the Scriptures, expounds each doctrinal topic as far as the biblical presentation goes, and then returns to the hub to begin a new topic. The absence of the rim is Calvin's deliberate choice not to impose a system upon the Scriptures but simply to expound its message. The *Institutes* in its earlier editions resembles Melanchthon's *Loci* closely. Its later editions become more elaborate. It differs from Luther in being less historically sophisticated in its use of Scripture, less paradoxical, less eschatological, and also in having a quite different understanding of law and gospel and of the relationship of creation to redemption.

Both the Lutheran and Calvinistic traditions turned away from the program of biblical exposition in the seventeenth century and adopted Scholastic methods. In both traditions the Scholastic tradition was challenged or modified from time to time by the recovery of insights of the Reformation. In the Lutheran church the challenge came from biblicists such as John Albrecht Bengel, J. T. Beck, and the Blumhardts, from Pietists such as Philipp Spener, Hans Nielsen Hauge, and C. O. Rosenius, or from a combination of Pietistic and historical concerns as in J. C. K. von Hofmann. It was left to the Luther renaissance to show more amply the methodical dimensions of the problem and to challenge Scholasticism as radically as Luther had done. Carrying out the hermeneutical program of Luther and the Augsburg Confession remains an unfinished task for Lutheran theology.

The story of biblical interpretation within the Lutheran church is not, however, only one of missed opportunities. There is a positive side to the story as well. If Lutheran exegetes and systematicians have not always realized the dimensions of the theological task set by the Reformation, they have entered into the heritage with energy. As noted above, there is a consistent assertion of the instrumental function of the Scriptures in the history of salvation. There is the constant awareness that the gospel is the invitation to participate in a redeemed community. Not always as constant is the recognition that in the new community the believer is called to a life of worship, witness, and service, and that the service takes place in the world and for the sake of the world.

Lutheran interpreters have also maintained the clarity of the Scriptures and the efficacy of the Word of God in the Scriptures. They have maintained that the Bible is a collection of books unified by the redemptive purpose of God. They have also understood this unity from a Pauline perspective, regarding Paul's exposition of justification as the most profound theological reading of the gospel.

IDENTIFICATION

The function of identification has also influenced exegesis. Positively it has contributed the sense of a Lutheran ethos in which worship, theology, patterns of witness and service, ethics, and an aesthetic are combined in an organic whole. An enumeration of distinctive points of Lutheran teaching or practice can always be challenged by the assertion that many others share these points. Yet there is a kind of Lutheran *oikonomia,* a distinctive life-style that permeates all aspects of life and gives a specifically Lutheran approach and perspective. There are recurrent themes, like motifs in a symphony, which can be identified as aspects of the music: the authority of Scripture, the priesthood of believers, the freedom of the Christian, the doctrine of vocation, law and gospel, creation and redemption, justification, faith, grace. The organic whole is more than the sum of its parts and it eludes the analysis of the spectator. Like idiomatic speech, it is not always responsive to rules and requires a sense of fitness.

The negative aspect of identification is easily pointed out. The defensive self-consciousness of all the churches after the Reformation produced biblical scholarship that could be easily identified by confessional labels. Until quite recently, Roman Catholic exegetes dutifully produced exegesis in accord with the standards set by the magisterium. Dom Chapman, for example, altered his reading of the relationships of the synoptic Gospels after the pontifical biblical commission asserted the priority of the Gospel of Matthew. More recently, scholars such as Bea and Lagrange have stood out as courageous islands of scholarly independence. With the encyclical *Divino afflante spiritu* and the Constitution *Dei verbum* of Vatican II, Roman Catholic exegetes have a mandate to produce sound literary and historical interpretation of the biblical message.

In the same period Lutheran exegetes produced commentaries in which the writers of Scripture not infrequently sounded like confessional Lutherans. There have been notable exceptions also in the Lutheran church, Luther himself leading the way. As long, however, as the view prevailed that the language of Scripture is uniform, and that the Bible presents only one theology, most exegetes unconsciously tended to show the agreement of the Scriptures with the doctrinal position of their church. With the growth of historical scholarship, the sharpened awareness of the relation of the biblical writers to their environment, new understanding of the complexity and cultural relativity of language, the development of a sociology of knowledge, a new situation has arisen. Exegesis is no longer branded with denominational markings but reflects instead the extent to which the tools of interpretation are used. The divisions among exegetes no longer run across traditional lines; the same differences appear in almost all church bodies.

NOTES

1. Formula of Concord, Epitome, 7–8 in *The Book of Concord: The Confessions of The Evangelical Lutheran Church*, trans. and ed. Theodore G. Tappert (Philadelphia: Fortress Press, 1959), p. 465.

2. Lennart Pinomaa, *Faith Victorious: An Introduction to Luther's Theology*, trans. W. J. Kukkonen (Philadelphia: Fortress Press, 1963).

3. See John Leith, ed., *Creeds of the Churches: A Reader in Christian Doctrine from the Bible to the Present* (Atlanta: John Knox Press, 1973).

Confessional Biblical Interpretation: Some Basic Principles

RALPH A. BOHLMANN

President and Professor of Systematic Theology
Concordia Seminary
Saint Louis, Missouri

Lutherans concerned about the current inter-Lutheran confusion and disagreement in matters pertaining to biblical authority and interpretation will no doubt applaud the fact that a group of Lutheran theologians has been assembled to consider the general theme "Confessional Propria as Hermeneutic." Although the theme reflects our common desire to be guided by our historic confessional writings, it also raises questions directly touching points at issue among us. For example, in the area of biblical interpretation, why should it be more useful to focus on the peculiar emphases, the "propria," of the Confessions rather than on those emphases they share with Christendom in general? How do we identify the confessional "propria"? How do we determine which "propria" have the greatest pertinence to the issue at hand? Does our focus on "hermeneutic" rather than "hermeneutics" suggest that we are to address broad questions of theological methodology more directly than principles of biblical interpretation per se?

A careful study of the confessional attitude toward and use of Holy Scripture can be of great benefit to the contemporary church. The eight theses of this essay are presented as summaries of the principles employed and advocated by our Lutheran confessional writings for biblical interpretation then and now. On the assumption that the basic confessional data underlying each thesis are well known to all of us, such data are generally summarized in the notes rather than incorporated in the body of the essay.[1] The paragraphs following each thesis offer some applications of the confessional principles to contemporary biblical interpretation.

THESIS 1

Subscription to the Lutheran Confessions includes acceptance of the confessional position on the nature and interpretation of Holy Scripture.

The first thesis assumes that there is in fact a confessional position on Holy Scripture and its proper interpretation. This assumption is by no means obvious. Students of the Confessions have long been struck by the absence of a specific article on this subject anywhere in the Book of Concord. Werner Elert and Arthur Carl Piepkorn have underscored the fact that in the sixteenth century virtually all confessional families had a high view of biblical authority. Elert emphasizes that although the confessional writings presuppose the traditional scriptural principle as self-evident, they also stress the truly reformational character of the Lutheran scriptural principle with their emphasis on justification by grace.[2] Edmund Schlink asserts that the absence of such an article "must be taken seriously as a theological decision" in order to stress that "the Gospel is the norm in Scripture, and Scripture is the norm for the sake of the Gospel."[3] While one can hardly quarrel with the focusing of Elert and Schlink on the christological and soteriological emphasis of the confessional writings, it is difficult to agree with Schlink's notion that this absence reflects a conscious "theological decision" designed to affirm the gospel as the norm for faith and life. There is simply no evidence in the Confessions or elsewhere to support that notion, and the suggestion that the gospel is a "norm" of any kind seems strangely out of tune with the confessors' understanding of the gospel.

Piepkorn is undoubtedly correct in emphasizing that one point of universal agreement among all the sixteenth-century Confessions was "the authority, the inspiration, and the inerrancy of the sacred Scriptures." Piepkorn continues, "It is not surprising, therefore, that we do not have an explicit article on the sacred Scriptures in the Lutheran Symbols."[4] Schlink is correct in acknowledging that "in the actual use of Scripture by the Confessions there is implicit not only a doctrine of Scripture, but also principles of interpretation, and even important hermeneutical rules for the exegesis of the Old Testament."[5] While the task of understanding and explicating the confessional position on the authority and interpretation of Holy Scripture is undoubtedly more difficult than in those doctrinal points treated explicitly and directly, the confessional position can nevertheless be derived not only from explicit confessional statements but also from the actual use of Scripture throughout the Book of Concord. Far too little attention has been paid to this important area in confessional research.

Our first thesis assumes not only that there is a confessional position on the nature and interpretation of Holy Scripture but also that this position is itself biblical. All Lutheran confessional writings ask to be understood and accepted as biblical exposition, and this holds true for the confessional position on Holy Scripture no less than for other points of doctrine. Moreover, our American Lutheran church bodies, like Lutheran churches around the world, accept the Confessions precisely because they are regarded as true expositions of Scripture. Implicit in this claim is that the principles of interpreting Scripture employed by the confessional writings are also consistent with the confessional view of the nature and authority of Holy Scripture. In other words, it is the claim of our first thesis that Lutheran church bodies today that seek to be faithful to their confessional heritage should subscribe to the confessional position on Holy Scripture and its interpretation no less than to the confessional position on other biblical truths. Moreover, we should do so not simply because this position is confessional but also because of the fundamental principle that what is confessional is biblical.

In this connection we should note the inadequacy of contemporary notions of confessional subscription that regard the Confessions as being only historically correct or treat them only as symbols of a movement, companions in our venture into an unexplored future, or expressions of the "spirit" of Lutheranism. Not only do such postures make confessional subscription a waxen nose, but they are also untrue to the very notion of subscription evident in the confessional writings themselves. For confessional subscription then, as well as now, was a pledge to uphold the doctrinal content of the Confessions, not merely to honor it or to regard it fondly as a position once viable but no longer valid. Thus our first thesis underscores *our* responsibility as confessional Lutherans not only to be familiar with the confessional position on biblical authority and interpretation but also to teach it, preach it, and live it, while rejecting and opposing whatever contradicts it as being inimical to God's own truth.

THESIS 2

Holy Scripture is the product of the unique and miraculous action of God the Holy Spirit upon his chosen prophets and apostles

191

whereby he spoke his Word in their words, so that he is the true author of their every word. Because of their divine authorship, the Scriptures are qualitatively different from every other form of human expression in every age.

The principles for interpreting any piece of literature are to a large extent determined by the nature, content, and purpose of that literature. Poetry is not prose, and a textbook on algebra has little in common with a book of science fiction. The same principle is true of Holy Scripture. If the interpreter regards it only as a collection of human documents, he will tend to interpret it only as documentation of the human religious experience or as important writings for the history of religions or something similar. If the interpreter regards Holy Scripture as a storehouse for bizarre divine information or as a collection of divine riddles, he will no doubt engage in some rather esoteric forms of interpretation. Thus, one's method for interpreting Holy Scripture is never neutral. How one regards the nature of Holy Scripture, in both its divine and human dimensions, will have a direct bearing on the principles of interpretation he chooses to follow.

The Confessions do not deal with the divine origin of Holy Scripture reflectively, abstractly, or philosophically, but reflect their doctrine of divine authorship existentially and functionally. The confessional writers work from the "that," the "given," of a divinely authored Scripture. They show little or no interest in explaining the "how" of divine inspiration, nor do they reflect on the process by which God caused his Word to be written in the words of men. In that respect the confessional writers differ somewhat from those stages in the church's tradition when the attempt was made to explain inspiration psychologically. Perhaps that explains why many of our contemporaries have an aversion to the use of the term *inspiration*. It should also be noted, however, that contemporary criticism of psychological theories of inspiration has frequently been too severe, often failing to understand the metaphorical intent of such terms as *pen, secretary, lyre,* or *amanuensis.*

When one reads the Confessions carefully and objectively it is impossible to miss their constant working assumption that Holy Scripture is the unique product of God himself and that his authorship and authority underlie every word of the Scriptures. With the Nicene Creed our sixteenth-century fathers acknowledged that the Holy Spirit "spoke by the prophets." The Scriptures are frequently identified as "divine," "holy," or "of the Holy Spirit."[6] The Apology of the Augsburg Confession acknowledges that the words of Holy Scripture consciously "fell from the Holy Spirit."[7] The Formula of Concord describes the article of Christian liberty as "an article which the Holy Spirit through the mouth of the holy apostle so seriously commanded the church to preserve."[8] Citations of this type could be multiplied.

Attention should also be given to the way in which the Confessions unabashedly call Holy Scripture the "Word of God." To be sure, the term *Word of God* is sometimes used with reference to Jesus Christ, or as the instrument of the Holy Spirit, or as the word of preaching, or with primary reference to the gospel. But a careful examination of the terminology of the Confessions shows unmistakably that the term *Word of God* most frequently identifies Holy Scripture. A comparison of the German and Latin texts of the Apology or the Formula of Concord shows the complete interchangeability of these terms in many contexts.[9]

Similarly, confessional references to the term *command of God* (*mandatum dei*) reveal how natural it was for the confessors to regard a biblical statement or principle as being from God himself.[10] Likewise, the concept of divine law (*ius divinum*) is closely linked to biblical statements.[11] Lutheran theologians who claim that the Lutheran Confessions have a purely functional view of biblical authority, or who imply that it is not truly Lutheran to regard the Scriptures as authored by God in any strong sense of the term, are simply misinformed about the actual statements of the confessional writings.

If we contemporary Lutherans wish to be faithful to our confessional heritage and to follow confessional principles of biblical interpretation, it is incumbent upon us to approach the Scriptures with the same high view of their divine origin and authority, recognizing that they are by virtue of that fact different from every other form of human expression in every age. We must therefore reject the view, common since the Enlightenment, that the Scriptures are purely human documents and which asserts, in fact, that in listening to the Scriptures we are not listening to God speak but are hearing men speak about their religious experiences of God. It is this fact that makes total acceptance of the historical-critical method, as that term is usually understood, an impossibility for a confessional Lutheran theologian. For that method, by approaching the Scriptures in *precisely* the same way one approaches other ancient historical literature, is in that very act incompatible with the confessional view which regards Holy Scripture as being uniquely from God.

Is this evaluation of the historical-critical approach to Scripture too negative? Not if we recognize that this method does in fact place Holy

Scripture on the same level as literature that is purely human in its origin and that it assumes that the interpreter sits in judgment over what he reads. In a recent book on the subject, Edgar Krentz of Seminex has acknowledged the accuracy of this description of the historical-critical method. He writes:

> It is difficult to overestimate the significance the nineteenth century has for biblical interpretation. It made historical criticism *the* approved method of interpretation. The result was a revolution of viewpoint in evaluating the Bible. The Scriptures were, so to speak, secularized. The Biblical books became historical documents to be studied and questioned like any other ancient sources. The Bible was no longer the criterion for the writing of history; rather history had become the criterion for understanding the Bible. The variety in the Bible was highlighted; its unity had to be discovered and could no longer be presumed. The history it reported was no longer assumed to be everywhere correct. The Bible stood before criticism as defendant before judge. This criticism was largely positivist in orientation, imminentist in its explanations and incapable of appreciating the category of revelation.[12]

Nor is this approach limited to the nineteenth century. As Krentz notes,

> the Bible's time-conditioned words speak to specific situations in the literary conventions and forms of their day. . . . This basic recognition about the nature of the Bible entails the axiom that one interprets the Bible by the same methods and procedures used on any other book. No serious Bible student denies this evaluation.[13]

To be sure, not every technique or activity carried out by historical-critical scholars is to be condemned. On the contrary! But honesty compels us to recognize that the confessional view of Holy Scripture is incompatible with an approach to the Scriptures that regards them as purely human literature over which the interpreter sits in judgment.

THESIS 3

Because God's authorship of Holy Scripture was accomplished through human authors living and writing at various times and places as men of their times, the Scriptures must be read as historical literary documents in order to discern God's intended meaning. That meaning is to be sought in the text, not behind it or apart from it. Careful literary exegesis is therefore not an option but a necessity for the Christian interpreter.

One of the cardinal emphases of Lutheran reformational exegesis was its insistence that the "letters" and "grammar" of Scripture must be understood and taken seriously before the Scriptures can be understood theologically. The opposition of the Reformers to the allegorical exegesis of their predecessors is well known and well documented. The polemics in the confessional writings against both Roman Catholic and enthusiastic exegesis is often quite severe, with the confessors complaining that such interpreters have failed to take the text of Scripture with the utmost seriousness and care.[14] The Confessions themselves manifest great care in dealing with and interpreting the text of Holy Scripture. Careful textual exegesis is not simply a matter of choice or style, nor is it merely the result of the flowering of humanism in the early sixteenth century, but it is the result of a conscious theological decision. For the confessors believed and confessed that God himself is speaking in the words of Scripture and that what he is saying can therefore be learned only by deriving the meaning from the text of Scripture itself.[15]

This insistence, not unlike the "incarnational principle" which one can discern in other theological accents of the confessional writings, means that the confessional exegete must diligently seek the intended sense of the text itself in order to get God's meaning. To do this the biblical exegete must attempt to understand the historical setting and context of the text as well as the intention of the author.[16] It was axiomatic for the confessional interpreters of Holy Scripture that God's intended meaning is the literal or intended sense (*sensus literalis*) of a passage. (The confessors recognize that the "sense of the letters"—the *sensus litterarum*— may not always be identical with the *sensus literalis,* or intended sense. It is most unfortunate that contemporary Lutherans so often fail to discern the traditional distinction between the literal meaning and the literalistic meaning of a text!) The confessional writings reflect the conviction that God's intended meaning is to be found *in* the text, not behind it or above it or alongside it. What God intends to convey through the Scriptures is conveyed by the words themselves; it is not to be identified with some kind of experience occurring in the consciousness of the interpreter, perhaps, but not necessarily, while he is occupying himself with the text. For the Lutheran confessors any other principle would have to be condemned as *Schwärmerei,* that is, the attempt to hear God apart from his Word.

With this principle the Confessions give historical-grammatical exegesis *theological* foundation and significance. That is, the careful exegesis of Holy Scripture is carried out by Lutherans not merely because it is the scholarly or customary thing to do but ultimately because of our theological conviction that careful exegesis helps us—and those we serve—to hear *God* speak in the words of Holy Scripture. To that end confessional exegesis is concerned to understand the historical dimensions of the biblical text. Our sixteenth-century fathers, however, derived their notion of history from God's own revelation. They viewed God as the Lord of history, who is not only its creator but its governor and guide and who intervenes in the history of mankind as he did with his chosen people in the Old Testament and as he did preeminently in Jesus Christ for the redemption of all mankind. God's saving acts for his people took place in history and are the focal point of all history. Because the confessional view of history acknowledges God's role in human history, it has no problem with miracles, divine causation, or prophecy. Thus the confessors could and did employ the best tools of their day to establish the text, to discern its literary form, to understand the historical situation in which it was first written, and to analyze its literary and historical content. For the confessional writings, sound historical-grammatical exegesis meant using every means to uncover and explicate the intended sense of the text itself. Historical exegesis thus stood in the service of the text, not the other way around. The *locus* of meaning is in the literary text itself, not in some functional re-creation of the original *Sitz im Leben* (important as that might be for understanding the meaning of the text).

When we apply this principle to our day we must acknowledge and affirm many advances in biblical scholarship since the sixteenth century. Our knowledge of the biblical world is much more complete today than it was in the sixteenth century, however fragmentary it still remains. Noteworthy advances have been made in understanding the biblical languages and their cognates in the ancient world. We no doubt understand ancient literary forms better than some of our sixteenth-century predecessors. Textual criticism has greatly enhanced our knowledge and use of the most ancient biblical texts. For all such advances Lutheran interpreters of the Bible should be truly grateful. But certain cautions are in order also as we examine some contemporary approaches to the Scriptures.

For one thing, we need to cultivate the sober recognition that the use of historical methods is never objective or free of presuppositions. It is important that our presuppositions be biblical, that is, our understanding of history itself ought to be derived from and shaped by God's revelation. Furthermore, historical methods, like other methods of interpretation, are to be used ministerially, never magisterially; that is, such methods serve to illuminate the divinely authored text, not to sit in judgment upon it. Furthermore, the use of historical techniques needs to be accompanied by the humble realization of the limits of *all* historical inquiry. It likewise needs to avoid all attempts to gain a vision of the past through speculative, conjectural, or intuitive attempts to become a part of the original audience. Three "maybe's" do not yield a "therefore"! A long list of conjectures, no matter how scholarly, does not permit any conclusion other than that the evidence is largely conjectural! Again, the attempt to read Holy Scripture on its own terms is to be warmly applauded only when it is recognized that such terms include its divine authorship and consequent truthfulness. The witness of the New Testament is in fact pertinent for Old Testament exegesis! No pericope or text of the Scriptures may be treated as though it were the product of a purely human situation.

The secularistic and humanistic notions of history that govern so many aspects of contemporary historical-critical methodology must be rejected not only as inadequate but also as wrong. The universe is not a closed system of cause and effect. God *does* act in the objective arena of nature and not merely in man's own self-understanding. Process views of history, which place God before, after, and even in the historical process, but not above it, are clearly incompatible with the biblical view of history with which our confessional fathers operate. Furthermore, faith recognizes that there is more to history than can ever be adequately measured by laws derived exclusively from empirical data and rational observation.

Caution must be used in employing extrabiblical materials in biblical exegesis, however essential they may be for certain tasks. Extracanonical traditions, sources, forms, and materials, however useful for understanding the text, are not the authoritative word for the church today—or for any other day. For example, in the Lord's Supper it is the canonical words of institution that are authoritative for the church, not some hypothetical reconstruction of the original words of Jesus based on conjectured traditions alleged to be earlier than other traditions. The *sola scriptura* principle with which our confessional fathers work does not imply that extrabiblical materials cannot be used in exegesis, but it does mean that such data do not determine the meaning of the Scriptures in opposition to the biblical data themselves.

Finally, this thesis implies that we, like our confessional fathers, will continue to recognize and condemn all forms of contemporary *Schwärmerei*, that is, all attempts to derive the meaning of the Scriptures from something other than the intended sense of the text. This is done, for example, by the existentialist reinterpretation of the Scriptures in purely anthropological terms, even when the text says something quite different. Elements of the so-called new hermeneutic are clearly enthusiastic in employing the text of Scripture as an occasion for man's self-understanding through the language event implicit in the text; stated another way, this approach suggests that the biblical text may be the situational illustration or locus of human understanding, even though what is understood may be in actual conflict with the intended meaning of the text itself. The notion that a sharp distinction must be drawn between the "meaning then" and the "meaning now" of a biblical text is another form of contemporary *Schwärmerei*. No less than our sixteenth-century fathers, we need to be reminded of Luther's warning in the Smalcald Articles that enthusiasm is "the source, strength and power of all heresy."[17]

THESIS 4

God addresses man in law and gospel throughout Scripture in order to lead him to salvation through faith in Jesus Christ. The *sola scriptura* principle focuses on the unfolding of Scripture's christological content for its soteriological purpose.

Thesis 4 emphasizes the great heart and center of the Lutheran confessional writings. The confessional data in support of this thesis are simply overwhelming.[18] From beginning to end, the Confessions articulate this important truth. Perhaps the greatest contribution of our sixteenth-century Lutheran fathers to biblical interpretation was that they emphasized the soteriological purpose and the Christocentric content of Holy Scripture with such clarity and force. This accent dare not be lost in our concern for other aspects of Scripture. Scripture is law and gospel, and it is that for man's salvation. This fact gives direction and purpose to Lutheran biblical interpretation and helps to keep it from distortion and fragmentation. The recognition of this great truth is a cardinal Lutheran presupposition for interpreting the Scriptures. This means simply that we always go to the Scriptures expecting to hear God speak law and especially to hear his gracious gospel—and we are not disappointed![19]

It means, furthermore, that we do not interpret the gospel as though it is law and vice versa. As we interpret passages dealing with the relationship between God's deeds and man's, between faith and works, between sin and grace, we are aided by the law-gospel distinction and the recognition of the soteriological intention of all Scripture so that we do not weaken the condemnation of the law or stifle the good news of the gospel. Lutheran biblical interpretation knows that any interpretation of the Scripture that does not minister to our hope in Jesus Christ is not true to God's intent in giving the Scriptures. This is as true of the Old Testament as it is of the New.[20]

On this account, confessionally Lutheran exegesis will reject a purely informational approach to Holy Scripture that loses sight of the overarching purpose and central content of the Bible. The biblical affirmation that Nimrod was a hunter is indeed true, but it is not as important for faith as its affirmation that Jesus is the Son of God. The doctrine of angels is important and comforting, but it is not as central as Christology. Both the fundamentalist and the higher critic sometimes tend to obscure this overarching purpose of Holy Scripture—the former with a basically rationalistic notion of faith and the latter with a purely historical notion of reality. The Confessions understand very well that the Scriptures "are written that you might believe that Jesus is the Christ, the Son of God, and that believing you might have life through His name" (John 20:31).[21]

For the Lutheran Confessions there is an indissoluble connection between Christ and the Bible. They constantly set forth and proclaim the Christ of *Scripture* even as they derive all theology from the Scripture that testifies to *Christ*. Lutherans are ultimately concerned about the Scripture principle, just as we are about all aspects of divine doctrine, because of our concern for the preservation and proclamation of the gospel of Jesus Christ.

THESIS 5

Because the Scriptures were authored by God they address man as God's own infallible, powerful, and authoritative speech. As such the Scriptures are the only source and norm for all doctrine in the church, serving the "purely" and "rightly" of the church's use of the means of grace.[22]

Holy Scripture is recognized as God's speech only by those who believe and know God, and God is believed and known only through Jesus Christ. In other words, the authority of Holy Scripture is not established by rational or logical processes; it is rather recognized and accepted by faith that accepts the Bible's testimony to Jesus Christ and then to itself. On the other hand, man's faith does not first establish the authority of Scripture; Scripture *is* authoritative simply because it is the speech of God, whether man recognizes it or not.

Furthermore, God's Word is never a static thing, but is rather creative and dynamic. The Scriptures have power to make men wise unto salvation as the Holy Spirit works through their message of law and gospel. The Lutheran confessional writings repeatedly accentuate the continuing dynamic power of the Word of God or what later dogmaticians came to call the "causative authority" of Holy Scripture.[23]

The Scriptures also possess "normative authority," and this fact is recognized and underscored in countless ways by the Lutheran Confessions. The writings of human beings "should not be put on a par with Holy Scripture."[24] Not only do the Confessions explicitly state this important theological truth, but the very use of Holy Scripture throughout the Confessions to settle points in dispute bears eloquent testimony to the confessional acceptance of the normative function of Holy Scripture as God's authoritative Word.[25]

Not only the explicit statements of Scripture, but properly drawn inferences are authoritative, and this fact, too, is underscored by our confessional writings.[26] The Confessions do not limit biblical authority to explicit biblical statements in any slavish or wooden way, but they ascribe it to the biblical message in whatever form it appears. The reason, for example, that our confessional writings can ascribe a measure of authority to creeds and confessions is that those writings express and summarize what is biblical, that is, what God himself has said.

In carrying out its normative functions Holy Scripture is infallible, and this fact too is underscored by many confessional references. Although God accommodated himself to human speech in giving us the Scriptures (and we thank God that he did)—just as he truly became a man in Jesus Christ—he did not accommodate himself to error. It was axiomatic for the confessional fathers that there is no human standard which can be used to sit in judgment on the Scriptures and call them wrong.[27] Rather it is Scripture as the speech of God which sits in judgment on man in order to call him to faith in the gospel of Jesus Christ. Because historical criticism expects the interpreter to judge the Scriptures, it is in sharp contrast to the confessional approach to Scripture at this point. Neither is it in keeping with the Lutheran confessional view of Scripture to limit biblical infallibility to matters pertaining to salvation, or to reinterpret it in a functionalistic direction.

For the Confessions, traditions, whether precanonical or postcanonical, are not the source and norm of doctrine. Nor should apocryphal writings, rabbinic literature, apocalyptic intertestamental literature, Ancient Near Eastern texts, or the writings of the apostolic fathers be placed on the level of the Scriptures or used to determine their meaning. The tendency of some contemporary scholars to base exegetical conclusions on something allegedly behind the canonical text, rather than on the text itself, is in flagrant opposition to the confessional position on Holy Scripture.

Likewise, distinctions of authority within the canonical text of the Holy Scriptures are to be avoided. Granted that it is impossible to prove the precise limits of the canon (and the Lutheran confessional writings nowhere attempt this), it is nevertheless true that what is canonical is regarded as God's own speech. It is therefore inappropriate to weaken the authority of supposedly late biblical material in favor of giving greater authority to earlier biblical material; this kind of primitivism has no place in confessional Lutheran biblical interpretation.

Confessional Lutheran acceptance of the Scriptures as the source and norm of all theology will reject all appeals to the church itself as the norm of Christian faith and life, whether this is the traditional Roman Catholic claim or the modern Protestant version which holds that the Lord's promise that the Holy Spirit will lead the church into truth is fulfilled in the corporate decisions of Christians, whether they are guided by the Scriptures or not.

Again, confessional biblical exegesis gives no warrant to the current tendency to allow certain literary forms to function as a criterion for the truth of the pericope in question rather than as a clue to aid us in understanding it. We must reckon with the possibility that God in his scriptural revelation may not only have modified conventional literary forms but also have created unique modes without analogy in other literature. For example, to treat the infancy narratives in Matthew and Luke as midrashic in form and on that account to deny the virgin conception of our Lord clearly does violence to the Lutheran confessional notion of Scripture as norm.

Excursus: The Locus of Biblical Authority

Thesis 5 and its antitheses need to be understood in their proper perspective. Put another way, we must be clear about the proper locus of biblical authority in confessional Lutheranism. Unless this is understood, our articulation of biblical authority can easily go astray.

Some, for example, argue for a very high view of Scripture and assert its infallibility and authority simply on the basis of the obedience and reverence man owes God, also when he speaks in his Word. In this understanding of biblical authority it is argued that because God is the author of Holy Scripture, Christians are obliged under the First Commandment to let God be God also in his Word. Such an emphasis is true, as far as it goes, and it can even serve to remind the church that every trifling with or departure from the Word of God is an act of pride and rebellion against God himself. But this view of biblical authority often stops short and fails to capture the gospel understanding of biblical authority so keenly perceived and articulated in the Lutheran confessional writings.

In seeking to avoid this problem many contemporary Lutherans have attempted to understand biblical authority in a purely functional way. That is, they have stressed what our fathers called the "causative authority" of Holy Scripture, accenting the fact that God works through the Holy Scriptures to accuse us with his law and to restore us through his gospel. In this view the normative authority of Scripture is either minimized or ignored. In fact, some proponents even criticize such normative views as legalistic! Again, one can hardly quarrel with this view's emphasis on biblical power or on the role of Holy Scripture in the context of the means of grace. But this view, with its virtual replacement of the normative authority of Holy Scripture by an accent on its causative authority, is also deficient in its understanding of the confessional locus of biblical authority.

As the Confessions understand this question, the primary function of the Scriptures is to serve as the God-given source and norm for the church's life-giving use of Word and sacraments. As Augustana VII reminds us, it is through the "pure" preaching of the gospel and the "right" administration of the sacraments that the Holy Spirit creates and sustains saving faith in Jesus Christ, the faith which is of the very essence of the church and its unity.[28] An impure or erroneous preaching of the gospel and administration of the sacraments deprives the church of God's very life-giving power. In order to keep the church's proclamation pure and its sacramental administration right, God has given the Holy Scriptures to serve as the source and norm of our use of the means of grace. Along this line we should note again the close connection between the confessional view of biblical authority and the confessional polemic against all forms of "enthusiasm," for the determination of what is pure or right in the proclamation and administration of the gospel and sacraments is determined by Holy Scripture, not merely by individualistic or corporate decision. To be sure, recognition of the divine authority of Holy Scripture is a fruit of our faith in the gospel of Jesus Christ; but the *biblical* content of the gospel we preach and administer is in turn our assurance that our gospel message comes from *God* and therefore expresses *his* will and possesses *his* power. Whatever is faithful to the message of Holy Scripture serves the gospel, and whatever opposes Holy Scripture threatens the gospel. In this view advocates of a fallible Bible or a Bible over which the interpreter sits in critical judgment not only dishonor God as the author of Scripture but also call into question the very means he has given to keep our use of his life-giving message pure and right. Far from making Holy Scripture an object of saving faith (as critics frequently charge), this confessional position professes a high view of Holy Scripture simply in order to allow it to carry out its God-intended servant role on behalf of the gospel.

It is indeed tragic that contemporary Lutheran attempts to articulate this confessional understanding of biblical authority have so often been treated with caricature and scorn by fellow Lutherans. One frequently heard misrepresentation suggests that this view in fact makes Holy Scripture, rather than the gospel, the object of saving faith. This caricature is evident throughout a recent work of Paul G. Bretscher, *After the Purifying*. Bretscher criticizes the view we have been explicating as involving "a dross faith, over and above the Gospel's one true faith." He writes, "For the dross, however, it follows that our faith and obedience must then be directed not to Christ through the Gospel, but to the Scriptures"! Or again, "The dross commands rather that our thoughts obey the Scriptures as a divinely authored book"! Again, "Thus faith and unbelief were made to turn, not on what men think of Christ, but on what they think of the Bible." Bretscher's utter confusion is clearly set forth in the following syllogism, which Bretscher claims is a description of the Lutheran Church—Missouri Synod position: "The Holy Scriptures are the Word of God. God's Word cannot err. Therefore the Scriptures contain no errors or contradictions, but are in all their parts and words infallible truth. From this it follows that I can accept Jesus Christ as my Lord and Savior." The author then continues, "The first theology directs our faith to the Scriptures; accepting them as inspired and inerrant is the basis of faith, including faith in Christ."[29]

This distortion is hardly the aberration of a single individual! One can find the same misrepresentation repeated all too often by Lutherans who should know better. The pre-1974 faculty of Concordia Seminary in Saint Louis in a booklet widely distributed throughout American Lutheranism repeats the same caricature. The former faculty claimed that "at the heart of the discussions in our Synod is the question of whether the Gospel of our Lord Jesus Christ is the sole source of our personal faith and the center of our public teaching." The faculty referred to alleged efforts "to supplement the Gospel so that it is no longer the sole ground of our faith" and criticized a "tendency to make the doctrine of inspiration or the inerrancy of the Scriptures a prior truth which guarantees the truth of the Gospel or gives support to our faith."[30] Small wonder that the Commission on Theology and Church Relations of the Lutheran Church—Missouri Synod found it necessary to issue an evaluation of such faculty statements which pointed out their gross misrepresentation of the synod's position.[31]

These examples have been cited not to inject a note of high controversy into our discussions but to underscore the importance of understanding that the confessional *locus* of biblical authority is to be found neither in the doctrine of the sovereignty of God nor in the doctrine of the object of faith, but in the recognition that the sovereign God has given us the Scriptures in order to preserve his church from the subjectivism and enthusiasm which would destroy the purity and rectitude of our use of the gospel and sacraments, through which he creates and preserves saving faith in Jesus Christ.

THESIS 6

Although the Bible is fundamentally clear in its language, man must have the Holy Spirit in order to understand its message.

No obscure or abstruse book can perform the functions which the Lutheran Confessions ascribe to Holy Scripture, namely, revealing God's soteriological will for man in Jesus Christ and serving as the source and norm for all doctrine and proclamation of the church. For this reason it is not surprising that the Confessions frequently emphasize the fundamental clarity of biblical language. Perhaps this fact is most strikingly evident in the confessional practice of simply citing scriptural passage after scriptural passage without extensive explanation or interpretation. But it is also evident in many explicit statements of the Confessions themselves.[32] In this respect, the Confessions affirm Luther's repeated emphasis on the "external clarity" of Holy Scripture, that is, its fundamentally clear and plain language.

The emphasis that Luther and the confessional writings place on the fundamental external clarity of the biblical text served as a potent reminder in the sixteenth century that the individual reader of Holy Scripture could understand its message without the official ecclesiastical magisterium. Today, scholars need above all to resist the subtle tyranny of the ivory tower. The Bible was written not only for the exegete but for all Christians. We are in real danger today of making the academy, and especially the exegetical department of the academy, the new

magisterium of the contemporary church. Likewise, although the multi-
plication of contemporary versions with notes and of commentaries
pitched at laymen may indeed signal a healthy trend if the effect is to
lead more and more readers to search the Scriptures with new and
deeper understanding, it may also reflect a growing pessimism of church
leaders over against the clarity of the Bible.

Thesis 6 underscores another truth of perhaps even greater importance,
namely, that our confessional fathers recognized that man must have
the Holy Spirit in order to understand the message of the Scriptures in
its fullness. This is a judgment on the limitations of man's understanding
rather than on the limitations of Holy Scripture. Darkened by sin, man's
investigative powers are not sufficient to grasp the "internal clarity," as
Luther referred to it, of Holy Scripture. The Confessions recognize that
the Christocentric message of Scripture, as well as its soteriological purpose, becomes internalized for the reader only through the power of the
Holy Spirit. As Luther once stated, "Nobody who has not the Spirit of
God sees a jot of what is in the Scriptures . . . the Spirit is needed for
the understanding of all Scripture and every part of Scripture."[33] This
means that not even the best of biblical scholarship can mine the depths
of God's saving message in the Scriptures without the Spirit's gift of
interpretation. To be sure, the best of scholarship is none too good for
such an important and rewarding task. But an exegesis devoid of the
Spirit is of limited value.[34]

THESIS 7

Because the same God speaks the same message of Christ and his
salvation throughout the Scriptures, the Scriptures present an organic
unity of doctrine both within and between the Old and New Testaments. The unity of authorship, content, and purpose is reflected in
the principle that Scripture interprets Scripture, whether applied
to individual passages or articles of faith.

It goes without saying that God has chosen to speak to us in Holy
Scripture in a variety of ways and with a rich diversity of concepts,
pictures, and forms. Even parallel accounts of the same event or saying
present us with different accents and emphases. This diversity should be
gratefully received and employed in our proclamation, rather than simply
smoothed out and flattened. Contemporary biblical studies can often help
us to recognize the rich diversity in the conceptuality employed by the
sacred writers.

As the Confessions together with virtually the entire catholic tradition recognize, however, diversity does not mean disunity or contradiction. The Confessions consistently recognize, accept, and bear witness to the unity of Holy Scripture. This unity is rooted in the fact that all Scripture has but one divine author; one central content, Jesus Christ; and one fundamental purpose, namely, eternal salvation. Biblical unity does not consist simply in the fact that Scripture relates one salvation history from the beginning of recorded history through the period of the early church, although it does indeed do this. No, the confessional concept of biblical unity recognizes a unity of doctrine both within and between the Testaments.

The unity of Scripture means that the ultimate context of every passage in Holy Scripture is the entire Scripture. This in turn is reflected in the historic Lutheran emphasis on the self-interpreting Scripture. This principle is very obvious in the actual exegesis employed by the confessional writings.[35] It is seen when the confessors use clear passages to clarify those that are less clear. It is practiced when an article of faith drawn from the Scripture is used to illuminate or explicate a problem or emphasis in another article of faith.[36] It can be recognized in the citation of the Old Testament to comment on, explicate, or clarify aspects of the work of Christ.[37] It is employed when New Testament passages are used to clarify concepts or passages in the Old Testament.[38] In short, the Confessions recognize a unity of content, authorship, and purpose throughout the Scriptures.

With this view it would be impossible for the confessional writings to affirm the contemporary notion that the Scriptures include diverse and even conflicting theologies. This notion has become increasingly acceptable to Lutheran scholars as a result of the growing acceptance of the historical-critical method of biblical interpretation, for that method not only encourages the search for diversity in the Scriptures, but frequently employs historicistic assumptions to claim that diversity in fact means disagreement and contradiction. Over against such practices, the confessional view of Holy Scripture and its unity would remind the exegete who has not interpreted a biblical passage or book or "theology" in terms of its *total* biblical context that he has in fact done an inferior and incomplete piece of exegesis.

Unfortunately, the contemporary accent on historical exegesis has had the effect of greatly reducing the use of "let Scripture interpret Scripture" as a working exegetical principle. Exegetes may concede the systematician's right to the principle, but even then they frequently object to its nonhistorical use. One who understands the secular historian's craft can readily understand why he might balk at its extended use. But for one who takes the unity of Scripture as seriously as the confessional writers did, the question of meaning cannot be settled on narrow historicist assumptions but rather must be referred to the literary context provided by the divine authorship of the entire canon of Scripture. (Without developing the point, let it also be noted that violence is done to the confessional notion of the self-interpreting Scripture by the reductionistic revision which reads, "Let the gospel interpret the Scripture." Although the intention of this revision may be proper, it represents a departure from and limitation upon the confessional understanding and practice.)

In this connection we should also lament the divorce that has often occurred between the Old and New Testaments as a result of the contemporary accent on historical exegesis. To be sure, contemporary exegetes, perhaps better than many of their predecessors, have recognized the need to interpret the New Testament against its Old Testament background. But the converse is not true, unfortunately, and the result is that the Old Testament is often not read as a truly Christian book. When the Old Testament is read apart from its fulfillment in the New, there is in fact little difference between rabbinic exegesis and such interpretation. For our confessional fathers, however, the Old Testament was a thoroughly Christian book.

THESIS 8

The law-gospel distinction and the doctrine of justification not only serve to clarify passages dealing with faith and works but are basic presuppositions for the interpretation of all Scripture, without, however, providing general criteria for the correctness or legitimacy of particular exegetical interpretations.

In many respects, Thesis 8 is simply the corollary of Thesis 4. It is important, however, to underscore the proper hermeneutical significance of justification as well as the law-gospel distinction. Far too much preaching, teaching, and writing, at both academic and parish levels, has lost sight of the need to relate all biblical exposition to the central issues of the Christian faith. By the same token, care must be taken that the law-gospel distinction and the doctrine of justification do not become reductionistic principles or norms in the practice of biblical interpretation.

In one sense the frequent confessional appeal to these doctrines is simply an important application of the hermeneutical principle that Scripture is to interpret Scripture. The Confessions often appeal to these articles of faith when discussing a difficult passage dealing with the relationship between faith and works. When this happens the Confessions are using the law-gospel distinction or justification not as independent hermeneutical principles but as doctrines drawn from the Scriptures that help to clarify other biblical materials. Such a practice allows the Scripture to interpret itself.[39]

This thesis also recognizes, however, that the law-gospel distinction and the doctrine of justification are broad presuppositions for the interpretation of *all* Scripture. The exegete approaches his task, no matter which passage or book he is dealing with, in the expectation that he will hear God speak to him in both law and gospel and that the meaning of all biblical passages, directly or indirectly, sheds light on the great central content and purpose of the Scriptures to make men wise unto salvation through faith in Jesus Christ. In this important way these doctrines at the very heart and core of biblical and Lutheran theology have a critical role to play in the task of all biblical interpretation.[40]

Care must be taken, however, particularly in Lutheran circles today, that the law-gospel principle and the doctrine of justification are not advocated as some kind of basic hermeneutical principle for deriving the meaning from the text. This is not done by the Confessions, in spite of their frequent appeal to the doctrine of justification or the law-gospel principle. For the confessors these two doctrines *are* the message of Scripture, not free-floating principles to be applied to a passage in order to derive meaning from it. Nor do the Confessions employ the law-gospel principle or the doctrine of justification in a reductionistic way, as though any interpretation is legitimate if it does not violate the doctrine of justification or confuse law and gospel. The confessors do not use these central doctrines of the faith as a kind of canon within the canon, for the confessors are convinced that *all* Scripture bears witness to Jesus Christ, that *all* Scripture is law and gospel, and that *all* Scripture serves to teach the justification of the ungodly through Jesus Christ. The meaning of a particular text can be discerned only through a careful exegesis of the text itself.[41]

CONCLUSION

What then are the "propria" of Lutheran confessional biblical interpretation? This essay has underscored four confessional principles and attempted to demonstrate that certain practices in biblical exegesis today are not compatible with them:

(1) The confessional emphasis on the divine authorship and authority of Holy Scripture is basic to the confessional view of the *sola scriptura* principle.

(2) The confessional emphasis on the authority of Scripture is intended to safeguard the "purely" and "rightly" of the church's use of the means of grace over against various forms of enthusiasm.

(3) The confessional attitude toward Holy Scripture is characterized by a recognition of its total unity and truthfulness.

(4) The confessional understanding of the words of Holy Scripture as the very Word of God places a greater premium on the literary character of Holy Scripture than on the historical circumstances of the composition of its various parts.

These great truths, along with many other insights that we learn from our confessional fathers, reach their apex in the recognition that all biblical interpretation in every age is to serve the high and noble purpose of heralding to the world the good news of God in Jesus Christ. Seldom in the history of the church has the interrelationship of Bible and gospel been understood and confessed as clearly as in the Lutheran confessional writings of the sixteenth century. *Te Deum laudamus!*

NOTES

1. A more complete presentation of the confessional data can be found in my *Principles of Biblical Interpretation in the Lutheran Confessions* (St. Louis: Concordia Publishing House, 1968). Abbreviations used in the notes to denote the Lutheran Confessions are: AC = Augsburg Confession; Ap = Apology of the Augsburg Confessions; SA = Smalcald Articles; SC = Small Catechism; LC = Large Catechism; FC = Formula of Concord; Ep = Epitome; SD = Solid Declaration.

2. Werner Elert, *The Structure of Lutheranism*, trans. Walter A. Hansen (St. Louis: Concordia Publishing House, 1962), pp. 190–91.

3. Edmund Schlink, *Theology of the Lutheran Confessions*, trans. P. F. Koehneke and H. J. A. Bouman (Philadelphia: Fortress Press, 1961), pp. 5–6.

4. Arthur Carl Piepkorn, "The Position of the Church and Her Symbols," *Concordia Theological Monthly* 25 (October 1954): 740.

5. Schlink, *Theology of the Lutheran Confessions*, p. 20, n. 18.

6. Bohlmann, *Principles*, p. 31.

7. Ap IV.107, in *The Book of Concord: The Confessions of the Evangelical Lutheran Church*, trans. and ed. Theodore G. Tappert (Philadelphia: Fortress Press, 1959), p. 107 (hereafter cited as *BC*).

8. FC, SD X.15, in *BC*, p. 613.

9. Bohlmann, *Principles*, pp. 33–35, offers several references to the various uses of "Word of God" in the Lutheran Confessions.

10. Ibid., p. 35, offers an examination of this important concept in the Augsburg Confession.

11. Ibid., p. 36.

12. Edgar Krentz, *The Historical-Critical Method* (Philadelphia: Fortress Press, 1975), p. 30.

13. Ibid., p. 62.

14. See Bohlmann, *Principles*, pp. 84–86, for several examples from the confessional writings. Typical is Melanchthon's comment from Ap IV.224 (in *BC*, p. 138): "Our opponents twist many texts because they read their own opinions into them instead of deriving the meaning from the texts themselves." The classic confessional text on "enthusiasm" is SA III.viii.3–13.

15. An examination of the exegetical practice of the confessional authors is very instructive at this point. They know the importance of word study and usage, sometimes employ extrabiblical data to help clarify the meaning of a term, call attention to the importance of grammar, and note the importance of both the closer and wider contexts of passages. For several examples of this practice, see Bohlmann, *Principles*, pp. 86–89.

16. There are many examples of this principle at work in the exegetical practice of the Confessions. Melanchthon notes that "allegory does not prove or establish anything" (Ap XXIV.35, in *BC*, p. 256) and frequently chides his Roman opponents for using it. Nowhere is the confessional appeal to the native sense of the text more evident than in the interpretation of the eucharistic words of institution; see particularly LC V.13–14, 19, as well as FC, SD, VII.38, 42, 43, 45, 48, 50–51, 92. What the Formula says about the words of institution is the general principle followed throughout confessional exegesis: "We must accept them in simple faith and due obedience in their strict and clear sense, just as they read. Nor dare we permit any objection or human contradiction, spun out of human reason, to turn us away from these words, no matter how appealing our reason may find it." (SD VII.45, in *BC*, p. 557.) The Confessions are also aware that the proper sense of a passage is the sense intended by the author and that the biblical authors do not always speak in literalistic terms; accordingly, the Confessions do not hesitate to recognize figures of speech in biblical statements. For a more extended treatment of this matter, see Bohlmann, *Principles*, pp. 89–96.

17. SA III.viii.3–13, in *BC*, pp. 312–13.

18. Among the clearest statements in the Confessions are Ap IV.5–6; XII.53; SA III.ii, iii; FC, SD V.1; AC IV, XXVIII.52; FC, SD III. See Bohlmann, *Principles*, pp. 69–80, for additional examples and a brief explication.

19. One of the clearest statements of the Confessions on this point is in the Formula of Concord: "The distinction between law and Gospel is an especially brilliant light which serves the purpose that the Word of God may be rightly divided and the writings of the holy prophets and apostles may be explained and understood correctly" (FC, SD V.1). The German text of Ap IV.2 states that the article of justification "is of special service for the clear, correct understanding of the entire Holy Scriptures, and alone shows the way to the unspeakable treasure and right knowledge of Christ, and alone opens the door to the entire Bible."

20. Several examples of the christological interpretation of the Old Testament in the Confessions are given in Bohlmann, *Principles*, pp. 78–79.

21. For a brief discussion of the hermeneutical function of the law-gospel distinction and the doctrine of justification, see ibid., chap. 7, pp. 111–25.

22. AC VII, in *BC*, p. 32.

23. The accent on the creative power of the Word of God is particularly evident in such references as LC I.100–101, where Luther states about the Word, "Such is its power that it never departs without fruit . . . for these words are not idle or dead, but effective and living" (in *BC*, p. 379). In Ap XXXIII.8 Melanchthon notes that the Word of God in Gen. 1:28 is still active, for "the Word of God did not form the nature of men to be fruitful only at the beginning of creation, but it still does as long as this physical nature of ours exists." For other confessional references on this point, see Bohlmann, *Principles*, pp. 50–55.

24. FC, Ep, Rule and Norm 2, in *BC*, pp. 464–65.

25. Perhaps the best-known confessional references on this point occur in the Rule and Norm sections at the beginning of both the Epitome and Solid Declaration of the Formula of Concord, which describe the Scriptures as "the only rule and norm according to which all doctrines and teachers alike must be appraised and judged" (Ep 1 in *BC*, p. 464) or "the pure and clear fountain of Israel, which is the only true norm according to which all teachers and teachings are to be judged and evaluated" (SD 3, in *BC*, pp. 503–4).

26. Several examples of such inferences are mentioned in Bohlmann, *Principles*, p. 48.

27. The preface to the Book of Concord frequently describes the Word of God as "pure," "infallible," "unadulterated," or "unalterable." Because we know that "God does not lie" and that "God's Word cannot err," Luther advises: "Believe the Scriptures. They will not lie to you." (LC IV.57, and V.76, in BC, pp. 444, 445). The Formula of Concord urges us "to abide by the revealed Word which cannot and will not deceive us" (FC, Ep XI.14, in *BC*, p. 496). For other examples of such expressions, see Bohlmann, *Principles*, pp. 47–48.

28. *BC*, p. 32.

29. Paul G. Bretscher, *After the Purifying* (River Forest, Ill.: Lutheran Educational Association, 1975), pp. 49, 74, 76. The syllogism is attributed to Bretscher by James G. Bauman in the brief study guide to Bretscher's book entitled "His Word and Our Ambiguities," LEA Monograph, vol. 3, no. 1 (Fall 1975).

30. *Faithful to Our Calling, Faithful to Our Lord*, pt. I: A Witness to Our Faith (St. Louis: Concordia Seminary, 1973), pp. 3, 21.

31. "An Evaluation of the Faculty Document," in the 1973 Convention Workbook of the Lutheran Church—Missouri Synod, pp. 39–40.

32. The confessional affirmation of the Bible's fundamental clarity is particularly evident in the well-known statement of the Formula of Concord that describes the Scriptures of the Old and New Testaments as "the pure and clear fountain of Israel" (FC, SD, Rule and Norm 3). But the confessional writers throughout the Book of Concord frequently appeal to the fact that their argument rests on "clear Scripture." The following statement from the Formula is particularly pertinent: "In the institution of his last will and testament and of his abiding covenant and union, he uses no flowery language but the most appropriate, simple, indubitable, and clear words, just as he does in all the articles of faith and in the institution of other covenant-signs and signs of grace or sacraments, such as circumcision, the many kinds of sacrifice in the Old Testament, and holy Baptism" (FC, SD, VII.50, in *BC*, p. 578). For further discussion of the confessional view of biblical clarity, see Bohlmann, *Principles*, pp. 60–64.

33. Martin Luther, *The Bondage of the Will*, trans. J. I. Packer and O. R.

Johnston (Westwood, N.J.: Fleming H. Revell Company, 1957), pp. 73–74; see also p. 124.

34. A number of confessional references emphasize the total incapacity of natural man to understand spiritual matters; see esp. FC, SD II.12 and Ep II.2. As FC, SD II.9 (and several other references) emphasizes, the enlightenment of the Holy Spirit is absolutely necessary if man is to comprehend spiritual things with his reason and not regard them simply as "mere foolishness and fables." Although natural man "can hear and read this Word externally" (FC, SD II.53, in BC, p. 531), the Spirit is necessary because "he opens the intellect and the heart to understand the Scriptures and to heed the Word" (II.26, in BC, p. 526). See Bohlmann, *Principles,* pp. 64–68, for other confessional references to this point.

35. For several examples, see Bohlmann, *Principles,* pp. 101–2.

36. Article I of the Formula provides a good illustration of this principle. Over against the contention of Flacius that original sin is man's *substantia,* the Formula argues that a distinction must be made between our nature as it was created by God and the original sin that dwells in the nature and corrupts it; this must be done because "the chief articles of our Christian faith constrain and compel us to maintain such a distinction" (FC, SD I.34, in *BC,* p. 514). Article I then proceeds to show how the articles of creation, redemption, sanctification, and resurrection are all opposed to the Flacian position. Each of the articles is set forth in the Formula on the basis of several passages from Scripture. The Apology also argues from the article of justification, based on clear passages of Scripture, to disprove a number of positions and practices of the Roman opponents. See Bohlmann, *Principles,* pp. 107–9, for other examples.

37. Passages from Habakkuk and Isaiah are used side by side with citations from Paul, John, and Acts in Ap IV. 88–89. Citations from Romans, Genesis, and Hebrews are used together to explain how Abraham was justified before God through faith alone (FC, SD III.33). Old Testament passages are used to describe the voluntary nature of the good works done by the "people of the New Testament" in FC, SD IV.17. A passage from Deut. 12 is used as the basis for the confessional assertion that believers should not "set up a self-elected service of God without his Word and command" (FC, SD VI.20, in *BC,* p. 567).

38. Eph. 5:9 and Col. 3:10 are used to interpret "image of God" in Gen. 1:27 (AP II.18, 20). Abraham's faith and Abel's sacrifice are explained on the basis of Rom. 4:9–22 and Heb. 11:4 (AP IV.202). The Formula cites Gen. 17:4–8 and 19–21 against the Anabaptist denial of infant baptism (SD XII.13 and Ep XII.8). For other examples, see Bohlmann, *Principles,* p. 104.

39. See Bohlmann, *Principles,* pp. 118–21, for further explication of how the Confessions use the biblical doctrine of justification and the biblical law-gospel distinction to define important biblical principles with reference to the relationship between faith and works as well as the Christian life in general.

40. The important role of presuppositions in exegesis is recognized by the Confessions, especially in the Apology's criticism of Roman Catholic exegesis. The faulty Roman Catholic understanding of soteriology and anthropology had its effect on the Scholastic exegesis of the Scriptures, leading them to interpret passages of Holy Scripture "in either a philosophical or a Jewish manner" (AP IV.376, in *BC,* p. 164) and to "maliciously twist the Scriptures to suit the man-made theory that by our works we purchase the forgiveness of sins" (AP IV.260). In reacting against this kind of exegesis, however, the Lutheran Confessions do not suggest another arbitrarily chosen set of presuppositions

but rather permit the Bible's own testimony to its content to provide the proper hermeneutical perspective. This the Confessions find in the justification of the condemned sinner by grace for Christ's sake through faith. As the Formula of Concord states, "any interpretation of the Scriptures which weakens or even removes this comfort and hope is contrary to the Holy Spirit's will and intent" (FC, SD XI.92, in *BC*, p. 632). See Bohlmann, *Principles*, pp. 121–24, for other examples of this point.

41. If the law-gospel distinction and the doctrine of justification by grace were hermeneutical principles of general applicability, or even the dominant hermeneutical principles, it is difficult to understand why the Confessions bring nonsoteriological questions to the Scripture for an answer, or answer such questions from the Scriptures without the explicit help of such soteriological hermeneutical principles. Moreover, it must be remembered that the chief issue for much of the Confessions is the interpretation of the gospel itself: what *is* the gospel according to the Scriptures? To suggest that the gospel served as a hermeneutical principle for answering this question is a *petitio principii*. No, the Confessions derive the meaning from the text itself; they do not force the text to say what they want it to say. This is very much in evidence in the way the difficult passages in James on justification are explained (see AP IV.244–53). For further discussion of this point, see Bohlmann, *Principles*, pp. 111–17.

The Influence of Confessional Themes
on Biblical Exegesis

HORACE D. HUMMEL

Associate Professor of Exegetical Theology
Concordia Seminary
Saint Louis, Missouri

The first part of this essay will address itself to the topic of confessional themes, understood broadly enough to include presuppositions, principles, method, or hermeneutic. The second part will attempt a few specific applications, especially to Old Testament studies, this writer's field of specialization.

CONFESSIONAL THEMES

We cannot pursue the vast topic of hermeneutic(s) extensively here. To speak only of "themes," however, might easily exclude legitimate aspects of the topic which are not explicitly or statistically very prominent in the Lutheran Confessions because of the very nature of confessional documents. The Confessions do not purport to be a complete *corpus doctrinae,* and they often discuss thematically or at length only issues that were in dispute at the time they were written.

First, there must be basic agreement in theological method or hermeneutics, or there is no basis for meaningful discussion beyond the mere contribution of various private, subjective viewpoints. I stress *theological* hermeneutics because the concern is not with philological methods or hypotheses as such. At least up to the point of contradiction in terms, quite a variety of these may be used by scholars who are equally committed to Scripture and the Confessions. The confessional scholar will strive both to be a good technician in the area of his speciality and to relate his endeavor to the symbols of his church. But we must have a common court of appeal in order to sift, weigh, and decide which differences count and which do not, which viewpoints are idiosyncratic and which really represent the consensus of the church, which are only traditional and which are really biblical.

Second, there must be a common understanding of the term *confessional*. That term must not be limited to personal or existential confess*ing*, important as that ultimately is. To speak only of the "Lutheran confession" is no full substitute for speaking of the "Lutheran Confessions." More disconcerting still is a tendency in some quarters to construe pejoratively the suffix on confessional*ism* whenever the suggestion is made that we cannot be selective among their teachings. Confessionalism so construed then appears alongside biblicism and, apparently using some Tillichian Protestant principle as the real norm, is actually even condemned as triumphalism or a theology of glory. Confessionalism is much more than a merely accidental ecclesiastical identification with one's heritage. Rather, "confessional" must include the doctrinal or propositional content of that confession. The *fides quae* dare not be entirely absorbed by the *fides qua*. Both Bible and Confessions are theoretically dispensable as far as private *fides qua* is concerned, but they are absolutely indispensable when it comes to the *fides quae*. The point is not, as often charged, some quasi-rationalistic subversion of the "evidence of faith," but confession of God's own gift for preventing faith from vaporizing into fideism or existentialist mysticism.

Neither may "confessional" be understood as only a study of the history of confessional exegesis, as a mere analogy to exegesis today (faithfully confronting our problems as the confessors confronted theirs—important as that ultimately is).[1] In fact, we could well distinguish a normative confessionalism from a merely historical confessionalism. Sometimes it is revealing to note whether teaching the symbols is assigned to the systematicians or to the historians.

The common divorce of exegesis and systematics in theological curriculums today is only another way of stating our problem. Allegedly scientific exegesis either limits itself to philological investigation or searches for some positivity, supposedly discoverable behind the text, for its real authority. Especially under the influence of existentialism, personal experience comes to be assumed to be the primary datum of revelation. Then the reference point for studying Scripture is not the text as such but whatever encounters it may trigger, more or less equal to other extrabiblical stimuli. Meanwhile, systematics reflects on whatever it feels like reflecting on, and the real source for theology and ministry becomes the social sciences.

The influence of the Confessions must really be in the nature of a *norma normata,* to use our traditional phrase (or *quia,* not mere *quatenus,* if you prefer). In other language, it must really function as hermeneutical circle, that is, both as our confession that the doctrines here enunciated are ultimately based on and normed by Scripture, thus representing how *Lutherans* understand Scripture, and as indicating the major direction and themes that Lutherans will pursue in their scriptural exposition. There is a danger, of course, that the Scriptures will be twisted and strained to make them "talk Lutheran" (and in the current climate, that charge is usually quick to come), but there is far greater cause to worry about consistent *under*interpretation of the Bible, as measured by full confessional sensitivity.

What does not really and fully norm is no norm. If the Confessions do not norm, something else inevitably will. It is a case where no position is a very vocal position; "presuppositionlessness" is an impossibility. If the Confessions (i.e., the Scriptures) do not provide the interpretation of their own primary symbols, something else inevitably will, and there will be no end to the alien paradigms imposed upon it, as well as of exegetical legerdemain with respect to the details. Correspondingly, theology proceeds not according to the *analogia fidei* but in "correlation" with "the questions everybody is asking today," letting "the world write the church's agenda," drawing on Scriptures only for a few serviceable quotes or symbols for a content that is really derived elsewhere. In fact, in confessional theology, law plays the role of forcing people to ask the right questions, the real questions.

One aspect of that understanding of "confessional" which we dare not shrink from reaffirming is the particularism represented by the *damnamus-improbant* structure of the Augsburg Confession and by the apologetic-polemic tone of the Book of Concord as a whole.[2] Here too we must be faithful, both formally and materially, or we are not even using the Confessions as good models. Clear, definite perimeters are implied, beyond which we may well be Christian but no longer confessionally Lutheran. The common problem with pleas that room be found for all is that we are never told clearly just who all that "all" includes or how one might decide. Questions of ecumenicity and church discipline are very near the surface here but beyond our purview at the moment.

There is, indeed, a danger of negativ*ism,* but in my judgment most modern temptations are in the opposite direction. It would be unusual

217

if this essay escapes that charge too, but I submit that the history of Christendom and specifically of Lutheranism, both in the past two or three centuries and perhaps particularly during the sixties just past, amply documents the assertion that the concerns expressed here are by no means exaggerated. (We could also adduce the vast amount of negativism in the Bible, especially in the prophets—so much so that critics still tend to think of that as a criterion for authenticity and true prophecy.) Mere positive statements invite abuse at both ends of the spectrum: subjective elasticity on the one side with everyone interpreting (or ignoring) as he sees fit, and on the other side, excessively literalistic and legalistic constructions beyond the original intent. In contrast, excluding statements alongside positive ones function both to establish clear boundaries and to indicate a "field" within which there will be considerable freedom for individual variation and exploration. Thus we have indicated here two major aspects of the hermeneutical function of the symbols, pointing out (1) the "field" within which the exegete carries on his investigations and (2) the perimeters or outside limits beyond which one is no longer confessional.

Perhaps the unique role of symbolics in the total theological enterprise needs to be enunciated too. That term implies neither an official systematics nor an official exegesis as such. One suspects that most of those who make charges of "Scholasticism" really know this and are really using the term as a code word, but let it be stressed once more that the Aristotelian-based system of orthodoxy is not synonymous with orthodoxy or confessionalism. Likewise with exegesis: it is hard to see how anyone even marginally literate in either the history or present practice of evangelical biblical study could make such a charge. (Perhaps "Antichrist" would suffice as one classical example.)

That is, there is freedom indeed within the confessional perimeters, but obviously not that of the autonomous, antinomian, or "liberated" exegete. Those ethical categories apply quite as much to exegesis. Here too confession and confessionalism must merge: the exegete who internally agrees with what the Confessions confess will experience its norms as genuinely liberating, while he who has no such convictions should align himself with another confessional group where he does feel free.

We have already employed those Aristotelian terms, formal and material, so if "themes" includes hermeneutical presuppositions, the first ones must surely be what we often refer to as the formal and material principles of Lutheran epistemology (roughly, *sola scriptura* and *sola gratia*, respectively). Ultimately the two are inseparable, and that is part of the problem with the terminology. The greater problem usually confronting us today, however, is the tendency to repudiate the formal principle or to collapse it and subordinate it entirely to the material principle.

This is not the place to demonstrate again that the symbols (like Luther) do identify the Bible with the Word of God.[3] Of course, "Word of God" has other facets to its meaning (gospel, Christ) which are ultimately just as indispensable, but its identifiability with the Bible remains one of them. God has revealed his truth in the Scriptures, in its noetic and propositional aspects as well as in its existential sense. He reveals there not only himself but also facts, history, and doctrine about himself. The Confessions, like the Scriptures, put quantitatively more accent on the functional or existential dimension because God's Word is first of all something to be believed and proclaimed, not explored theoretically, but the latter is obviously desiderative too in its proper place.

If one thus agrees with the legitimacy of placing the adjective "propositional" before "revelation," two other adjective-noun couplings in order to avoid ambiguity follow synonymously: factual inerrancy (i.e., not only functional) and verbal (or special) inspiration. Because of the jingoism and sloganeering often accompanying those terms—sometimes on both sides of the fence![4]—it would possibly be better to speak of objective revelation, but that too would have to be defined correctly. If we use that terminology we have a fine parallel to Lutheran sacramentology. At least for theologians, however, the issue is anything but merely semantic!

Because of the current scene we must insert parenthetically here the caveat that inerrancy not be confused with literalism, as it often appears to be. That the Bible often uses all kinds of figures of speech, symbols, and popular modes of speaking is not at all in dispute. There is a more substantial issue, however, when it comes to historicity or facticity. Form criticism quite characteristically "proves" its own secularistic and skeptical presuppositions by arbitrarily declaring materials parabolic, or mythical, and that is an entirely different matter. It has almost become axiomatic in modern biblical scholarship that the Bible exhibits one species of mythical thinking that characteristically personalizes, historicizes, "eventifies" its theology (places *mythos* before *logos*). What we really have then is a return to allegorism, which provided much of the provocation for the Reformation (and thus the Confessions) to begin with.[5]

If we retain the traditional (and confessional) understanding of revelation, a whole host of traditional hermeneutical axioms then ensue (or, really, are only restatements of the same postulate). Perhaps the most significant one for our purposes is the unity of Scripture, the assumption that ultimately it has only one theology because it has only one Author. Mind you, this does not mean uniformity, failure to recognize the many theologies in Scripture in the sense of varying formulations or accents, nor above all the development involved in the difference between the promise and the fulfillment. Up to the point of contradiction in terms, we can even thank historical criticism's fresh exploration of the variety and historical conditionedness (not conditionality) of the various parts of Scripture. That is part of what is implied by the "historical" part of "historical-grammatical," which many Lutheran conservatives urge as a label for their hermeneutics instead of "historical-critical"; the Reformation itself usually spoke only of the grammatical (over against the allegorical). Today, however, the common problem, as one sees it constantly in the literature, is an almost reflex rejection of any attempt to unify or harmonize different biblical expressions or accents as necessarily fundamentalistic.

The current popularity of the term *trajectory*,[6] implying that the Bible is really only another part of the universal historical flux and that scriptural tradition is only a springboard for later ecclesiastical tradition with no essential qualitative difference between canonical and extracanonical, is virtually a priori unacceptable, at least in that form. When it is combined, as it ordinarily is, with a virtual dogma of theological pluralism within Scriptures (in order to justify our own pluralism), it is obvious that we are several light-years removed from the Reformation's *sola scriptura.*

It is our basic contention that one cannot really speak of confessional theology without such presuppositions as the above, at least not without a radical redefinition of terms. If there is no fundamental unity in Scripture, how does one speak of biblical teaching or biblical theology on much of anything? How does one ultimately define terms, other than on the basis of personal whim and subjectivity? On what basis then does one defend Lutheran doctrine other than on the basis of mere tradition (which, of course, is about as un-Lutheran as imaginable)? How can one have dogmatic theology or systematic theology in any traditional sense (versus, I suppose, what today is often called constructive theology) other than on such a deductive basis, that is, drawing equally on *tota scriptura* wherever it speaks to the subject at hand, and then collating and summarizing in language that will be biblical in essence even if not always in form?

220

Or, if we put the question in slightly different form, unless *scriptura sui ipsius interpres est*, how shall we even agree on what is the basic, appropriate paradigm for biblical interpretation? If it is not the soteriological or christological one (in the sense of vicarious atonement) that the Bible itself provides, why should it not be the political, social, or liberation one, which has always been more or less synonymous with liberalism and which today enjoys perhaps as great a vogue as ever? The radical difference is probably most apparent with respect to the interpretation of the prophets (basically, messianic prophecy vs. prophetic ministry), but not infrequently it involves Christology and Pauline theology as well.

And it is an almost omnipresent, simply determinative factor with respect to Old Testament theology, that is, whether or not the Old Testament proclaims basically the same gospel as the New, as confessional Lutheran theology has always stoutly insisted and as the New Testament plainly assumes. When with the Reformation we stress *unus sensus literalis*, we neither resort to allegory nor blind ourselves to the many obvious differences in formulation and degrees of clarity and the obvious need to hear them in their original historical context. But here too the clear must interpret the unclear, the patent the latent (Augustine), the explicit the implicit. Scripture as its own interpreter here does not imply elimination of the historical aspects of that latency, but would indicate how all facets are finally unified christologically (e.g., *logos incarnandus* vs. *logos incarnatus;* "what Christ is" vs. "who he is"). In general, *unus* might better be rendered "unified" than "one" in this context. One it ultimately is, however, not only chronologically and linearly but also organically and intrinsically.

When we insist that Scripture must interpret Scripture, that is, provide its own basic paradigm, we are by no means excluding all use of external evidence, such as that richly provided by archaeology, and even history of religions, for fuller understanding of vocabulary, metaphors, and secondary symbolism. While it is historically demonstrable to a certain degree, the Bible's uniqueness is ultimately a matter of confession. The question is whether external (historical) evidence may be used to test *whether* or not the Bible is true or whether its legitimate use is limited to helping us better understand *what* truth is revealed there, as defined by the canon's own internal self-testimony.

Let us turn now to the so-called material principle. This may be formulated in more than one way, among the most common being justification by faith, law-gospel, and possibly theology of the cross. Not only for the active mission of the church, but also for our theoretical purposes at the moment, this is no less important than the proper prolegomena. It is often pointed out, and rightly so, that the confession of inerrancy or verbal inspiration does not suffice to guarantee full confessional truth, as witnessed by the veritable host of positions that appeal to it. Not only do Lutherans confess *that* the Bible is God's Word, but they also confess specific things about the content of that revelation. Both Scripture and gospel, however, readily become a matter of private interpretation if not controlled by the other.

Thus one might say there both is and is not a canon within the canon. In the sense of the gospel or justification by faith as the central paradigm to which all details must be related, one might say there is. The usual sense of the phrase, however, implying that the interpreter has freedom to choose which parts of *tota scriptura* are true, must be rejected, in a way precisely because the canon in the other sense, that is, the gospel, soon becomes adulterated or attenuated as a result. One hears it intimated repeatedly that if conservatives would just abandon their dogged insistence on inerrancy no significant differences would remain. We have no reason to deny that in many individual instances that may be true, but as a generalization anyone who has ears to hear what really goes on can only respond, "Would to God it were the case!" Then our problems would be trivial indeed. At best one often notes the substitution of exclusivity for centrality: what is indeed indispensably central is about all that remains of the original substance as a sort of spiritualistic sole survivor.

My judgment is that contemporary Lutheranism is, on the whole, much more threatened by a "gospel reductionism" than by any "bibliolatry." The same one-sided existentialism we noted above with respect to the definition of confessional plagues us with respect to gospel. Both the *norma normans* and the *norma normata* are set adrift by the same sabotage. Some drift far from real biblical and confessional moorings, others hardly at all. Even if the actual drift is slight, the potential for more is always there. The *method* remains unsound even if the proper answers are still reached by other, subjective means.

Let it be stressed again that we are not asserting that this aberration necessarily implies shipwreck of saving faith. That verdict belongs to God anyway. Nor are we subscribing to any mechanical domino theory, as though one aberration inevitably leads to total error. Personal, saving faith (*fides qua*) and creedal sufficiency (*fides quae*) must be distinguished, but the Bible gives us ample warrant to insist that subversion of

222

the latter may well be deleterious, if not ultimately fatal, for the former as well. The ultimate concern here is pastoral.

Even if the right syllables are repeated, one is never quite sure which lexicon is being used, nor do we lack for explicit appeals to the modern study of language, which would further dissolve theological communication into private preferences for objectification or articulation of the same religious experience. If we abandon the correspondence theory of language and of truth, that is, its ultimate rationality and consistency (even if a species of symbolism is always being employed), so that words may mean whatever anybody wants them to mean, how can we ever communicate with anyone about anything? Such an approach may be handy for the ecumenists, but is not this a relapse into mysticism?

The one-sided subjectivism characteristically also expresses itself in a certain antisupernaturalism and/or demythologization. To be sure, there is no salvation in supernaturalism as such any more than in inerrancy as such. The important thing is our relation to the supernatural which, of course, will have to be defined correctly. Nevertheless, it eludes me altogether how a genuinely biblical and confessional accent on the relational is possible without supernatural content.[7] Care must be taken that all our phrases in this context like gospel, law-gospel, justification by faith, and theology of the cross are not emasculated, psychologized, and universalized by such desupernaturalization. Virtually all biblical themes—for example, reconciliation, resurrection, hope, and covenant—are subject to the same horizontalization and trivialization. Our symbols remind us that the Bible's primary orientation is vertical and *coram Deo*, and any horizontal, ethical accents are meaningful only in that context. I, for one, am not at all satisfied that many of the new liturgical proposals before us are sufficiently guarded in this respect.

As we noted above, neither the Confessions nor the Bible requires any specific metaphysical or philosophical system as such (including Aristotelianism), but it remains to be demonstrated how any of the post-Cartesian and post-Kantian systems can be considered remotely adequate for the presentation of the total Christian verity. There is no doubt that the subject-object antithesis as such was unknown in Reformation times, but that justifies the subjectivism of modern nonconfessional hermeneutics no more than it did the objectivism (*opus operatum* sacramentalism, and such) that the confessors found objectionable in their day.

All reductionism aside, however, the importance of the material principle as a major, positive hermeneutical guide can scarcely be overstated.

HORACE D. HUMMEL

It both provides an indispensable center and focus to which all exegetical conclusions must be integrally related and vetoes many centrifugal interpretations that secular scholarship often proposes. Christological exegesis is one of those fine epithets that will really be serviceable if defined in this context, upholding both Jesus' own messianic self-consciousness and his ontological relationship with the Father, and avoiding both mere immanentalism and allegorism.

SPECIFIC APPLICATIONS

Now let me attempt a few applications. Being primarily an Old Testament specialist, I shall offer the bulk of my illustrations in that area.

Law-gospel consciousness, used together with confession of Scripture's ultimate unity in its one Author, will be very helpful in demonstrating exegetically, and perhaps even making more functional, our confessional stress that both Testaments are equally canonical Scripture. Illumination of the whole troublesome semasiology of law will be one of the major advantages: "torah" will be seen as more parallel to our "gospel" or "Word" than to our usual usage of "law." The difference between the Testaments will be understood primarily as an eschatological one (sometimes with correspondingly different but ultimately synonymous vocabulary), not one of basic theological structure. The real difference between the Testaments is not theological at all; instead, it consists basically in the fact that ancient Israel was *both* "church" and state, while in the new Israel the political and ceremonial scaffolding falls away. New Testament increments will be seen as a filling (fulfillment), not as any fundamental evolution in the ordinary sense. Hence, the many laws (statutes, judgments) in the Old Testament will be interpreted not as in any way legalistic in intent but as essentially what we know as the "third use of law," indicating concretely to the faithful how they should respond in gratitude. All due difference will be made between the Testaments (moral vs. ceremonial and political law), but it will not be possible to label all the prescriptive parts of the Bible as law, at least not in the sense of the de facto repudiation of a *tertium usum* which that accent often appears to imply (e.g., ordination of women).

The purely moralistic—if not eudaemonistic and expediential—reading to which especially the wisdom literature is often subjected will be replaced by one which sees it as simply an alternate expression of genuine covenant ethics. With the New Testament, wisdom will be seen as exhibiting its ultimate meaning in the person of Jesus Christ, versus its

224

merger both with halakah in rabbinism and with *haskalah* (the enlightenment of mere human rationalism and empiricism) in most modern critical study, especially much of that of the sixties when wisdom study suddenly came into vogue.

"Covenant" will not be misread as legalism, as perhaps Lutherans especially are prone to do (although "covenant" does imply a legal, forensic paradigm), but it will be read in the light of the promise and as an articulation of the meaning and application of election and expiation. A law-gospel texture will be seen throughout: in the relation of Genesis 1–11 to virtually all that follows, in the radicalization of the theme of judgment (the obverse of messianism) in classical prophecy and later in apocalyptic, in the outlines and internal arrangements of much of the prophetic literature (e.g., the frequent pattern of alternation of weal and woe, the positioning of the Gentile oracles between the oracles of judgment and salvation upon Israel).

On any purely philological basis it is impossible to demonstrate irrefutably that this Christian reading of the Old Testament is more faithful to its real spirit and intention than the halakic and semi-Pelagian one of traditional Judaism or than the variety of historicistic versions that modern criticism often serves up. It will be confessed only when the Spirit removes the veil (2 Cor. 3:14–16).

A correlary of law-gospel is "two kingdoms." In the hermeneutical circle we again have there not only confessional social theory derived from Scripture, but also a fundamental interpretative guideline for properly expounding Scripture. The whole understanding of the nature of biblical eschatology, of prophecy-fulfillment and of the nature of the unity in diversity of the two Testaments, is involved here. Its major application will be in connection with the adjective "prophetic." As the prophetic endeavor was eschatologically and messianically oriented, so prophetic ministry will devote itself primarily to the proclamation of Christ and his eschatological kingdom. The prophetic oracles of judgment and promise apply primarily via the cross to the church, the "kingdom on the right," not to America or Russia or any of the kingdoms of this world on the "left." Any suggestion that capitalism or Marxism or any other system will as such contribuite one iota to the coming of the Kingdom will have to be considered blasphemous. Literalistic and this-worldly applications of the many prophecies about the "land" by both right-wing millennialists and left-wing liberation, social action, or ecology ideologues will be regarded as equally horrendous perversions of biblical theology.

Another basic way of expressing the same hermeneutical principle is in terms of the "now–not yet" nature of the fulfillment, that is, a certain dialectical relation between the two Testaments. Some types of recent *Heilsgeschichte*, and perhaps especially Oscar Cullman,[8] have given this manner of expression considerable recent currency, but I submit that it corresponds quite exactly to traditional understandings of promise-fulfill-ment.[9] It also corresponds to the *simul iustus et peccator* dialectic of Lutheran anthropology.

Properly understood, we can say that we still live in the old covenant as well as in the new. Hence, the promise, hope, wait themes of the Old Testament still apply to the Christian, indeed, in a sense, with even greater poignancy and urgency than for the Old Testament saints. The New Testament is so preoccupied, if you will, with the proclamation of the good news of the "now" that it devotes relatively little space to the ques-tions of order and structure, of cult and even sacraments in the interim of the "not yet." Nonspiritualistic exegesis will neither spurn what little the New Testament does say on these subjects as law, early catholicism, or the like, nor entirely ignore the relevant portions of the Old Testament. The New Testament itself apparently assumes that much of Old Testa-ment ethics needs little reiteration. Old Testament structures, institutions, and cult no longer apply in any mandatory way, of course, but they do serve as theological structural models and examples of more than ordinary significance. If typology and fulfillment are not misunderstood as simply exhausting themselves in Christ, the Old Testament types, transmuted and transfigured in Christ, remain important sources for the ethics and wor-ship also of the body of Christ.

Before we leave the topic of eschatology, personal eschatology or belief in an afterlife must not be overlooked. It is no secret that most critical scholarship reads the Old Testament in this respect about as differently from precriticism as is imaginable. We can concede that precriticism char-acteristically glossed over differences in clarity and fullness of revelation also in this respect, but the almost total disjunction that modern scholar-ship posits is not the alternative. Again it is largely a matter of which lens the exegete uses. At the very least a cogent case can be made for a lively awareness already in the Old Testament of the living God's power over death also, and a conviction that death did not end all, especially not for the faithful (this without recourse to the recent reconstructions of Dahood, which remain to be thoroughly tested).

The confessional exegete and theologian will take all due care not to read into the ancient texts more than is there, but he will also not hesitate to read out of them all the fullness of subsequent revelation (Augustine's formula of latency and patency). He will distinguish but will not divorce. This principle, of course, will have vital applications across the board, if positivistic exegesis is being replaced by the confessional type.

Apocalyptic will not be treated with the consummate horror which much liberal exegesis has accorded it. It will be viewed not as fundamentally different from classical prophecy (as even a minority of critics will agree) but rather as a climactic sharpening and dramatization of all that prophecy, yes, biblical theology, was all about. And while some critics have overstated apocalyptic's formative role in early Christian articulations, it is quite clear that the New Testament as we have it is incomprehensible apart from it. In fact, no full biblical doctrine of prophecy-fulfillment is possible without reference to the two-aeon dualism. Finally, it must be observed here that what biblical apocalyptic highlights is precisely what liberalism generally minimizes, so that a simple equation between biblical apocalyptic and confessionalism would ultimately not be too far off target.

The confessional accent on Word and sacrament also has hermeneutical significance. In both Testaments, one always notes to what extent the interpreter's sympathy for sacramental and liturgical accents in theology and practice tends to influence his attitude toward possibilities in the biblical text. It is one of those areas where the text must check unbridled speculation, of course, but also an area where sensitivity to symbolism and nuance is of the essence of the art of exegesis alongside its more scientific aspect. One suspects that nothing more profound than plain anti-Catholicism ("Romanizing tendencies") has often played a major, subliminal role in inhibiting Lutheran exegetes in this respect. Nor can Lutherans expect much encouragement either from conservative—but still very Reformed—evangelicals or from typical liberalism with its various spiritualistic and antiinstitutional proclivities.

The entire prophet-priest antithesis that has often seemed virtually endemic to biblical higher criticism, the disparaging judgments about the priestly, and the instinct to regard such materials as late and ungenuine (e.g., the priestly code; see the pastoral Epistles) cannot survive in a truly confessional context. The laws of cleanness, for example, will be seen not as primitivism but as a "sacramental" expression of the theology of holiness.

The entire sacrificial cult will be viewed as analogous to and typical of Christ's expiation and the Christian sacraments, not as an unassimilated bit of paganism in ancient Israel. Even the various cultic reconstructions of Mowinckel, Weiser, and Kraus, for example, may receive a sympathetic hearing, although when it comes to details their highly hypothetical and sometimes theologically objectionable nature will have to be recognized too. Especially the exegesis of the Psalms cannot but be profoundly affected by such perspectives.

The idea of typology as one of the main lines of unity between the Testaments runs very parallel to sacramental theology. Certainly the confessionalist will neither be able to abandon it to the dispensationalists nor confuse it with allegory. The symbols speak little to this issue as such, but it is implicated in Luther's and the confessors' sense of the preexistence or "real presence" of Christ in the Old Testament. The *logos incarnandus* who is really present "in, with, and under" Old Testament events, institutions, and personages is also he who fulfills them in his incarnation and who bodily actualizes them *pro nobis* in baptism and in the Eucharist.

One could continue at length in illustrating the exegetical applications of the confessional hermeneutical circle for virtually every article of the faith. If we proceed holistically rather than reductionistically, the principle must finally be applied to all the parts. We shall limit ourselves to only two other applications.

We surely cannot neglect theology proper. It is certainly not irrelevant to today's theological scene. The God of Abraham, Isaac, and Jacob is far removed from the theistic construct of many biblical practitioners. Scarcely any of the various theories of the evolution of the Israelite god-hypothesis out of paganism will pass muster. Both the more personalistic and *heilsgeschichtliche* construct of a patriarchal God of the fathers growing up to be regarded as Israel's redeemer and only much later being regarded as universal creator, and the monism and immanentalism toward which process and Teilhardian thinkers tend (where very often god = change), will be seen as, at very best, only very myopic visions of the totality.

God as Spirit, that is, as "person," is so central to biblical theology that almost everything is changed if this tenet is altered. The God of the Bible can neither be banished to the pure interiority of the individual soul nor be buried within the historical process. In either case "God" soon becomes only a personification for the great ideas and ideals of men, minus only the mythology of ancient pagans. Freud and Feuerbach, Marx and Comte were then in essence indisputably correct. If God-as-person is kept in view, the phenomenal parallelism, *mutatis mutandis*, between the Yahweh-

Baal conflict and many of orthodoxy's struggles with modern syncretisms or even de facto paganisms will readily come into focus.

We cannot refrain from a brief note about "original sin." It is no secret that most modern scholarship, like traditional rabbinic exegesis, finds no such doctrine in the Old Testament, not even in different dress. That such teaching is absolutely pivotal in the Confessions, as it was in the struggles with medieval Romanism in general, needs no demonstration. Nor will we have to demonstrate that exegesis and theology are intimately involved in the question of hamartology almost across the board.

Perhaps that makes as good a conclusion as any. It is because the question of sin always remains *the* question, in a sense even the only question for the church, that our endeavor does not represent any kind of repristination but remains as relevant and timely as ever. We believe, teach, and *confess* that the answer for all time comes only in the gospel, as revealed and defined in the Holy Scriptures and as correctly expounded in the Book of Concord.[10]

NOTES

1. If we really are confronting today's problems confessionally, it would appear obvious to me that this would often and characteristically take the form of *statements* specifying their contemporary application and to which a confessional body might rightly require allegiance or subscription, at least provisionally. These would be construed in no way as additions to the Book of Concord but rather as ongoing efforts to keep it relevant. I fear that I must judge most contemporary appeals to the "sufficiency" of the confessional statements we already have as code words for a de facto relativization or other reductionism of their authority, as traditionally understood. On this point the first chapter of Edmund Schlink's *Theology of the Lutheran Confessions,* trans. P. F. Koehneke and H. J. A. Bouman (Philadelphia: Fortress Press, 1961), remains required reading.

2. The major study of this aspect of the symbols is Hans-Werner Gensichen, *We Condemn: How Luther and 16th-Century Lutheranism Condemned False Doctrine* (1955), trans. Herbert J. A. Bouman (St. Louis: Concordia Publishing House, 1967). Some of the biblical antecedents of this stance are noted in Gensichen's first chapter. For a "gospel-reductionist" reading of the *damnamus* clauses, see Edward H. Schroeder, "Current Implications of the 'We Condemn' Statements in the Lutheran Confessions," *Currents in Theology and Mission* 2, no. 1 (February 1975): 5–9.

3. Perhaps the most recent, succinct, and readable such demonstration is *Gospel and Scripture: The Interrelationship of the Material and Formal Principles in Lutheran Theology,* A report of the Commission on Theology and Church Relations, Lutheran Church—Missouri Synod, November 1972. For the same in brief form, see Harry Huth's review of Paul Bretscher's *After the Purifying, Lutheran Quarterly* 27, no. 3 (August 1975): 262–64. Also generally

pertinent is Harry Huth, "One Savior and One Confession," *Concordia Journal* 2, no. 2 (March 1976): 61–68. Among the many other titles that could be cited, we mention the following: Ralph A. Bohlmann, *Principles of Biblical Interpretation in the Lutheran Confessions* (St. Louis: Concordia Publishing House, 1968); Holsten Fagerberg, *A New Look at the Lutheran Confessions (1529–1537)*, trans. Gene L. Lund (St. Louis: Concordia Publishing House, 1972), esp. chap. 1, "The Basis of the Confessions"; Eugene F. Klug, *From Luther to Chemnitz: On Scripture and the Word* (Grand Rapids: Eerdmans Publishing Company, 1971); and Robert D. Preus, *The Theology of Post-Reformation Lutheranism: A Study of Theological Prolegomena* (St. Louis: Concordia Publishing House, 1970).

4. Those who reject our position commonly try to pin the label "fundamentalist" on it, with the implication that it is not really confessional or Lutheran. The classic refutation of that charge remains: Milton Rudnick, *Fundamentalism and the Missouri Synod* (St. Louis: Concordia Publishing House, 1966). Nevertheless, it appears obvious that the death of that canard is about the last thing in the world some people want to happen!

5. Hans Frei has recently analyzed this shift in *The Eclipse of Biblical Narrative: A Study in Eighteenth and Nineteenth Century Hermeneutics* (New Haven: Yale University Press, 1974).

6. E.g., James M. Robinson and Helmut Koester, *Trajectories through Early Christianity* (Philadelphia: Fortress Press, 1971), passim.

7. Perhaps Edward H. Schroeder has been as vocal and articulate as anyone in defense of the existentialist posture in this respect—of course defended as genuine Lutheranism. See especially his "Is There a Lutheran Hermeneutics?" in *The Lively Function of the Gospel: Essays in honor of Richard R. Caemmerer*, ed. Robert W. Bertram (St. Louis: Concordia Publishing House, 1966), pp. 81–97, as well as later articles already cited above.

8. Oscar Cullmann, *Christ and Time: The Primitive Christian Conception of Time and History* (Philadelphia: Westminster Press, 1964).

9. A good example of confessional Lutheran adaptation of the scheme—in spite of its technically Calvinistic roots—can be found in Peter Brunner's *Worship in the Name of Jesus*, trans. M. H. Bertram (St. Louis: Concordia Publishing House, 1968).

10. The following major English-language literature may be noted in addition to what has already been cited: Herbert J. A. Bouman, "Some Thoughts on the Theological Presuppositions for a Lutheran Approach to the Scriptures," in *Aspects of Biblical Hermeneutics: Confessional Principles and Practical Applications*, Occasional Papers 1 of *Concordia Theological Monthly* (St. Louis: Concordia Publishing House, 1966); Nils A. Dahl, "The Lutheran Exegete and the Confessions of His Church" in *Lutheran World* 6 (1959–60): 2–10; John Warwick Montgomery, *Crisis in Lutheran Theology* (Grand Rapids: Baker Book House, 1967), vols. 1 and 2; Arthur Carl Piepkorn, "The Position of the Church and Her Symbols," *Concordia Theological Monthly* 25 (October 1954): 738–42; Jürgen Roloff, "The Interpretation of Scripture in Article IV of Melanchthon's Apology of the Augsburg Confession," *Lutheran World* 8 (1961): 47–63; and various publications of the Commission on Theology and Church Relations of the Lutheran Church—Missouri Synod—"Gospel and Scripture," "The Inspiration of Scripture," "Seven Theses on Reformation Hermeneutics," "Revelation, Inspiration, and Inerrancy," and "A Lutheran Stance toward Contemporary Biblical Studies."

Allow me also to mention some of my own publications in this area, many echoes and derivatives of which may be found in the present essay: "The Bible and the Confessions" (a review of Ralph A. Bohlmann's *Principles of Biblical Interpretation*), Dialog no. 8 (Winter 1969): 51–55; "No Other Gospel," *Lutheran Forum* no. 3 (October 1969): 4–9, plus exchanges with correspondents in subsequent issues; "Is There a Lutheran View of the Bible?" *Lutheran Scholar* 27, nos. 1 and 2 (January and April 1970): 29–32 and 2–13; and "The Outside Limits of Lutheran Confessionalism in Contemporary Biblical Interpretation," *The Springfielder,* 35, no. 2 (October 1971): 103–25; 35, no. 4 (March 1972): 264–73; 36, no. 1 (June 1972): 37–53; and 36, no. 3 (December 1972): 213–22.

Confessional Propria as Hermeneutic—
Old Testament

FOSTER R. MCCURLEY
Professor of Old Testament and Hebrew
Lutheran Theological Seminary
Philadelphia, Pennsylvania

LUTHER'S CHRISTOLOGICAL EXEGESIS

One cannot begin a discussion of interpreting the Old Testament in light of the Lutheran Confessions without paying some attention to the exegetical principles of Luther himself. Heinrich Bornkamm's *Luther and the Old Testament*[1] is particularly helpful in spelling out the complexities of Luther's approach to the Old Testament and serves as the basis for the following observations preliminary to moving into the topic proper.

Luther had worked his way through and above medieval theology's "four senses of Scripture" to the point that the only legitimate exegetical goal was "to make Christ, the content of Scripture, present for the individual in judgment and grace."[2] This "spiritual" sense of Scripture renders as useless arbitrary allegorization. It is *upon history* and not false allegory that faith rests, and it is *in history* that we find hope and help in time of need. In fact, allegory and history are opposites; only by avoiding allegories and by following the literal sense can we recognize history wherein the physical suffering of our ancestors and their liberation enables us to draw comfort for our spiritual suffering today.

In his discussion of the Song of Songs, Luther exhorts theologians to concentrate on what the texts of Scripture say.

> I leave allegories alone. A young theologian should avoid them as much as he can. I think that in a thousand years there was no more economical allegorist than myself. . . . Become a text critic and learn about the gram-

matical sense, whatever grammar intends, which is about faith, patience, death, and life. The Word of God does not deal with frivolous things.[3]

By a literal sense of Scripture, however, Luther meant a christological exegesis whereby Old Testament texts of varied types point in a prophetic way to the coming of Christ. This approach was worked out in two ways: (1) direct predictions of Christ and (2) indirect permeation of the gospel.

Direct predictions of Christ went far beyond the so-called messianic texts to include passages from the first book of the Old Testament to the last. (a) From the "Books of Moses" Luther listed such predictive passages as Genesis 3:15 (the promise of victory over the serpent); Genesis 22:18 (the promise of blessing on Abraham's seed); Genesis 4:1 (Eve's cry of triumph, "I have the man of the Lord"); Genesis 49:10 (the messianic prophecy about Judah); and Deuteronomy 18:15, 18 (the promise of a prophet like Moses). Beyond these "messianic" texts Luther found christological promises in Exodus 33:18-19 ("I will let all my goodness pass before your eyes, and I will preach in the Lord's name before you") as well as in Exodus 34:5ff. and 8ff. (the appearance of God and the covenant of God, which point to the promise of Christ).

(b) From the prophecies of David, Luther listed 2 Samuel 23:1ff. (where the "one who rules justly over men" is not David but Christ) and 2 Samuel 7:16 (where "your house and your kingdom shall be made sure for ever before me" must apply to the king who will replace the earthly house of David). Moreover, since David is traditionally held as the author of most of the Psalter, he spoke of Christ in poetic ways through a multitude of psalms, especially Psalms 110 and 2.

(c) From the prophets themselves, Luther cited Isaiah 9:6, 51:4-5, 51:6, and 60:19-20, and Daniel 9:24ff. and 7:13-14, as pointing to Christ in his twofold nature: divine and human.

In the course of the Old Testament revelation, Luther believed, God expressed himself more and more clearly through ever-new allusions to the promised Christ. Passage after passage was interpreted as a promise of Christ through Luther's insistence on the grammatical, historical, and literal meaning of texts. It is somewhat ironic, therefore, that those of us who have heeded Luther's exhortation to become text critics and learn the grammatical sense now interpret many of those Old Testament texts quite differently. Our present-day knowledge of Semitic languages, in particular, of Hebrew expression, the nature of idioms and of poetic parallelism—all lead us to judge much of Luther's interpretation as a misunderstanding of the language and its forms, that is, "the literal-grammatical sense."

Indirect permeation of the gospel throughout the Old Testament was seen by Luther because of the many prophecies that, he believed, pointed to Christ. In fact the gospel can be said to be present and indeed flood the whole Old Testament land and thus go beyond individual prophetic passages. But if historical exegesis now understands these prophetic passages differently, in what sense can one speak of "gospel" in the Old Testament?

Luther himself offers some clues: maintain a tension between law and gospel throughout the Old Testament and the New. This tension is not an equation of Old Testament with law and New Testament with gospel— a feature of medieval hermeneutics that Luther overcame.[4] On the contrary,

> there is no book in the Bible that does not contain both. God has placed them side by side in every way—law and promise. For he teaches through the law what there is to do, through the promise whence it should be taken. But the New Testament is primarily called gospel above other books because it was written after the advent of Christ, who fulfilled God's promise and through oral preaching publicly disseminated that promise which was before hidden in the Scripture. Insist, therefore, upon this difference; and read whatever book is before you—be it Old or New Testament—with such a difference so that you may notice: where there are promises, that is a gospel book; where there are commandments, that is a law book. But because there are a heap of promises in the New Testament and a heap of commandments in the Old, we call one the gospel book and the other the law book.[5]

Equally instructive is Luther's discussion of the First Commandment. "I am the Lord your God" is the promise of promises which embraces the gospel of Christ. The same commandment can result in either judgment or comfort and thus became law or gospel—depending on the human situation. To the person who thinks he is his own lord and master, the commandment comes as judgment: *I* am the Lord your God. But to the lost and despairing soul who fears God, the word comes as comfort: "I am the Lord *your* God." Thus the same message comes as command and affirmation, as law and gospel.

It was because Luther knew what the gospel was on the basis of the New Testament witness to Christ that he looked back to see the *gospel as promise* witnessed throughout the Old Testament as well. In God's faithful relationship to his people Israel, pointing them again and again to the establishment of his reign, God acts in terms of the *gospel* "preached . . . beforehand to Abraham, saying, 'In you shall all the nations be blessed'" (Gal. 3:8).

We shall now turn to selected theological issues in the Book of Concord in order to demonstrate continuity and discontinuity between the Confessions and the Old Testament.

THE SPOKEN WORD

The gospel is primarily what is spoken and thus heard. The Confessions are unambiguous about the gospel as a message that through the Holy Spirit brings faith (Augsburg Confession, V)[6] and that, when *preached* aright, provides for the true unity of the Christian church (Augsburg Confession, VII).[7] The observance of the holy day in the explanation to the Third Commandment is based solely on the *preaching, teaching,* and *hearing* of the Word of God (Large Catechism, I.91, 92; 95–97).[8] Indeed, the basis of election is the *preaching* of the Word for repentance and forgiveness of sin (Formula of Concord, Solid Declaration, XI.27–28).[9]

Likewise in the Old Testament the Word of God is primarily a message that is addressed to individuals or to nations through the mouth of one of God's spokespersons. Of the 241 times that the expression "Word of the Lord" occurs, 123 texts state that "the Word of the Lord came to . . ." such and such a person, usually a prophet. In many cases this oft-occurring formula simply introduces in editorial fashion the message of God that follows (Jer. 33:19; Hos. 1:1; Joel 1:1; Jon. 1:1; Mic. 1:1; Zeph. 1:1). In other cases the formula seems to be part of the message itself, especially in the autobiographical style "the Word of the Lord came to me" (Jer. 1:4, 11, 13; 2:1; 16:1; Ezek. 6:1).

In either case, however, the major point is this: the Word never says the same thing twice. The context of the message itself is never a neat formula but instead a direct address to a particular person or group at a particular time in history situated at a particular place. This dynamic character of the Word enables God to command Hosea to "take to yourself a wife of harlotry and have children of harlotry" (Hos. 1:2) and to order Jeremiah by contrast, "You shall not take a wife, nor shall you have sons or daughters in this place" (Jer. 16:1). Obviously we would not wish to absolutize either of those expressions of the Word, and so we are challenged to deal with the particularity of each message as it comes to hearers in various conditions of human existence.

That this Word has power to effect what it promises in the many situations of life is of primary import in the Confessions. Pondering the Word, hearing it, and putting it to use enables humans to experience its power of awakening understanding and devotion and of cleansing the heart.

"For these words are not idle or dead, but effective and living" (Large Catechism, I.100–101).[10] In the Old Testament, God's spoken Word effects creation itself (Gen. 1; Ps. 33:6) as well as deliverance and judgment (Jer. 1:9–10). It never returns empty but accomplishes God's intended purpose (Isa. 55:10–11) and even directs history according to his desires and plans (the whole Deuteronomistic history).[11]

The primacy of the spoken Word and its effectiveness is indeed basic to the Lutheran Confessions and to the Old Testament witnesses.

Therefore only the Word makes significant what is seen. The Confessions make it clear that visible signs can serve as means of grace, provided they are instituted with God's command and have added the promise of grace, that is, the spoken Word (Apology XIII.3–4).[12] More specifically, "where the Word is separated from the water, the water is no different from that which the maid cooks with and could indeed be called a bathkeeper's baptism. But when the Word is present according to God's ordinance, Baptism is a sacrament, and it is called Christ's Baptism," (Large Catechism, IV.22).[13] Likewise in his discussion of the Lord's Supper, Luther states, "The Word must make the element a sacrament; otherwise it remains a mere element" (Large Catechism, V.10).[14]

This principle is of utmost importance in interpreting the Old Testament where likewise the Word gives significance to what is seen. Obviously we cannot parallel the application of the principle to sacraments in the Old Testament, but the issue becomes crystal clear in the case of theophanic descriptions. With only one exception (Exod. 24:9–11) every theophany ("God appearance") is played low-key so that the Word of God to his people stands out as the purpose for telling the story.

The classic theophany text is, of course, Exodus 19, where the appearance of God in Mount Sinai is described in terms of a storm and a volcano (vv. 16–18). Yet God is not seen; only the signs of his presence are visible. But even in the midst of these powerful signs what stands out is speech. "And the Lord *called* . . . saying, Thus you shall *say* . . . These are the *words* you shall *speak* . . . Moses . . . *called* . . . and set before them these *words* . . . And all the people *answered* together and *said*, 'All that the Lord has *spoken* we will do.' And Moses *reported* the *words*. . . . And the Lord *said* to Moses, 'Lo, I am coming . . . that the people may *hear* when I *speak* with you' . . . Then Moses *told* the *words* of the people to the Lord. And the Lord *said* . . . Moses *spoke* and God *answered* him in thunder . . . And the Lord *called* to Moses . . . And the Lord *said* to Moses . . . So Moses went down to the people and *told* them."

This monotonous exercise makes the point: The emphasis in the Sinai theophany lies in what is said and heard. The visible signs of God's coming merely pave the way for his Word to be spoken. This issue became so important in Israel's history that the Deuteronomistic historian makes it unconditionally explicit in his description of the event. "Then the Lord spoke to you out of the midst of the fire; you heard the sound of words, but saw no form. There was only a voice" (Deut. 4:12). Indeed, when Elijah fled to Mount Horeb, apparently expecting to experience what Moses did in the past (Exod. 33:21–22), the refugee prophet saw all the signs of a good old theophany—wind, earthquake, and fire—but the Lord was not there except when he spoke, "Go, return on your way . . ." (1 Kings 19:9–18).

Such an emphasis in the Old Testament itself and consistent with the Lutheran Confessions should warn us against false emphases in treating theophanic passages and against truncating the story before the author's own intention is fulfilled. In the call of Isaiah (Isa. 6), the prophet-to-be experiences a glorious theophany in the temple. All the earmarks of a God-appearance are present in the first four verses. Then after his confession of sinfulness Isaiah is treated with a burned lip as the seraph announces forgiveness. But only then does the Lord speak to introduce the reason for the whole spectacle: "Whom shall I send, and who will go for us?" Obviously the text cannot end there! Isaiah responds, "Here am I! Send me." That's where most lectionaries stop—with the result that a prophet is called with no message to speak. In fact, the text goes on in verses 9–13 to explicate the Word of God that Isaiah is to proclaim to the people.

Likewise, failure to apply the principle that the Word gives significance to what is seen can distort the story of Jacob and the proverbial ladder (Gen. 28:10–17). The theophany is highlighted by truncating the pericope at verse 17 with Jacob's exclamation, "How awesome is this place! This is none other than the house of God, and this is the gate of heaven." Tucked away in the middle (vv. 13–15) is the Lord's express promise that he would give to Jacob and his descendants the land and that he will be present with Jacob in a foreign land until he himself brings home the fugitive. Perhaps this message, rather than the theophany and sanctity of the place, would be enhanced by continuing the pericope to include verses 18–22, wherein Jacob responds with a promise of his own to the promises God had made earlier. Nevertheless, with or without the addition of verses 18–22 in a lectionary, the Christian interpreter must concentrate, as the story itself does, on the Word of God addressed to Jacob. This message of God's protection and restoration provides the content and emphasis for a sermon or lesson on this text that is best known in people's minds for its theophany ("We are climbing Jacob's ladder").

The spoken Word of grace, not the deeds and merits of people, brings salvation to the needy. It hardly need be pointed out that Article IV of the Augsburg Confession states without reservation that "we cannot obtain forgiveness of sin and righteousness before God by our own merits, works, or satisfactions, but that we receive forgiveness of sin and become righteous before God by grace, for Christ's sake, through faith. . . ."[15] The proclamation of the cross is the means by which the forgiveness of sins comes to us. "Although the work was accomplished and forgiveness of sins was acquired on the cross, yet it cannot come to us in any other way than through the Word. How should we know that this has been accomplished and offered to us if it were not proclaimed by preaching, by the oral Word?" (Large Catechism, V.31).[16]

There is not, to be sure, in the Old Testament a once-for-all event, the proclamation of which accomplishes forgiveness of sin. But the Old Testament is quite consistent in its understanding that salvation comes by God's grace, as a gift, and not as a result of human endeavor. Particularly instructive in this regard is the use of the word *therefore*. That simple word is indeed a technical term in the form-critical category called "announcement of judgment." That literary genre describes (1) the reason for the accusation followed by (2) the announcement itself, consisting of the intervention of God and the results of his intervention. The reason always describes the activities of people, and the judgment itself is always a portrayal of the activity of God. Between (1) and (2) occurs the word *therefore*, sometimes accompanied by "thus says the Lord" or by "behold." The announcement of judgment is "therefore" always based on the people's behavior (see Isa. 8:5–8; Mic. 3:9–12).

By contrast, an announcement of salvation is not based on the acts of the people. Usually salvation announcements are simple statements about what God will do. "I have seen the affliction of my people who are in Egypt, and have heard their cry . . .; I know their sufferings, and I have come down to deliver them . . ." (Exod. 3:7–8). Sometimes the salvation to come is based on the relationship God had earlier established with his people.

> Behold I will bring them from the north country,
>   and gather them from the farthest parts of the earth, . . .
> *for* I am a father to Israel,
>   and Ephraim is my first-born. (Jer. 31:7–9)

> Fear not, for I have redeemed you;
>   I have called you by name, you are mine.
> When you pass through the waters, I will be with you;
>   and through the rivers, they shall not overwhelm you;
> When you walk through the fire you shall not be burned,
>   and the flame shall not consume you.
> *For* I am the Lord your God,
>   the Holy One of Israel, your Savior. (Isa. 43:1–3)

And indeed there are some announcements of salvation which include the word *therefore.*

> *Therefore,* behold, the days are coming, says the Lord, when men shall no longer say, "As the Lord lives who brought up the people of Israel out of the land of Egypt," but "As the Lord lives who brought up and led the descendants of the house of Israel out of the north country and out of all the countries where he had driven them." Then they shall dwell in their own land. (Jer. 23:7–8)

Of course "therefore" always assumes that some reason precedes the transitional word. What precedes in this case is God's announcement that he will establish his kingdom and raise up a Davidic ruler (23:5–6). Thus it is the gracious activity of God and not the benevolent deeds of the people that provides the basis for salvation from exile and restoration to the land.

Likewise at Isaiah 37:33, "therefore" introduces an announcement of salvation from Sennacherib, whose army has Jerusalem under siege. The Lord's promise to "defend this city to save it, for my own sake and for the sake of my servant David" is based upon the rejuvenation of Judah (vv. 30–32). But that rejuvenation is not Judah's own doing; "the zeal of the Lord of hosts will accomplish this." Immediately there follows our familiar "therefore."

Thus the confessional understanding of the spoken Word that announces judgment on human sinfulness and salvation by God's grace is consistent with the Old Testament witnesses. Indeed, the clear statements in the Confessions drive us back to the Old Testament to interpret its texts according to their theological importance as the Word of God which judges and saves. But it is the *content* of judgment and salvation that presents a contrast between the Old Testament on the one side and the New Testament and the Confessions on the other.

THE GOSPEL, THE WORLD, AND GOOD ORDER

The gospel teaches not an outward and temporal mode of existence but an inward and eternal one. In the discussion of civil government, the Augsburg Confession (Art. XVI.4) indicates that governmental rule and law were instituted and ordained by God for the sake of good order and that Christians may without sin occupy civil offices and perform civil duties. In order to show that the gospel advocates neither overthrow of the government nor forsaking of home and family, the Confession argues: "Actually true perfection consists alone of proper fear of God and real faith in God, for the Gospel does not teach an outward and temporal but an inward and eternal mode of existence and righteousness of the heart."[17] Thus, the gospel does not reject civil authorities, for example, except when their demands cannot be obeyed without sin. A person or group of persons who have been given the gospel must obey God rather than men. But believers neither overthrow nor institute civil authority. That person or group of persons does not withdraw from the world but manifests Christian love in whatever his station in life, even though that station is not identifiable with the gospel.

In the Old Testament one might say that the "church" and state are identical. The people of God is the nation Israel. The effects of his Word of judgment and grace are, therefore, empirical. Salvation and judgment take outward and temporal forms. The "announcements" of the preceding section point to destruction of land and temple and to restoration of city and country. The exodus event itself is a deliverance from the physical bondage of slavery in Egypt to the wide-open spaces of the fruitful land in Canaan. To be sure, there is more at stake in Exodus 1–15 than a change in sociological status. What lies beneath the whole story is a conflict between Yahweh, the God of the Hebrews, and Pharaoh, the god of Egypt. Yahweh's consistent message through Moses to the god-king of Egypt is clear about this: "Let my people go that they may serve *me!*" But the salvation itself is an outward and temporal change of status, without which there is no deliverance.

Throughout the preaching of the preexilic prophets, judgment by God for the people's apostasy, injustice, idolatry, and complacency will be effected by destruction of the land or by loss of land through exile (e.g., Amos 6:1–7; Jer. 4:23–28). And when that exile occurred salvation would take a form which all the world would see (Isa. 52:10), even restoration to the land (see Jer. 31:7–9, above).

All this is not to say that forgiveness of sin is never part of salvation in the Old Testament. On the contrary, Second Isaiah begins his powerful proclamation of the end of Babylonian captivity by announcing that Israel's "iniquity is pardoned" (Isa. 40:2). He continues that emphasis when he reports, "I have swept away your transgressions like a cloud, and your sins like mist; return to me, for I have redeemed you" (44:22). These and a host of other passages from the prophets make clear that since judgment came because of the people's sins, then salvation would follow only by God's forgiveness. But again, that judgment and that salvation take on empirical form; these acts of God are experienced empirically.

Apart from those direct prophecies of judgment and salvation, the motif of "rest" demonstrates the outward nature of the Old Testament over against the inward and eternal mode of the gospel. In the Deuteronomistic corpus in particular the motif of rest plays an important role. In the days of Joshua, David, and Solomon, God gave rest to Israel, a weary people. This rest took the form of the gift of land (Deut. 3:20; 12:9; Josh. 1:13, 15; 21:44), and in that land he gave security or rest from enemies round about (Deut. 12:10; 25:19; Josh. 23:1; 2 Sam. 7:1; 1 Kings 5:4; 8:56). Thus in one specific period in time God brought about a condition of *shalom* in the empirical land.

In 1 and 2 Chronicles God gave rest (as security from enemies) intermittently. Under pious kings Israel experienced this empirical condition (1 Chron. 22:9, 18; 23:25; 2 Chron. 14:5), but in between there was war and chaos. At Isaiah 28:12 the people rejected God's gift of rest (= security from enemies), and in Psalm 95:11 God refused to let the people enter "my rest" (apparently the land) because they rebelled in the wilderness. Only at Exodus 33:14 is it possible that "rest" is something other than land or security from enemies: "My presence will go with you, and I will give you rest." Is this verse a synonymous parallelism whereby God's presence with Moses is itself rest? Or is it sequential in the sense that after the guidance in the wilderness God will give the land? If the former is the correct interpretation, it is the only such understanding of rest in the Old Testament.

This motif is used in two significant places in the New Testament. At Hebrews 3:7–4:13 there is a nicely developed argument to show that hearing the gospel and believing enable people to enter the eschatological rest which God experienced from the creation of the world. Here "rest" seems to be equivalent to the kingdom of God in the eschaton. The second instance is striking. Matthew puts on the lips of Jesus the sayings of Wisdom (see Sir. 6:23–31; 24:1–12; 51:23–30): "Come to me, all who labor and are heavy laden, and I will give you rest. Take my yoke upon you, and learn from me; for I am gentle and lowly in heart, and you will find rest for your souls. For my yoke is easy, and my burden is light" (Matt. 11:28–30). Here rest is not an empirical piece of turf or repose from enemy attack; rather, it is a relationship with Jesus, the Son of God, and through him with God the Father. Rest is unloading the burdens of toil and being confident in the knowledge of God that Christ gives.

But even here the invitation of Jesus does not draw men out of the world, for the Jesus who said, "Come to me . . . and learn . . .," is the resurrected Christ who, at the end of this same Gospel of Matthew, commands his disciples to "go . . . and teach" *in* all the world (Matt. 28:19).

What does a Christian preacher today do with those empirical manifestations of judgment and salvation so common in the Old Testament? He should not, it seems to me, christologize them so that they become prophecies of the New Testament event. Neither should he ignore them as having no significance for Gentiles. Rather, he should heed that good advice of Luther to "learn about the grammatical sense," that is, what it actually meant in the situation for which it was originally intended. Having performed that task, the Christian can begin to see that the physical suffering and empirical liberation of the Old Testament enables him to draw comfort for "spiritual" suffering today. To leave Luther's words, one might say that the problems of the Old Testament people and the response of God to their dilemmas both must be interpreted theologically, so that exile, for example, is not simply a sociological and historical problem of the sixth century B.C. but a theological disaster in which hope and confidence in God's power and concern are lost (see Ezek. 37:11). Understanding exile in such a theological sense opens up

243

possibilities for preaching to theological exiles today. And in doing so some of the concreteness, vitality, particularity, and even empiricism of the Old Testament texts might guarantee that we do not turn the New Testament into an otherworldly mystery religion.

People possess a measure of free will to make decisions on the basis of reason. Article XVIII.1–2 of the Augsburg Confession asserts that while human deeds are not capable of making man acceptable to God, of fearing God and believing in God with his whole heart, man does have a "measure of freedom of the will which enables him to live an outwardly honorable life and to make choices among the things that reason comprehends."[18] The relationship of this article to that concerning civil government (Art. XVI) seems to lie in the area of "good order," that is, one can make good decisions in life for the orderly functioning of government, society, labor, marriage, occupation, and so on.

On the basis of this principle the Christian can look positively at several parts of the Old Testament witness that are too often totally disregarded. One such area of concern is codification of laws which, to the extent that they are in harmony with natural law, are useful for the preservation of society. I would like, however, to concentrate to some extent on another part, namely, proverbial wisdom.

Wisdom was an international, prephilosophical attempt to understand life which includes the human and natural worlds as one realm. By observation of empirical data a person could understand the characteristics that make up life. Inductive reasoning was, therefore, the way ancient man confronted order and acknowledged it. Such indeed was its goal: to understand and participate in order. All order was created by God and belonged to him in the full sense, but man could discipline himself to attain a measure of that order. Thus education was important, for by teaching and learning one gathered together experiences that served as the guide on how to get along in the world in harmony with other people and with nature.

Since wisdom was international it is not surprising to find in the Old Testament Egyptian wisdom (Prov. 22:17–24:22), Aramaic wisdom (the words of Ahiquar scattered throughout Proverbs), Ishmaelite wisdom (words of Agur and of Lemuel in Prov. 30 and 31, respectively) and knowledge of Babylonian (Jer. 50:35), Canaanite (Ezek. 28:3, 17), and Edomite (Jer. 49:7) wisdom. Because wisdom was nonhistorical in its approach and noncultic in its interest, such borrowing by one culture from another presented little problem—particularly because it was also anthropocentric rather than theocentric.

It was a basic contention of wisdom teaching that the good (i.e., the wise) will be rewarded, and that the wicked (i.e., the fool) will be punished. That such a neat system did not always work out in life led to reactions such as those contained in Job and Ecclesiastes. From the point of view of the gospel, of course, that old wisdom tradition is completely unacceptable. The gospel of forgiveness of sins is given not to the righteous but to sinners as God's free, unmerited gift.

But from the point of view of anthropology, that is, that area of life in which man has a measure of free will "to live an outwardly honorable life and to make choices among the things that reason comprehends," wisdom can be quite useful. Indeed, wisdom is good for what it's good for! It is good on a variety of levels, some of which are importance of skill at one's occupation, humanitarian concern for the poor and needy, value of discipline, and use of a variety of pedagogical methods.

For these reasons we Christians should perhaps not be upset when pericopes from Proverbs appear in the lectionary or come up for discussion in teaching a class. While many of the old proverbs will not enable the preacher to proclaim the gospel on the basis of their teaching, nevertheless they might indeed offer helpful advice on an anthropological level to maintain order by the use of free will.

Finally, Jeremiah's letter to the exiles in Babylon (Jer. 29:4–23) is likewise instructive in the use of free will and sense at the same time that it promises salvation and restoration.

> Thus says the Lord of hosts, the God of Israel, to all the exiles whom I have sent into exile from Jerusalem to Babylon: Build houses and live in them; plant gardens and eat their produce. Take wives and have sons and daughters; take wives for your sons, and give your daughters in marriage, that they may bear sons and daughters; multiply there, do not decrease. But seek the welfare [*shalom*] of the city where I have sent you into exile, and pray to the Lord on its behalf, for in its welfare [*shalom*] you will find your welfare. (Jer. 29:4–7)

The Word of the Lord exhorts the people to deal with the reality of judgment of exile. Contrary to the message of prophets in Babylon, Jeremiah writes that this is no passing phase. On the contrary, the people will be in exile a long time, and so on the basis of that reality Jeremiah urges them to carry on normal lives and multiply their numbers (just as the Hebrews became a multitude in the land of Egypt before the Exodus). As regards their attitude toward the city of their captivity, the people are exhorted to pursue *shalom* for it, indeed, to pray for it, because in Babylon's *shalom* the exiles will find their *shalom*. There is nothing here about meriting a deliverance in the near future; and surely there is nothing to indicate that reality was only back home or that captivity was a worldly matter about which God was unconcerned. On the contrary, the Word of the Lord calls upon the exiles to exercise free will and common sense in order to make the city and life in it not only bearable but "complete" (*shalom*).

But there's more. The letter goes on to promise a restoration to the land—in seventy years—and so to give the people "a future and a hope" (vv. 10–11). The promise of restoration in the distant future is the hope and assurance that the Lord has not forgotten, neither will he forget, the exiles whom he sent away in judgment. The exiles thus live in the confidence that God will restore everything and himself be found when they seek him. That hope for future salvation provides the context for the pursuit of happiness in their present situation of exile.

While the details of such a text should not be allegorized, it seems that on the basis of Articles XVI and XVIII of the Augsburg Confession the Christian preacher could use Jeremiah's letter to good advantage by reinterpreting restoration in light of the gospel and by regarding Babylon as life in the world, that is, life apart from paradise.

THE GOSPEL AND COVENANT

The only covenant coexistent with the gospel is that new covenant established by Christ for the forgiveness of sins. References in the Confessions to the word *covenant* are so rare that the General Index in the Tappert edition of the Book of Concord contains no mention of the term.[19] To my knowledge, "covenant" appears in only two passages in Book of Concord—all in reference to the covenant that God established in Christ. As might be expected, greatest attention is given to the "new covenant" in the discussion of the Lord's Supper. In the first instance, the Lord's Supper was instituted "to be observed with great reverence and obedience until the end of the world and . . . to be an abiding memorial of his bitter passion and death and of all his blessings, *a seal of the new covenant*, a comfort for all sorrowing hearts, and a true bond and union of Christians with Christ their head and with one another" (Formula of Concord, Solid Declaration, VII.44).[20] The same article, in the second instance, asserts that Christ added "given for you, shed for you" to prevent misunderstanding; nothing is to be added by way of interpretation or change (VII.50–52).[21]

In like manner—but apart from the words of institution—Article XV.5 of the Apology of the Augsburg Confession states, "to the covenant of God, promising that he will be gracious to us for Christ's sake, we dare not add the condition that we must first earn our acceptance and justification through these observances."[22]

In these statements concerning covenant the Confessions are in complete accord with Pauline theology. In fact, the last quotation is derived from Galatians 3:15: "No one annuls even a man's will [*diathēkē*], or adds to it, once it has been ratified." Moreover, in their insistence that the new covenant is a promise of grace from God, that it is "given," the Confessions are consistent with Paul's sharp distinction between the covenant of promise given to Abraham and the covenant of law given to Moses (Gal. 4:21–31). The "old covenant" that was made with Moses and that leads to condemnation has been surpassed, indeed *replaced*, by the new covenant, which leads to life and freedom (2 Cor. 3:4–11; Gal. 4:21–31). Thus Christians are not the children of Moses but, like Isaac, children of promise, children of Abraham.

All this leads us back into the Old Testament to analyze the various kinds of covenant and to determine their usefulness for the Christian community.

Present-day obsession with "covenant" began in 1954 when George Mendenhall published his profound article on the relation between the outline of the second-millennium Hittite treaties and covenant forms in the Old Testament.[23] The familiar pattern consisting of preamble, historical prologue, stipulations, blessings and curses, witnesses, and provision for reading the treaty has been found in Joshua 24, the structure of the Book of Deuteronomy, and in the Sinai narrative of Exodus 19–24, especially 19:3–8. This covenant type establishes a relationship between two parties on the basis of which the superior pledges protection or support in exchange for the inferior's obedience to the imposed stipulations. Failure to obey the regulations leads to a curse upon the inferior partner.

It is important to note in this treaty form that the initial relationship is based on a historical prologue. The covenant was not made at Sinai until the redeeming act at the Red Sea had already taken place. This sequence is attested to not only by the structure of the Book of Exodus but also by specific texts within:

You have seen what I did to the Egyptians, and how I bore you on eagles' wings and brought you to myself. Now therefore, *if* you obey my voice and keep my covenant, you shall be my own possession among all peoples; for all the earth is mine, and you shall be to me a kingdom of priests and a holy nation. (Exod. 19:4–6)

The salvation event, in other words, does not arise out of the people's obedience; rather, the deliverance serves as the basis for the relationship. After the relationship has been established, it seems, its continuation depends on the obedience of the people. Their subsequent vow, "All that the Lord has spoken we will *do*," seals the agreement, and since that formula appears at Exodus 19:8 and again at 24:3 and 7, *what* they will do is keep the Ten Commandments and the Book of the Covenant—or else! This is the nature of the Mosaic covenant (as well as that of Joshua), which Paul and the Confessions consider contrary to the gospel and the new covenant.

The other type of theological covenant in the Old Testament is the one in which God puts the obligation not on Israel but on himself. In other words, God promises in such a way that the fulfillment is not dependent on obedience to stipulations, although, of course, it is accepted and believed by faith. Such covenants of promise without stipulation are made to Noah (Gen. 9:8–17), to Phinehas (Num. 25:10–13), to David (2 Sam. 7; 23:5; Ps. 89:3, 28–29), and most especially to Abraham (Gen. 15:7–21; 17:1–14; see 12:1–3; 15:1–6). It is not simply this type, but this covenant, of promise with Abraham that God continues and brings to fulfillment in the new covenant in Christ.

Besides those two theological covenants between the Lord and Israel (or individuals), there are attested many covenants between two human partners: Jacob and Laban (Gen. 31:44–50); Abraham/Isaac and Abimelech (Gen. 21:25–32; 26:27–31); Joshua and the Gibeonites (Josh. 8:3–27). Political covenants are made between David and Abner (2 Sam. 3:12); David and the Israelite elders (2 Sam. 5:3); and Nebuchadnezzar and Zedekiah (Ezek. 17:13). None of these covenants is made between members of the same group; they are always made with a member of another group, usually foreigners.

The only covenant made between members of the same group is that between Jonathan and David (1 Sam. 18:1–5). This one is different from all the others listed above because it is based solely on the love between them. Their covenant consists of no specific agreements but only of a deep personal (exclusive?) love, similar in nature to the covenant of marriage described in Malachi 2:13–16. Its content then is one of mutual fidelity.

On the basis of covenant in the Bible and in the Confessions, one must ask serious questions about all the covenant-making in the church today whereby synods and church colleges, synods and congregations, and congregational members themselves make mutual agreements to work together effectively. In the first place, there is no biblical covenant for members of the same group that can be used as a parallel for the accomplishment of projects, fund raising, or the like. In the second place, for the New Testament people of God there is only one covenant that has validity in terms of the gospel: the one promised to Abraham and fulfilled in the death of Christ. This new covenant is already "a true bond and union of Christians with Christ their head and with one another." That union itself, already established, is motive enough to love one another, treat one another with dignity and respect, and work together for the sake of the Kingdom. Thus, we are not called to be makers of covenants but rather to be *"ministers* of a new covenant" (2 Cor. 3:6).

Beyond the issue of our covenant-making fad, a study of the biblical concept of covenant demonstrates several issues of hermeneutical significance. First, there is no need to christologize the Old Testament texts in order to have them point to the New Testament. On the contrary, the element of promise inherent in the Abrahamic type of covenant itself points forward to the time when God will bring to fulfillment his promises, plans, and purposes. Looking back from the New Testament, from the standpoint of faith, we Christians allow those Old Testament texts to speak for themselves and at the same time understand them more clearly in light of God's revelation of himself in his Son. That is to say, the texts had meaning for the original authors and audience apart from the Christ event; they take on meaning for us insofar as they witness to a promise that we believe to be ultimately fulfilled in Christ.

Second, the covenant theme crystallizes the law-gospel issue. The Mosaic covenant in which God places responsibility and obligation on people, insofar as it is consistent with natural law and not simply Jewish folk law, accuses us of our failure to be the creatures God made and intended us to be. In this sense the Mosaic covenant is law, and in this sense it is not excluded. We always stand under its judgment because we are always sinners.

The Abrahamic covenant, on the other hand, addresses us as gospel because it consists of the promise of God's faithfulness and grace which comes to climactic fulfillment in Christ. It is a covenant in which God takes upon himself the burden of faithfulness and continues toward his intended goal, not because of us but in spite of us.

Thus the Confessions are consistent with the New Testament's understanding of covenant, by which one Old Testament type is surpassed—even replaced—and one other type is continued and brought to fulfillment. Like Paul, the Confessions determine what from the Old Testament is yet valid for the saints on the basis of the gospel and what is relevant for sinners on the basis of the law. In this question of covenant the relationship between the Confessions and the Old Testament must be described as both continuous and discontinuous—depending upon the judgment of the gospel.

The issues isolated in this essay are limited, to be sure. One should go on to deal with the nature of ordination viewed over against the Levitical priesthood, the once-for-all effectiveness of the sacrifice of Christ, the nature of sin, and a host of similar issues. It is hoped nevertheless that the issues discussed here and the methodology employed can serve as a paradigm for such further work.

The confessional principle of interpreting all Scripture in light of the gospel serves to enhance the meaning of the Old Testament as well as reinterpret it for appropriate Christian proclamation.

NOTES

1. Heinrich Bornkamm, *Luther and the Old Testament,* trans. Eric W. and Ruth C. Gritsch (Philadelphia: Fortress Press, 1969).
2. Ibid., p. 89.
3. Ibid., p. 92.
4. James S. Preus, *From Shadow to Promise: Old Testament Interpretation from Augustine to the Young Luther* (Cambridge, Mass.: Belknap Press, 1969), pp. 2, 5, 191, 223.
5. Bornkamm, *Luther and The Old Testament,* p. 83.
6. *The Book of Concord: The Confessions of the Evangelical Lutheran Church,* trans. and ed. Theodore G. Tappert (Philadelphia: Fortress Press, 1959), p. 31.
7. Ibid., p. 32.
8. Ibid., pp. 377, 378.
9. Ibid., p. 620.
10. Ibid., p. 379.
11. Gerhard von Rad, *Studies in Deuteronomy* (London: SCM Press, 1953), pp. 74–91.
12. *Book of Concord,* p. 211.
13. Ibid., p. 439.

14. Ibid., p. 448.
15. Ibid., p. 30.
16. Ibid., p. 450.
17. Ibid., pp. 37–38.
18. Ibid., p. 39.
19. Ibid., pp. 651ff.
20. Ibid., p. 577.
21. Ibid., p. 578.
22. Ibid., p. 216.
23. George E. Mendenhall, "Law and Covenant in Israel and the Near East," *The Biblical Archaeologist* 17, no. 2 (May 1954): 26–46; no. 3 (September 1954): 49–76.

Confessional Propria in Relation to New Testament Texts

JOSEPH A. BURGESS
Philadelphia, Pennsylvania

Lutherans, when they explicate their position, might well begin with *sola scriptura*. Yet *sola scriptura* dare not be understood as an assertion of biblical positivism, as an assertion that in a wooden fashion the Bible in all its parts is equally valid. Luther's practice is helpful at this point. When he published his translation of the New Testament in 1522 he placed Hebrews, James, Jude, and Revelation at the end. In contrast to the other New Testament writings, they were not numbered in the table of contents. Like the Apocrypha of the Old Testament, these four books were clearly separated from the previous material by an empty space.

More important were Luther's reasons for doing this. After citing Hebrews 6:4–6, 10:26, and 12:17, Luther concludes: "This seems, as it stands, to be against all the Gospels and St. Paul's Epistles; and although one might make a gloss on it, the words are so clear that I do not know whether that would be sufficient."[1] Concerning James he writes: "Directly against St. Paul and all the rest of Scripture, it ascribes righteousness to works, and says that Abraham was justified by his works. . . . In summary: he wants to guard against those who relied on faith without works, and he is too weak for this task in spirit, understanding and words. He rends the Scriptures and thereby resists Paul and all Scripture."[2] Jude he praises, but "it is an epistle that need not be counted among the chief books which are to lay the foundation of the faith."[3] Revelation he criticizes in the same fashion: "Finally let everyone think of it as his own spirit gives him to think, my spirit cannot fit itself into this book. There is one sufficient reason for me not to think highly of it, that Christ is not taught or known in it."[4]

What Luther did was *Sachkritik*—content criticism. Is what he did to be rejected as an arbitrary and limited viewpoint, or is it part of what is called "discerning the spirits" (1 Cor. 12:20; 1 John 4:1)? Luther himself did not consider his judgments about these four books to be slips of the pen or purely occasional opinion. To be sure, he later modified what he had written about James and Revelation, but the preface to Hebrews remained the same. As is well known, for the rest of his life he was very critical of James; for example, in 1542 in Table Talk he says that James "has no syllable about Christ."[5]

None of this is to imply that Luther did not take Scripture very seriously, for he did, and in its literal sense. To the contrary, precisely because he took Scripture seriously and in its literal sense, he faced the fact that there were problem passages. We, as his spiritual and intellectual heirs, are called upon to do the same.

The issue, of course, is not whether the New Testament is made up of twenty-three books, or even of twenty-two books as in the eastern Syriac church or of thirty-three books as in the Ethiopian canon, although each subtraction or addition is obviously a matter of concern. The issue is whether an individual book is added or subtracted because it does or does not conform to that "something" which makes *scriptura* to be *scriptura*.

The issue, to put it in traditional terms, is that of the canon within the canon. One dare not be apologetic about this much-disputed concept, for there always is a canon within the canon. An examination of the ways various Christian groups use Scripture indicates that no matter what counterclaims may be made each in fact operates with a canon within the canon. It has sometimes been said that each part of Scripture has been found to be useful to some part of the Christian church at some time and (a) therefore there are no impossibly problematic passages in Scripture, (b) therefore there is no "center," such as justification, which governs the rest of Scripture, and (c) therefore Scripture in each of its parts must equally be considered "canon." However, such a concept of the "useful" is very elastic and could just as well be stretched to include such books as 1 Clement and Barnabas, which were included in the canon in some parts of the ancient church. Furthermore, what happens in practice is that a choice is always made, as it must be, between Paul and James.

How is it possible to discern what the "center" of the New Testament is? Can we leave it to the New Testament scholars (or, for that matter, to the systematicians)? As a matter of fact, scholars add to the complexity of the problem.

Take Paul, for example. Stephen Neill writes: "Yet, when we have done our best, we shall always find that the apostle goes beyond us. When we think that we have caught him, like Proteus he escapes from our grasp. . . . We know that we shall always fail."[6] Does this mean that Paul is inconsistent in a way which goes beyond the inconsistency into which each of us as human beings falls? Or does this mean that we have not yet discovered the categories which are needed in order to interpret his theology? Or, more probably, that the categories which are needed can no longer be discovered because we no longer have access to the materials needed for the task?

The problem becomes more complex when we face the question of context. The New Testament scholar tries to find the context of each word in the paragraph, and of the paragraph in the letter Paul has written. But the task does not end here. It is essential also to discover the historical context of each letter, if the material allows, and when this has been done, it turns out, some would say, that each letter applies only to a specific and concrete situation.[7] An additional difficulty is the fact that New Testament scholars often do not agree about these historical contexts. Moreover, once certain less specific, that is to say, more universal lines of Paul's thought have been discovered, it may turn out that they are so foreign (apocalyptic, *heilsgeschichtlich*, Gnostic, or whatever) to our ways of thinking that we would have to de-apocalypticize, de-heilsgeschichticize, de-gnosticize, or de-whatever them before they could apply to our present-day concerns. And all the above has to be said *mutatis mutandis* about every New Testament writer.

The history of the interpretation of New Testament texts adds another dimension to the complexity. The variations in the interpretation of each verse down through church history make evident the problem of depending on the scholars to discern what the "center" of the New Testament is. We today, for example, would not accept many of the exegetical conclusions from the sixteenth century. Even the same scholar within the space of a few years will vary; for example, Krister Stendahl has recently announced basic changes in his exegetical position.[8] And when and if some agree about certain passages or about the New Testament as a whole, their agreement seems to be on the basis of schools of thought, and the opposing camps play the game of "here is a passage which does not fit your analysis" and "you have not dealt with all the evidence."

What is the preacher supposed to do? He knows that right preaching is preaching the "center" of the New Testament. Yet he cannot stop preaching until the scholars somehow agree on this center, for it may be years or the Parousia before that happens. Nevertheless the church has continued down through the centuries.

Then does historical scholarship have any role to play in discerning the "center"? Much in every way. For historical scholarship helps to keep *Sachkritik* honest. It forces us to take the text seriously. As such it is a deadly weapon against any "infallible" tradition which tries to impose itself upon the text.

Sola scriptura equals *solus Christus*. Luther in his Table Talk describes Christ as the *"punctus mathematicus"* of Scripture.[9] More definitive is his famous sentence from 1535: "If the opponents use Scripture against Christ, then we use Christ against Scripture."[10] Christ himself is the foundation on which everything rests, and no other foundation is possible (1 Cor. 3:11). He is "the way, the truth, and the life" (John 14:6). Thus the "center," the truth, is a historical person of a particular time and place. No information about him, even if within the New Testament, is in itself the "center," for he is not the equivalent of information about him. No ideas or combinations of ideas about him, even if within the New Testament, determine who he is, for he is the "truth" who determines what all other truth is. Luther's phrase *was Christum treibet* has become a kind of slogan to summarize this whole approach.

> All the genuine sacred books agree on this, that all of them preach Christ and deal with Him. That is the true test, by which to judge all books, when we see whether they deal with Christ or not, since all the Scriptures show us Christ (Romans 3) and St. Paul will know nothing but Christ (I Corinthians 2). What does not teach Christ is not apostolic, even though St. Peter or Paul taught it; again, what preaches Christ would be apostolic, even though Judas, Annas, Pilate and Herod did it.[11]

This whole approach, however, does not prove to be as useful in determining the "center" as it seems it ought to be, for any and all camps agree that Christ is the "center," and therefore the problem of determining the "center" is no closer to resolution than before. Luther's *was Christum treibet* is in itself simply a phrase, an empty vessel, ready to be filled with whatever each camp is convinced is part of the "center."

Christ as the *punctus mathematicus* of Scripture remains precisely that, without dimension, like the *x* in an equation.

Solus Christus may also be stated as *the gospel.* Once again, however, "gospel" is but a word. It indicates the "something" that is the "center" of the New Testament, but does not in itself establish that "something." In practice "gospel" often serves as a kind of ecumenical wallpaper, covering a host of differences. A look at the New Testament usage of the word shows that we cannot find there a unified sense (such as "the historical person of Christ") which would establish the meaning of this "center." To be sure, the "gospel" is closely identified with Christ in Mark 8:35 and 10:29; in Paul it often means the living power of God in Jesus Christ that effects salvation in the world now (Rom. 1:16; 1 Cor. 1:24; 2:5; 9:16;[12] Gal. 2:5, 14;[13] probably Mark 1:14–15, "kingly rule"). But "gospel" can also mean the revelation about Christ (2 Cor. 2:12; 9:13; 10:14; 11:4; Gal. 1:7–9; Phil. 1:27), the life of Jesus (Mark 1:1; 14:9), teaching about Christ (in pre-Pauline creedal formulas, Rom. 1:3–4; 1 Cor. 15:1–2), and sound doctrine (1 Tim. 1:10–11).

A more generalized approach that is not tied to the concordance asks if there is not an idea, theme, or theology which is the "center," the *gospel.* Some of the proposals have been: Jesus is Lord (Rom. 10:9; 1 Cor. 8:6; 12:3; Phil. 2:11); the tension between already and not yet (although Qumran has this as well); the kingdom of God (Luke 11:20);[14] the resurrection (1 Cor. 15:14); and justification (Rom. 1:16–17).

But each of these formulas, even when it is used as the "central" theme, has relationships to the other formulas and to the other ideas in the New Testament. In Romans 10:9–10 "Jesus is Lord," resurrection, justification, and salvation are all together within one short passage. 1 Corinthians 1:30 has righteousness, sanctification, and redemption in close association with Jesus Christ as our life and wisdom. In Matthew 5:20 the kingdom is based upon a righteousness which exceeds that of the scribes and Pharisees. The distinctive meaning of each concept must, of course, be determined in each verse according to the context.

The question still remains: how is it possible to discover which of these formulas is the "center"? Or is it impossible? Stendahl writes: "I am not sure that 'the gospel' can be so easily summarized under the rubric of 'the justification of the ungodly' (Rom. 4:5; see 5:6; Käsemann, pp. 75, 78 and passim)—or, for that matter, in any other single theme, Pauline or not."[15] The metaphor of the cut diamond is helpful for understanding what is meant by this kind of thinking. The gospel is the diamond. The many facets are the various ideas, themes, and formulas—all of them integral to the diamond. Together they reflect light and are brilliant. It would be impossible to take one facet to be the "center." Metaphors such as the diamond result in equating the gospel with the historical canon of the New Testament.[16]

Stendahl understands that those who emphasize the justification of the ungodly and who think that for Paul the Jew typifies the religious man living by the law are anti-Semitic.[17] Paul was asking not how one finds a gracious God but how his mission to the Gentiles fits into God's plan for the world.[18] One must fault Stendahl for psychologizing Paul (Paul's "innate arrogance" and "elitism")[19] and for not heeding his own warning that New Testament issues are specific and may not apply later[20] when he analyzes Paul's reflections about God's plan. But the most serious error Stendahl makes is not discerning the cosmic dimension of justification for Paul: what is at stake in justification is not primarily conscience but God's lordship over the world and therefore concretely over the individual and also necessarily over Israel.[21]

The gospel equals justification by grace, not works—that is, *sola gratia*. Therefore the proper distinction between law and gospel must be maintained. For Lutherans the justification of the ungodly is the canon.[22] "Justification is no peripheral incident in Pauline thought given a false importance by the Reformation."[23] This does not mean, however, that Paul becomes the canon within the canon, for it is not Paul but justification which is the canon. Nor does this mean that justification as the canon within the canon can in some way still be thought of as one doctrine among others, even though more important, more fundamental, or the necessary first step. Not simply the doctrine, but the event of justification is the canon for all proclamation, doctrine, and life in the church.[24]

The doctrine of the justification of the ungodly (Rom. 4:5) guarantees that grace remains grace and sin remains sin. Justification is pivotal. In *Christ* we become the *righteousness* of God (2 Cor. 5:21); we are justified by his blood (Rom. 5:9). The gospel, the power of God for salvation, reveals the *righteousness* of God (Rom. 1:16-17).

"But now the righteousness of God has been manifested apart from law" (Rom. 3:21). The law does not lead to righteousness; it is not a way of salvation. To distinguish between law and gospel (i.e., to distinguish between salvation through my own righteousness and salvation through the righteousness of God, which is Christ) Luther calls the highest art in Christianity.[25] "All Scripture should be divided into these two chief doctrines, the law and the promises," says the Apology.[26] Galatians 3:18 also contrasts the law and the promise. Similar distinctions are made by Paul between the law and faith (Rom. 3:28; 4:14; Gal. 2:16; 3:11; Phil. 3:9) and between Moses and Christ (2 Cor. 3:7–12; Gal. 4:21–31). Analogous are the contrasts in Paul between the flesh and the spirit (Gal. 5:17) and between the letter and the spirit (Rom. 2:27–29; 7:6; 2 Cor. 3:6), which combine with the distinction between the two aeons (Rom. 12:2; 1 Cor. 1:20; 2:6; 3:18; 2 Cor. 4:4; Gal. 1:4).

For Paul the law brings knowledge of sin (Rom. 3:20; 7:7). The law makes sin increase (Rom. 5:20; see 5:13; 7:5) and revives sin (Rom. 7:9). The law was added because of transgressions (Gal. 3:19); we were confined under the law, under restraint, as a custodian, until Christ came (Gal. 3:23–26). The law is a curse (Gal. 3:10, 13). The law cannot make alive (Gal. 3:21). The law brings wrath, sin, and death (Rom. 4:15; 8:2; see 7:23; 2 Cor. 3:6). Some have sought to establish their own righteousness (Rom. 10:3), but "we hold that a man is justified by faith apart from works of law" (Rom. 3:28; Gal. 2:16; 3:11–13). But now we are "not under law, but under grace" (Rom. 6:14; 7:6). "For Christ is the end of the law" (Rom. 10:4) and we are redeemed from the law (Gal. 4:5; see 3:13).

In order that no one pretend that Paul only wrote such things concerning the law because of particular concerns he had for Rome and Galatia, other striking references must be mentioned: "The sting of death is sin, and the power of sin is the law" (1 Cor. 15:56); Moses brought a dispensation of death carved in letters on stone, but the dispensation of righteousness has a splendor that causes the old covenant "to have no splendor at all" (2 Cor. 3:7–18); "not having a righteousness of my own, based on law, but that which is through faith in Christ" (Phil. 3:9).

In Qumran justification was also "of the ungoldly" and by grace alone. But this does not mean that Paul builds on Qumran. In contrast to Paul, sin stands in opposition to the law (1QH 4:10), justification means taking up once again salvation by the law, and thus there is no antithesis between faith and works. Faith in Christ, of course, was also not a factor.[27]

It must be mentioned that there are a few uses of the word *law* that do not seem consistent in Paul. There is no guarantee that Paul could never be inconsistent, but it is also true that we must not expect in him a computerlike use of language (in every case we must understand a word in context) and we must always try to follow the flow of his argument. Most of the places where Paul's use of "law" seems inconsistent are in Romans 7:7–25. It would seem strange if in this passage Paul suddenly took back what he had said about the law in the previous four chapters and especially in the immediately preceding chapter: "For sin will have no dominion over you, since you are not under law but under grace" (Rom. 6:14). When Romans 7:7–25 is seen as parallel to Romans 5:12–21 and as the working out of the antithesis between the law and the Spirit announced in Romans 7:1–6, and when therefore Adam is the subject in Romans 7:7–11 and the non-Christian seen from a Christian point of view is the subject in Romans 7:13–25, then the varieties of "law" in Romans 7:7–25 fall into place.[28] Because of Romans 7:1–6, the use of "law" in Romans 8:4 and 13:8–10 is best seen as based on formulations he adopted from elsewhere.[29] Galatians 5:14 and 6:2, in view of 3:13, 4:5, and 5:4, should be understood in a similar fashion. Romans 3:31 seems paradoxical until one notices that it is a transition to Romans 4; it picks up the point raised in Romans 3:21b and sets the theme for the next chapter that God's will in the Old Testament can only become visible where the "law" is no longer a way of earning salvation. In this sense the "law" does not contradict justification by faith but points to it (see Gal. 2:19).[30]

It may be suggested that Paul teaches justification by faith now but then at the final judgment salvation will be by works (Rom. 2:6–11; 5:9–10; 2 Cor. 5:10).[31] There can be no question that Paul holds to an eschatological judgment according to works (Rom. 2:6–11; 1 Cor. 3:13–15; 9:17; 2 Cor. 5:10; 9:6; Gal. 6:7–9). But there can also be no question that for Paul the eschatological judgment according to works is to be understood from the perspective of justification.[32] "God's forgiving grace is that of the judge, and faith may not, before it becomes sight, lose sight of God the judge, which simply means that faith is always based only on grace, and thus justification never becomes a quality which one possesses."[33] At the same time God the judge cannot be separated from God who is grace; the righteousness of God which we receive as a gift through faith is a power active in the present calling us constantly to responsibility, and to that extent every day is the last judgment.[34]

After Paul his doctrine of justification continues only within the so-called Deutero-Pauline literature and more as fixed formulations. Ephesians 2:8–9: "For by grace have you been saved through faith; and this is not your own doing, it is the gift of God—not because of works, lest any man should boast." Titus 3:5–8: "He saved us, not because of deeds done by us in righteousness, but in virtue of his own mercy . . . so that we might be justified by his grace and become heirs in hope of eternal life. The saying is sure." At the same time the word *righteousness* turns into "uprightness": "But as for you, man of God, shun all this; aim at righteousness, godliness, faith, love, steadfastness, gentleness" (1 Tim. 6:11; see Eph. 4:24; 5:9; 2 Tim. 2:22; 3:16). "Nevertheless one sees in this process that the internal validity of Paul's doctrine of justification does not depend on standing in historical opposition to Judaism."[35]

The Book of Acts, although it reports about Paul, reflects a theology of salvation history rather than Paul's doctrine of justification. Cornelius is "a devout man who feared God" (Acts 10:2), "an upright and God-fearing man" (Acts 10:22), and Peter concludes: "Truly I perceive that God shows no partiality, but in every nation any one who fears him and does what is right is acceptable to him" (Acts 10:34–35). Forgiveness and grace are supplements to what our own works cannot achieve (Acts 13:38–39; 15:7–11). Paul is said to have circumcised someone who was already a Christian, Timothy (Acts 16:1–3; see Gal. 2:3!). A sermon attributed to Paul says that God "is not far from each one of us," for we are "God's offspring" (Acts 17:22–31; see 14:15–17; 2 Pet. 1:4).

Although the Letter to the Hebrews has also been associated with Paul, its doctrine of no second repentance stands in contradiction to Paul's doctrine of justification: "For it is impossible to restore again to repentance those who have enlightened . . . if they then commit apostasy" (Heb. 6:4–6); Esau "found no chance to repent" (see Heb. 10:26; Mark 3:28–30; 1 John 5:16–17).

The Book of James may actually have intended to correct Paul or a "misunderstood" Paul; in any case, it does not agree with Paul's doctrine of justification. Since faith means agreeing with objective facts (James 2:19), then faith alone is not enough and must be supplemented with works (James 2:24; 1:22–25).[36] It is not possible to say that these are simply terminological differences (i.e., that "faith" means something different in James from what it means in Paul), for James 5:19–20 ("whoever brings back a sinner from the error of his way . . . will cover a multitude of sins"; see 1 Pet. 4:8) can hardly be made to fit into the Pauline doctrine of justification, no matter what the terminology.

The proper distinction between law and gospel is derived from the cross. *Crux sola est nostra theologia.*[37] " 'The crucified Jesus is the Christ' is the center which defines Paul's whole thought and thus also what he says about the law"; and his negation of the law is a direct result of the meaning of the cross: "If justification were through the law, then Christ died to no purpose" (Gal. 2:21).[38]

There is no cross in the Old Testament; we are not Jews.[39] In the New Testament, Paul has the only developed theology of the cross. Just as he juxtaposes law and gospel when he writes against his opponents in Galatia, so he juxtaposes wisdom and the cross in writing against his opponents in Corinth. Thus he writes, "For Jews demand signs and Greeks seek wisdom, but we preach Christ crucified, a stumbling block to Jews and folly to Gentiles, but to those who are called, both Jews and Greeks, Christ the power of God and the wisdom of God" (1 Cor. 1:22–24; see Rom. 5:6; Gal. 5:11; Phil. 2:8). The centrality of the cross, which corresponds to the centrality elsewhere in Paul of Christ, the gospel, and justification, is expressed in another famous passage: "For I decided to know nothing among you except Jesus Christ and him crucified" (1 Cor. 2:2; see Gal. 6:14). The perfect-passive participle used here indicates an event which happened in the past but also that the one who was crucified is always present in proclamation and worship.[40] The word of the cross is the *power* of God "to us who are being saved" (1 Cor. 1:18). We carry in our bodies "the death of Jesus, so that the *life* of Jesus may also be manifested in our bodies" (2 Cor. 4:10; see 13:4; Rom. 6:3–11; Gal. 2:19–29; 5:24; Phil. 3:9–11).

This *power* and this *life* are manifestly not power and life according to the standards of worldly wisdom. There is a "foolishness" about them. Preaching the gospel cannot be by human wisdom, for it is precisely in our foolishness from the world's viewpoint that the power of the cross, which is God's power, can be effective through the Holy Spirit (1 Cor. 1:17, 19, 24–25; 2:3–5, 13). The same point is made by Paul about signs (miracles); the cross is a stumbling block to any worldly understanding of signs, for it is in the weakness of the cross that God is strong (1 Cor. 1:22–29). When we are weak, we share Christ's weakness, but precisely in this weakness is God's power (2 Cor. 1:4–6; 4:10–11; 11:30; 12:7–10; 13:2–4; Phil. 3:10).[41]

To be sure, the cross, precisely because it is "weakness" in this world of flesh, continues (*sub contrario*) as before to be involved with sin, sickness, ambiguity, and death. Christians continue (*simul*) to sin (Rom. 6:12–13 [in spite of 6:14, 16–18; 7:5–6]; 8:10–13; 13:14; 1 Cor. 3:3; Gal. 5:17), become sick (1 Cor. 11:30), face ambiguity (Rom. 8:23; 1 Cor. 13:9, 12; 2 Cor. 4:7; 11:14!), and die (1 Cor. 11:30; 1 Thess. 4:13). Although Christ's death and resurrection have taken place (Rom. 4:25;

8:33–34; 14:9; 1 Cor. 15:3–6; 1 Thess. 4:14), we have joined him only in his death, not in his resurrection (Rom. 6:3–8; 1 Cor. 15:52; Phil. 3:9–11; cf. Col. 2:12–13; 3:1, 7–10); we shall surely join him in his resurrection, but at the Parousia.

In Ephesians 2:16 and Colossians 1:20 and 2:14 the cross has become the "means of reconciliation."[42] The word is lacking in the Pastorals. In Hebrews 12:2 the cross is exemplary, as it is in Mark 8:34 (par. Matt. 10:38; Luke 14:27; John 15:12–13). In Acts 3:17 and 13:27–28 the cross is a miscarriage of justice, caused by the fact that the Jews were ignorant of the Old Testament; in Acts 2:23 and 4:28 the meaning of the cross is that it is part of predestined salvation history. In John the death on the cross is the "departure" to another sphere of existence (John 13:1; 14:3). To be lifted up on the cross is to be exalted into heavenly glory (John 3:14; 8:28; 12:32–34), and whoever believes in this exalted one has eternal life; he will participate in the heavenly glory (John 14:1–3). The "hour" of being glorified means being lifted up, exalted on the cross (John 7:30; 8:20; 12:23; 13:31–32); the Father has appointed this "hour" of glorification (John 12:27–28; 18:11; 19–11; see 8:28).[43]

Sola cruce leads necessarily to *sola fide*.[44] Since life in the power of the cross is "foolishness" and "weakness," we live by the *certainty* of faith, not by *securitas*. We have no guarantees as the world reckons guarantees; all experience, including the experience of faith itself, is ambiguous. The *certainty* of faith based upon God's faithfulness to his promise stands over against a *securitas* based on faith or any other experience. Not even the canon within the canon can be the canon for us unless "the Holy Spirit produces faith, where and when it pleases God, in those who hear the Gospel" (Augsburg Confession, V).[45] The *testimonium internum Spiritus sancti* has traditionally been a Calvinist proprium; the Lutheran stress has been on *faith* effected by the Holy Spirit *in the gospel*.

The word *faith* is used in many ways in the New Testament, and it must in each case have its meaning not only in the immediate context but also in the total context of the author's theology. Paul does use the word to mean *fides quae* (Rom. 10:8–9; 1 Cor. 15:11; Gal. 1:23; 6:10) and virtue (1 Cor. 13:13 [formula?]; 1 Thess. 1:3). But he also uses the word to mean a state of faith and "having faith in" (Rom. 4:20; 14:22; 1 Cor. 2:5; 16:13; 2 Cor. 1:24; 13:5; Gal. 2:20; 1 Thess. 3:2, 5–7; Philem. 6). What he means by this usage is shown by the contrast he draws between law and faith (Rom. 3:22, 28, 31; 4:14; Gal. 2:19–20; 3:12, 23, 25), sin and faith (Rom. 3:25; 14:23), and works and faith (Rom. 3:20–22, 27; 4:2–6; 9:32; Gal. 2:16; see Rom. 9:11–12; 11:6), a contrast identical to the contrast noted earlier between law and gospel.

Faith is an empowered faith, for it is in the gospel which is the power of God for salvation (Rom. 1:16); it is not an abstract faith, a mere assent. The righteousness of God that is ours as a gift through faith cannot be separated from the God who gives, who is effective, and who is also God the judge; thus the righteousness of God is "a power active in the present calling us constantly to responsibility."[46] Thus there is an "obedience of faith" (Rom. 1:5), "obedience in acknowledging the gospel of Christ" (2 Cor. 9:13), "faith active in love" (Gal. 5:6), and therefore the "work of faith" (1 Thess. 1:3; see 1:8; 3:6; 5:8; Gal. 5:22; 1 Cor. 13:13). Nevertheless, faith is faith in the cross, which is foolishness and weakness and not "sight" (2 Cor. 5:7). There can be grades of faith (Rom. 12:3), lacks in faith (1 Thess. 3:10), and weakness in faith (Rom. 14:1; see Phil. 2:12–13; 3:12–14).

Once again literature in the Pauline trajectory echoes Paul, but in a formulaic fashion (Eph. 2:8–9; 2 Tim. 1:9; Titus 3:5). Faith has become "the faith," *fides quae* (Col. 1:23; 1 Tim. 1:4; 3:9; 4:1; 6:20–21; 2 Tim. 4:7; Titus 1:1, 4; see 1 John 5:4–5) and a virtue (Col. 1:4; 1 Tim. 1:5, 14; 2:15; 4:12; 6:11; 2 Tim. 1:3; 2:22; Titus 2:2; see Rev. 2:19). Although faith and works are listed together in the same verse in Hebrews 6:1, they are not set in opposition; faith is another work, assent, as it is in Hebrews 11:6 (see Heb. 4:2; 10:26; 11:27), and has become a virtue allied closely with hope (Heb. 10:22; 11:1; see Rom. 4:18–20). In James faith is not even a work and is useless without works (James 2:14–26); its testing produces steadfastness (James 1:2–3).

In Mark man does his part, Jesus does the rest: "I believe; help my unbelief" (Mark 9:24; see 2:5; 4:40; 5:34, 36; 6:6; 10:52; 11:22–23). Matthew has the same pattern: "According to your faith be it done to you" (Matt. 9:28–29; see 8:10, 13; 15:28; 17:20); so does Luke: "Your faith has made you well" (Luke 17:19; see 17:6). In John faith is a curious mixture. Faith may begin with signs (John 11:45–48) and may be based, at least to some degree, on "earthly things" (John 3:12). Yet faith is in Jesus (John 5:38, 46; 8:45–46; 10:37–38; 4:11), his word (John 2:22), and his works (John 10:38; 14:11), as well as in the doctrine (*fides quae*) about Jesus (John 11:27). He who believes in Jesus has life (John 3:15; 5:24; 11:26), and to believe in Jesus means to depart this world in order to participate in Jesus' heavenly glory (John 14:1–3). The believer is at this point, however, still in the world and endangered by the evil one

(John 17:15); he is exhorted to good works (John 5:29; 6:28–29) and given a new law (John 13:34; 15:12, 17), although the old law has not been rejected (John 1:45; 3:14; 5:39, 46; 1:17 must be understood in this context). Nevertheless it is God who causes men to hear (be born) (John 1:13; 8:47; 18:37; see 6:44, 65), it is Jesus who has chosen them out of this world (John 1:12, 15, 19; 17:14), and it is by the Spirit that one is born (John 3:5–6).

Is there sometimes the need to preach against the text? In what possible sense can one say that every text contains law and gospel? These questions apply first of all to the Old Testament. "Not only the law, but all Old Testament prophecy and all the institutions of Jewish religion are reinterpreted in the light of Paul's vision of Jesus as the righteousness of God. . . . Justification thus provides perspective for a comprehensive hermeneutics of the Old Testament."[47] We can use the Old Testament because we reinterpret it. In the second place these questions apply to the New Testament. Not every text in the New Testament can be taken as it stands. Where the text, after being carefully examined, does not stand for *sola gratia,* something radical must take place. The text must be either reinterpreted or preached against or omitted. This has important implications for what is usually understood by expository preaching.

Do we find the propria in the Scripture or do we bring them to the Scripture? The decision for justification by grace through faith in the cross of Jesus Christ is a gift; it "cannot be settled by the historian according to the results of his investigations but only by the believer who is led by the Spirit and listens obediently to the Scripture."[48] Furthermore we cannot wait for the historian to decide and for the historians to come to a consensus.

Is it possible to describe this position as triumphalism or arrogance? This question is asked with a kind of uncomprehending astonishment. For those who stand at the foot of the cross, whose lives are centered in the cross, all triumphalism and arrogance are impossible.[49]

NOTES

1. *D. Martin Luthers Werke,* Deutsche Bible (Weimar, 1906–61), 7: 344 (hereafter cited as WA, DB). See *Luther's Works* (St. Louis: Concordia Publishing House; Philadelphia: Fortress Press, 1955–   ), 35: 394–95 (hereafter cited as *LW*).

2. WA, DB 7: 384. See *LW* 35: 396–97.

3. WA, DB 7: 384. See *LW* 35: 398.

JOSEPH A. BURGESS

4. *WA, DB* 7: 404. See *LW* 35: 399.
5. *D. Martin Luthers Werke,* Tischreden (Weimar, 1912–21), 5, no. 5443 (hereafter cited as *WA,* TR). See *LW* 54: 424.
6. Stephen Neill, *Jesus through Many Eyes: Introduction to the Theology of the New Testament* (Philadelphia: Fortress Press, 1976), pp. 72–73.
7. See Krister Stendahl, *Paul among Jews and Gentiles and Other Essays* (Philadelphia: Fortress Press, 1976), pp. 48, 75–76. As a consequence, what Paul writes is so localized that it is no longer possible to draw any conclusions or even to distinguish truth from error!
8. Ibid., p. vi.
9. *WA,* TR 2, no. 2383.
10. *Urgemus Christum contra scripturam. WA,* DB 39: 1, 47. See *WA,* DB 40: 1, 458–59.
11. *WA,* DB 7: 384. See *LW* 35: 396.
12. See Gerhard Friedrich, "*Euanggelion,*" in *Theologisches Wörterbuch zum Neuen Testament,* ed. Gerhard Kittel (Stuttgart: Kohlhammer, 1935), 2: 729.
13. See Peter Stuhlmacher, *Das paulinische Evangelium: I Vorgeschichte* (Göttingen: Vandenhoeck & Ruprecht, 1968), pp. 90, 106–8.
14. The "kingdom" is a popular proposal today for the "center," but like "gospel," "kingdom" means many differing things in the New Testament. To be sure, some deal with these differences by redefining "kingdom" in terms of justification, Jesus is Lord, and the like.
15. Stendahl, *Paul among Jews and Gentiles,* p. 130.
16. With the diamond analogy and similar devices that equate the themes of the New Testament, the "center" is lost. It is assumed that the "center" is all, so that in a fundamentalistic fashion the historical canon is the "center."
17. Stendahl, *Paul among Jews and Gentiles,* pp. 127, 131–33. By implication, Bornkamm and Käsemann. In logic this is called poisoning the well.
18. Ibid., pp. 130–32.
19. Ibid., pp. 73, 76.
20. Ibid., pp. 48, 75–76.
21. Ernst Käsemann, *An die Römer, Handbuch zum Neuen Testament,* vol. 8a (Tübingen: J. C. B. Mohr, 1974), p. 254.
22. Wilhelm Dantine, *Justification of the Ungodly,* trans. Eric W. and Ruth C. Gritsch (St. Louis: Concordia Publishing House, 1968), pp. 138–39. Inge Lønning, "*Kanon im Kanon*": *Zum dogmatischen Grundlagenproblem des neutestamentlichen Kanons,* Forschungen zur Geschichte und Lehre des Protestantismus 43 (Munich: Chr. Kaiser Verlag, 1972), p. 272. See, e.g., Augsburg Confession, XXVIII. 52; Smalcald Articles II.1, in *The Book of Concord: The Confessions of the Evangelical Lutheran Church,* trans. and ed. Theodore G. Tappert (Philadelphia: Fortress Press, 1959), pp. 89, 292.
23. Warren A. Quanbeck, "Justification and Baptism in the New Testament," *Lutheran World* 8 (1961): 12.
24. Hermann Diem, *Was Heisst Schriftgemäss?* (Neukirchen Kreis Moers: Verlag der Buchandlung des Erziehungsvereins, 1958), p. 74; Lønning, "*Kanon im Kanon,*" p. 156.
25. *WA,* DB 36: 9.
26. Apology, IV.5, in *Book of Concord,* p. 108.
27. Günther Klein, "Rechtfertigung: I. Im NT," in *Die Religion in Geschichte und Gegenwart,* 3d ed., vol. 5 (Tübingen: J. C. B. Mohr, 1961), cols. 825–26.
28. Käsemann, *An die Römer,* pp. 182–202.

29. Ibid., pp. 207, 345–46.

30. Ibid., pp. 97–98.

31. It should be noted, however, that Paul writes not only of salvation coming at the end but also of salvation as a present activity (1 Cor. 1:18; 15:2; 2 Cor. 2:15; 6:2; see Rom. 10:10).

32. Käsemann, *op. cit.*, pp. 52–53.

33. Rudolf Bultmann, *Der zweite Brief an die Korinther*, Kritisch-Exegetischer Kommentar über das Neue Testament (Göttingen: Vandenhoeck & Ruprecht, 1976), p. 146.

34. Käsemann, *op. cit.*, p. 53.

35. Klein, "Rechtfertigung," col. 827.

36. Ibid., cols. 827–28.

37. WA, DB 5: 176. See "Crux Christi unica est eruditio verborum dei, Theologica syncerissima"; WA, DB 5: 217.

38. Walter Gutbrod, "*Nomos*," in *Theologisches Wörterbuch zum Neuen Testament*, ed. Gerhard Kittel (Stuttgart: Kohlhammer, 1942), 4: 1063.

39. Often the cross is reduced to every *thlipsis* or to the general idea of suffering. For example a "cross" can be said to be any trouble or difficulty. As a consequence the radicality of the cross of Jesus Christ is lost. We will of necessity have ideas about the cross, but it is also necessary to keep in mind that we start from the "meta-event" of the cross, not from ideas or combinations of ideas about it.

40. Johannes Schneider, "*Stauroō*," in *Theologisches Wörterbuch zum Neuen Testament*, ed. Gerhard Kittel (Stuttgart: Kohlhammer, 1964), 7: 582.

41. The rhetorical irony in 1 Cor. 4:10 should be noted. Rom. 5:6 refers to the non-Christian, as the exact parallel in Rom. 5:8 indicates.

42. Schneider, "*Stauroō*," p. 576.

43. Georg Bertram, "*Hypsoō*," in *Theologisches Wörterbuch zum Neuen Testament*, ed. Gerhard Kittel (Stuttgart: Kohlhammer, 1969), 8: 608–9. Peter Stuhlmacher, *Gerechtigkeit Gottes bei Paulus* (Göttingen: Vandenhoeck & Ruprecht, 1965), p. 196, holds that "glory" in John is the same as "justification" in Paul.

44. It might be asked if any one of the five Lutheran "*solas*" is superior to the others. But they are all equal and all really mean the same thing.

45. *Book of Concord*, p. 31.

46. Käsemann, *op. cit.*, p. 53.

47. Quanbeck, "Justification and Baptism in the New Testament," p. 13.

48. Ernst Käsemann, *Essays on New Testament Themes*, Studies in Biblical Theology 41, trans. W. J. Montague (London: SCM Press, 1964), p. 223.

49. Some may reject the position held in this essay by calling it "hyper-Paulinism," but they are left with these questions: What is their alternative? Will it be relativism? Or will it simply be the historical canon and therefore a kind of fundamentalism? Or John? Or James? Or Matthew? Or Luke? Or will it be a hollow vessel labeled "Jesus" or "kingdom"? Or will it be an abstract idea, such as "grace"? Or will the "church" decide, so that Christology is made subordinate to ecclesiology?

PART III

Methods of Interpretation — The Historical-Critical Method as Hermeneutic?

Methods of Interpretation: Old Testament Texts

RONALD M. HALS

Professor of Old Testament
Trinity Lutheran Seminary
Columbus, Ohio

The names of methods are not of the essence of interpretation. More important is what we do. Even more important is why we do it. Here two different kinds of "why" questions are relevant. To the question about why we do it at all, the response is that we come from the experience of having been addressed, and so we do it in expectation. The second "why" aspect is why we do precisely what we do. There the response is that the text itself suggests it. There is no pattern for exegesis. Every answer to every question must be reevaluated continually in the light of further questions and further answers. Here I propose to sketch first the "doing" of a text, Ezekiel 18, and then to reflect on what it was that was done.

EXEGETICAL CONSIDERATIONS

Ezekiel 18 seems to present an argument between God and his people. The people express an experience of God's injustice (vv. 2, 19, 25, 29). To this, God via his prophet opposes an affirmation of God's justice and more. While the people see in the events a challenge to God's justice, God sees a challenge to Israel to repent.

Along the way something else provides the pattern for verses 5–24, the section which comes between the initial posing of the argument's two sides in verses 2–4 and the final summation in verses 25–32. What appears in this middle section is manifestly a series of three hypothetical cases. The beginning of each case (vv. 5, 10, 14) is given in a traditional, priestly, legal formulation.[1] Further, the end of each case (vv. 9b, 13b, 17b) reflects the style of a declaratory verdict, verse 13b that of a death sentence picking up the end of verse 4, and verses 9b and 17b that of a corresponding verdict of life. Verse 9b prefixes "he is righteous" to the verdict of life, thereby picking up the beginning of verse 5. The list in between in verses 5b–9a is patently an elaboration of what "righteous" means. It calls to mind similar lists in Psalms 15 and 24, which reflect a liturgical ceremony conducted at the sanctuary gate, the so-called gate liturgy or entrance *torah*. There, in a dialogue between a priest and a worshiper seeking admission, an avowal of loyalty in the shape of a confession of obligation was required. Those who participated in such an entrance rite were admitted to the "congregation of the righteous" (Ps. 1:5), presumably by means of the declaratory verdict "He is righteous" pronounced by the priest after the pattern of similar such declaratory priestly pronouncements in Leviticus 1:17, 2:15, 13:3, and possibly Genesis 15:6. It should be clear from its liturgical function that such a confession is one of allegiance or obligation, not of achievement. It should also be clear that Ezekiel has quite likely modified the materials of these old lists by adding, particularly at the beginning, phrases that disavow precisely those sins of which he has been accusing his contemporaries.

The content of the list of corresponding sins in verses 10–13a is simply derived from verses 6–9a by selecting a sampling of opposites. Then in verses 15–17a we encounter verses 6–9a virtually repeated in slightly condensed form.[2] What follows in verses 18–24 is a kind of assessment of what can be concluded from these three cases. In verses 18–20 it is pointed out that, contrary to what the people are reported to say, the fate of a son is not tied to that of his father. Instead each person, whether righteous or wicked, is seen to be responsible for his own fate. It is further noted in verses 21–23 that a wicked person can change and that when he does his fate will change, this being in fact what God really wants to happen. Of course, as verse 24 adds, it is also possible for a righteous person to change, his fate then also changing.

In verses 25–32 the entire course of the argument is summed up. The people's claim that God is not just (v. 25a) is countered by God's claim that his people are not just (v. 25b). It is again noted that a righteous person can change his fate (v. 26) and that the wicked can also change (vv. 27–28). Once again the people's claim (v. 29a) and God's claim (v. 29b) are repeated. Then in verse 30a a judgment of every individual is announced, followed by a call to repent and live through getting a new heart in verses 30b–31. This in turn leads to the final repeated affirmation that it is the life of his people that God really wants. On this note of invitation the argument closes.

We can assess this chapter as a kind of preaching to despondent exiles (see Jer. 31:27ff. and frequently in Second Isaiah, e.g., 40:27ff.), but also as a type of preaching going back earlier (Mic. 2:6–11) and continuing on later (Mal.). Also familiar and frequent is the using of a pattern borrowed from worship life. Again Second Isaiah uses hymns (42:10ff.) and Isaiah 63:7ff. uses a lament. Often such borrowings are parodies (Amos 4:4; Isa. 33:14–16). This use of a worship pattern would have been especially meaningful in exile, where a cultic assurance of righteousness and life was no longer possible in the old way. Now a new way is offered— and by a priest! Similarly a priest whose office involved legal practice now uses hypothetical cases for a transformed, what we would call pastoral, purpose.

In all this, little that is basically new appears. Individual responsibility of sons and fathers appears in Deuteronomy 24:16 and was prominent in the record of Israel's recent past, if an early edition of the Deuteronomistic history can be assumed. Repentance and apostasy as schematized possibilities involving a reversal in verdict are found in Jeremiah 18. God's overwhelming preference for the repentance and life of his sinful people and his willingness to change his mind are prominent already in Hosea 11. Life and death as the basic alternatives to which people are challenged are characteristic of psalms like 30 and 88, and especially of wisdom material, whether in Proverbs or in Psalm 1, and of homiletical appeal as in Deuteronomy 30:15ff. Even the specific image of a new heart is no unique phrase, as Psalm 51:10, Jeremiah 24:7, Jeremiah 31–32, and other passages here in Ezekiel show.

It is interesting, though, to note how verse 31 stands in some contrast to the other passages about a new heart and spirit elsewhere in Ezekiel. What appears as a demand in 18:31 comes as a promise in 36:26ff. and in 11:19ff. While we recognize the profound theological truth that God does graciously give what he demands, for that is the only way obedience can come, we also note a progression in the presentation of Ezekiel's preaching. Before the fall of Jerusalem in 587 b.c., he faces a stubbornly confident audience to whom he preaches judgment and repentance. After 587 he speaks consolingly to a despairing audience, promising a gracious new act of God. Chapter 36 comes in the section of Ezekiel's book following the year 587, and chapter 18 in that section preceding. Chapter 11 is initially a message of judgment, but verses 14–21 add a brief condensation of the good news of chapter 36, possibly by way of advance sampling but more likely as a later elaboration, perhaps by the prophet himself, when his message was collected.

A parallel kind of rounding out of the assembled message of Ezekiel may be what lies behind the condensed summarizing of chapter 18 in 33:10–20, this time in order to spell out the setting of judgment preaching over against which the message of hope begins in chapter 33ff. This conclusion may be supported by the presence of a kind of brief rehearsing of the prophet's role in 33:1–9 parallel to the more extensive call account in chapters 1–3.

But the understanding of a biblical text is not finished when its content and background are looked at. The ongoing history of that text's meaning is important, for in a real sense a text's context extends into the rest of the Scriptures. This is especially true of a text from the Old Testament, for the very label *Old* Testament confesses the perspective of the *New* Testament.

No biblical material is preserved apart from an intention for its future use. When we ask what significance Ezekiel 18 would have as used by the later community of Israel, we enter the realm of the virtually totally conjectural. And yet if we are to consider the bits of information of possible significance in reconstructing the process of the preservation of a prophetic message of judgment (Isa. 8:16–18; 30:8ff.; and Jer. 36), it seems likely that such a message was preserved in the light of its fulfillment. That is, the twin aspects of doxology of judgment ("God was right to destroy us") and of admonition ("Don't let it happen again") would be inescapable, viewing subsequent history as the vindication of this message of judgment. Nonetheless, the hope for a fulfillment which would pick up on the offer of life, the possibility of change from wickedness to righteousness, and God's desire for life rather than death, seems also an inescapable part of the process of preservation. Within the New Testament we encounter a witness to a making alive of the dead by the God who loves even those dead in their sins (Eph. 2:4ff.) and an affirmation of the way God still finds joy nowhere as much as in the repentance of the sinner (Luke 15). Also in the New Testament we find a challenging summons to choose between the two ways, life and death, by choosing life (Matt. 7:13–14) and by expressing that choice in appropriate deeds (Matt. 7:15–27). In fact, we even find model lists of those virtues that are to characterize the ones belonging to God (Matt. 5:3–16), and even a facing of the same fact faced in Ezekiel 18, that a falling away from righteousness can indeed occur in behavior (Matt. 25:31–46). But what strikes me as the most consistent aspect in the New Testament's taking up of the message of Ezekiel 18 is the way the declaratory verdict of righteousness is still seen as the decisive factor (*dikaioō*).

There is, however, also an element of discontinuity in the way the message of Ezekiel 18 is picked up in the New Testament. I sense this most clearly in the repeated use of the phrase "O house of Israel" in the latter part of Ezekiel 18 (vv. 25, 29, 30, 31). This stands in marked contrast to the "whosoever" of the New Testament. The narrower focus of the Old Testament is understandable as the direct expression of that peoplehood which was rooted in the past saving acts of God, but it is the surprising attestation of the New Testament that the way through which the goal of God's love was reached led to a new and greater saving act on the basis of which a new peoplehood has been established. And yet this is actually the very kind of new saving act for which Ezekiel 36 calls exilic Israel to hope, and in fact it is explicitly promised that it is by such a new saving act that peoplehood is to be reestablished.[3]

In view of these continuities and discontinuities, every listening to this text must involve an encounter with the God whose will for judgment and love finds expression in his invitation to the joy of repentance. Still, no method of listening can by itself bring about that encounter.

METHODOLOGICAL REFLECTIONS

It is now time to reflect from a methodological perspective[4] about what procedures were actually involved in the preceding treatment of Ezekiel 18.[5] The starting point that got the study of the text underway was an answer to the question, What is it? This is the question about form.[6] The answer that the whole chapter seemed to present an argument was the giving of a genre label, that of "argument saying." The subsequent survey of the makeup of the chapter constituted; an analysis of the structure, which then confirmed the accuracy of the genre label but also discovered that a pair of borrowed structures had been employed in the course of the argument, namely, a series of three hypothetical cases and the pattern of a gate liturgy. It was the noting of technical formulae that enabled this discovery. But now matters became more complex, for it was necessary to trace—albeit very briefly—the history of three genres: argument saying, priestly casuistry, and gate liturgy. This was essential, for only when the appropriate material for comparison is found can comparison be fruitful. Further, in my opinion a knowledge of genre pattern is vital to effective comparison, for only when one knows what is typical does one know when to be surprised by the nontypical. Thus I regard form

275

criticism as simply an inescapable necessity, whether done under that name or not. Presupposed by the method of form criticism (or perhaps, better, form history) is simply the conviction that a recurring sociological situation will produce a standard type of oral literature having a typical vocabulary.[7]

The borrowing by a prophet of these patterns from other areas of life meant a change in their setting in life, however. A significant shift was noted in the way a ceremony from the temple cult was now reinterpreted in the preaching of a priest-prophet in the midst of a templeless exile. Similarly, priestly cases were now made the vehicle not so much of legal as of pastoral concern. But by noticing this we found our exploration of the text leading us from the study of the history of genres into an examination of the way traditional material had been picked up and reapplied, that is, the method of tradition history.

Tradition history is the most comprehensive of all the methods of interpretation. In employing it

> the tradition historian begins with a *critical analysis* of the tradition, trying to determine and describe each of the stages through which it passed in its process of development. The effort should be made to trace the tradition back as far as possible, although it will seldom be possible to reach its origins. The second step consists of *historical synthesis,* the diachronic consideration of the analytical findings in the attempt to present a relative chronology of the growth of the tradition up to the point of its inclusion in a written composition. The first step is called "tradition criticism"; the second is "tradition history." For both, attention is directed to all the aspects of *traditio* and *traditum.* . . .
>
> Despite all our efforts to carry out this examination with as objective, thorough, and sophisticated means as are at our disposal, we must have no illusions about the fact that we are working in a domain of hypotheses and conjectures. Certainty is elusive, if not even unattainable; the great variations among suggested solutions to certain problems give silent witness to this fact. This hypothetical character of traditio-historical work makes caution essential also in our attempts to draw historical and theological consequences from our results.[8]

As it was used here, the method of tradition history led to a recognition of the way a common heritage of traditions known from elsewhere in the Old Testament has been utilized in the shaping of the argument saying in Ezekiel 18. As so often in the prophets, the old becomes the vehicle for the presentation of something new, in this case the confrontation of a despairing and doubting exilic audience with a new and wooing admonition to repent.

The individual elements in Ezekiel's message in chapter 18 were seen to involve widely known traditions and emphases. But it was also observed how prominent at this time was the struggle with the problem of how God's just punishment of the nation of Israel could be squared with his ongoing concern for individual members within that nation. Although the treatment of Ezekiel 18 was content to point out how prominent a matter this struggle was during the seventh and sixth centuries, especially in Jeremiah and in Deuteronomy, a fuller treatment would have gone on to trace this matter further.[9] In so doing, the contrasting emphases of Ezekiel, Deuteronomy, and Chronicles would have come to attention, but no challenge to the authority of the biblical message would have been involved. It is not the intention of the tradition-historical method to challenge the authority of the Bible.

> The issue is a hermeneutical one having nothing to do with critical study. Rather the issue is what is meant by the word of God in the text, whether it is a live word addressed to a particular historical moment, or an eternal word without reference to history. The latter position is a denial of the historical character of the gospel, a position long ago rejected by the church.[10]

The actual verse-by-verse comments on the text of Ezekiel 18, which would be the central part of any interpretation, have been virtually totally omitted in the exegetical sketch presented here, not only for reasons of space but also because the methods employed (e.g., word studies and usage analysis) are relatively beyond dispute.

The basic principle that the procedure of exegesis is determined by the text itself is nowhere more obvious than in the case of the method of redaction history. This method "traces the path the unit has taken from the time it wast first written down until the time it achieved its final literary form."[11] Clearly this method embodies a presupposition that may or may not be valid in the case of a particular text. Bluntly stated, it assumes that a biblical book does not come to us in the same shape in which it was originally written down. In the case of some New Testament letters this assumption is quite likely not valid. Further, the nature of the process by which the pentateuchal editors or the evangelists blended together the relatively fixed traditions with which they worked was doubtless far different from that followed by those responsible for shaping the prophetic books. Here more than anywhere else the interpreter is called to follow the implications of the particular circumstances of the writing with which he is working. In the case of Ezekiel 18 two observations seem to me especially worth pursuing.

The first is the surprising observation that what appears as a demand in 18:31, "Get yourself a new heart and a new spirit," appears as a promise in 11:19 and 36:26, "A new heart I will give you, and a new spirit I will put within you." This phenomenon, that is, repentance being seen both as a command and as a gift, is not unique to Ezekiel. Virtually the same summons, "Circumcise yourselves to the Lord, remove the foreskin of your hearts" (Jer. 4:4), and the same promise, "I will give them a heart to know that I am the Lord" (Jer. 24:7), appear in the nearly contemporary Book of Jeremiah. The theological issue of the place of repentance in the preaching of the prophets, whether within the message of accusation or within the message of salvation, is an issue dear to my heart, and I set it aside only reluctantly.[12] For the purposes of this essay, however, it is more appropriate to note that chapters 18 and 36 are to be found in two different parts of the Book of Ezekiel. That book is among the most clearly arranged of all the prophets, chapters 1-24 dealing with the prophet's message of judgment prior to 587 B.C., chapters 25-32 with a collection of foreign-nation oracles, and chapters 33-48 with the prophet's message of hope following the year 587. It seems likely that we have a redactional arrangement that may well go back to the prophet himself. And yet this pattern of the arrangement of Ezekiel's message is not quite as neat as the preceding general observation might suggest. In our particular case this is shown by the presence in 11:19—at the end of a large section of judgment materials in chapters 8-11—of the same promise of a new heart as that which occurs in chapter 36. Two possibilities of redactional interpretation occur to me. Either the promise material in 11:14-21 may reflect that Ezekiel's earlier preaching of judgment did indeed contain on occasion (whatever preaching occasion the vision of 8-11 may reflect) a sampling of what was later to be the prophet's message of hope, or this section of promise in 11:14-21 may be the later filling out of the prophet's message, possibly so that the section 8-11 might be used as a kind of complete message in itself. In view of the prophet's struggle before the year 587 to convince a fantastically overconfident audience that God could indeed bring to fulfillment his verdict of judgment on his people, the second possibility mentioned above seems more likely. What is involved here is not the unwillingness to accept the genuineness of a passage, because its logic seems strange. The bizarre complexities of the Book of Ezekiel rapidly chasten such naive love of consistency out of any interpreter. Instead the intention of this exercise is solely to confront the interpreter with the full complexity of the issue so that the alternatives might be faced with all their complications.

The second observation calling for redaction-critical conjecture is that a condensed summary of the whole of chapter 18 occurs in 33:10-20. It seems again that two major possibilities confront us. Either the passage 33:10–20 is an instance in which the prophet in an actual preaching situation repeated in briefer scope something he proclaimed earlier—a by-no-means-impossible occurrence—or the section 33:10–20 is editorially repeated for some reason. In view of the structural development of chapter 33 as the beginning of the salvation section, the latter option again seems more likely. Chapter 33 leads up to the announcement of the fall of Jerusalem as the turning point in the prophet's ministry in verses 21–22. As preparation for the understanding of the nature of this part of the prophet's function, verses 1–9 present his role as watchman in a manner corresponding to the function of the account of his call in chapters 1–3 as background for understanding his ministry in chapters 4–24. Because the watchman role centers on the duty to "warn the wicked to turn from his way" so that he may not "die in his iniquity" (33:8), the subject matter of chapter 18 is the natural and even vital elaboration of what this preaching of repentance involved during the pre-587 part of his ministry; hence the appropriateness of the insertion of this summary in verses 10–20. Once again, what is involved is not an unwillingness to accept the text as a faithful record in chronological order of what the prophet said. Rather, facing the redaction-critical question is simply an attempt to take the obligation to listen to the text with the fullest seriousness by asking what the implications of the arrangement of the text are. Naturally, two interpreters facing the same question may come to different conclusions, and they may even change their minds about the relative likelihood of the alternatives involved, but they do so as joint participants in the same task of weighing arguments in their common struggle to be faithful to their common calling by letting the text speak in all its fullness.

That part of the study of a text which reflects on the ongoing history of its meaning within the stream of interpretation following its reaching of its final shape is sometimes called canon criticism, for it deals among other matters with how a text is understood within the context of the Christian canon. I know no one who denies the importance of such investigation, but many feel it is not their area of competence or not an essential part of the exegesis of a text in the strict sense. It is my conviction here that every Christian student of a text must deal with this area to the best of his ability and do so within the process of exegesis. I believe we know no God apart from the God we know in Jesus Christ, and I find it simply impossible to study any Old Testament passage without asking how this relates to the revelation of God in the New Testament. Although opinions may diverge about precisely where continuity and discontinuity exist, however, I do not find these divergences methodologically significant and I assume that the further treatment of them would belong to the discussion of the canon anyway.

In summary, I find all the various methods of interpretation employed and discussed here to be essentially neutral and their results open to revision. I find that to be true for both scientific and theological reasons. From the point of view of strict scientific objectivity, the text itself must always be the starting point. Otherwise there can be no real listening. Where the text itself suggests it, it may be necessary to go behind the text to its background in earlier tradition, but "the study of the prehistory has its proper function within exegesis only in illuminating the final text."[13] Further, from the viewpoint of simple scientific integrity, the stream of tradition history must be traced beyond the text in the light of both evidence and conjecture, ending for Old Testament texts with the interpreter's own response (whether affirming, rejecting, or reinterpreting) in the light of his own position. From a theological viewpoint, we confess that in the text we are addressed, and that interpretation is the process by which listening takes place and in the light of which response is made. Inherent in the hermeneutical circle[14] is one reason why this process is a never-ending one. No *method* can guarantee that this dialogue of address and response will take place, but every method must reflect both in its openness and in its responsibility an accountability to the place where it is practiced, and for us that place is within the church of Jesus Christ.

NOTES

1. V. 5 has *'ish ki* as in Lev. 19:20, and vv. 10 and 14 have *hōlīd,* which recalls the Genesis *toledoth.* In addition, v. 10*b* poses a textual problem. Probably for *weʿāsāh āh meʾahad mēʾelleh* one ought to read *weʿāsāh ʾehad mēʾelleh.* See *Biblia Hebraica Stuttgartensia,* ed. K. Elliger and W. Rudolph (Stuttgart: Württembergische Bibelanstalt, 1971), fasicle 9; and Walther Zimmerli, *Ezekiel* (Philadelphia: Fortress Press, forthcoming), 1, ad loc.

2. *Mēʿānī* in v. 17*a* seems to be a transmissional mistake for the *mēʿāwel* of v. 8.

3. It was not only the early Christian tradition that believed itself to be heir to the ongoing process of preserving the Old Testament traditions. The synagogue was also the locale of a similar process. The synagogue was, however, the setting for a twofold kind of exegetical tradition, the one focused on rules for daily living (a sort of legal tradition or halakah) and the other on edifying illustration (a variety of homiletical tradition or Haggadah). In the latter vein two items strike me as worth sharing. The first comes in a discussion of what kind of skill or mastery is of the greatest value. The conclusion is that the greatest master of all is the master of repentance (*baʿal teshūbāh*). The second is a story about a drought-stricken village searching for an effective intercessor.

It was clear to the town's leaders that God would hear the prayer of a righteous man, and yet the prayers of the leading scholars and other notables in the community were unavailing. In desperation a systematic search was undertaken in which each male resident was canvassed and asked "Are you a righteous man?" As the persisting drought became more serious, the search became more desperate. Finally the canvassers approached the last man on their list, a bathhouse attendant, whose occupation—involving human nakedness as it did—made him the least likely to be righteous. When asked, "Are you a righteous man?" he could only reply in amazement, "You've got to be kidding!" Then his questioners persisted, "Try hard to think if you ever in your whole life did anything righteous." He shook his head—and then hesitated. "Maybe once," he replied. "One time I heard a woman weeping because she'd have to sell her body to pay off a small debt, and I loaned her the money." Immediately the rain began to fall, and the committee of elders went away rejoicing and saying, "Praise to the Holy One (Blessed be He!), for we went looking for righteousness, and he showed us mercy."

4. To give as objective as possible a treatment of the issues involved I have confined my citations to what are in my judgment the most widely accepted works dealing with methods of Old Testament interpretation.

5. The procedures of textual criticism, that is, the attempt to determine as surely as possible the original Hebrew text of a given passage, are here confined to the notes. This is done for two reasons: to affirm that the issues involved in this text are of minimal significance and to express the conviction that great unanimity exists in the way in which such questions are to be handled. This should not obscure the fact, however, that even here we deal with conflicting witnesses to an inaccessible original text. The closest we can get to the original text is an editorial effort at critical restoration based on diverging traditions and employing hypothetical conjectures.

6. That no strictly-speaking literary criticism should be undertaken at the beginning of an exegesis may strike some as startling. And yet it is of the essence of critical exegesis that it goes where the text leads, and Ezekiel 18 does not lead the interpreter in a literary-critical direction (at least in the sense of source analysis or separation of glosses). The basic point of departure for this phase of criticism is the recognition of material that reflects doublets, inconsistencies, or divergent historical backgrounds. While there may indeed be glosses in the text of Ezekiel 18, there is no evidence of multiple sources. And the glosses involved, such as *ya'aseh wāhāy* ("if he does that, shall he live?") in verse 24 or *wehāshībū wih'yū* ("so turn and live") in verse 32, are of such an insignificant sort as far as the text's meaning is concerned that they are really better seen as solely matters of text-critical minutiae, for the words in question are in fact not attested by some of the major witnesses. Apart from the Pentateuch and Second Isaiah, strictly literary-critical questions often receive more attention in Old Testament study than they deserve. Finally, the issue of divergent opinions which might surface here will arise later anyway in connection, for example, with redaction criticism, and I have accordingly dealt at some length with a couple of such questions within that framework.

7. "It [form criticism] depends on the observation that in each individual literary form, as long as it remains in use in its own context, the ideas it contains are always connected with certain fixed forms of expression. This characteristic connection is not imposed arbitrarily on the material by the literary redactors of a later period. The inseparable connection between form and content goes back behind the written records to the period of popular oral compo-

sition and tradition, where each form of expression was appropriate to some particular circumstance amongst the regularly recurring events and necessities of life." (Albrecht Alt, "The Origins of Israelite Law," in his *Essays on Old Testament History and Religion*, trans. R. A. Wilson [Oxford: Oxford University Press, 1966], p. 87.) The standard recent handbook on form criticism is Klaus Koch, *The Growth of the Biblical Tradition*, trans. S. M. Cupitt (New York: Charles Scribner's Sons, 1969).

8. Douglas Knight, *Recovering the Traditions of Israel*, SBL Dissertation Series 9 (Missoula, Mont.: Scholars Press, 1973), pp. 30–31. An excellent discussion of this method from a very practical perspective, together with some outstanding instances of the results of its use, can be found in Walter Brueggemann and Hans Walter Wolff, *The Vitality of Old Testament Traditions* (Atlanta: John Knox Press, 1975).

9. See esp. Hans Walter Wolff, "The Kerygma of the Deuteronomic Historical Work," in Brueggemann and Wolff, *Vitality of Old Testament Traditions*, pp. 83–100; and idem, "Das Thema 'Umkehr' in der alttestamentlichen Prophetie," *Zeitschrift für Theologie und Kirche* 48 (1951): 129–48.

10. Walter Brueggemann, "The Continuing Task of Tradition Criticism," in Brueggemann and Wolff, *Vitality of Old Testament Traditions*, p. 125.

11. Koch, *Growth of the Biblical Tradition*, p. 58.

12. See again the idea of "the end of the road of return" in Wolff, "Das Thema 'Umkehr.'" In passing it might also be noted that the statement in Ezek. 18:20, "The soul that sins shall die," can scarcely be viewed as only the bottom line in a legal process of judgment and condemnation. The subsequent observation, "Have I any pleasure in the death of the wicked, says the Lord God, and not rather that he should turn from his way and live?" (v. 23), makes it plain that the intended function of v. 20 is rather as a preliminary step on a road that is aimed to lead to repentance and forgiveness. See here Karl Barth, "Gospel and Law," in his *God, Grace and Gospel* (Edinburgh: Oliver & Boyd, 1959), p. 5.

13. Brevard S. Childs, *The Book of Exodus* (Philadelphia: Westminster Press, 1974), p. xv.

14. See, e.g., Claus Westermann, "Zur Auslegung des Alten Testaments," in his *Forschung am Alten Testament, Gesammelte Studien* (Munich: Chr. Kaiser Verlag, 1974), 2: 9–67.

Methods of Historical Inquiry and the Faithful Interpretation of the Christian Scriptures

DAVID L. TIEDE

Associate Professor of New Testament
Luther Theological Seminary
Saint Paul, Minnesota

INTRODUCTION: LET US BOAST IN OUR WEAKNESS!

Perhaps only a fool would attempt to address the topic of methods of biblical interpretation at a time when that question has already been used to tear at the fabric of Lutheran unity. Perhaps the battle has already been fought elsewhere and the unity of a Lutheran witness has been destroyed. Perhaps it is impossible to resist inflammatory rhetoric about the historical-critical method. But if it is possible to believe that even at this late hour one can risk honest discussion and debate about methods of historical inquiry and the faithful interpretation of the Christian Scriptures, then perhaps it can be acknowledged that the problem of the interpretation of the Scriptures is one which unites as well as divides. Perhaps this is a time for the humble confession of a common weakness in the face of the pressing needs of the world for a word of the Lord. Rather than touting the glories of the "historical-critical" or "historical-grammatical" or "historical-biblical" methods as if a particular method were the *vade mecum* for all current problems, the inadequacy and brokenness of all human attempts to state the truth must be acknowledged, without disparaging the sincerity or value of those efforts.

One does not need to listen very long at the keyhole of a much larger Christian discussion to hear a common murmur about a "strange silence of the Bible in the church"[1] or a "crisis in biblical theology"[2] or an uncertainty about whether the unity of the church is founded upon the biblical canon,[3] or even the assertion from voices that are poles apart theologically that "historical criticism" is at an end[4] or is, at least, "bankrupt."[5] Perhaps Lutherans have a distinctive service to render in the larger fellowship of believers, but it probably does not lie in the recognized strength of our European tradition of biblical scholarship or the virtue of doctrinal solidarity. Rather, the fact that Lutherans largely represent immigrant churches who are recently emerging on the scene of American Christianity and that they have a theological heritage of confessing sins openly and regularly probably holds more promise.

"Boasting in weakness" is more than a tactic. It is a confession that pride in the good workmanship of scholarly studies may have blinded us to a crisis of the spirit in our churches. When people were hungering for the bread of the gospel, they have been handed the stones of prideful attacks on biblical teachers or the sterile "assured results" of "scientific historical research." When the questions have become more and more difficult, the strident voices have incriminated themselves by becoming more shrill and self-justifying. We have been slow to listen.

Who more than we can boast in our weakness? Who can face the painful and difficult questions that post-enlightenment culture has brought to bear on our Scriptures graced only with an unwavering trust in the God who revealed himself to us in Jesus Christ? Who better than we can press forward in the liberated pursuit of these questions, aware of our limitations and sinful proclivity to set ourselves up as the arbiters of the truth, yet confident of the abiding presence of the Holy Spirit? Foolish as it seems, let us boast in our weakness.

WHAT DID THE TEXT SAY?

What did the text say? has not always been a problem for the church. In the time of the domination of the Vulgate in Western Christianity, or in the time of the early vernacular translations by the Reformers when only a few Greek manuscripts and a standardized Hebrew text were available, or even in the centuries when the Luther Bible and the King James Version were broadly accepted as based upon the "text received by all,"[6] discussing "what did the text say?" was not a cause of anxiety. Appeals could always be made to the standardized and broadly circulated text and theological rhetoric about the "inerrant" and "infallible" text could be used with little restraint.

Even as increasing numbers of manuscripts were discovered, the pressure to deny the complexity of the matter was immense. Thus, for example, when Johann Albrecht Bengel, the pious superintendent of the Evangelical Church of Württemberg, sought to defend the text of the New Testament by a carefully reasoned analysis of the manuscript evidence, he was treated as an enemy of the Scriptures for opening the issue.[7] He did not create the problem, nor did he want to disturb the faith of the church. Rather, Bengel merely sought to give a faithful and honest and assuring response to the thirty thousand variant readings that had been published in Mill's edition of the Greek New Testament.

But the idea of the "inerrant" Greek text resisted honest admission of the problem. For a century and a half after Bengel's appraisal of the situation, efforts to appeal to earlier or more accurate manuscripts than those that lay behind the *Textus Receptus* were largely unsuccessful, until finally the work of Tischendorf and Wescott and Hort could not be silenced by theological assertions. The question of what the author originally wrote was open to debate, and the discussion of criteria and methods of the reconstruction of the history of the text was pursued vigorously in many quarters in the church.

Of course one only has to compare the King James Version and the Revised Standard Version to see that the coherence of the testimony of the divergent manuscripts is still very impressive. Most students of the text would agree that the variants pose no substantial threat to the message of the Scriptures. In fact the history of the transmission of the text provides an eloquent testimony to the care and diligence and affection with which the scribes and scholars of the early church preserved and forwarded the Scriptures to us.

But we seem to want the Scriptures to be something else. Like Peter who was bold to make the glorious confession of the messiahship of Jesus but unwilling to accept a messiah who would suffer and die (see Mark 8), we are inclined to make lofty theological claims about the Scriptures but then feel embarrassment that once again God has chosen to reveal himself to us through human and historical means. Perhaps we had thought we were defending the integrity of the Scriptures by loud claims for their divine origin, almost as if we believed in a transsubstantiated text, but now we find that we must readjust our rhetoric lest we be guilty of despising the vital human testimony we encounter both in the texts and in their transmission to us.

Gerhard Maier attempts to deal with the difficulty that the long process of textual transmission presents to a static view of revelation:

> We understand the "infallibility" of Scripture, of which the fathers spoke, in the sense of authorization and fulfillment by God, and not in the sense

of anthropological inerrancy. Insofar as textual difficulties are concerned, we also accept the continuation of divine guidance and foresight (*providentia Dei*), without indulging in the idea of progressive or unterminated revelation and without being relieved of searching for the best possible form of the text.[8]

Of course, some would argue for the verbal inerrancy of the original inspired text of which we possess only imperfect copies. But there is less and less comfort in that as the thousands of manuscripts increase and the detailed complexity of collecting the readings gnaws even at the relative confidence that Wescott and Hort had of recovering the original. Why would we despise the Scriptures that God has preserved to us through the service of his saints in favor of an elusive, unrecoverable original? Plato may have demeaned the mundane and earthly in favor of ideal types, but apparently the God of Abraham, Isaac, and Jesus does not.

WHAT SOURCES WAS THE AUTHOR USING?

When the discussion moves from "text criticism" (analysis) to "source criticism," the theological issues become more complex, and some will suggest that now we have passed to the plane of "higher criticism." Clearly there are reasons for being on the alert, but the distinction between "lower" and "higher" criticism may only confuse the question of the value of source analysis for the faithful interpretation of the Scriptures. The goal or purpose for seeking to identify sources is crucial.

In the later nineteenth and the early twentieth centuries, a great deal of source-critical work was done in both Testaments in rather strict service of a positivistic historiography that intended to arbitrate the truth strictly in terms of its determination of "what really happened." Energized by a reaction to what was perceived as a rigid ecclesiastical dogmatism, the new "criticism" may be faulted for its too willing service to the dogmas of historicism. Whether in quest of the historical Jesus or of the "real" authors of the Pentateuch, the confidence that was often shared of discovering the historical kernel of truth by peeling off the husks of theological accretion now appears naive and reductionist. Karl Barth, Walter Wink, and Gerhard Maier can all agree that such "historical criticism" is theologically mute and at an end.[9]

But source criticism need not be done only in the service of such a narrow concept of truth nor used merely as a tool to identify later materials in order to dismiss them in favor of "more primitive" or "more original" traditions. Such positivistic "historical criticism" shares the bias of the old dogmatists in favor of the ideal original (now the original "objective event" instead of the original text) over against the living witness of faith. But once again the quest to pin down that objectively verifiable "original," whether to prove the text right or wrong, led gradually to the awareness of the vast chorus of witnesses, each speaking the Word of the Lord to a particular time and place, drawing upon the wellsprings of earlier testimony and heralding that Word in a new context. As my colleague Terence Fretheim states it,

> The theory and practice of the historical-critical method is not bound to an understanding which views history as a closed continuum in which there is no room for divine activity. Source criticism must recognize that the biblical literature emanated from a religious community. The intention of its authors was never merely literary or historical, and due consideration must be given to theological intentions, which inevitably affected literary composition. Moreover, this means that source criticism cannot be an end in itself, but must stand in the service of the explication of the full meaning of the biblical text.[10]

Thus the efforts and discoveries of those who have struggled to unravel the complex strands of the cord of biblical tradition remain of great interest even to those who regard the hermeneutic of positivistic historiography as too narrow and reductionist. Not that the basis in "fact" or "actual occurrence" is a matter of indifference, for the reality of the past is not dissolved into a mere complex of significances. But those "mere facts" are mute until given voice.

So Israel crossed the sea, but by attending to the discipline of source criticism fresh access has been gained into the long process by which that story was given shape in song, poetry, prophecy, and prayer in various situations and times in the history of the people of God. The dependence of an author on the oral tradition or of a prophet upon a school of prophecy, or an evangelist who sees Jesus in the light of the prophecies accomplishing a new exodus—all that interdependence and connectedness bespeaks a "living voice" that bears witness with the voices and spirits of the people of God to the significance of those "facts" or that "history" to a host of contexts.[11]

The question concerning the literary relationships among the Gospels—which is at least as old as Augustine—was perhaps reopened in the service of finding which was most likely the first and therefore the most trustworthy for writing a biography of Jesus. But the incredible diligence poured into that effort did not produce such a result. It did yield a much more detailed picture of the relationships among the Gospels, but even more important it led scholars to a recognition that the Gospels could not be reduced to being mere records of the life of Jesus. They are also the living testimony of the people of God. To describe Mark as "a passion narrative with an extended introduction" is not merely a counsel of despair for those who want to write a biography, it is also an insight into the *theologia crucis* that the evangelist intended to proclaim.[12]

WHAT WAS THE AUTHOR INTENDING TO SAY?

The previous section demonstrates that the question of sources is being asked very consciously in the service of discovering the message of the text. But it should be noted carefully that the methods of historical inquiry have not thereby been abandoned by recourse to homiletical flourishes or "spiritual exegesis" in contrast to historical-grammatical analysis. Privatistic interpretations, no matter how attractive or inspiring, must be judged in terms of their consistency with the intention of the text, and the historical integrity of the books of Scripture always provide a check against arbitrarily subjective uses of the text.

Of course no one approaches a text without hermeneutical agenda. The fiction of disinterested inquiry need not trouble the discussion. Nevertheless, historical exegesis is first of all a *descriptive* enterprise, attempting to do justice to what the author intended to say to his immediate audience and seeking to proceed in a disciplined manner or method so that the exegete may be accountable for that description.

The exact ground for attending so carefully to the historicity of the text or its message to its own time no doubt needs more exploration by those trained in systematic and historical theology. But in the hands of the biblical theologians and pastors of the church the exegetical process clearly is not merely a matter of researching religious antiquities.[13] Rather, the discipline is pursued with deep convictions about the specific historical character of divine revelation and an awareness that the distinguishing mark of the true biblical prophet or proclaimer of God's Word was often not so much the abstract content of the statements (the false prophets and the devil also quoted the Scriptures) but their appropriateness to a given situation.

Furthermore, every exegetical step involved in describing what that author intended to say to his reader is open to scrutiny and debate. No private revelations are allowed to shortcut or compromise the open analysis of the grammar, syntax, vocabulary, and context of a passage. The exegete is not necessarily charged with being the sole arbiter of the value of meaning of a given text, but the church and the world have a right to turn to the exegete and ask, "But what did Paul intend to say to the church in Corinth about the *charismata,* and how do you know that?"

One of the most telling consequences of such descriptive work has been the increasing sense of the diversity of biblical theologies. Again the hue and cry has gone up that the unity of the Pentateuch has been mutilated or that the integrity of "biblical theology" has been jeopardized by the technicians or that the scholars of the Gospels have a perverse if not sadistic interest in dwelling upon discrepancies. First the inerrant text, then the historical facts, and now the unified kerygma has become problematic.

Again it is true that the diversity of biblical theologies has been perceived by some as incriminating evidence of inconsistency, and many Christians who have been taught to think of the Bible as a seamless cloth are amazed and perplexed when they actually read it or hear the several Gospels preached in the new lectionary.

But modern scholars did not dream up the diversity. Whether the compelling hypothesis of multiple sources behind the Pentateuch can be finally proved or not, the four Gospels are explicit and ample testimony to that diversity. Apparently Marcion was embarrassed by it and tried to eliminate three and clean up the one according to "the gospel." Tatian tried to create a harmony. But the church said, "No!" Sharply aware of the differences, the church preserved the *four* Gospels to us. Simply reading Chrysostom's sermons on the Gospel of *Matthew* will also indicate the care and insight with which an ancient "redaction critic" handled the text.

Thus the enterprise of "redaction criticism," which seems to have appeared within the past quarter-century, is in the first instance merely the old Bible-study method of "book studies" brought back with more intense attention to the methods by which the theology of a book may be ascertained.[14] Furthermore, by using the methods of historical inquiry to establish the sources and specialized vocabulary and theological agenda with which the evangelist was concerned, redaction criticism then aims to ask concerning what in particular that author did with what was available to him in the tradition.

Thus it is not a perverse interest in discrepancies that leads to such careful attention to the place where the author has restated or rearranged his sources. Rather, in analogy to assessing what a modern evangelist does with a text, the question is, How did this evangelist reformulate what he received in order to speak the Word of the Lord for a new time and season?

Of course historians and students of the Scriptures cannot resist the urge to inquire why the evangelist may have restated a text in a given way, and thus redaction criticism quickly produces a number of imaginative reconstructions of the situation that was being addressed. Such reconstructions must always remain tentative and must not be allowed to dominate the interpretation of the text, but they may prove valuable at least as suggestions for the preacher who is faced with the task of heralding the Word of God in new times and situations. Thus even descriptive redactional work presumes to make tentative suggestions about the appropriate word to particular settings.

HOW WAS THE MESSAGE FORMULATED?

Form criticism was once primarily a tool of the quest for sources in the effort to pursue the kind of positivistic historiography described above. Surely a significant debt is owed to those groundbreaking efforts to reconstruct the history of the patriarchal and subapostolic traditions in particular, although the results of that research are still subject to heavy criticism and review.[15]

But the task of assessing the forms in which the traditions were recited before they were placed in literary contexts need not be done simply in service of an effort to isolate the earliest traditions. A clearer picture of the modes of telling the story of Jesus, for example, can also be suggestive and helpful for finding appropriate forms for proclaiming and reciting the stories in the modern world. The close connection between message and medium is not a new insight, but a more differentiated picture of the preliterary traditions about Jesus is particularly valuable for those who interpret snippets or pericopes of the tradition orally week by week.[16]

Furthermore, the very real possibility that collections of sayings of Jesus or miracle stories or apocalyptic discourses existed prior to our canonical Gospels has raised the question of the genre or *Gattung* of the Gospel very sharply. Even by the process of the formation of a Gospel tradition, the cross-resurrection shape of Christian preaching was apparently being assured in contrast to a variety of other ways of telling the story of Jesus.[17]

Clearly a great deal more study is required in this area, but the point to be emphasized in the present discussion is that methods of historical inquiry are leading us into direct conversation with the theological issues and struggles of the first-century church. Surely this is not the theologically mute or disinterested research to which Karl Barth and the kerygmatic theologians objected in the 1920s. Biblical theology is perhaps becoming more complex, but clearly new theological and hermeneutical issues are bursting upon us. Whatever method has been laid to rest by Wink and Maier, the questions raised by historical research have only changed, they have not gone away.

CONCLUSION: "TE TOTUM APPLICA AD TEXTUM: REM TOTAM APPLICA AD TE" (J. A. BENGEL, 1734)

The book on assured results of historical-critical research is far from written; indeed, if ever such hope was invested in "the method," the misplaced optimism now seems amusing. In fact, the one lesson that we should have learned is well stated by Gerhard Maier: "We refrain from saying more than we can say honestly."[18]

Each of the methods of historical inquiry discussed above (text, source, redaction, and form criticism) at first seemed to tempt us with a promise of some externally verifiable ground for faith, whether an inerrant text, an objective history, the original kerygma, or the most primitive tradition. But again and again we have been brought up short in our attempts to impose our agenda on the text. Neither lofty doctrines which all but transform the Bible into an otherworldly reality, nor attempts to treat it simply as a resource for historical reconstruction, are adequate to the texts of Scripture. And as Carl Braaten states correctly: "The ultimate criterion of an appropriate hermeneutic is a material one; that is, does the hermeneutical method do justice to the matter to be interpreted?"[19]

Historical criticism, like all other human enterprises, has been required to learn to serve the subject matter of the text rather than dominate it, and needless to say, that process continues. In some sense finally the interpreter is interpreted, and the process of careful historical inquiry becomes the occasion for hearing as well as asking.

No, the "original and inerrant text" could not be fixed in place for all time. But out of a long living history of the people of God preserving, cherishing, perverting, and transmitting these Scriptures, an amazingly coherent textual tradition can be recovered.

No, the sources do not lead us back to a purely objective record of "what really happened," but as we pursue the evidence of sources we encounter a process of transmitting the words and works of Jesus that is both careful to conserve reminiscence and alive to the possibilities of applying those stories to a variety of situations in the life of the community.

And no, we are not able to comprehend the variety of messages in the texts by one set of theological categories or metaphors. Even our most noble efforts to state "the biblical theology" run aground on the particularities of the several books. Our need to isolate a canon within the canon is frustrated and challenged by the catholicity of the collection.

But as we ask and listen, as we attend carefully to what a given author intended to say and ponder the relevance of that message for our times and situations, the Word of the Lord breaks into our inquiry. Through, in the midst of, or in, with, and under the rich diversity of voices in the Scripture, the living Lord speaks to us, to our times and condition.

The fault is not that we have brought the strange or inappropriate questions of the modern world to the text, nor that our methods of historical inquiry were more debased than the hermeneutics of other times. In fact, it may be the peculiar function of the church's Scripture scholars to pursue such difficult questions with as much or more diligence as those who are not concerned with the faithful interpretation of the Christian Scriptures. The questions will not simply go away, and even our poor efforts are not despised but are redeemed by the Lord of the church as the earthen vessels for the transmission of treasure.

The fault is rather that we have been wont to speak, to tell the text what it must be or what we would hear, to master and even silence the text, often by means of glorious claims in its behalf. We have despised the earthen vessel of the church which transmitted the text to us, formulated the gospel traditions and addressed a host of situations. If nothing else, the past century of historical inquiry has humbled us by forcing us to attend carefully to the text and allowing the text to call our reductionist inquiries into question. The discipline of listening to the text does not come easily to any of us.

NOTES

1. See James D. Smart, *The Strange Silence of the Bible in the Church: A Study in Hermeneutics* (Philadelphia: Westminster Press, 1970).

2. See Brevard S. Childs, *Biblical Theology in Crisis* (Philadelphia: Westminster Press, 1970).

3. See Ernst Käsemann, "Begründet der neutestamentliche Kanon die Einheit der Kirche?" in *Das Neue Testament als Kanon*, ed. Ernst Käsemann (Göttingen: Vandenhoeck & Ruprecht, 1970).

4. Gerhard Maier, *The End of the Historical-Critical Method*, trans. Edwin W. Leverenz and Rudolph F. Norden, with a foreword by Eugene F. Klug (St. Louis: Concordia Publishing House, 1977).

5. Walter Wink, *The Bible in Human Transformation: Toward a New Paradigm for Biblical Study* (Philadelphia: Fortress Press, 1973), p. 1.

6. This phrase was used in the publisher's blurb that prefaced the 1633 edition of the Greek text printed by the Elzevir brothers in Leiden, and it lies behind the concept of the *Textus Receptus*, which still is regarded as equivalent to the "inspired and inerrant" text in some circles. Any church that has adopted the Revised Standard Version has abandoned the notion of the *Textus Receptus*.

7. See Bruce Manning Metzger, *The Text of the New Testament* (New York: Oxford University Press, 1964), pp. 112–13.

8. Maier, *End of the Historical-Critical Method*, p. 72. In a note Maier qualifies what he means by "anthropological inerrancy" as "in the sense of a doctrine of man."

9. See also Carl E. Braaten, *History and Hermeneutics. New Directions in Theology Today* (Philadelphia: Westminster Press, 1966), 2:11–52; Edgar Krentz, *The Historical-Critical Method* (Philadelphia: Fortress Press, 1975), pp. 73–88.

10. Terence E. Fretheim, "Source Criticism, O. T.," in *The Interpreter's Dictionary of the Bible*, Supplementary Volume (Nashville: Abingdon Press, 1976), p. 838.

11. Clearly, the objectives of the early form critics to reconstruct the history of the tradition are also being appropriated under the rubric of the source question. In the section on forms that follows, the attempt is made to move beyond the significance of that work for such reconstruction and to describe the value of that contribution in terms of forms and genera of proclamation.

12. See Hans Conzelmann, "Present and Future in the Synoptic Tradition," trans. Jack Wilson, *Journal for Theology and the Church* 5 (1968): 85–96.

13. See the discussion of the purpose and limits of "descriptive" exegetical work in Krister Stendahl, "Biblical Theology, Contemporary," in *Interpreter's Dictionary of the Bible*, ed. George A. Buttrick (Nashville: Abingdon Press, 1962), 1: 418–32. See also James Luther Mays, "Exegesis as a Theological Discipline," Inaugural address delivered 20 April 1960, at Union Theological Seminary, Richmond, Virginia.

14. The title of Joachim Rohde's volume on redaction criticism states the objective nicely: *Rediscovering the Teaching of the Evangelists* (Philadelphia: Westminster Press, 1969); see Norman Perrin, *What Is Redaction Criticism* (Philadelphia: Fortress Press, 1969); and Robert Stein, "What Is Redactionsgeschichte?" *Journal of Biblical Literature* 88 (1969): 45–66.

15. For a good resumé of this earlier work, see Edgar V. McKnight, *What Is Form Criticism?* (Philadelphia: Fortress Press, 1969). Unfortunately, McKnight still treats the contribution of New Testament form criticism largely in the light of the concerns of such positivistic historiography.

16. The work of Martin Dibelius, *From Tradition to Gospel*, trans. Bertram L. Wolff (Greenwood, S.C.: Attic Press, 1972), was particularly sensitive to the proclamatory function of the oral tradition.

17. See in particular, Helmut Koester, "One Jesus and Four Primitive Gospels," *Harvard Theological Review* 61 (1968): 203–47, also reprinted in James M. Robinson and Helmut Koester, *Trajectories through Early Christianity* (Philadelphia: Fortress Press, 1971). See also William A. Beardslee, *Literary Criticism of the New Testament* (Philadelphia: Fortress Press, 1970).

18. Maier, *End of the Historical-Critical Method*, p. 18.

19. Braaten, *History and Hermeneutics*, p. 52.

Theology and Hermeneutics

DUANE A. PRIEBE

Associate Professor of Systematic Theology
Wartburg Theological Seminary
Dubuque, Iowa

Hermeneutics is the science of interpretation. It deals with the question of understanding and the process by which understanding takes place. Theology is a hermeneutical discipline since it seeks to understand God's revelation, focused in Jesus Christ, in relation to our present history, and to understand our present history in the light of God's revealing Word. This Word, which constitutes Christian tradition, has come to expression in Israel's history culminating in Jesus Christ and has been precipitated in Scripture. It is not surprising then that the question of appropriate methods of interpretation of Scripture is a significant issue for theology. Today the use of the historical-critical method has become an issue from different standpoints. From a conservative side the use of the historical-critical method seems to threaten the role of the Bible in the church as the inspired Word of God. But also people who regard the historical-critical method as an important tool for interpreting Scripture are asking whether its use merely leaves the Bible a remote and irrelevant book, dissolving its religious significance as Scripture. As a result there has been an interest in less-historical methods of interpretation, such as structuralism.

The question of interpretive methods can be dealt with adequately only within the context of a broader treatment of the relationship of theology and hermeneutics. Theology's interpretive task involves a double movement: the understanding of language and understanding by means of language.[1] If words are to help us understand something, we must first understand the words being used. Often that takes place directly. But at other times we might not understand the words being used or the precise meaning they have for the person using them. Furthermore, the context of what is said, the appropriate connections between ideas, and the underlying unspoken assumptions that belong to the meaning of what is said may not be adequately known. Then both understanding and mis-understanding are interwoven, and the task of interpretation is first of all to determine just what it is that is being said. In this task the words spoken or the words of the text remain the primary means by which understanding is sought. Since the Bible was written in languages foreign to us, in historical settings no longer immediately apparent to us, and utilizing conceptual frameworks no longer identical with our own, the dimension of hermeneutics that focuses on understanding what is said by the text has played a major role in theology. Biblical hermeneutics has normally treated the methods and techniques for understanding what the language of the Bible means. This is of course an essential endeavor if we are to take the Bible seriously. If that is the end of the hermeneutical task relative to Scripture, however, it does not take account of the basis for such interest in the Bible and it leaves us with little more than historical curiosities. It also allows our present horizon of theological understanding to remain relatively untouched and safe from any claim Scripture might make on us as God's Word.

A second essential movement in theology's hermeneutical task then is to learn to understand ourselves, our world, and our history anew in the light of God's Word in Jesus Christ by means of the language of Scrip-ture. In this sense hermeneutics is a matter of hearing the claim of the text on us and our understanding, and thus being placed in question by the text. It presupposes that understanding is not something we already possess but something we seek with the help of the text. It means that we expect to hear something more from the text than that which we al-ready know. We listen for a Word from God in which the text that once was God's Word to people in a different time and place might again become God's Word for us.

In treating the topic of hermeneutics, we shall discuss the necessity of hermeneutics in the relation between Scripture and theology, the polarity of distance and participation that belongs to understanding, the signifi-cance of historicity for understanding the hermeneutical circle, and the evocative power of the text to interpret the present and create new dimen-sions of meaning.

SCRIPTURE AND THEOLOGY: THE NECESSITY OF HERMENEUTICS

Christian faith is rooted in Israel's history, culminating in the activity and fate of Jesus of Nazareth. This particular history is understood to be the definitive history in which God has approached all humanity, revealing himself as God and acting for our salvation. Through his activity in this history God is present as God to all other human history. It is God's once-for-all saving action. The relation of our life and history to God then is given in its relation to Israel's history, so that Christian life and thought is essentially involved with Israel's history in memory and interpretation. Christian tradition is inherently constituted by the dialogue with that history as we seek to understand our life, our world, and our history in its relation to God. The history of Christian theology, especially as the history of doctrine, is an aid in this hermeneutical task. It is a history in which biblical tradition has helped people understand their own situations in relation to God's action in Jesus Christ. The history of theology involves both understanding and misunderstanding. It helps provide pointers for the proper appropriation of Israel's history and sets up warning signs against certain misinterpretations. The history of theology also transmits biblical tradition to us as a living tradition that shapes our world and understanding, providing us with powerful, and at times unconscious, understandings of God's Word to us in Jesus Christ. Both as a guide to interpretation and as a transmitter of biblical tradition, the history of the church and its doctrine forms an essential dimension of theology's hermeneutical endeavor. But it does this as an aid to the dialogue with the past history culminated in Jesus, not as a substitute for it. For it is that particular history which mediates God and his judgment and grace to our history and to all other history. That it does so is related to the power of Israel's history to take up our history into itself, interpreting our history in such a way that God becomes present to us anew in Jesus Christ both in judgment and grace.

The relation of Christian faith to history corresponds to the role of a historically given, essentially closed canon of Scripture. The formation of Scripture was one expression of the conviction that the definitive history has ended, whether that be expressed in the idea that the time of prophecy had ceased or in the Christian emphasis on apostolicity. At the same time the emphasis on apostolicity expressed a concern for the preservation and transmission of an authentic memory of the revelatory history. Such "authentic memory" was not merely a matter of preserving historical "facts," but it was also concerned with the continuing representation of that history in its meaning for faith as God's approach to humanity in judgment and grace. Thus Scripture gives us access in a continuing way to the revelatory history. But it also makes that history present to us in a particular way, namely, as a history that is transparent to God and his action and thus as a history that has meaning for all human history vis-à-vis God. There certainly could be other ways of representing Israel's history, as, for example, the presentation provided by a modern critical reconstruction. While such a presentation may be "true" in a certain sense, it tends to bypass the actual fabric of that history in its historic significance for those participating in it as well as for future generations. It cannot replace or be a substitute for the representation of Israel's history in the biblical text. The truth that Israel's history and Jesus' activity and fate is God's action toward all human history is conveyed to us through the particular way in which Israel's history is represented in Scripture. Thus the dialogue between theology and practice and the revelatory history through which God approaches us is at the same time a dialogue with Scripture.

This structure of meaning was not externally imposed onto Israel's history, but it was a part of the fabric of that history as it took place. In his presentation of Old Testament theology Gerhard von Rad[2] has shown that Old Testament materials took shape in a process of transmission and reinterpretation of historical traditions. When he speaks of the Old Testament as a history book, he understands history as a hermeneutical process, involving the dynamic interaction of historically shaped traditions and new events. The meaning of these new events as they happen is related to their context in the history of traditions, and they in turn transform the meaning of those traditions. Thus, for example, Israel interpreted its present history vis-à-vis God by means of narratives of its past history as God's action. These historical narratives and their re-presentation, whether in the cult or in extended narrations, were the context for interpreting the present in its relation to God. In turn the historical narratives were constantly reshaped by God's continuing activity in the course of Israel's history. In a somewhat different way the prophets used Israel's historical traditions to interpret the situation in their time in the light of God's future action of judgment or grace. Conceptions of reality in relation to God and anticipations of the future as threat or promise contained in Israel's traditions provided the context within which events were experienced as God's action toward his people. These events in turn modified and reshaped Israel's traditions, even negating some interpretations. Thus, for example, the prophetic message of impending doom as God's judgment made it possible for Israel to experience the destruction of Jerusalem by the Babylonians and the exile as God's judgment on Israel for its sins. Some interpretations of Israel's situation in the light of God's action in the past represented by the false prophets were also negated by these events. Thus the true meaning of Israel's traditions in relation to God can only be understood properly in retrospect in the light of the future of those traditions in history. This is reflected in one way by Jeremiah's suggestion that the future will determine the true and the false prophet, although prophecies of judgment are more probable in the light of the prophetic tradition (Jer. 28). It is also reflected in the Christian conviction that the Old Testament is most properly understood only when it is interpreted in the light of Jesus as the goal and fulfillment of Israel's history with God.

In the actual historical process of the transmission of traditions, the historical distance between the past and the present is dissolved—a situation that is true of memory as well as of tradition. The past is remembered and is transmitted to the future in its significance for the constantly changing present. The past is remembered with the meaning it has acquired in history, and the present is interpreted by the way in which the past is remembered. Thus, for example, the Pentateuch presents us with the end product of a long process in the history of the transmission of traditions, involving new combinations of traditions, the interweaving of various strands of traditions, and the interpretation and reinterpretation of those traditions in the course of Israel's history. Critical methods have made it possible to distinguish earlier strands of the tradition and, to some extent, to trace the history of theological interpretation contained in these traditions. But this is possible only with ambiguity and debate as is reflected, for example, in the divergence between the presentations of Israel's history before the monarchy by John Bright and Martin Noth.[3] The same situation is reflected in the difficulty of distinguishing the historical Jesus and the theological overlay of the early church's interpretation in the Gospels' presentations of Jesus. This process as such is not a matter of falsification, although falsification is possible. Rather, it expresses the fact that the future of an event belongs to the meaning of that event in history. What any event is as a phenomenon of human history is tied up with the future course of history produced by that event and related to it. Its meaning as a historical event is not locked up in its original time and place and in the original course of events, although it is always related to that origin. Any interpretation of events in history that

299

isolates them from their proper context in the web of history and from the flow of history that proceeds from them distorts the historical reality. It is this complex of meaning, not archaeological facts, that Scripture transmits to us.

David Noel Freedman has argued that a primal history, including the Pentateuch and the Former Prophets, was written in a form that acquired the status of Scripture shortly after the middle of the Babylonian exile.[4] The written form of this history became fixed around that time, and the documents were no longer extensively reworked, as had been the case earlier. Instead, new interpretations took the form of new documents, such as Chronicles or, later, the Book of Jubilees. Regardless of the details of the argument, Freedman's point reflects the difference between the process of traditions and the character of Scripture as written. The difference between Scripture and tradition is that in Scripture, tradition becomes fixed. As a written document Scripture presents us with a fragment of past history, preserved essentially unchanged, like an artifact. The past continues to be present as something that belongs to a past time, in its difference from the present form of tradition. This means that we have the possibility of a double relationship to history: one through tradition with its tendency to dissolve the distance between past and present, preserving the past in the form in which it continues to be significant in the present (although that dynamic is modified to some extent by the extensively written character of Christian tradition), and the other direct access to history through the written documents of Scripture. (This may be compared with Luther's distinction between the written and the oral Word of God, in which the accent on authority lay with the written Word, while the primary form of the Word of God was the oral word, which dissolves the boundaries between what God said then and what he says now.) Thus it is the written character of Scripture that makes dialogue with Israel's history in its difference from the present possible as an essential dimension of the structure of Christian theology.

This dual relation to the history presented in Scripture is reflected in the tradition of the fourfold sense of Scripture with its distinction between literal and spiritual exegesis. The latter included allegorical exegesis related to the church and its doctrines, moral exegesis related to Christian behavior, and anagogical exegesis related to metaphysical and eschatological mysteries. The balance between the accent on literal and spiritual interpretation varied between exegetes, although heresy was often associated with an insistence on literal interpretation. The presupposition for spiritual interpretation was the inspiration of Scripture and the presence of the Spirit in the Christian community and its tradition. Along with tradition, spiritual interpretation provided the bridge between the historicity of the text and the present, enabling the text to embrace and interpret the present. As Luther correctly saw, however, spiritual interpretation ultimately meant that what Scripture said was finally conformed to the theological tradition of the church, which became the criteria of the meaning of Scripture. Hence Scripture was no longer able to function as the authoritative word that made possible the dialogue between theological tradition and the historical revelation of God. In contrast, Luther argued for a single sense of Scripture, the literal sense, which he connected with the christological focus of Scripture. For Luther the literal grammatical-historical sense of Scripture was its sole authoritative sense, and it also had the power to embrace the present as God's Word, transcending the difference between then and now.

While Luther's understanding of Scripture restored the dual relationship between theology and God's historical revelation in Jesus Christ, it was still possible for him to understand his own theology as essentially identical with the theology of the biblical texts, without a strong sense of historical distance. The Enlightenment and the subsequent development of historical methodology, coupled with the emergence of historical consciousness in its modern form, have made us much more aware of historical relativity and historical distance. While that distance may be stressed to a greater or lesser degree, it is no longer possible for many people today to assume that we can preserve any past theology, whether that of the Bible or of the Reformation, by simply repeating their formulations. Nor is it possible to identify our theology with that of Scripture or the Reformation in any simple way. Historical context and meaning are closely interwoven, so that even to repeat past theological formulations in a new historical context alters their meaning in significant ways. This introduces new dimensions to an understanding of theology as a hermeneutical dialogue with Scripture.

THE POLARITY OF DISTANCE AND PARTICIPATION

In nuclear physics the principle of complementarity in the Heisenberg uncertainty principle says that there are certain properties necessary to an adequate description of physical reality that cannot be measured simultaneously with exactness, such as position and momentum. The more precisely an experimenter measures position the less he knows about momentum, and the more precisely he measures momentum the less he knows about position. This is an aspect of the nature of physical reality, and it reflects the fact that the observation of nature is itself an effective part of the results obtained. This is connected with the emergence of quantum mechanics and the duality of the wave (associated with momentum) and particle (associated with position) representation of physical reality. While there is some debate about the precise significance of this for our understanding of physical reality, it is clear that the questions asked of nature in an experiment are not neutral but determine the results in significant ways.

Something like complementarity exists in theology's hermeneutical enterprise in the two dimensions of distance and participation. Distance is associated with the historical character of Scripture and revelation and thus with its difference from any possible contemporary theological construct. That is, it is related to the character of Scripture as a written document and thus as a historical artifact, which is an essential dimension of its meaning for theology. Participation is associated with the power of Scripture to take up our reality and to interpret it vis-à-vis God. That is, it is related to the power of Scripture to dissolve the distance between then and now and to create new understanding. In that sense it is similar to the living function of traditional as an aid to understanding. Both these dimensions are necessary for Scripture to function properly as a hermeneutical aid in theology. The accent on distance by itself tends to leave the Bible an irrelevant archaeological artifact. On the other hand, the accent on participation, including the function of tradition and the dissolution of the distance between then and now, tends to lose a sense for the otherness of Scripture as God's authoritative word of address which always stands over against us. In either case, the methods of interpretation used are not neutral to the results obtained but shape the interpretation in significant ways.

The power of tradition to shape our understanding of the Christian message is such that it normally has been difficult in the history of interpretation to see Scripture in its difference from our own theological understanding. We read it in the context of traditions that provide us with powerful presuppositions about the message of Scripture. The result is that without considerable care we almost automatically find in the Bible what our presuppositions lead us to expect, and we fail to notice the oddities that stand in tension with our expectations. For example, we have a tendency to read Paul in the light of our Western tradition of the introspective conscience, oriented to the themes of guilt and forgiveness.[5] The result is that we fail to take serious account of the fact that Paul does not ordinarily use these themes or of what that might mean for the interpretation of Paul. Even our Lutheran tradition, with its emphasis on the sole authority of Scripture, can easily slip back into a pre-Reformation domination of Scripture by the interpretive power of tradition, with the result that Scripture cannot say anything to us that is different from what we already know through our tradition.

It is therefore necessary to have interpretive tools that help us see the Bible in its difference from our own theological framework for the sake of a genuine practice of theology as a dialogue with Scripture. For the Reformation the authoritative sense of Scripture was its literal grammatical-historical sense. In our day the historical-critical method provides us with a set of interpretive tools for understanding biblical texts in their historical contexts and thus in their distance from our own theological thought. This involves the attempt to understand the process by which the text took shape and was transmitted to us, the question of the original form of the text, the endeavor to see the text in its original historical setting as well as to see the significance of new historical contexts within Scripture for its meaning, the quest for a historical understanding of the language and grammar used, the study of the text in relation to the conceptual world of the time within which it was written, and so on. All this belongs to the endeavor to understand the literal historical sense of Scripture in terms of what it meant for the author and for the people to whom it was originally written as God's Word. In this way the historical-critical method functions positively in carrying out the Reformation's concern for the literal grammatical-historical sense of the text as its authoritative meaning. Of course, this is not the only way the Bible can be seen in its difference from our own theological tradition, and theology has not had to await the development of the historical-critical method for this dialogue to take place. But given our historical setting with the availability of historical methodology, the interest in the historical meaning of Scripture impels us to make use of all the tools available to us for gaining access to that meaning.

The accent on the difference between Scripture and the dogmatic tradition of the church has accompanied the development of modern biblical studies from the beginning. The Reformation accented the difference between the Bible and the prevailing form of the Roman Catholic church's dogmatic tradition. When people began to write biblical theologies at the time of Pietism, there was an emphasis on recovering the simple message of the Bible in contrast to the complexities of the dogmatic tradition of Protestant orthodoxy. At times, especially during the nineteenth century, the difference took the form of active hostility to the church's dogmatic tradition. But even research done in hostility contributed to methodologies for gaining access to the historical context and meaning of biblical material.

The development of the historical-critical method was, however, also accompanied by the presupposition that the sense of historical distance gained was synonymous with methodological objectivity and neutrality. This was contrasted with the subjective prejudice of the dogmatic tradition and of attempts to understand Scripture in the context of that tradition. At the beginning of the twentieth century Albert Schweitzer[6] and others demonstrated that the interpretive tradition and interest of the historical school itself functioned as a dogmatic prejudice that led in its own way to an unhistorical interpretation of the biblical material. Later Adolf Schlatter, Karl Barth, Rudolf Bultmann,[7] and others exposed the inadequacy of the historical-critical method as the sole approach to understanding the biblical text. They stressed the hermeneutical power of the presuppositions with which the text is approached, and rejected the assumed objectivity of the historical-critical method and its alleged neutrality in relation to the meaning of the text. As a result they emphasized the importance of moving beyond a distancing encounter with Scripture to a dialogue in which its claim on our present understanding of ourselves and our history could be heard effectively.

Taken by itself, in its isolation from the church's tradition of the Bible as the Word of God, the distancing aspect of the historical-critical method tends to dissolve the character of Scripture as God's revelation to us.[8] In this way it makes it possible to avoid the claim of the text on our present understanding of our world and its history. We can easily fall prey to the temptation to explain away the claim of the text on us by understanding its origins in history. That is nothing new. Already in Jesus' day there were those who dismissed Jesus because they knew his historical origins. But, as the church's emphasis on Jesus' humanity maintained, it was only in Jesus, whose human, historical origins were known and accessible, that the transcendent mystery of God was redemptively present to all human history. Also, while the Bible's meaning as God's Word of address is not given in the historical-critical interpretation of it, it is also found not by avoiding historical interpretations in which its origins are known but only in relation to such interpretations. For what is discovered by such methodology is also true, and thus essential to an adequate interpretation, even though it does not say all there is to say in the task of interpreting Scripture. As is indicated in the image of complementarity, both the distancing function of the historical-critical method and the dimension of participation associated with tradition and the concern for present meaning belong essentially to the reality of the Bible and to the nature of theology as a hermeneutical dialogue with Scripture. Both are necessary for an adequate representation of the Word of God in Scripture as it addresses us. In addition, our own historicity means that many people would find it neither possible nor helpful to attempt to return to a precritical approach to history and to Scripture. If that were necessary for the Bible to be God's Word for us, that would of itself make faith in God, who has approached us in Israel's history and in the person of Jesus Christ, difficult if not impossible for many people in our historical context.

HISTORICITY AND THE HERMENEUTICAL CIRCLE

Hans-Georg Gadamer in *Truth and Method*[9] has described hermeneutics as a process of the fusion of horizons. At any given point in our history each of us sees and understands our world from a certain perspective or viewpoint that makes it possible for us to see things in a particular way and that also hides some things from our view. This is like looking out over the landscape that can be seen from a view point. As we walk through the world of that landscape our horizon changes and we see it in new ways that may significantly alter our initial perception of it, although that initial view remains a part of that perception. Similarly, as we move through history the horizon for our understanding of the reality within which we live constantly changes. Different people and different times also have different horizons. The encounter with different horizons of understanding alters our own horizon if we enter into serious dialogue with them. A conversation is one model of such fusion of horizons in which two people seek to understand each other and thus to enlarge their own horizon of understanding. The process is similar with texts, but with at least one significant difference. In a conversation each person can make sure that what he says is not misunderstood by being taken to say something he does not intend. One can ask the other person to explain himself, or he can say that what one understood is not what he really means to say. Each person takes responsibility for making sure that what he says is properly heard by the other. With texts, however, the interpreter himself must take responsibility for establishing the strange horizon of the text in its validity over against the horizon of thought he brings to the text. The interpreter must take responsibility for letting the text speak for itself and correct his understanding.

The process of understanding as a fusion of horizons involves three aspects that are closely interwoven. First, the material to be understood must be grasped precisely in its distance from the horizon of the interpreter. As has been argued above, this is the role of historical and grammatical exegesis and of the historical-critical method. Its goal is to establish the literal meaning of the text within its own historical matrix in its distance from our present. Second, in the process of interpreting the text a new common understanding emerges, establishing an embracing horizon that incorporates the initially strange horizons of the interpreter and the text. This is not an additional step, but it takes place in the process of interpretation itself. Third, in this way the interpreter moves beyond the boundaries of his initial question and preliminary understanding of the subject matter.

This is, of course, a form of the hermeneutical circle with its dialogue between preunderstanding and text. But in the movement of human existence through history as an irreversible process—not necessarily progress—horizons within which people understand the reality of their world alter. Horizons of understanding that once were natural for people are no longer immediately understandable for us. Pictures we have of the world we live in change, and the meaning they had for human self-understanding is forgotten. For example, cultic and sacrificial systems, as well as laws of ritual purity, often appear to us to be merely external and formal matters, for we have lost the sense for the profound human meaning they once had for people. Those horizons of understanding are available to us only indirectly as they have been transmitted to us historically in the way they have continued to have significance through tradition, as for example the Christian transformation of Israelite cultic systems, and more particularly as they have been precipitated in texts. If history were simply progress, the former would be sufficient. Texts preserve the human resource of forgotten horizons of meaning, however.

This means that in the interaction of Scripture and theology the hermeneutical circle is relatively complex. It includes the text as a given fact, the impact of Scripture as a whole on the theological traditions of the church, and our own theological horizons within those traditions. But since context and meaning belong together it is also important to attempt to reconstruct the historical horizon(s) of thought out of which the biblical writers wrote and which came to expression in what they said in the situations they addressed by means of formulating biblical theologies. This is required by the historical distance between our own theological horizon and that of the biblical writers. The projection of such theologies is a dimension of the quest both to understand the text of Scripture historically and to understand the present by means of a dialogue with the biblical text. The projection of such theologies is not simply historically descriptive, but it takes place in a dynamic dialogue with the text as something given and the present theological and historical tradition of the interpreter. In this entire hermeneutical process, the criterion of any interpretation is the text itself in its givenness. Does the text itself shape the interpretation and come to expression in it? Or is the interpretation imposed onto the text?

THE EVOCATIVE POWER OF THE TEXT

As a process of the transmission and transformation of traditions, history involves the fusion of horizons. Human history is a constant quest for the embracing horizon of thought that provides the context for a genuine understanding of the reality within which we live. For Christian faith, Israel's history culminating in Jesus is, as God's once-for-all approach to human history, the proper interpretive context for understanding all human history vis-à-vis God. On the other hand, in view of the universal character of God's action in Israel's history and in Jesus, all human history itself is the proper context within which God's saving action in Jesus is ultimately understood in its full meaning.

The issue of the proper context for understanding is already involved in the question of a proper understanding of Scripture. The historical interpretation of Scripture has made it clear that there are more or less diverse, if not contradictory, theologies in the Bible itself. As such, this awareness is not entirely new, but it has been intensified by Ernst Käsemann's argument[10] that denominational diversity is related to theological diversity within the canon. Whether one stresses or minimizes the differences between biblical writers, it seems clear that on the surface of the text there are differences in accent and emphasis, differences in perspective on the meaning of God's saving action in Jesus Christ, and at times even apparent contradictions. On one level this variety belongs to the richness of the meaning of God's action in Christ for human history, so that its representation in Scripture reflects its many facets rather than presenting us with a single, homogeneous picture. The unity of Scripture then has a mosaic character and is best represented as a dynamic dialogue of the parts, in which Scripture as a whole is taken into account.

As soon as such differences are recognized, however, even though in minimal form, we are confronted with the question of the proper inner-biblical context for the appropriate interpretation of the parts. If the context is a significant factor determining meaning, then those portions of the Bible that provide the center in relation to which the whole Bible is interpreted shape its meaning in significant ways. Indeed, theological traditions as well as particular theologies can be analyzed in terms of the parts of Scripture that provide the integrating focus for the interpretation of the whole. One need only think of the role of Paul for Lutheran theology, or of the different theological tendencies that result when Romans 4:17, which speaks of God "who gives life to the dead and calls into existence the things that do not exist," is taken as the central definition of the relation between God and humanity in contrast to Revelation 3:20, which pictures Jesus standing at the door and knocking. Since such differences in perspective are given within the Bible with no simply defined statement of *the* central perspective, this theological diversity belongs to the meaning of Scripture and thus to its unity and to the unity of theology and the church. Of course there are criteria that are possible within this diversity. One is the power of a perspective to integrate and bring to expression Scripture as a whole. A second criterion, suggested by Wolfhart Pannenberg,[11] would be the inherent meaning of Jesus' history within its context in the history of Israel's traditions. A negative criterion given by the history of the formation of the canon is the conviction that an integrating perspective should not be derived from those books more ambiguously present in the canon, such as James or Revelation, lest the message of Scripture be distorted. But these criteria leave a significant measure of diversity in the proper theological appropriation of Scripture in the church and its history, a diversity that belongs to the meaning of Scripture itself.

The interrelation of context and meaning also presents us with the issue of theological diversity in another way. The historical situation of the interpreter is a context within which the text takes on a particular meaning. The interpreter and his history are a part of the interpretive process. Hans-Georg Gadamer illuminates this by discussing the reenactment of an artistic production in the performance of a play or a concert. What takes place on the stage is a product of the text of the play itself, the interpretation given it by the directors and performers, and the reaction of the audience. In each production of a play, the play is reenacted and made present in a new way with new dimensions of meaning, resulting from the interaction of the play and a new historical situation, which were not there before. There may, of course, be effective and poor reproductions. But these new dimensions of meaning belong to the meaning of the play itself as it continues to take shape in reenactments in history. An archaeological reconstruction of the play as it was originally produced would not be a more effective presentation of the play, nor would it be a genuine reenactment of the meaning the play had in its original production. Similarly, theology as an interpretive process is concerned with the reenactment of the text of Scripture as an effective Word of God in the present history of the interpreter. That reenactment is a product of the interaction of the text itself with our history and horizon of thought, creating new insight and understanding not there before. This process involves the interaction of our present horizon both with the language of the text and with its historical meaning, although each may take place in different measure on different occasions. In that interaction the text becomes the Word of God in a new way in the new situation, and it illuminates and transforms that situation, creating a new understanding of our history as it is addressed by God's Word.

Thus, the dialogue with the text interprets the present, creating new dimensions of meaning with regard to the present, and the text in turn acquires new dimensions of meaning in the context of the present. This is another way to talk about the traditional themes of the effectiveness of Scripture or of Scripture as the living Word. If the history of theology is the history of the interpretation of biblical texts or the history of the interpretive power of biblical texts in relation to changing historical situations, then the history of theology belongs to the meaning of the texts, even when that history involves misunderstanding. Indeed, important new insights may even arise through creative misunderstanding. At the same time, interpretive methods that effectively represented the message of Scripture in some historical contexts, such as the fourfold interpretation, may cease to be possible at other times, while new methods may emerge in the history of interpretation.

By being written and fixed, the language of a text acquires a life of its own in history, which is somewhat independent of the history that gave rise to the text. Thus, at the time when parts of the Bible were incorporated into the canon, they had already acquired new dimensions of meaning through Israel's history and were no longer read in a way that necessarily corresponded to the original intention. Similarly, by being incorporated into the canon they acquired a context that gave them new dimensions of meaning not necessarily foreseen in the original intention of their authors. This development is part of what the text is as God's Word to all human history. But it also means that the text does not have a simple single meaning. It has its original historical meaning, which may or may not be recoverable. But it also has other meanings in the context of Israel's history and in the context of the canon, as well as a multiplicity of new dimensions of meaning that have emerged in new historical contexts. Every preacher who has used the same text on more than one occasion is familiar with that fact. That multiplicity of meanings belongs to the text itself as it interprets changing historical circumstances.

Gerhard von Rad suggests[12] that one distinction between the true and false prophet was that the latter used Israel's traditions to close the future and to orient the people to the past, while the former used those traditions to anticipate the new future action of God in judgment and grace. That suggests that one criterion of the truth of the Christian message and of Scripture lies in the power of God's action in Jesus Christ as it is presented in the Bible to take up our particular history into itself, opening it to the future of God's judgment and grace and thus transforming it by his presence in Jesus Christ. This plurality of meaning, however, stands in a dialectical relation to the emphasis of the Lutheran tradition that the normative sense of the text as authoritative Word is the literal grammatical-historical sense, a sense that has the power to embrace and interpret the present. The stress on the literal grammatical-historical meaning ought not, of course, to lose sight of the hermeneutical history of Scripture in the Christian tradition as a dimension of the meaning of Scripture. The criteria of this history, however, lies not in the tradition itself but in the historicity of Scripture in its literal grammatical-historical sense.

The power of Scripture to evoke new meaning in new historical situations is, then, an essential dimension of its role in the life and thought of the Christian community. It is important for it to be a part of our hermeneutical horizon and to be correlated with our interpretive methodologies, even though it is not simply contained or controlled by scholarly methods. Ultimately the evocative power of Scripture to provoke new meaning and thus to create new life is, in theological language, the work of the Holy Spirit. This corresponds to what we have called the dimension of participation. The evocative power to illuminate the world in which we live is, of course, also characteristic of all great literature and art. If that were all that mattered in the relation of the Christian community with Scripture, then historical study would merely be an interesting but optional sideline for theology and we could content ourselves with the mythical and symbolic functions of biblical language and imagery. The message of the Christian community, however, is that God has entered human history once for all in the course of Israel's history and above all in the person of Jesus of Nazareth. This message of God's entry into our world roots our life and thought in a past history. Historical methodology, of which the historical-critical method is at least an aspect, is important to maintain and re-present that tie to history in Christian theology. In any adequate set of interpretive methods in Christian theology both the dimensions of present participation and those of historical distance are necessary for an adequate dialogue with God's saving work in history as that is presented to us in Scripture.

NOTES

1. Gerhard Ebeling, "Word of God and Hermeneutic," in *Word and Faith,* trans. James W. Leitch (Philadelphia: Fortress Press, 1963), pp. 305–32, esp. p. 318.
2. Gerhard von Rad, *Old Testament Theology,* trans. D. M. G. Stalker, 2 vols. (New York: Harper & Row, 1962–65).
3. John Bright, *A History of Israel,* 2d ed. (Philadelphia: Westminster Press, 1972); Martin Noth, *History of Israel: Biblical History* (New York: Harper & Row, 1960).
4. David Noel Freedman, "Son of Man, Can These Bones Live," *Interpretation* 29 (1975): 171–86, esp. 181–84.
5. Krister Stendahl, "The Apostle Paul and the Introspective Conscience of the West," in *The Writings of St. Paul,* ed. Wayne A. Meeks (New York: W. W. Norton & Co., 1972), pp. 422–34. Originally published in *Harvard Theological Review* 56 (1963): 199–215.
6. Albert Schweitzer, *The Quest of the Historical Jesus* (New York: Macmillan Company, 1960).
7. Adolf Schlatter, "The Theology of the New Testament and Dogmatics," in *The Nature of New Testament Theology,* ed. and trans. Robert Morgan, Studies in Biblical Theology, Second Series, 25 (Naperville, Ill.: Alec R. Allenson, 1973), pp. 117–66; Karl Barth, *The Epistle to the Romans,* trans. Edwyn C. Hoskyns (London: Oxford University Press, 1933); Rudolf Bultmann, "The Problem of Hermeneutics," in his *Essays Philosophical and Theological,* trans. James C. G. Greig (New York: Macmillan Company, 1955), pp. 234–61; idem, "Is Exegesis without Presuppositions Possible?" in *Existence and Faith: Shorter Writings of Rudolf Bultmann,* trans. Schubert M. Ogden (Cleveland: World Publishing Company, 1960), pp. 289–96.
8. See Hendrikus Boers, "Historical Criticism versus Prophetic Proclamation," *Harvard Theological Review* (1972): 393–414.
9. Hans-Georg Gadamer, *Truth and Method* (New York: Seabury Press, 1975).
10. Ernst Käsemann, "The Canon of the New Testament and the Unity of the Church," in *Essays on New Testament Themes,* trans. W. J. Montague, Studies in Biblical Theology, First Series, 41 (Naperville, Ill.: Alec R. Allenson, 1964), pp. 95–107.
11. Wolfhart Pannenberg, "The Crisis of the Scripture Principle," in his *Basic Questions in Theology,* trans. George H. Kehm (Philadelphia: Fortress Press, 1970), 1:1–14.
12. See his discussion of prophetic eschatology in *Old Testament Theology,* 2:112–19.

The Incompatibility between Historical-Critical Theology and the Lutheran Confessions

KURT E. MARQUART

Associate Professor of Systematic Theology
Concordia Theological Seminary
Fort Wayne, Indiana

The present essay submits and argues three specific propositions, namely, that historical-critical theology or theologizing, seen in the perspective of the Lutheran Confessions, (1) subjects Scripture to reason, (2) introduces a deeply antiincarnational split between history and theology, and (3) relativizes all dogma into doubtful human opinions. My basic working assumption is that any theology which cannot or will not subserve the faithful proclamation and celebration of Christ's life-giving gospel and sacraments in the churches, in the sense of the Lutheran Confessions, has thereby declared itself insolvent and forfeited any claims to churchly validity or attention.

SCRIPTURE AND REASON

By "historical-critical theology" I mean a theology that accepts the so-called historical-critical method as a valid and necessary, or at least permissible, instrument of biblical interpretation. The hermeneutical issue involved here could not be more far-reaching. Let us begin by reassuring ourselves, in the first place, that there really is such a thing as "the historical-critical method." This is sometimes doubted. Yet writers as diverse as Karl Barth, Gerhard Ebeling, Hans-Joachim Kraus, Willi Marxsen, Gerhard Maier, Ernst and Marie-Luise Keller, Edgar Krentz, Peter Stuhlmacher, Ferdinand Hahn, Norbert Lohfink, Bengt Haegglund, John Warwick Montgomery, Horton Harris, and with reservations

George Eldon Ladd—an arbitrary selection of authors whose works I happen to have at hand—speak without any hesitation simply of "the historical-critical method," often in titles of books, chapters, or articles. Werner G. Kümmel generally prefers the terms "critical," "scientific," or "historical" to the phrase "historical-critical" or its derivatives.[1] Clearly, just about everybody writing on the subject assumes that "the historical-critical method" is an intelligible term corresponding to an identifiable entity.

What then is this historical-critical method? What is its essence or the distinguishing characteristic by which it can be defined and identified? Some discussions become confusing at this point because of the common fallacy of mistaking descriptive examples for definitions. Thus we are sometimes offered a list of scholarly "techniques" as if this were a definition. But this "techniques" approach does not get to the heart of the matter and tends toward a pragmatic short-circuiting of meaning. For one thing, most of the techniques (e.g., literary criticism, redaction criticism) can be used up to a point also by anticritical scholars. For another, particular techniques come and go, but historical criticism goes on. Third, once the discussion is abducted off the open highway of first principles onto booby-trapped jungle paths of esoteric techniques, people tend to frighten themselves and each other with abstruse technicalities and counter-technicalities. As a result the wearied disputants are tempted to take refuge in the bland evasion that since the techniques differ, and even more so their applications by individual scholars, there really is no such thing as *the* historical-critical method.

If we are looking for definitions rather than illustrations, we shall have to ask what it is that distinguishes historical criticism from other methods. While some have labored to find the seeds of historical criticism in Luther or in ancient Antioch or even in Alexandria, it is generally acknowledged that in point of fact "historical method is the child of the Enlightenment."[2] Werner Kümmel maintains that "it is improper to speak of scientific study of the New Testament or of a historical approach to primitive Christianity prior to the Enlightenment."[3] Gerhard Ebeling is even more explicit:

> For historical criticism is more than lively historical interest. Even the early and medieval churches concerned themselves more or less with history and the study of its sources. . . . It was not what we know today as the critical historical method. For the latter is not concerned with the greatest possible refinement of the philological methods, but with subjecting the tradition to critical examination on the basis of new principles of thought. The critical historical method first arose out of the intellectual revolution of modern

times. It is—not just, say, where it oversteps its legitimate limits, but by its very nature—bound up with criticism of content.[4]

Ferdinand Hahn, in a most penetrating essay, draws attention to historical criticism's chameleonlike "adaptability" and "flexibility" on account of which "one could again and again deceive oneself about the premises which were taken over without reflection and accordingly were only latently active." He makes no bones about the fact that the very first such premise was and is "the concept of autonomous human reason, taken over, as a rule, without reflection. . . ."[5] That of course is what the Enlightenment was all about.

What this adds up to is that the distinctive feature of the historical-critical method or approach is simply the supremacy of human reason or, in dogmatic terms, the magisterial use of reason. Edgar Krentz remarks helpfully that the rationalist "Semler rather than Ernesti is usually regarded as the father of historical-critical theology, since Ernesti denied the possibility of inspired Scripture ever erring."[6] Clearly, biblical inerrancy is incompatible with the magisterium of reason, hence also with historical criticism. For as Krentz also observes,

> the Scriptures were, so to speak, secularised. The biblical books became historical documents to be studied and questioned like any other ancient sources. The Bible was no longer the criterion for the writing of history; rather history had become the criterion for understanding the Bible. . . . The history it reported was no longer assumed to be everywhere correct. The Bible stood before criticism as defendant before judge.[7]

This *judicial* function of magisterial, critical human reason was highlighted in Abraham Kuenen's 1880 essay "Critical Methods," which Kraus regards as representing "the 'methodology' of historical-critical scholarship at the apex of its unfolding."[8] Comments Kraus:

> The biblical witnesses are first and foremost witnesses of a historical process which the "judge" must reconstruct, because he is dealing—and that is the secret presupposition of all research for Kuenen—with the "case" of a "false historiography" in the Old Testament. At this point lies the real life-nerve of historical-critical scholarship in the phase of its powerful unfolding. Already with De Wette there begins the great cross-examination by the historical-critical "judge.". . . Here one encounters the innermost impulse of scientific questing and questioning.[9]

Science of course cannot cope with sacrosanct texts or privileged authorities. If scientific method is to be applied at all, it must be applied without exceptions or exemptions. The Bible henceforth becomes one set of data among others. Stripped of its majesty, it is reduced to the status of a private citizen in the great republic of letters, all of them equally answerable to the supreme court of inquisitive human intelligence and ingenuity. One of the most clearheaded formulations of the leveling implications of historical criticism is to be found in a set of theses on the historical-critical method which formed the basis for a discussion between the Protestant and Roman Catholic theological faculties in the University of Munich:

> . . . If exegesis is to be practised historico-critically, it must use the methods of secular historical science, i.e. criticism, which allows only probable judgments, and the principles of analogy and correlation (cf. Troeltsch). Thereby it subjects itself in principle to secular-historical judgment. . . .
>
> Historical-critical exegesis presupposes the equal historical value of all sources, i.e., it prescinds from the self-witness or the special status of a writing. . . . The biblical books count as ancient near-eastern sources, and the concepts contained in them are ancient near-eastern. . . .
>
> From the historical integration into general history there follows the religio-historical integration. Yahweh is a semitic divinity (about whose introduction into Israel the historian may offer conjectures); this applies in principle also to the *Theos* of the NT. Phenomena and concepts (e.g. charismatics, kingship, prophecy, discipleship, apostolate; commandments, ethos, prayer, virgin birth, resurrection, ascension) are subject to the principles of correlation and analogy. Jesus is a late-Jewish figure. The forms of religion in the biblical texts count, since they developed historically, as syncretistic. . . .
>
> Through the abolition of the boundary of the canon for historical research, the concept "unity" or "centre of Scripture" becomes questionable. . . .
>
> Events which are not subject to the criteria of analogy and correlation (miracles, raisings of the dead, resurrection) cannot be regarded as historical in a strict sense.[10]

Ernst Troeltsch's principles of analogy and correlation seek to simulate for history the objectivity of the exact sciences, to reduce historical events to the coveted regularities of physics. This dogmatic immanentism, however, has now been completely undermined by the fading of the mirage of "scientific" history, and especially by the dramatic collapse of nineteenth-century scientistic materialism. A universe in which matter is but a visible foreground merging into an imponderable background of pure energy is a very different sort of place from the intractably, irreducibly solid machine imagined by the Victorians! The German mathematics professor Hans Rohrbach argues that the allegedly biblical ("three-story universe") world view is not that of the Bible, and that the so-called modern scientific world view is not that of modern science but that of nineteenth-century scientism. The latter, it is true, had no room for God and miracles. But of the genuinely contemporary scientific view of nature Rohrbach says not that there is "room in it for God" but rather that it finds room "in" God, that is, in God's reality.[11]

In the wake of this disintegration of erstwhile scientific certainties, biblical criticism too has become more hesitant, particularly about the principle of correlation, with its rigidly immanentist causality. Books like *Miracles in Dispute* by Ernst and Marie-Luise Keller, with their rigorous exclusion of miracles in the name of the historical-critical method, are really anachronisms.[12]

It would be a mistake, however, to assume either that radical criticism was a brief, self-correcting lapse into extremism or that a rejection of this extremism means that the historical-critical method has thereby been purged of its inherent subjugation to magisterial reason. An Eastern Orthodox observer, Konstantinos E. Papapetrou, notes:

> Today's theology is certainly less "liberal" than the "liberal theology" of yesterday. . . . In comparison with the leading ideas of the liberals, "demythologization" appears to be very pious. Nevertheless it would be an error if one came to the conclusion on that account that theology was becoming more conservative with the passage of time. Liberal theology was the fruit of an acute process of secularization and reigned in a few academic and ecclesiastical circles. The people of the church were for the most part less affected by this liberalism; they saw in the pioneers of this liberalism in the first place enemies of the church or even atheists. . . . Meanwhile, however, much has changed. The acute stage of the liberalization of theology is over, but on the other hand this liberalization has become chronic, more deeply penetrating, more thorough. It has embraced broad sections of the people of the church and the majority of the young West European pastors. "Demythologizing" (and we may not understand thereby simply the program of Bultmann!), together with its liberal features, has for some time been more than the affair of a few academics; rather, it largely shapes the consciousness of the Protestant churches. . . . Today all Christendom is being gradually and slowly but surely secularized. Even the Second Vatican Council seems in a certain respect to be the great Council of the secularization of the Roman Catholic church. . . .
>
> The Protestant Christian today hears sermons which are possibly less liberal than some theological-scientific lectures at the turn of the century. But this subdued liberalism of the present is no longer the content of lectures but of sermons; it has even become self-evident.[13]

One is reminded of the comment of Hans Asmussen, president of the chancery of the Evangelical Church in Germany from 1946 to 1948:

> But this is in fact the picture of wide sectors of our Lutheran Church to-day: clergymen read aloud the Christmas story, which they consider a

317

fairytale. They read aloud the Easter story, to which they find access only after several reinterpretations. At the grave, they witness to the resurrection of the dead, which they consider a myth.[14]

Whether one holds to a strict or loose application of the principle of correlation (the concept of a closed, nonmiraculous chain of cause and effect), it comes to the same thing if one is still free to reject biblical miracles while not denying their possibility in theory. In other words, magisterial reason is still in the saddle. Abraham Kuenen, the classic formulator of the critic-as-judge theme, took precisely that position. He did not rule out miracles a priori but he did reserve his right as a critic to determine whether a given biblical report of a miracle was to be accepted as probably authentic or not.[15]

In other words, to let reason rule magisterially one need not with Ebeling object to "metaphysical beings in the sense of the older picture of the world as internal factors in the world and its history."[16] It is enough to make oneself the judge in principle of the validity of biblical statements. So then, whether criticism happens to be more radical or less radical in given circumstances does not alter its essential nature. But how can one distinguish between criticism's essence and extreme, radical versions of it? I suggest that it might be useful, on the analogy of the narrow and the wider cosmological principles in astronomy, to speak of a "narrow critical principle" and a "wider" one. The narrow principle would denote the acceptance of critical human intelligence as arbiter of truth, inasmuch as the critical approach demands that the Bible be treated exactly like all other literature. But this narrow principle would involve no a priori bias against miracles or the supernatural as such. The wider critical principle would include the further refinement that miracles are simply to be ruled out *e limine* on the grounds either of a heuristic historicism or of a dogmatic one, based on a secular-scientistic (and probably antiquated) world view.

It follows from this analysis that the narrow critical principle is the bare, irreducible minimum of the historical-critical method, which cannot be surrendered without destroying the method itself. One can certainly sympathize with Peter Stuhlmacher's suggestion of "the frame of reference of the Third Article of the Creed" as an antidote to the current historical-critical impasse.[17] For in Krentz's paraphrase of Stuhlmacher, "There are mutually exclusive opinions on every topic or question in the discipline, a scandal in a scientific discipline"![18] And Ferdinand Hahn, in a penetrating analysis in the very same issue of *Zeitschrift für die neutestamentliche Wissenschaft* in which Stuhlmacher writes, speaks darkly of "the end or at least a late phase of a process of dissolution which has been going on for centuries."[19] Nevertheless it is futile to suggest the third or any other article of the creed as a way out. For either this would be so vague as to impose no real controls at all, in which case the exercise would amount to no more than a bit of rhetorical cosmetic, or else, if effective controls were imposed, the resultant procedure would no longer be the historical-critical method. The whole point of the method has been and is emancipation from all theological authorities or controls. Or, in Krentz's understatement, "the method tends to freedom from authority."[20] It is a wild horse that cannot endure the bit and bridle of external authority but is instinctively bound to follow the dictates of free scientific inquiry alone. If it were caught flirting with authority principles or making special allowances for some writings in preference to others, the method would thereby forfeit its scientific credentials, hence its whole raison d'être.

In light of the above I take it that no one will seriously contend that the *wider* critical principle is compatible with bona fide subscription to the Lutheran Confessions. The burning issue is whether the narrow principle, representing the quintessence of the historical-critical method rather than "accidental" excrescences or epiphenomena, can be brought into harmony with the confessional commitment. To this basic question we must now turn.

Peter Brunner has written:

> In the last 250 years, the Lutheran Church has not been able to overcome the theological crises through which it has had to pass. It is still largely unaware of the depth of its plight. All talk of confessional allegiance is meaningless, if Holy Scripture is lost as the concrete judge over all proclamation and teaching. The Confession presupposes Scripture, and Scripture not as an historically given phenomenon, but as a speaking authority! This presupposition has become problematic for many pastors, theologians, and non-theologians. For this reason confessional loyalty has also become problematic.[21]

This language alludes first of all to the Formula of Concord (Rule and Norm), which acknowledges "Holy Scripture alone as the sole judge, rule, and norm" (*sola sacra scriptura iudex, norma et regula*), according to which "all teachings and teachers" must be judged.[22] Here already is foreshadowed the irreconcilable conflict with the historical-critical method: either *sola sacra scriptura* will be *iudex* or else critical human reason and scholarship, but not both. The two principles are mutually exclusive. One must inevitably rule and the other serve; one function magisterially, the other ministerially. The issue is nonnegotiable. *Tertium non datur.*

A characteristic feature of the critical approach, as we shall see in the next section, is the splitting up of the Bible into "divine" and "human" elements. "The root of the evil" in theology, said Johann Salomo Semler, the father of historical-critical theology, "is the confusion of Scripture and Word of God."[23] The Formula of Concord also insists on a clear distinction between divine and human elements—but in a totally different sense. While criticism drives the separating wedge *into* the biblical text itself, the Formula drives it *between* Holy Scripture and all other writings. The Latin version of the Solid Declaration (Rule and Norm) uses very pointed language: there is a clean break or *"discrimen"* between *"divina et humana scripta"* such that "the sacred Scriptures [*sacras litteras*] alone must be acknowledged as the single [*unica*] rule and norm of all teachings, and no man's writings whatever [*nullius omnino hominis scripta*] be put on a par with them, but rather all must be subjected" to them (par. 9).[24] And the "sacred Scriptures" here stands for the German *Gottes Wort*.

The Formula's decisive distinction, be it noted, is not between gospel content and nongospel content but between "divine and human *writings*" (*scripta*). The biblical text, as God's Word, stands over against all "human beings' writings"—even if the latter are gospel-centered and gospel-permeated creeds, catechisms, and confessions! To be sure, the distinction between law and gospel is an "especially brilliant light" for the proper understanding and application of God's holy Word or Scripture.[25] But this light is not something imposed on the text from without —some "Lutheran insight" perhaps—but an inner-biblical radiance and illumination issuing from and demanded by Scripture itself, as the proof-texts of Article V show. By the same token, Scripture is not some other authority principle in addition to or in competition with the gospel; it is simply the gospel's own instrument of self-definition. Law and gospel are the chief "kinds" or "heads" of doctrine;[26] but the sole judge, rule, and norm for *all* doctrines is Holy Scripture alone.[27] Law and gospel are only what Scripture defines as such; anything else is fraud and fantasy. For as the Smalcald Articles insist, "The Word of God ['Word' and 'Scripture' are interchangeable in context!] shall establish articles of faith, and no one else, not even an angel"![28]

This means too that the "rule" for interpretation is not some abstract gospel floating above, beyond, or behind the text but the "sure and clear passages of Scripture," in other words, concrete biblical texts.[29] It is instructive in this connection to note the Formula's high praise for Abraham because he took an express word of God literally rather than looking for a "tolerable and loose interpretation," even though the divine command to sacrifice Isaac on the face of it ran counter "not only to reason and to divine and natural law but also to the eminent article of faith concerning the promised seed, Christ"![30] Abraham, despite his appalling dilemma, "gave God the honor of truthfulness."

Giving God "the honor of truthfulness" is really the whole point of the much maligned and misunderstood doctrine of biblical *inerrancy*. Without it the principle of *sola scriptura* becomes an empty pretense. If the sacred text is subject to error, and therefore to human correction, then it is no longer the standard, rule, and norm of truth but is itself in need of such a standard. It is no longer judge but defendant—precisely the historical-critical concept. Inerrancy therefore means no more and no less than what Luther asserts in the Large Catechism on baptism: "I and my neighbour and in sum all men are capable of erring and deceiving, but the Word of God can neither err nor deceive—*nec potest errare nec fallere*"![31] And it is quite clear that Luther is here arguing from inerrancy to baptism, not from baptism to inerrancy! The inerrancy attaches to God's Word as such, not to particular topics only (else why to these and not those?). Vergilius Ferm, incidentally, while energetically taking issue with the Lutheran Confessions on this and other points, freely admitted that an "infallible Bible . . . verbally inspired" was in fact "an assumption implied throughout the Lutheran symbols."[32]

An example will illustrate the hopeless self-contradiction involved in the affirmation of the Bible's authority and the simultaneous denial of its inerrancy. A historical-critical commentator on the parable of the sower (Luke 8:4–15) notes: "Since [Luke's] interpretation of the parable is not factually correct, it dare not determine the sermon. But since it is, after all, written there, it must also be heard and taken seriously as God's Word"![33] This is not a minor question of wording, but a schizophrenic crisis of meaning. I think James Barr puts it as well as anyone:

> (i) First, the Bible was traditionally tied up with a whole view of the world as God's world; and through this it furnished a world-view, a total orientation for life.
> (ii) Secondly, the Bible served as a resource-book, to which one could turn for guidance on all questions of truth, morality, etc.
> (iii) Thirdly, the Bible was an authority for theology.
> According to [G. D.] Kaufman, if I have understood him rightly, (ii) depends on (i) and (iii) depends on (ii). The first sense, however, has now departed: we no longer orientate ourselves to the world through a biblical framework. The framework through which we see the world is that furnished by science, by sociology and so on; what was once taken as God's truth is now seen as Hebrew or early Christian customs and folklore.
> The loss of the first sense has caused a deep crisis in the second and

third. The demand for biblical theologies, and other kindred approaches, and the whole modern reassertion of biblical authority, can be seen as a demand for authority on levels (ii) and (iii), after level (i) is known to have passed away. But in fact the attempt to reassert biblical authority in modern terms is a nostalgia for the good old days: the real question is the breakdown of the Bible as the fundamental orientation for western man.[34]

In other words, the problem is not with inerrancy as such, however one might define it. The crisis involves rather the whole notion of divine authority, which, as Barr says in the same connection, "no longer fits the intellectual structure in which theological work is carried on."[35] There is, however, a naive fallacy involved in the reference to "the breakdown of the Bible" simply "for western man"—as if secular Western man were the same as Christian Western man or ever had been. Neither during the sixteenth century nor at any other time was it simply self-evident that one should accept the Bible as one's "fundamental orientation." The Lutheran confessors did not do so simply for lack of alternatives. The Apology of the Augsburg Confession, for instance, makes a most illuminating remark about the sophisticated popes of that time: "How many of them care anything for the Gospel or think it worth reading? Many openly ridicule all religions, or if they accept anything, accept only what agrees with human reason and regard the rest as mythology, like the tragedies of the poets."[36] Apart from bona fide biblical inspiration and inerrancy there is no way out of Barr's dilemma—

either that we abandon the whole concept of any special status of the Bible and admit that it no longer matters very much; or that we continue to affirm for it the sort of special status that it used to have, but do so in an essentially irrational way, saying that it has for us this status but that we cannot really explain why.[37]

Krentz seems fully aware of the problem when he writes, "The introduction of historical criticism constituted 'the most serious test that the church has had to face through nineteen centuries' about the nature of authority."[38] There is, however, no solution except a forthright reassertion of the Reformation's *sola scriptura* against the rival pretensions of critical, magisterial human reason. It may be of interest to note that the Lutheran Church of Australia was able to declare with virtual unanimity in 1972, after years of painstaking study and discussion:

We therefore find ourselves opposed to many assumptions of "higher" criticism, assumptions which have increasingly shaped the methods and conclusions of biblical scholarship in the last two hundred years. Some of these assumptions are:
(a) That the biblical documents must be treated in principle like all

other historical documents, without regard to their claim to inspiration and authority;

(*b*) That science, history, and other disciplines are valid and legitimate norms and standards by which the truthfulness and reliability of biblical statements can and must be judged;

(*c*) That the miraculous aspects of the witness of the biblical writers may be discounted as an element of primitive culture;

(*d*) That the Apostles' and even our Blessed Lord's own understanding and interpretation of particular texts of Scripture may in principle be regarded as defective or questionable, and as subject to progressive correction by subsequent biblical scholarship.

Such assumptions as these constitute an attack not only on the *apostolicity* of the Church (Ephesians 2:20), but on the very Lordship of Christ. For this reason we reject them unconditionally.

This does not mean that we reject either reason or scholarship. Quite on the contrary. We hold that it is the function of biblical interpretation to understand and apply the Bible as a whole and in all its parts. But everyone who takes the Reformation's *sola scriptura* seriously must insist that the proper function of reason, and thus of scholarship, is in every respect *under* and not *over* Scripture—as handmaid, and not as mistress. As emphatically as we reject any use of reason as master or judge over Scripture, so we affirm the fullest use of reason, with all its scholarly tools, as a servant, to understand and make clear what the sacred text says and means.[39]

HISTORY AND THEOLOGY

Since it is self-contradictory to take issue with God's Word, but since the right to take issue with biblical statements is an inherent, constitutive necessity for the historical-critical method—precisely in its "narrow" sense!—it is clear that the application of criticism to Scripture cannot theoretically be justified so long as the biblical writings are regarded as inviolable, divinely inspired truth given in human language. That is why, as we have seen, Semler declared, "The root of the evil is the confusion of Scripture and Word of God."[40] Before any historical-critical operation can begin, a wedge must first be driven between that which is divine and that which is human in Scripture. Once such a beachhead has been gained, in terms of an isolable "human side," then criticism can go to work on it, leaving "faith" to tender its courtesies to an ever more vague "divine side." Kraus puts it well when he traces to Semler "the critical splitting up into divine and human elements, whereby alone free biblical research is guaranteed."[41]

The "human side" of Scripture naturally came to be understood as the whole realm of fact, history, geography, and the like. Theology, "faith," or the "divine side" had to withdraw to the limbo beyond Lessing's "nasty ditch" if it wished to remain unmolested by historical-critical debunkings. A painstaking monograph by C. Hartlich and W. Sachs on the origin of the notion of "myth" in "modern biblical science" shows that this notion was first applied to the opening chapters of Genesis. What is significant is that the motive for the "surrender of the historical-factual" dimension was not anything textual or exegetical but "in the first instance the insight into the incompatibility of the biblical proto-history with the newly-won scientific and historical knowledge concerning the primordial condition of the world and of mankind."[42] This mythical infection could not, of course, be contained in Genesis, but spread at once to the whole Bible, including the New Testament.[43] It is undoubtedly this heirloom that lies behind contemporary commonplaces like Joseph Sittler's pronouncement that "if we equate the Word of God with the Scripture, we are confusing things heavenly with things historical"[44] or Paul G. Bretscher's dichotomy between a "vertical" (theological) line and an "horizontal" (historical) one.[45] Elsewhere, Bretscher specifically rejects the proposition that "the historical framework . . . in Scripture is an essential part of the Word of God."[46]

Ferdinand Hahn has summed up this historical-critical dilemma in a splendid understatement: "The renunciation of the theological relevance of the factual element . . . has meant for exegesis something like a loss of reality."[47] One of the most consistent representatives of this tendency was undoubtedly Rudolf Bultmann, who said of John, for instance, that "the evangelist while making free use of the tradition, creates the figure of Jesus entirely from faith."[48] It was this sort of thing, no doubt, that Walter Künneth had in mind when he said that historical criticism had reached "completion [Zuendefuehrung] and perfection" in Bultmann.[49] The evacuation of factual-historical content clearly leaves theology holding empty verbal bags—an intolerable state of affairs that is only very poorly disguised by recourse to the fraudulent category of "religious language." The real point and essence of this pseudosemantic subterfuge was made perfectly clear in an Abingdon Award–winning essay on the language and phenomenology of religion by Sten H. Stenson.[50] The author speaks of the "punlike character of miracle stories and religious legends" and compares "religious language" to "puns and witticisms" which "are irrelevant to truth and falsity in the usual propositional sense."[51]

With such "friends" of Christian theology, who needs enemies? It need not surprise us to find avowed enemies of the faith gleefully exploiting much "Christian" scholarship. Israeli Supreme Court Justice

Haim Cohn, for example, is able to argue as follows in his anti-Christian reconstruction of the New Testament:

> In short, the Gospel traditions are "messages of faith and not historiography": any historical material in their hands the authors used "to add detail and graphic quality," but on the whole, they freely exercised their fantasy "in presenting, and in meaning to present, not history but theology."[52]

Nor is anything gained by substituting "Easter experience" for "fantasy"!

Naturally not everyone was as rigorous or radical as Bultmann. But on the other hand it should not be suggested that the problem concerns only a few unrepresentative extremists. After World War II, American Lutheranism was deeply influenced, not to say corrupted, by the movement unhappily dubbed "neo-orthodoxy." In defining the movement for *A Handbook of Christian Theology* Langdon B. Gilkey made these highly significant observations:

> Neo-orthodoxy agrees with liberalism that the whole area of spatio-temporal fact and event is the valid object of scientific inquiry, with the result that the hypotheses of science in the area of natural and historical fact are regarded as authoritative. Thus, although such doctrines as "Creation out of Nothing," and the "Fall of Adam" have again become important theologically, neo-orthodoxy does not quarrel with scientific explanations of the origin of nature and of man's life. Likewise, although the Incarnation has become the central theological doctrine of all neo-orthodoxy, the factual manifestations and explanations of the Incarnation (e.g. the miracles, the Virgin Birth, and the Empty Tomb) have not played such a central role in contemporary theology as they did in "orthodoxy." In other words, to the contemporary thinker theological doctrines are statements containing symbolic rather than literal truth, propositions pointing to the religious dimensions of events rather than propositions containing factual information about events (see Niebuhr's use of "myth," Tillich's use of "symbolic language" and Dodd's "fact and interpretation").[53]

Let me emphasize the sentence that follows immediately upon this characterization: "The intricate relation between the historic fact and the religious, 'mythical' or symbolic interpretation of the fact *remains as an important and as yet unresolved problem for neo-orthodoxy*"[54] (emphasis mine). Elsewhere Gilkey has portrayed even more starkly the widespread historical-theological schizophrenia, which has by no means disappeared from the scene:

> For us, then, the Bible is a book of the acts Hebrews believed God might have done and the words he might have said had he done and said them— but of course we recognise he did not. The difference between this view of the Bible as a parable illustrative of Hebrew religious faith and the view

of the Bible as a direct narrative of God's actual deeds and words is so vast that it scarcely needs comment. . . .

What has happened is that, as modern men perusing the Scriptures, we have rejected as invalid all the innumerable cases of God's acting and speaking; but as neo-orthodox men looking for a word from the Bible, we have induced from all these cases the theological generalisation that God is he who acts and speaks. This general truth about God we then assert while denying all the particular cases on the basis of which the generalisation was first made. Consequently, biblical theology is left with a set of theological abstractions, more abstract than the dogmas of scholasticism, for these are concepts with no known concreteness. Finally, our language is self-contradictory because, while we use the language of orthodoxy, what we really mean is concepts and explanations more appropriate to liberal religion. For if there is any middle ground between the observable deed and the audible dialogue which we reject, and what the liberals used to call religious experience and religious insight, then it has not yet been spelt out.[55]

Any retreat from facts and history as such is of course a retreat from the incarnation. The divorce between facts and faith, between history and theology, is deeply antiincarnational, yet this fatal divorce is endemic to the historical-critical orientation. To see historical criticism as removing "the idolatry that confuses the temporal and the eternal"[56] is to take one's stand on docetic and/or Nestorian ground. One might be able to justify this sort of thing on the basis of the Zwinglian-Calvinistic *extra Calvinisticum* but not on the basis of the full, unmutilated christological Mystery confessed by the Lutheran church (Formula of Concord, VIII) in harmony with Christian antiquity. What historical criticism combats as an "idolatry that confuses the temporal and the eternal" is precisely the point of the most solemn confession of the Virgin Mary as being not in name only but in very truth the Mother of God.[57] John Meyendorff has recently again underscored the crucial significance of the term *theotokos* for the ancient orthodox Christology.[58]

It is the radical, that is, consistent application of historical criticism (the "wider principle") which not unnaturally reveals most clearly the destructive christological implications of the method:

It makes a difference to the way one thinks of Jesus. Is he a mighty being of superhuman power, who can manipulate [sic] the elements as he wills, stilling the storm and the waves, conjuring [sic] fish into the fisherman's net, abolishing the force of gravity, and altering his own material substance so that at one moment he is a man who can be touched and can eat and drink, and at the next a spirit who can pass through closed doors? Or is he an ordinary man who did nothing like this at all, and never wanted to; a man whose enormous significance expressed itself not in any physical abnormality [sic] but merely in his behaviour and in his destiny?[59]

The Lutheran Quarterly published as a perfectly legitimate exercise in historical criticism a piece entitled "A Fresh Look at Jesus' Eschatology and Christology in Mark's Petrine Stratum," by a J. S. Setzer. The author calmly presented the option of seeing the transfiguration "as an occasion on which Jesus, who had deep rapport with his psychic disciples, hypnotised them, and presented them with illusions of Moses, Elijah, and the voice of God, in order to convince them of his unusual messiahship."[60] The general christological conclusion was:

> There is nothing to be heard about a second person of a divine trinity, nothing of a virgin birth. And, once the Son of Man tradition is seen as an interpolation, or as a special delaying device used by Jesus, then also nothing is to be heard from him about the descent of a heavenly being to become Messiah. We hear, rather, about a marvellous but human child of God. . . .
>
> It seems that a strong argument would be generated for considering adoptionist christology and realisationist eschatology the positions of the historical Jesus.[61]

It is easy to dismiss such sub-Arian blasphemies as unrepresentative, extreme aberrations. But do they really differ in *kind*—as distinct from *degree*—from milder-seeming critical formulations such as those of Roy A. Harrisville endorsed by Krentz?[62] Harrisville presented "faith" as so independent of fact and dogma that it suffered no loss even by accepting the critical opinion that the historical Jesus neither claimed to be nor thought of himself as being the Christ or Messiah! Apart from better rhetorical padding, the substance differs hardly if at all from the Setzer and Keller views cited above.

No doubt such and similar views were included under the broad umbrella of "a variety of positions" envisioned by the 1968 Lutheran Council discussion report *Who Can This Be?* on the basis of "the conviction that biblical criticism is here to stay."[63]

Summing up, it is difficult to avoid the conclusion that historical criticism affects Christology somewhat paradoxically. In the short term, as it were, its brash reductionism leads to Arian or at least kenotic reconstructions of the historical Jesus. The long-term effect of such unsatisfactory results, however, is a docetic theologizing that no longer regards the historical facts—such as they are—as very important or relevant to "faith." A quest initiated by the conviction that the facts matter a great deal ends up being justified theologically by the assurance that the facts are really harmless and do not matter after all. Both phases of this anti-incarnational (1 John 4:2, 3) critical enterprise are beyond the pale of the Lutheran Confessions:

Since the Holy Scriptures call Christ a mystery over which all heretics break their heads, we admonish all Christians not to pry presumptuously into this mystery with their reason, but with the holy apostles simply to believe, close the eyes of reason, take their intellect captive to obey Christ, comfort themselves therewith, and rejoice constantly that our flesh and blood have in Christ been made to sit so high at the right hand of the majesty and almighty power of God.[64]

DOGMA AND PROBABILITY

"The inevitable result" of the critical division of the biblical materials into fact and fancy, writes R. P. C. Hanson,

> is that all the facts might as well be fancy because, while it is agreed that *some* of them are almost certainly facts, nobody can produce any satisfactory reason why his selection should be regarded as facts and not fancy, rather than that one, or that one, or that one. It is not merely that every critic plays the game differently from the others, but that every critic makes his own rules.[65]

This demotion of all historical facts from certainty to probability and hence, from a dogmatic point of view, to doubt and uncertainty is inherent in the critical principle itself, which demands the right to question anything and everything. Let us recall the fourth of the Munich theses cited above:

> If exegesis is to be practised historico-critically, it must use the methods of secular historical science, i.e. *criticism which allows only probable judgments*, and the principles of analogy and correlation (cf. Troeltsch). Thereby it subjects itself in principle to secular-historical judgment.[66] [Emphasis mine.]

The term *criticism* here corresponds to what I have called the "narrow critical principle," while a rigorous application of the principles of analogy and correlation represents the "wider critical principle." It is of course in the sense of the wider principle that the thirteenth Munich thesis goes on to formulate as follows:

> If historical-critical exegesis subjects its findings to secular-historical judgment, then *the requirement that it be bound* to an ecclesiastical teaching office or *to confessional writings contradicts its very starting point*.[67] [Emphasis mine.]

This applies equally to the narrow critical principle, however, for the critical insistence that *all* facts are always subject to review and reappraisal cannot be squared with the confessional assertion that *some*

328

facts are a priori certain and settled, namely, by divine authority and revelation.

Krentz has defined the problem admirably: "Historical criticism produces only probable results. It relativises everything. But faith needs certainty."[68] Apart from a few tiny and ambivalent nibbles at the problem, however, Krentz offers no cogent way out of the dilemma but falls back on Harrisville's notion of "the true nature of faith." And that, as we have seen, amounted simply to a retreat from the relevance of the historical facts. Given the priority of the historical-critical commitment, there really is no other choice, for as Günther Bornkamm put it: "Certainly faith cannot and should not be dependent on the change and uncertainty of historical research."[69]

This unresolved historical-critical embarrassment has led even to the extraordinary attempt to portray belief in biblical facts as the *fides historica* "which the Book of Concord condemns"![70] In this view it is wrong to regard as an act of faith the belief that "the incarnation and other events took place"! The Augsburg Confession, however, leaves no doubt about what it teaches on this score: "Here the term 'faith' does not signify *merely* knowledge of the history . . . but it signifies faith which believes *not only* the history but *also* the effect *of the history*, namely, this article of the forgiveness of sins."[71] Luther's explanation of the Second Article revels in the gospel's historicity and speaks of the need for dealing at length in sermons with "such *articles* as the birth, passion, resurrection, and ascension of Christ."[72] Nor does the Formula of Concord know a de-historicized gospel. The narrow understanding of gospel versus law presupposes the historical framework of the gospel in the wider sense, that is, the total teaching and narrative, as in Mark 1:1, "The beginning of the Gospel of Jesus Christ."[73] And, after all, the Lord himself has guaranteed concerning an incident at Bethany that "wherever this gospel is preached throughout the world, what she has done will also be told, in memory of her" (Matt. 26:13).

But does not this very historicity of the gospel invite and validate the use of the historical-critical method? In a word, no. The historicity of the gospel indeed makes it possible to point the inquirer to the factual-historical moorings of the faith—for as Paul said, "these things were not done in a corner" (Acts 26:26; see 1 Cor. 15). It also affords the unbeliever the opportunity to question and challenge the historical evidence in an effort to explain it away. The gospel's historical "infra-structure," however, does not entitle the believer, least of all a public teacher in the church, to "keep an open mind," that is, to cultivate doubt about the correctness of the gospel's historical framework. One must therefore carefully distinguish between the realms of apologetics and theology proper. In the former realm it suffices to show, as the London University legal authority J. N. D. Anderson does so well, that the New Testament is not a collection of doubtful legends but an impressive documentary record of valid evidence that establishes the Christian case beyond a reasonable doubt.[74] That, however, is totally insufficient and sub-Christian in the area of theology proper, where the lordship of Christ and consequently the truthfulness of Christianity are no longer in dispute but are confessed with the Spirit-given certainty of faith. Before faith the prophetic and apostolic Scriptures may appear simply as venerable old documents; after faith they are seen to be divine, authoritative truth. In apologetics it suffices to say, "This is most likely true." In theology anything short of "this is most certainly true" is sacrilege. Hence the narrow critical principle has valid uses in the pre-Christian, pre-evangelical realm, but is intolerable in the realm of gospel-dogma, that is, "the doctrine and . . . all its articles."[75] For faith cannot live on empirical probabilities but "must have a very definite Word of God."[76] "Good consciences cry for the truth and proper instruction from God's Word, and to them death is not as bitter as is doubt in one point."[77]

A good illustration of the incompatibility of historical criticism with doctrinal confession was the Arnoldshain agreement on the Sacrament, where it was "no longer possible to connect the institution of the Supper with the night in which He was betrayed"![78] The Lutheran church, by contrast, is convinced that her sacramental teaching "rests on a unique, firm, immovable, and indubitable rock of truth in the words of institution recorded in the holy Word of God and so understood, taught, and transmitted by the holy evangelists and apostles, and by their disciples and hearers in turn."[79] The critical and the dogmatic attitudes are mutually exclusive. *Tertium non datur.*

Lutherans above all must treasure the incarnational-sacramental unity of history and theology in the one gospel. We cannot countenance any scheme by which the gospel is degraded into "a mere tissue of significances, . . . dissolves into a mere SIGNIFICAT and has lost the force of the EST!"[80]

NOTES

1. Werner G. Kümmel, *The New Testament: The History of the Investigation of Its Problems* (Nashville: Abingdon Press, 1972), p. 13.
2. Edgar Krentz, *The Historical-Critical Method* (Philadelphia: Fortress Press, 1975), p. 55.

3. Kümmel, *The New Testament*, p. 13.

4. Gerhard Ebeling, *Word and Faith* (Philadelphia: Fortress Press, 1963), pp. 22ff.

5. Ferdinand Hahn, "Probleme historischer Kritik," *Zeitschrift für die neutestamentliche Wissenschaft*, 63, no. 1/2 (1972): p. 13.

6. Krentz, *Historical-Critical Method*, pp. 18–19.

7. Ibid., p. 30.

8. Hans-Joachim Kraus, *Geschichte der historisch-kritischen Erforschung des Alten Testaments*, 2d ed. (Neukirchen: Neukirchener Verlag, 1969), p. 249.

9. Ibid., p. 254.

10. *Korrespondenzblatt* (Pfarrerverein, Bavaria), 1969, pp. 128ff., theses 4, 6, 8, 10, 12.

11. Hans Rohrbach, *Naturwissenschaft, Weltbild, Glaube* (Wuppertal: Theologischer Verlag Rolf Brockhaus, 1974).

12. Ernst and Marie-Luise Keller, *Miracles in Dispute* (Philadelphia: Fortress Press, 1969).

13. "Über die anthropologischen Grenzen der Kirche," in *Arbeiten zur Geschichte und Theologie des Luthertums*, ed. W. Maurer, Karl H. Rengstorf, E. Sommerlath, and W. Zimmermann (Hamburg: Lutherisches Verlagshaus, 1972), 26: 132–33.

14. *Lutheran World* 13, no. 2 (1966): 186.

15. See Kraus, *Geschichte*, p. 253.

16. Ebeling, *Word and Faith*, pp. 22ff.

17. Peter Stuhlmacher, "Thesen zur Methodologie gegenwärtiger Exegese," *Zeitschrift für die neutestamentliche Wissenschaft*, 63, no. 1/2 (1972): 21.

18. Krentz, *Historical-Critical Method*, p. 85.

19. Hahn, "Probleme historischer Kritik," p. 3.

20. Krentz, *Historical-Critical Method*, p. 4; see p. 76.

21. *The Unity of the Church*, Papers presented to the Commissions on Theology and Liturgy of the Lutheran World Federation (Rock Island, Ill.: Augustana, 1957), p. 92.

22. *The Book of Concord: The Confessions of the Evangelical Lutheran Church*, trans. and ed. Theodore G. Tappert (Philadelphia: Fortress Press, 1959), pp. 464–65.

23. Quoted in Gerhard Maier, *Das Ende der historisch-kritischen Methode* (Wuppertal: Theologischer Verlag Rolf Brockhaus, 1974), p. 9.

24. *Die Bekenntnisschriften der evangelisch-lutherischen Kirche* (Göttingen: Vandenhoeck & Ruprecht, 1959), pp. 767–69.

25. Formula of Concord, Solid Declaration, V.1, in *Book of Concord*, p. 558.

26. Ibid., pp. 558, 562–63.

27. Ibid., VI, p. 465.

28. Smalcald Articles, Pt. II, Art. II.15, in *Book of Concord*, p. 295.

29. Apology of the Augsburg Confession, XXVII.60, in *Book of Concord*, p. 279.

30. Formula of Concord, Solid Declaration, VI.46, in *Book of Concord*, p. 577.

31. Large Catechism, Baptism, 57, in *Book of Concord*, p. 444 (translation mine).

32. Vergilius Ferm, ed., *What Is Lutheranism?* (New York: Macmillan Company, 1930), p. 279.

33. Quoted in *Lutherischer Rundblick* 18 no. 4 (1970): 325.

34. James Barr, *The Bible in the Modern World* (New York: Harper & Row, 1973), pp. 110–11.

KURT E. MARQUART

35. Ibid.
36. Apology of the Augsburg Confession, VII–VIII.27, in *Book of Concord*, p. 173.
37. Barr, *Bible in the Modern World*, p. 111.
38. Krentz, *Historical-Critical Method*, p. 4.
39. Lutheran Church of Australia, "Genesis 1–3: A Doctrinal Statement," *Report*, 1972, p. 362.
40. See above, n. 23.
41. Kraus, *Geschichte*, p. 112.
42. C. Hartlich and W. Sachs, *Der Ursprung des Mythosbegriffes in der modernen Bibelwissenschaft* (Tübingen: J. C. B. Mohr, 1952), p. 35.
43. Ibid., pp. 61ff.
44. Joseph Sittler, *The Doctrine of the Word* (Philadelphia: ULCA Board of Publications, 1948), p. 11.
45. Paul G. Bretscher, *After the Purifying* (River Forest, Ill.: Lutheran Education Association, 1975), pp. 86–87.
46. Paul G. Bretscher, "An Inquiry into Article II," *Currents in Theology and Mission* 1, 2 (October, 1974): 41.
47. Hahn, "Probleme historischer Kritik," p. 6.
48. Quoted in Sten H. Stenson, *Sense and Nonsense in Religion* (Nashville: Abingdon Press, 1969), p. 153.
49. Walter Künneth, "Die Grundlagenkrisis der Theologie Heute," Essay read to the Council of the European Evangelical Alliance, London, 1968, p. 6.
50. Stenson, *Sense and Nonsense in Religion*.
51. Ibid., pp. 233, 146.
52. Haim Cohn, *The Trial and Death of Jesus* (London: Weidenfeld and Nicolson, 1972), p. xv.
53. M. Halverson and A. Cohen, eds., *A Handbook of Christian Theology* (London: Meridian Books, 1958), pp. 260–61.
54. Ibid.
55. Langdon B. Gilkey, "Cosmology, Ontology, and the Travail of Biblical Language," *Concordia Theological Monthly* XXIII, 3 (March 1962): 146–53.
56. Krentz, *Historical-Critical Method*, p. 67.
57. Formula of Concord, Epitome, VIII.12, in *Book of Concord*, p. 488.
58. John Meyendorff, *Christ in Eastern Christian Thought* (Tuckahoe: St. Vladimir's Seminary Press, 1975), pp. 18, 21ff., 157, and passim.
59. Keller and Keller, *Miracles in Dispute*, p. 177.
60. *The Lutheran Quarterly* 24 (August 1972): 248.
61. Ibid., pp. 252–53.
62. Roy A. Harrisville, *His Hidden Grace* (Nashville: Abingdon Press, 1965), pp. 52, 53. See Krentz, *Historical-Critical Method*, p. 67.
63. *Who Can This Be? Studies in Christology* (New York: Lutheran Council in the U.S.A., 1968), p. 10.
64. Formula of Concord, Solid Declaration, VIII.96, in *Book of Concord*, pp. 609–10.
65. Quoted in J. N. D. Anderson, *Christianity: The Witness of History* (London: Tyndale Press, 1969), p. 33.
66. See above, n. 10.
67. See above, n. 10.
68. Krentz. *Historical-Critical Method*, p. 67.
69. Quoted in H. P. Hamann, "History: A Proof for the Christian Faith," *The Springfielder* XXXVI, 3 (December 1972): 200.

332

70. Walter R. Bouman, "History and Dogma in Christology," *Concordia Theological Monthly* XLII, 4 (April 1972): 211.

71. Augsburg Confession, XX.23 (Latin), in *Book of Concord*, p. 44; emphasis mine.

72. Large Catechism, Creed, 31–33, in *Book of Concord*, pp. 414–15.

73. Formula of Concord, Solid Declaration, V.4, in *Book of Concord*, pp. 558–59.

74. Anderson, *Christianity*; and idem, *A Lawyer among the Theologians* (London: Hodder and Stoughton, 1973).

75. Augsburg Confession, VII, and Formula of Concord, Solid Declaration, X.31, in *Book of Concord*, pp. 32 and 616.

76. Apology of the Augsburg Confession, IV.262, in *Book of Concord*, p. 145.

77. Apology XII.129 (German); see *Die Bekenntnisschriften der evangelisch-lutherischen Kirche*, p. 279.

78. Marc Lienhard, *Lutherisch-Reformierte Kirchengemeinschaft Heute* (Frankfurt: Lembeck, Knecht, 1972), p. 54.

79. Formula of Concord, Solid Declaration, VII.42, in *Book of Concord*, p. 576.

80. Quoted in G. Glöge, *Mythologie und Luthertum* (Göttingen: Vandenhoeck & Ruprecht, 1963), p. 183.

The Parables of the Leaven and of the Mustard Seed: A Suggested Methodological Model

MARTIN H. SCHARLEMANN

Graduate Professor of Exegetical Theology
Concordia Seminary
Saint Louis, Missouri

The application of interpretation, and not the theory, lies at the heart of this presentation. We shall proceed in a general way as though this were a class at Concordia Seminary in Saint Louis.

The two parables of the leaven and of the mustard seed were selected for this demonstration because the former is found in Matthew and Luke but not in Mark. This means that it includes material to which the label "Q" is often applied. The parable of the mustard seed occurs in all three Synoptics with some variations in the wording of each account. Furthermore, both parables are offered by Luke within a context quite different from that of Matthew in the case of the parable of the leaven, and from those of both Matthew and Mark in the instance of the mustard seed.

In working terms this means that we shall have to deal both with what is called the synoptic problem and with the question of a presumed source referred to as Q, which, it is said, both Matthew and Luke used in addition to some version of the Gospel according to Mark. While we do not necessarily want to prejudge the case, it would be less than honest to say that by the time a class at Concordia Seminary would deal with the two parables under consideration its members would have behind them a course in the art of biblical interpretation. This course is devoted to spelling out in detail a method of interpretation known as radical orthodoxy. During these sessions five major points are developed as they appertain to the text before us, namely, (1) that an exegete is a theologian and not just a historian; (2) that the canonical text, and *not* some point in the trajectory behind it, is the seat of authority; (3) that God's truth is deposited there by his Spirit to be uncovered rather than discovered; (4) that the Gospels offer us the words of the exalted Christ standing in continuity with the earthly Jesus;[1] and (5) that it is a sociological heresy to hold that a community can produce anything of consequence unless it has within it a person or persons of creative genius.[2] Just how these observations apply to a treatment of the two parables under discussion will become clear as we move along through the texts. It seems advisable to sound this alert ahead of time, since the presuppositions here stated constitute a conscious rejection of major ingredients found in much of contemporary New Testament interpretation. We shall begin with the parable of the leaven and then proceed to a consideration of the parable of the mustard seed. It will be essential to keep in mind, as we move through these materials, that the truth to be taught by a parable is drawn from the point of comparison arrived at by a careful study of the canonical text.

Since both parables describe some aspect of what the New Testament refers to as "the kingdom of God [or heavens]," it may prove useful to set forth at the outset the observation that this is a shorthand expression for all the bother God has gone to in order to reestablish his rule of grace in, over, and among men. What the parables offer is a description of what happens when God was and is at work in this way.

THE PARABLE OF THE LEAVEN

Having said all this by way of introduction, we shall proceed to take up the parable of the leaven (Matt. 13:33 and Luke 13:20–21). That is to say, we shall first take up the one that is given as the second of a pair by both Matthew and Luke. We do so for the reason that the one on the leaven seems to be more simple than the one about the mustard seed.

Textual Matters

To get our bearings properly we shall start with some notices about the verses in question. We shall note that the last eight words of each rendering are exactly the same. Before that, however, there are a number of differences in both wording and construction.

In this context we ought to note that the rendering of this parable as given by the Gospel of Thomas does not have the last words at all. It simply reads as follows: "Jesus said: The kingdom of the Father is like a woman. She took a little leaven, hid it in dough and made large loaves of it. He that has ears to hear, let him hear!"[3]

In Matthew the opening words are just like those used to begin verse 31, where the evangelist introduces the parable of the mustard seed, except for the *elalēsen* taking the place of the *parethēken* of verse 31. (The Western text omits the verb completely.) At Luke 13:20 the opening statement is a question that is rabbinical in form: "With what shall I compare the kingdom of God?" This is an abbreviated version of the double question that introduces the Lukan version of the parable of the mustard seed (see v. 18).

Matthew uses his usual expression, "the kingdom of the heavens," while Luke has "the kingdom of God." Now this kingdom, Jesus said, is not like a woman. Instead it is similar to what happens when a woman hides some yeast in three measures of flour and the dough is leavened throughout.

One of the problems in this parable is the use of the word *zymē* (yeast). Everywhere else in Scripture it connotes something evil (see 1 Cor. 5:6–8; Matt. 16:6, 11, 12; Mark 8:15; Luke 12:21). This fact has moved some persons to arrive at such a strange interpretation as that found in G. H. Lang's *The Parabolic Teaching of Jesus:* "Thus from the small grain of leaven, the elevating of one elder above the rest of the brethren, there developed the vast hierarchical system of the Papacy, with its corruption in doctrine and its depraved practice."[4] In the section below dealing with exegetical considerations we shall return to the subject of the yeast. It is a term of crucial importance for a proper interpretation of this brief parable.

The *labousa* in each of the two renderings might be called a kind of Semitic redundance except that it suggests an action separate from the *enekrypsen* (Matthew) or *ekrypsen* of Luke. In the case of the latter, some manuscripts have the fuller *enekrypsen*, including such important ones as Papyrus 75, the Codex Sinaiticus, and even the Beza Codex (Western text). The shorter form is probably more original since it is the more difficult reading and is supported by the Vaticanus and the Chester Beatty Papyrus. The critical apparatus suggests that the compound form of the verb is derived from the parallel in Matthew.

In passing it may be of interest to note that one of the Syriac versions calls this woman "wise" or "thoughtful" *(phronimē)*. That is an indigenous "kingdom word," as is evident, for example, from the parable of the ten bridesmaids (Matt. 25:2). While Clement of Alexandria quotes it as one of the Syriac versions has it, there is no solid manuscript evidence for the inclusion of this adjective.

The word *aleuron* connotes the kind of wheat flour required for an acceptable cereal offering at the temple (Lev. 2:1, 4, 7). The occurrence of the word within the parable is a reminder that the action described by the parable takes place within the context of the arrangements made by God to deal redemptively with his people. In other words, it provides a kingdom touch.

Exegetical Considerations

At least two exegetical points have already been touched upon as we discussed the words for "leaven" and "flour." We must get back for a moment to the word *zymē* (leaven).

While acknowledging that "yeast" is normally part of the "bad news" in Scripture, it is clear that in the present parable it cannot have connotations of evil. In other words, it may not be interpreted by the other passages that have this word. The immediate context is of decisive importance. (This, incidentally, is an extremely important hermeneutical operating principle, all by itself!) At this point a rabbinic saying, quoted by William Barclay in *And Jesus Said,* may prove helpful: "Great is peace; and that peace is to the earth as is leaven to dough."[5] Unfortunately he does not tell us his source for this quotation. In their *Rabbinic Anthology,* however, Montefiore and Loewe offer this statement: "If they had occupied themselves with the Law, the leaven which is in it would have brought them back to me."[6] Here we have at least two references from rabbinic Judaism to indicate that "leaven" could be understood in a good sense and as relating to God's gracious activity.

Even more intriguing is the use of the expression "three measures" (*sata tria*). The Hebrew for this kind of measure is *se'ah* and is equal to forty liters. As Jeremias has pointed out, three measures of flour used for dough is enough to feed 162 people.[7] That is to say, the parable is told in terms of banquet proportions, just as other parables liken the kingdom to a dinner that a king prepared for his son's wedding (see Matt. 22:2). Incidentally, this is the amount of flour and dough used by Sarah when Abraham saw three guests coming down the road, one of them being the Lord himself, and dashed into the tent to tell his wife, "Make ready quickly three measures of fine meal, knead it and make cakes" (Gen. 18:6). Once again we are in kingdom territory, for on that day God came to Abraham as a guest, offering his grace but also ready to execute judgment over Sodom and Gomorrah. Hence this chapter became the inspiration for Rublev's famous icon "The Old Testament Trinity."

In Bishop Richard C. Trench's famous volume *Notes on the Parables of Our Lord,* various allegorical interpretations are put on these three measures of meal.[8] Augustine, for example, argued that they referred to heart, soul, and spirit. Theodor of Mopsuestia believed that the three meant Greeks, Jews, and Samaritans. Since the days of Adolf Jülicher, the art of New Testament interpretation has abandoned this kind of nonsense. Our business is to work from within Scripture itself. Peace, law, banqueting— these are all kingdom concepts! The kingdom of God is like a woman who took some yeast and "mixed [it] in" with three *se'ahs* of flour until the whole was leavened.

Against the Jewish backdrop indicated, those who could "hear" Jesus recognized the symbolism of yeast. It represented "torah," instruction by revelation. This is inserted into the assembly of guests taking part in the banquet of the kingdom. The *zymē* keeps working its ferment in everything it touches: the meal (Sacrament of the Altar), the participants, and all that they come into contact with.

The word *enekrypsen* literally means "hid in." It is a reminder that the power of God's kingdom comes as an intrusion into human affairs. It gets "mixed in" from the outside and does not have its source in human idealism or achievements. As Luther puts it in his explanation of the second petition of the Lord's Prayer: "The kingdom of God comes indeed without our prayer, of itself. . . ."

As indicated before, the last phrase about permeating the whole is missing in the rendering of this parable as given by the Gospel of Thomas. And for a good reason! Gnostics worked without any kind of eschatology that relates to history. The parables of Jesus as given in the New Testament do, as a rule, have an eschatological thrust. While C. H. Dodd errs in limiting this dimension to what he called realized eschatology, that is, to the time of Jesus' own ministry, the following comment is still useful: "The ministry of Jesus was like that. There was in it no element of external coercion, but in it the power of God's kingdom worked from within, mightily permeating the lump of Judaism in his time."[9]

In point of fact the period of the *eschaton,* as the New Testament indicates, extends from the time of Jesus' ministry to the moment of his *parousia.* During this period of time God is busy reestablishing his rule in grace in, over, and among men. As that activity is carried on, something happens like that which is described in this parable.

The point of comparison, therefore, might be formulated as follows: When God is busy with the work of reestablishing his rule of grace a process is set in motion like that of yeast mixed in with a large amount of dough—its fermenting and penetrating power permeates from within everything it touches. The truth to be taught by this parable, then, could be formulated as follows: the gracious rule of God as proclaimed by Jesus and his church is at work here on earth in such a revolutionary way as to transfigure everything it touches.

Homiletical Possibility

Since the chief task of our seminary is to prepare men for the pastoral ministry, we usually conclude our work with a parable by suggesting at least one homiletical possibility, mostly to show how one moves from the text through the point of comparison and the central truth to an acceptable sermon outline.

MAGNIFICAT MOMENTUM

Introductory: Stanley Jones once called the Magnificat the most radical of all revolutionary statements, even more dynamic than *The Communist Manifesto.* The permeating power of God's kingdom in terms of its internal effects is set forth in the present parable. Its force is—

I. Introduced from the outside as a quiet transfiguring power
  A. The kingdom of God is not a cosmic process secreting its own solutions as it moves forward
  B. The messianic age
    1. Was anticipated in the Old Testament (Abraham, Gen. 18)
    2. Began with Jesus of Nazareth
    3. Continues "without observation"
    4. Differs from human expectations, such as moral, political, and social utopias
II. An all-pervasive power in terms of
  A. Scope ("until the whole is leavened")
    1. Individual inversion of values (Malcolm Muggeridge)
    2. Social and cultural changes
      a. Justice with charity, and not just equity
      b. Bishops and Constantine: prohibition of child exposure
  B. Time
    1. Inaugurated eschatology
    2. Division into B.C. and A.D.
    3. An open future

Conclusion: Acts 17:6 reads, "They dragged Jason and some other brothers to the city authorities and shouted, 'These that have turned the world upside down are come here, too.'" There, in one sentence, you have a statement on the revolutionary effect of the gospel.

A Few Critical Observations

Before taking up the parable of the mustard seed it may be in order to give some brief considerations to items of literary and redactional criticism as applied to the study of the parable of the leaven. We do so not because such observations offer us some new points of departure but because they move us to look at the text more closely and, at times, even shed light on the movement that was part of the church's life from the beginning.

Going back to Luke 13:20 we note that the parable, as Luke has it, begins with a question that sounds very rabbinical: "To what shall I liken the kingdom of God?" This way of beginning a bit of parabolic instruction unquestionably brings us nearer the *ipsissima verba Jesu* than Matthew's rendering, which omits the question and makes the opening statement conform to verse 31, the beginning of the parable of the mustard seed, thereby giving us the *ipsissima vox Jesu*.[10]

By putting things this way, we do not want to imply that Jesus told this parable only once and that the differences in wording have their source either in the tradition of a single series of statements or just in modifications introduced by the respective evangelists using a source called Q. The two parables occur in rather different contexts. When considered as individual items in the respective synoptic Gospels, the variety itself goes back to our Lord himself. For what great teacher or preacher would not use certain central materials over and again with whatever variations suggested themselves at the moment? And never was there a greater master of instruction than Jesus himself. As Geraint V. Jones has noted:

> It should not be forgotten that Jesus was not only a religious teacher but a creative artist of unusual skill and penetration, the author of some of the world's classics in short stories and fables, and one whose distinction in this field was as unique as the rest of his mission.[11]

All this suggests that we need not necessarily resort to some hypothetical item known as Q to account for the slight differences in wording and form that occur in the two accounts as they are given in Matthew and Luke. Nor need tradition be injected at this point. The variety may well go back to Jesus himself.

THE PARABLE OF THE MUSTARD SEED

Having made the point once more of Jesus' creative skill, the moment has come to take up the parable of the mustard seed, which is found in all three Synoptics.

Preliminary Observations

In the present instance the preliminary observations must include a word on the *context*. This will indicate to what extent the Synoptics diverge in placing these particular materials. In both Matthew and Mark the parable of the mustard seed occurs in the chapters where other parables are included (Matt. 13 and Mark 4). But Luke gives the matter a very different setting. This parable does not appear in chapter 8, where we might expect it, since that is the section which is roughly similar to Matthew 13 and Mark 4. Instead Luke offers the parable of the mustard seed in chapter 13, where the context describes the teaching and healing activities of Jesus on his way to Jerusalem.

Mark does not offer the parable of the leaven at all, possibly because the rest of the parables in chapter 4 of his book deal with seed: the sower, the seed growing secretly, and the mustard seed. A story about leaven would hardly fit here, in view of his decision to include only such items as liken the kingdom to seed.

In the fuller Markan context the sequence of materials is the following:

At Mark 3:31–35 the mother and the brothers of Jesus look for him.

There follows the parable of the sower (4:1–9).

Jesus then explains the function of parabolic instruction (4:10–13).

Then comes an explanation of the parable of the sower (4:14–20).

After this we read a *logion* (a word) on the light to be put on a candlestick (4:21–23).

This is followed by another *logion* on the right way of hearing (4:24–25).

The parable of the seed growing secretly takes up verses 26–29.

At that point we confront the parable of the mustard seed (4:30–32) with a further note on teaching in parables (4:33–34).

Chapter 4 of Mark ends with the account of Jesus stilling the storm (4:35–41).

When we take a look at Matthew we discover the following sequence:

The mother and brothers of Jesus look for him (Matt. 12:46–50).

The parable of the sower (13:1–9).

Jesus describes the function of parables (13:10–15).

Then comes a beatitude on the disciples for hearing and seeing what prophets and kings had hoped to experience (13:16–17).

Jesus then explains the parable of the sower (13:18–23).

There follows the parable of the tares among the wheat (13:24–30) (which neither Mark nor Luke has).

Matthew then gives us the twin parables of the mustard seed and the leaven (13:31–33).

At this point there is added a statement on speaking in parables as fulfillment (13:34–35).

Jesus explains the parable of the tares when the disciples ask (13:36–43).

There follows another pair of parables, the treasure and the pearl of great price (13:44–46).

Then comes the parable of the dragnet (13:47–50).

This is followed by the *logion* on the scribe who is taught to be a disciple of the kingdom (13:51–52).

Jesus then returns to Nazareth to be shocked by the unbelief prevailing there (Matt. 13:53–58).

In passing we should note that Matthew makes no reference to the stilling of the storm. At this point he differs considerably from Mark.

In Luke the mustard seed and the leaven occur as a pair of parables, but in a very different context: Jesus was teaching in a synagogue and had just healed a woman crippled for eighteen years. At that point Luke introduces the two parables under discussion.

As indicated previously, we might have expected to find the parable of the mustard seed in Luke 8, where there are given some of the other materials that we already referred to in our outlines of Mark 4 and Matthew 13. There Luke gives us the parable of the sower (8:4–9), preceded by some verses on the women from Galilee who followed Jesus (8:1–3). As in Matthew 13 and Mark 4, Jesus is then described as indicating the function of parables (8:9–10). There follows an explanation of the parable of the sower (8:11–15). Then comes the *logion* on the light and the candlestick (8:16–18). Luke then introduces the item on the mother and brothers of Jesus looking for him (8:19–21); and that is followed by the account of Jesus stilling the storm (8:22–25) as well as by the healing of the demoniac in Gerasa (8:26–39) and the raising of Jairus' daughter (8:40–56).

It should be quite clear from all this how differently the parable of the mustard seed is placed in Luke. Luke relates both parables, the mustard seed and the leaven, to Jesus' teaching and his work of healing. These were the evidences for the presence of the kingdom among men. But Jesus himself was on his way to Jerusalem. We know what is about to occur there; he will be crucified. At this juncture we read the parable of the mustard seed.

Seed is a symbol for life springing out of death. Paul uses it that way

343

in 1 Corinthians 15:35–40, where he discusses the resurrection and makes the following comment:

> But someone will ask, "How are the dead raised? With what kind of body do they come?" You foolish man! What you sow does not come to life unless it dies. And what you sow is not the body which is to be, but a bare kernel, perhaps of wheat or of some other grain. But God gives it a body as he has chosen, and to each kind of seed its own body.

The symbol of sowing (or planting) occurs a number of times in the Old Testament to depict God's action of creating Israel. In at least one intertestamental context the people itself is called "the sown."[12]

We are to conclude, therefore, from Luke's placement of the parable of the mustard seed that Jesus' death will be a source of life. It will be the kind of event that will have large consequences for the nations of the world, which, as we shall see, are symbolized by the birds of the air that come to seek shelter in the branches of this tree. His death and resurrection will be the source of "the sown," his new people, the church.

Textual Matters

So much by way of preliminary observations. We must now proceed to matters of the text. In the present instance it will be necessary to include some comment on structure too.

First, then, matters of the text itself. The only meaningful variant in Mark is given at verse 30. There the Lake family of manuscripts (Caesarea) has the wording *homoiōmati parabalōmen autēn* ("To what likeness shall we compare it?") instead of the standard text *autēn parabolēi thōmen* ("In what parable shall we put it?"). The sense is not altered. These look like two different translations of an Aramaic question.

In verse 31 the Beza Codex (D) uses the accusative *epi tēn gēn* for the genitive of the text *epi tēs gēs* ("onto the ground" instead of "on the ground").

The only variant in the apparatus to Matthew is the *elalēsen* ("he spoke") in verse 31 instead of the *parethēken* of the Aland text ("he offered"; "set before them"—as in the case of a table).

In the Lukan account the Chester Beatty Papyrus, the Koine tradition, the Koridethi as well as many Latin codices, and the Syriac Peshitta describe the tree in verse 19. In this same verse a few codices offer *autou* for *heautou* ("his" for "his own").

None of these variants is supported strongly enough to warrant a change in the text as Aland gives it. Hence we shall use the reading as given in Kurt Aland's *Synopsis Quattuor Evangeliorum*.

But now a brief word on structure. You will note that Mark introduces this parable with two questions put by Jesus: "How shall we draw an analogy of the kingdom of God? In what kind of parable shall we present it?" These queries sound very rabbinical, as we noted previously in the case of the parable of the leaven. That is how a Jewish teacher would normally begin.

Luke offers the same two questions, but in a more simplified form, when he writes, "To what is the kingdom similar and with what shall I compare it?" Matthew has no introductory questions at all. His opening words attach this parable to the previous ones by saying simply, "He placed another parable before them, saying . . ." Matthew's own editorial work is clearly in evidence here.

Let us for a moment return to the subject of Q as the source for things which Matthew and Luke have in common. The other source for the first and third evangelists is said to have been Mark. This two-source hypothesis constitutes an attempt to explain both the similarities and the differences among the Synoptics. Like most theories it has its weaknesses. Here we have such a case. Matthew is different from both Luke and Mark. That will not do of course! It does not fit the requirements of the hypothesis. Matthew and Luke ought to be more similar to each other. So Vincent Taylor, for example, suggests that Luke's wording comes from Q and that Matthew conflated Q and Mark at this point.[13] Shall we call this a counsel of despair?

It is also one of the cardinal presuppositions of form and redaction criticism that any variations may be due to the treatment given a parable of Jesus during the time of the oral tradition or when a given pericope was written down. Behind this view lurks the assumption that Jesus told a parable only once and that the changes occurred in the process of transmission.

Such an approach is bound to be inherently false for the simple reason that no great teacher would use basic instructional materials only once. Jesus was an exceptionally creative genius. Why should he not have enjoyed the freedom that comes with such creativity? By what sensible rationale would a community or even an evangelist exhibit a genius superior to that of the Lord himself?

Exegetical Considerations

At this juncture we must proceed to a consideration of some exegetical items offered in and by the three accounts of the parable of the mustard seed.

As in the case of the parable of the leaven, the story of the parable is a very simple one. It describes the great contrast between the small seed when it is sown, on the one hand, and the full-grown shrub, or tree, on the other. In fact what is usually reckoned to be a garden herb (*lachanon*) actually develops into a tree with so many large branches that the birds come to rest there and, as Mark adds, take up their residence in its shadow.

There has always been some discussion as to just what kind of seed this was. Did it belong to the species called *khardel* (*salvadore persica*), or should it be classified as *sinapis nigra*?[14] In the former instance, it would be the kind that could reach a height of twenty-five feet; in the latter case, it could be expected to grow to twelve feet. Neither the question nor the answer materially affects the truth to be inculcated by the parable. For an understanding of the parable it makes little difference precisely what kind of seed this was in any technical sense. The point is the same: one of the smallest of all seeds grows up to outdistance all garden herbs by turning into a tree. From the smallest of beginnings there develops this large shrub.

Let us now take a closer look at some of the details of the text as they apply to interpretation. Mark does not repeat a word of comparison after the two opening questions. He proceeds directly to the point: "Like a seed of mustard." Then he resorts to the impersonal passive of the verb *speirō* ("to sow"). He does not include a reference to a man taking the seed and sowing it. Matthew and Luke do. But it should be noted that Luke has *ebalen* instead of the word for sowing.

"The man" of any parable is a symbol for God. The impersonal passive is frequently to be understood as signifying divine activity. All three evangelists, therefore, tell us that God is to be thought of as at work sowing.

Mark reports that the seed was sown on soil. In Matthew it is a field; in Luke it has become the man's garden, which is a word to designate what one might find in a Greek rather than a Jewish setting, Luke being the evangelist to the Gentiles.[15] Matthew's "field" is a symbol of the place where God is at work, as we can tell from previous parables. In Mark the accent is more on the action than on the place where the seed is sown. He has it being sown just on soil, without becoming more specific.

Mark's description of the process of growth is more detailed than the descriptions of Matthew and Luke. Mark wrote: "It comes up and gets to be larger than all herbs, and produces large branches, so that the birds of the air [heaven] can take up residence under its shadow." It should be noted that the Markan account does not contain the word for tree which the other two evangelists use.

Matthew's account lacks some of the Markan flavor. There the smallest of the seeds is described as getting bigger than other herbs and turning into a tree for the birds of the air to come and rest in its branches. Nothing is said by Matthew about the shade of the tree.

The chief difference in Luke is his use of past tenses in the case of the two words for growing and becoming. The nuance created by this difference exhibits a greater interest in both the fact and the final outcome of the man's action in sowing the mustard seed. Matthew and Mark suppose the case; Luke describes it in terms of actually having already happened. That is to say, his wording puts greater weight on the eschatological aspect of God's redemptive work. In short, as Jesus was telling the parable during his earthly ministry, he could and did at that point already envision and describe the progress of his ministry as carried forward by the church to the end of the age.

All three canonical gospels have the eschatological term (*kataskēnoō*) (Mark 4:32; Matt. 13:32; Luke 13:19). It has been translated as birds "making their nests in the branches and under the shadow of the tree." It is a word for the incorporation of the Gentiles into the people of God. There is a passage in a work called *Joseph and Asenath* where the word occurs in this sense and in this kind of context! "From now on you shall no more be called Asenath, but your name will be 'City of Refuge,' because in you many nations will take refuge and they shall [and now comes that word!] make their abode [there]."[16] You may recall that at the first council in Jerusalem, James used a quotation from Amos which has the "tent" word. He applied it to the extension of the church to the Gentiles (Acts 15:16). It is a word used in Daniel 4:21 of the birds of heaven nesting in the branches of a great tree as wild beasts dwell under it. In this Daniel context the tree is the symbol of the king (Nebuchadnezzar) and the size of his empire. That tree was so tall that it reached to the sky and covered the earth. In that same dream the birds represent the nations being incorporated into this kingdom.

In Ezekiel 17:23 the prophet speaks of Israel as a sprig of cedar that has become a tree, under which will dwell all kinds of beasts and in the shade of whose branches birds of every sort will nest. As we can tell from other parts of this book, especially chapters 40–48, the prophet was given a view of the greatness of the new Israel, which is the church, standing as it does in continuity with and succession to God's ancient people.

The tree and the birds are kingdom symbols. That is what makes them so appropriate for use in a parable dealing with God's rule of grace among men. It has grown from the most inauspicious beginnings to become a force at work among the nations.

This kind of symbolism could readily be understood by the people to whom Jesus spoke the parable of the mustard seed. Whenever it was told in the primitive church many of the hearers were well-enough versed in their Old Testament to grasp the meaning of the tree and of the birds making nests in its branches. Those among them who had been Gentiles would be glad to hear it again and again, for it provided the Lord's assurance that they were included among God's new people. This parable would offer them an insight into God's ways as seen not only from where they were at that moment but also from the end of history. That is what we call eschatology; it is a word for looking back from the end. Jesus had a way of interpreting things from that perspective; so do the Scriptures in general. Such a view of events helps us to see how things look from that future moment we call the last day. It provides a clue to the hidden agenda God has for history.

Matthew's and Luke's statement that the kingdom of God (heavens) is like a mustard seed is to be understood as a datival introduction: "It is the case with the kingdom of God as with what happens when a man sows a grain of mustard seed," etc. That is to say, the comparison is made not to the seed directly but to what happens when it is sown. The whole action described by the parable is to be taken into account.

The point of comparison of this parable may therefore be put as follows: When God is at work establishing his rule over, in, and among men, something happens that is like the surprising contrast between the mustard seed when it is sown and later when it has grown into a tree large enough for birds to find shade and shelter there.

From this we might formulate the central truth as follows: Do not be misled by the humble beginnings and the slow growth of God's kingdom. It is the end and outcome that matter. That is surely the point which Jesus intended to teach his followers. Like the first disciples we often expect the kingdom to be an impressive affair. Being God's very own rule, we argue, it should come amid earthquake and whirlwind. But in fact it is heard as a still, small voice. It is like a mustard seed, among the smallest of seeds. It grows, sprouts branches, and then gets to be a tree outdoing all other garden herbs.

What are we to understand by the sowing and growing? How do these take place? These basic questions have been answered in at least four different ways, depending on the assumptions of the respective interpreter.

The first approach says that a gradual and evolutionary process, working out from a small spark of man's innate goodness, will in time change men in sufficiently large numbers to bring in the kingdom of God. Idealism and the ethics of Jesus are to be the instruments for extending the rule of God.[17]

The existentialist view holds that the *kerygma* is the force by which men are brought to decision and self-understanding.[18] The rule of God extends to men everywhere as they come to comprehend the structures of their existence in the light of the model that Jesus provided.

C. H. Dodd and his followers see the story of Israel in the sowing of the seed. It grew until it became a tree in the ministry of Jesus. This is what is meant by "realized eschatology": the kingdom of God arrived fully with the coming of Jesus.[19] The period of slow and hidden growth, representing the activity of seers and prophets of old, came to an end as Jesus entered his ministry and began to proclaim, "The time has been fulfilled; the kingdom of God is upon you" (Mark 1:14). When interpreted in this way the parable of the mustard seed has nothing to say for the history of the church except as a kind of extension of Jesus' ministry. For the end came with Jesus Christ; his work constituted not only fulfillment but also the consummation of the kingdom.

But there is a fourth way.[20] It flows from an understanding of the central thrust of Scripture as the story of God's dealings with his people. In this view the fulfillment of what the Old Testament adumbrated took place in Jesus Christ. The rule of God for the last age of history came with him. By his ministry, death, and resurrection he manifested the grace of God to men. As John puts it: "Grace and truth came by Jesus Christ" (1:17).

His ministry was the time of sowing. His mission had the lowliest of beginnings. Yet his words and works, as proclaimed and celebrated in the church, have by now created a people, a tree, into which have come many Gentiles. The consummation is still ahead of us. It will come on the day of judgment. Birds are still gathering. In the meantime the tree keeps growing as more and more persons find a place to settle down on its branches and under its shade.

What makes it grow? The proclamation of the kingdom of God by Word and sacrament. The people of God assemble around these means of grace to constitute the *ekklēsia*, the church. They go out from there, strengthened by the words of grace, to carry out their tasks among men, exhibiting their commitment to God's rule of grace.

This parable, then, does not just illustrate the preaching of Jesus. It also proclaims God's rule—how insignificantly it began and how vast its outreach has become. The contrast intended, therefore, is that between beginning and end. In a sense, then, the story of the church is the account of the seed growing into a tree.

In conclusion, it will prove useful to read this parable in the way as it is told in the Gospel of Thomas:

> The disciples said to Jesus: Tell us what the kingdom of God is like. He said to them: It is like a grain of mustard seed, smaller than all seeds. But when it falls on the earth *which has been cultivated*, it puts forth a great *branch* and becomes a shelter [*skepē*] for the birds of heaven.[21] [Emphasis mine.]

The crucial difference between this way of telling the parable and that of the Synoptics is to be found in the words that have been italicized. Cultivated soil is a Gnostic concept for the illuminated individual, the elite, who is saved by the esoteric knowledge of that religious system. It should be noted, moreover, that the growth is depicted as that of a branch, meaning that such an enlightened person becomes a "shelter." There is no hint here of the corporate nature of the church and its members, nor is there any suggestion of an eschatology. As told in Thomas, this parable offers something of a primitive version of existentialism built on Gnostic presuppositions.

Homiletical Suggestions

Now that we have done the text of this parable and its exegesis it might be helpful to offer a few homiletical suggestions. In other words, we shall go from interpretation to preaching.

This long step is taken by selecting a thought from the text and examining it in the light of a felt need. In this way we get what we might call the arrow thought that will run through the whole sermon. That thought is a combination of text and application. It must be so stated as to make possible a logical division into parts. That is to say, the arrow thought does not always follow the sequence of statements in the text; it is a reworking of them for the purpose of presenting a coherent and persuasive sermon or homily.

The present parable invites us to reflect on the worldwide expansion of God's rule of grace by forces inherent in Word and sacrament. Here is a development which began with Jesus in a way that may be compared to the sowing of a grain of mustard seed which outgrows all other garden herbs to become a huge tree. The crucial homiletical question is, How do you take this thought and combine it with an application to a problem of the church today? When these two items have been brought together, the arrow thought must be so formulated as to yield to logical division into two or three units.

Such an arrow thought might be the conviction that the church provides a point of assembly for men of every nation, kindred, and tongue. Her work and influence transcend every border, whether it be that of a nation or race or color or age. This realization provides a healing focus for people everywhere, haunted as they are by the ghosts of meaninglessness and frustration. This parable invites them to find rest in the shade of the huge tree that symbolizes God's rule of grace at work in and through the church.

A title for all this might well be "Shelter and Shade for Us." That is the arrow thought in capsule form. It can be divided into the two parts of intent and consequence. An outline for a sermon would then look like this:

SHELTER AND SHADE FOR US

Introductory: Seed is a biblical symbol of life by way of death. Jesus himself once said, "Verily, verily I say to you, unless a grain of wheat falls into the earth and dies, it remains alone; but if it dies, it bears much fruit" (John 12:24). The grain that fell along the path in the parable of the sower was snatched up by birds. It had no chance to die and grow. The mustard seed was sown and grew. The man who sowed it intended it to die and grow so that it might offer shelter and shade. The kingdom of God works just that way in terms of his intent and result.

I. Intent
  A. As intrusion: God's grace comes to us by his choice as an act of intrusion.
    1. In the way that seed enters the soil to produce.
      a. At man's fall the ground came under a curse.
      b. Our existence is under the same divine judgment.
    2. In the way that life comes out of death.
      a. Seed must die to produce life.
      b. Jesus died to be raised and to give us life.
    3. In the way that a grain of mustard seed turns into a tree.
      a. It outdistances the ordinary things of existence.
      b. It has grown to create a place of refuge against the buffetings of life.
    4. In the way that birds find a nesting place in the tree grown out of seed.
  B. As an offer: God offers his rule of grace as an opportunity for meaning and hope.

351

1. Men suffer from meaninglessness and frustration; like stray sheep each one tries to go his own way (1 Pet. 2:25).
2. The parable invites them to find in Word and sacrament a focal point for their lives (1 Pet. 2:25) and an assembly place in the gathering of God's people (communion of saints).
   a. The means appear unimpressive (no pomp and circumstance).
   b. But by them God is working out his agenda for and in history (1 Cor. 15:23–28).
   c. Like birds of every kind, coming to the tree to enjoy its shelter and shade, men come from all nations to find healing in association.

II. Consequences
   A. The rupture of existence
      1. Life normally leads only to death; it goes nowhere.
      2. The structures of existence constitute a closed system.
      3. Liberation can come only from the outside.
      4. God's grace is that liberating force; it has opened history toward the future.
         a. The creation of Israel.
         b. Prophets spoke of the day of the Lord to come.
         c. That day came with the incarnation, death, and resurrection of God's Son.
         d. It continues in the assembly of those who gather around Word and sacrament.
      5. In this way the kingdom of God is like the mustard seed that grew into a sheltering tree for birds.
   B. The conquest of structures and divisions
      1. There are rich and poor; there are races and men of various colors; there are ethnic and national divisions.
      2. This tree outgrows them all.
      3. The church transcends all these divisions (Gal. 3:28).
      4. Into it flow men from everywhere; they fly across all boundaries, so to speak, for they have a place to go in order to become part of an abiding community.
      5. All this is God's doing; he is at work in and through the church.

Conclusion: Why, then, be discouraged, downhearted? Our destiny has been shaped and is assured. There is no note of sadness or depression in birds assembling to nest on the branches of a mighty tree. They sound glad to have found such a place. They enjoy it and chatter about it. The tree is for them. The kingdom of God is like that. It is for us to enjoy and celebrate.

NOTES

1. The expression *"earthly* Jesus" is here used to avoid the pitfalls of all the work that has gone into the quest for the *historical* Jesus. The earthly Jesus is the one proclaimed by Peter in Acts 2:32 as the one whom God raised up. Not only is there historical continuity between "Jesus" and the "Christ," but there is also a personal identity. To that the apostles were witnesses.

2. Edwyn Hoskyns and Francis Noel Davey, *The Riddle of the New Testament* (London: Faber & Faber, 1947), pp. 51–115.

3. Logion 96.

4. G. H. Lang, *The Parabolic Teaching of Jesus* (Grand Rapids: Eerdmans Publishing Company, 1955), p. 103.

5. William Barclay, *And Jesus Said* (Philadelphia: Westminster Press, 1970), p. 61.

6. C. G. Montefiore and H. Loewe, *Rabbinic Anthology* (Cleveland: World Publishing Company, 1963), p. 138.

7. Joachim Jeremias, *The Parables of Jesus*, trans. S. H. Hooke (New York: Charles Scribner's Sons, 1963), p. 147.

8. Richard C. Trench, *Notes on the Parables of Our Lord* (Westwood, N.J.: Fleming H. Revell Company, 1953), pp. 120–21.

9. C. H. Dodd, *The Parables of the Kingdom* (London: Nisbet & Company, 1950), p. 193.

10. The distinction between *ipsissima verba* and *ipsissima vox* is crucial for a proper understanding of the materials offered in the Gospels. In the first place, the Gospels are in Greek; Jesus spoke Aramaic. His words were put into Greek very early. Even so, as soon as there is a translation one is no longer dealing with a *verbatim* report, except in those instances in which the evangelists specifically offer the Aramaic, as in the case of the "Talitha Koum" of Mark 5:41 (the raising of Jairus' daughter) and in the instance of the word from the cross, as given in Matt. 27:46. Furthermore, the Gospels were written by the evangelists with the benefit of Easter and Pentecost at work in the church. As a result they give us the words of Jesus as he intended them to be understood and applied in the church of all ages by way of the apostolic witness. (See the three stages in the growth of the written Gospels as Luke refers to them in his preface, Luke 1:1–4).

11. Geraint V. Jones, *The Art and the Truth of the Parables* (London: S.P.C.K., 1964), p. 113.

12. See *The Book of Enoch,* trans. R. H. Charles (London: S.P.C.K., 1974), p. 82 (Enoch 62:8 "And the congregation of the elect and holy shall be sown").

13. Vincent Taylor, *The Gospel according to Saint Mark* (London: Macmillan Company, 1953), p. 269.

14. See Leopold Fonck, *The Parables of the Gospel* (New York: Frederick Pustet, 1914), pp. 160–61.

15. Here see Trench, *Notes on the Parables*, p. 112.

16. *Joseph and Asenath* 15. The Greek text of this is given in Jeremias, *Parables of Jesus*, p. 147.

17. Albrecht Ritschl might represent this particular approach, for he understood the kingdom of God to be a kind of moral commonwealth, or, as he put it, "a fellowship of moral attitude and moral properties." (See his *Rechtfertigung und Versöhnung* (Bonn: Adolph Marcus, 1888–89), 3:271. George Buttrick's *The Parables of Jesus* (New York: Richard R. Smith, 1931), p. 161, would be another, though more superficial, exhibit.

18. The work of Herbert Braun would be illustrative of this approach. See his *Jesus, der Mann aus Nazareth und seine Zeit* (Berlin: Kreuz Verlag, 1969), pp. 59–61. The following is a crucial sentence from Braun: "Der Mensch verfehlt sich oder verfehlt sich nicht, je nachdem, was er in seinen Augen ist und wie er von diesem Selbstverständnis aus handelt" (p. 61). Helmut Thielicke's *The Waiting Father* (New York: Harper & Row, 1959), must be classified as an exercise in Christian existentialism on a more popular level.

19. Dodd, *Parables of the Kingdom*, pp. 41–46.

20. See Martin H. Scharlemann, *Proclaiming the Parables* (St. Louis: Concordia Publishing House, 1963), pp. 26–27. It ought to be noted that Dan Otto Via's *The Parables: Their Literary and Existential Dimension* (Philadelphia: Fortress Press, 1967) fails to consider the two parables of the leaven and the mustard seed. It would have been interesting to see the principle that parables are "works of art, real aesthetic objects" (p. ix) applied in these instances.

21. Logion 20.

The Parable of the Mustard Seed

DONALD H. JUEL

Assistant Professor of New Testament
Luther Theological Seminary
Saint Paul, Minnesota

The first decision an interpreter of the parables must make is in what context the parables will be studied. Even a cursory reading of the parable of the mustard seed indicates the need for such a decision. This parable, like many others, occurs in more than one form in the New Testament; in fact, it occurs in three forms. In which of the canonical forms will the parable be interpreted? There are differences in wording among the three versions, some of which are minor, some of which may be major. This parable occurs in different contexts. Sometimes the context can decisively affect the meaning of a parable. In Luke, for example, the parable of the lost sheep (15:3-7) is a defense of Jesus' association with sinners and tax collectors in answer to objections of Pharisees and scribes (15:1-2). In Matthew the same parable illustrates to what lengths Christians should go to bring back errant brothers or sisters (18:10-14).

We cannot ask simply what a given parable means. We must ask what it means in Matthew, Mark, or Luke. Though differences among the three versions of a parable may be slight, we cannot assume in advance that a particular parable will have only one meaning or one function. The history of interpreting the New Testament is eloquent testimony to the ease with which the richness of the biblical witness may be concealed by premature harmonization. Even without raising the issue of settings of the parables in tradition prior to their incorporation in the written Gospels, or of their translation from Aramaic into Greek, or about possible changes that have occurred in the process of retelling, we recognize that our first task must be careful comparison of the parables that occur in more than one Gospel.

Since the parable of the mustard seed occurs in all three synoptic Gospels, we will begin with a synoptic comparison.

SYNOPTIC RELATIONSHIP

There are several patterns of agreement and disagreement among the three versions. In several instances Matthew and Luke have identical wording where Mark differs (*homoia estin, hon labōn anthropos, dendron, en tois kladois autou*; "is like," "which a man took," "tree," "in its branches"). Mark and Matthew agree at several points where Luke differs (*mikroteron . . . pantōn tōn spermatōn, meizon tōn lachanōn, hōste*; "smallest of all the seeds," "greatest of [all] shrubs," "so that").

These patterns of agreement and disagreement are familiar to students of the New Testament and need not be discussed in detail. Most agree that the data are best explained by a literary theory, that is, that one or more of the Gospel writers had access to one or more of the other written Gospels, or that all three evangelists had access to a common source no longer extant. Renewed interest in the synoptic problem has exposed weaknesses in old theories and has demonstrated that the evangelists probably used more than written sources and that understanding their precise interrelationship is highly complex. Nevertheless, the standard two-source hypothesis does account for most of the data in the case of our parable:

(1) Agreements in wording between Mark and Matthew and Luke can be explained if Matthew and Luke used Mark as a source. This would also explain any agreements between Mark and Matthew or Mark and Luke where the other Gospel has a different reading.

(2) Agreements between Matthew and Luke where Mark diverges are explained if the two authors had access to the parable in another form—the so-called Q. Both follow this parable with another, the parable of the leaven, which is not found in Mark, thus lending additional support to this hypothesis. The radically different contexts in which the twin parables are found in Matthew and Luke make direct borrowing of one from the other less likely than use of a common sayings source.

WORDING

(1) There are stylistic differences among the three versions. In Mark the extended simile is narrated as a truism: When someone plants a

mustard seed, the following happens. In Luke the parable is narrated as a past occurrence: When a man planted a mustard seed, the following happened. Matthew is inconsistent. The planting is described as a past event, but the future of the tiny seed is still only a possibility.

(2) Both Matthew and Mark emphasize the contrast implicit in the simile by calling the seed "the smallest of all seeds" and the full-grown plant the "greatest of [all] shrubs." Luke's version of the parable includes no such modifiers.

OLD TESTAMENT ALLUSIONS

In all three Gospels the parable concludes with what appears to be an allusion to one or more Old Testament passages, although it is unclear to which specific passage allusion is made. Candidates include Ezekiel 17:23 and 31:6 and Daniel 4:12 and 4:21. Matthew and Luke refer to the resultant plant as a "tree," which seems to derive less from agricultural expertise than from biblical images.

CONTEXT

(1) The setting of the parable is similar in Matthew and Mark. It is included as part of a collection of parables about the kingdom of God. In Luke the parable (together with the parable of the leaven) is not included in a collection of parables but follows the story of Jesus' healing of a crippled woman (13:10–17) in the context of warnings about the impending judgment (12:35–59; 13:1–9; 13:22–35).

(2) In Mark and Matthew the collection of parables is preceded by a story about Jesus' mother and brothers and followed by Jesus' rejection at Nazareth. In Mark, Jesus' calming of the sea precedes the rejection at Nazareth, while in Matthew it is placed earlier in Jesus' ministry (Matt. 8:23–27).

(3) In both Matthew and Mark the problem of understanding parables is posed by the disciples. In both Gospels, Jesus' enigmatic explanation for speaking in parables (Matt. 13:10–17; Mark 4:10–12) seems to apply to the parable of the mustard seed as well as to the parable of the sower. "Parable" is understood as an enigmatic form of speech. In Matthew, however, the disciples do not ask Jesus for explanations. They ask only why he speaks to the crowds in parables (13:10). And when, at the conclusion of the discourse, Jesus asks his disciples if they have understood everything, they reply, "Yes" (13:51). In Mark the disciples do not understand the meaning of the parables and require explanations

(4:10, 13). And their response to the stilling of the sea indicates that they do not yet understand Jesus (4:41).

Comparison of the three versions suggests several possible lines of study. One would be to examine the use of "kingdom of God" in the parable ("kingdom of heaven" in Matthew). This crucial expression is never defined in the New Testament, and it is used in somewhat different ways by the Gospel writers. There are passages that seem to view the kingdom as a present reality (e.g., Luke 11:20 and 17:21), while in most it is portrayed as future. We do not know whether the expression always means "kingly rule of God" or if it may also mean "territory" ruled by God, that is, whether "kingdom of God" can refer to a place as well as to a state of affairs.

Definitions were not provided by Jesus or the New Testament authors, probably because they were not needed. Knowledge of the expression "kingdom of God" could be assumed. What Jesus and the evangelists sought to do was provide a particular interpretation of a traditional conception. That means, however, that we must reconstruct from Jewish sources the background the New Testament presupposes simply in order to understand what the expression "kingdom of God" means.

Along the same line, we might examine in Jewish literature contemporaneous with the New Testament the place of biblical images like those in the parable (a tree that offers shelter for the birds of the air). Do such images occur elsewhere in portraits of the coming kingdom of God? The use of biblical texts and images in Jewish eschatological tradition might shed light on their use in Jesus' parables. Our task is not to reduce the meaning of New Testament imagery to what can be found in Jewish sources but to suggest a range of meanings within which the distinctive character of Christian language can be understood.

Another avenue of approach would be to study the use of verbs in the versions of the parable. The similitude in Mark portrays a typical situation; it is an expression of conventional wisdom. The parable is not an allegory. Narration of the parable with aorist verbs leaves open the possibility of allegorical interpretation. Matthew's departure from stylistic consistency may provide a clue that he has read the parable in this way, making Jesus the sower.

Yet perhaps the most obvious place to begin is with the matter of context. The short similitude was not important to Christian interpreters as an expression of conventional wisdom ("Large oaks from small acorns grow"). It was worth preserving because it sought to make a point about the kingdom of God—that is, because it was set within a Christian and, more broadly, a Jewish eschatological tradition. Yet that broad tradition does not provide a sufficiently precise context within which to study the parable. The various nuances of "kingdom of God" can be determined only within a specific literary setting. The precise aspect of the kingdom to be clarified by the parable can be ascertained only from within each of the Gospels.

This feature of parable study has not been central to most recent scholarship.[1] Scholars like Amos Wilder and Dan Otto Via have been more interested in the function of parabolic language as such. The parable is viewed as an entity with a structure and a reality sufficient to itself. Such study has demonstrated that parabolic language cannot be reduced to a communication of propositional truth. Emphasizing the complex function of figurative language provides a healthy corrective to overly rationalistic approaches to biblical interpretation. But it does little to aid in the interpretation of our parable. The parable of the mustard seed, abstracted from its setting, communicates nothing that would pass for divine reality. If the similitude points up the contrast between a small beginning and a glorious conclusion, we must know on what reality the image seeks to shed light.

We shall begin, therefore, by inspecting the context in which the parable is narrated, asking about the meaning and function of the similitude in its present canonical settings. In the interest of space, we will examine the parable as it occurs in the Gospel of Mark.

OBSERVATIONS

(1) The parable of the mustard seed occurs in a small collection of parables and sayings that provides the first real sample of Jesus' teaching as it is introduced programmatically in Mark 1:14–15: ". . . preaching the gospel of God, and saying, 'The time is fulfilled, and the kingdom of God is at hand; repent and believe in the gospel.'" The first occurrences of "kingdom of God" after 1:15 are in 4:11 and in the two kingdom parables (4:26–29; 4:30–32).

(2) The two kingdom parables, the mustard seed and the seed growing secretly, conclude with biblical allusions (both imprecise), drawing on imagery familiar to Jewish eschatological tradition.

(3) The parable discourse in Mark emphasizes contrasts: the time of sowing and the time of harvest; hidden-revealed; tiny seeds and large shrubs.

(4) Twice in the chapter the narrator reports that Jesus explains the

parables to his followers (4:10–12; 4:33–34). Parables require explanation. Jesus' disciples cannot understand the parables without private instruction. Parables are thus viewed as riddles, forms of discourse chosen for their ability to conceal meaning (4:10–12). The consistent use of the plural "parables" in 4:10–12 indicates that the explanation applies to all the parables in the chapter.

(5) In addition to parables, the chapter contains metaphors (4:21–23) and a nonfigurative warning: "Take heed what you hear; the measure you give will be the measure you get, and still more will be given you. For to him who has will more be given; and from him who has not, even what he has will be taken away." The saying in particular has a paranetic tone that seems strangely out of place in the chapter. Its presence, as well as the selection of parables in the chapter as a whole, requires some explanation.

(6) One link between the parable chapter and its larger context in Mark is the theme of understanding-misunderstanding. The chapter is introduced by repeated examples of misunderstanding. While demons know who Jesus is (3:11), Jesus' relatives (or friends) think that he is crazy (3:21); scribes who have come down from Jerusalem believe that he is possessed (3:22–30); and his mother and brothers appear to be in the dark as well (3:32). Although the crowds flock to Jesus, they are presumably not enlightened by Jesus' teaching, for he has chosen to speak in figures (4:10–12). The disciples seem to be the only ones to learn anything. They have been given the "mystery of the kingdom of God"; they receive explanations. Yet even they appear to have missed something. In the dramatic boat scene that follows, the disciples graphically demonstrate that they do not have faith (4:40), and they respond to Jesus' command of nature with stunned amazement, "Who is this, that even the wind and the sea obey him?" (4:41).

INTERPRETATION

The parable of the mustard seed has not been included in Mark as an example of how Jesus communicated to his contemporaries the nature of the kingdom of God. In Mark, Jesus says that he speaks in parables to conceal his message. Presumably the real meaning was explained to the disciples—though it is unclear what the secret meaning of this parable is and Mark includes no explanation. Yet not even the disciples are enlightened in Mark. While Matthew follows the parable discourse with a statement by the disciples that they have understood, Mark follows with an expression of their continued bewilderment. Their inability to understand is consistent in Mark. Jesus later calls them blind, seemingly comparing them to the outsiders (8:18; see chap. 4).

The parable of the mustard seed is included in Mark because it reveals something about the kingdom of God—but only for the reader, who understands what the characters in the story cannot. In the first place, the parable interprets Jesus' ministry as Mark narrates it. Jesus Christ, the Son of God (1:1), begins and ends his career as an enigma to friend and foe alike. He does not seem to fit in any category. He does not teach like the scribes and he demonstrates a sovereign attitude toward tradition. He performs wonders like Elijah and Elisha of old. Yet there is little about him or his movement that would convince anyone that he is the Christ. His career, which allegedly marks the inauguration of the kingdom, ends in apparent disaster. He is deserted by his followers, betrayed by one of the inner circle, and denied by Peter, the "rock." He is tried and condemned by religious and political leaders. He dies rejected, alone, ridiculed by everyone. Even his cry of desperation is misunderstood by the crowd (15:34–35). Can this one have anything to do with the glorious kingdom of God?

Upon closer inspection, however, the story reveals another dimension. Jesus' end, however desperate it may appear, has been predicted in detail on three occasions (8:31; 9:31; 10:33). His trial and death fulfill scriptural prophecies. Even Peter's denial fulfills an earlier prediction (14:30 = 14:66–72). Jesus has promised a turning of the tables (12:10–11; 14:62), and portents at his death suggest that the story is not quite over (15:38–39). There is more to Jesus and his mission than appearances suggest.

The parable of the mustard seed is one of the many places in Mark where this peculiar ambiguity of Jesus' ministry is dealt with, where contrasts between Jesus' ministry and traditional conceptions and expectations are interpreted. Do not be confused by appearances, says Jesus. It may seem that my preaching and my small circle of followers have nothing to do with the kingdom of God—but appearances can be deceiving. Although the mustard seed is exceptionally small, once planted it sprouts and produces a shrub large enough to offer protection for the birds. Once the seed has been planted the outcome is assured.

The point of the contrast between the tiny seed and the large shrub, emphasized in Mark, is not simply the inevitability of the magnificent plant but the organic link between the time of small beginnings and the time of full growth. The same contrast of two times is found elsewhere in the parable discourse. Jesus may tell parables to conceal his message for the moment, but the time of unveiling will come when the lamp is placed on the lampstand. What is hidden will one day be revealed. Once the seed has been planted the harvest is a certainty. The kingdom, present in germinal form, will emerge with all its expected glory. There will be a time of bounty and light and safety. The time of Jesus, however, is not yet that time. It is the preliminary stage of sowing and hiddenness and small beginnings.

It is conceivable that in Mark the parable is intended to explain the contrast between the time of Jesus and the time of the church. Perhaps in the author's mind the time of unveiling anticipated by Jesus, the time of harvest and safety, has now come. There is ample preparation for such a view in Mark. From the outset promises are made about great things to come. Jesus describes himself as the stronger one who has come to despoil Satan (3:27). On five occasions he predicts that he will be raised from the dead; once he tells his followers, Peter, James, and John, to keep information about his transfiguration secret until after his resurrection (9:9). Jesus is the "stone which the builders rejected" who will become "the head of the corner" (Ps. 118:22 in Mark 12:11; see Acts 4:11). It might seem, therefore, that Mark's readers were to view the parable as an explanation for the course of revelation: Jesus intended that his ministry should remain an enigma, but the time of fruition and openness has now come after Jesus' resurrection.

But that is not the way Mark chooses to tell Jesus' story. We never reach the great unveiling. Even when the resurrection is announced by an angel at the empty tomb the women flee in terror (16:8). The disciples of Jesus are not simply foils for Jesus' enemies; their steadfastness is not contrasted with the inappropriate responses of others. Throughout the story they exemplify a lack of fidelity and preparation. Even insiders have difficulty remaining faithful. Even those to whom the secret is given, who receive explanations, are not safe. They too must be encouraged to hold fast and warned about the consequences of a lack of preparation.

The time of the church is for Mark the time not of safety and bounty but rather of small beginnings and danger. Mark 13, Jesus' farewell speech to his disciples, provides the clearest glimpse into the situation of the author and his contemporaries. Here Jesus warns of the difficult times ahead. There will be extraordinary temptations for the elect—false Christs and false prophets. Terrible trials await everyone, but particularly those who await the return of the true Christ on the clouds of heaven. Families will be torn apart (13:12); believers will be persecuted (13:9). Only those who endure to the end will be saved (13:13). But endurance is possible. Jesus has told all these things beforehand (13:23), and he will return to gather his elect. The glorious era of the kingdom of God will come. In this context the message of the mustard seed is that believers should not be discouraged by a lack of signs. Even if the prospects in the present are not good the promised consummation is certain—as certain as the harvest after sowing and as sure as the protection afforded by the shrub that comes from the tiny seed.

MATTHEW AND LUKE

The parable of the mustard seed has a different function in Matthew and Luke. In the parable discourse, Matthew is much more concerned to stress the contrast between disciples and outsiders. As insiders they are genuinely enlightened. They ask not what Jesus means by the parables but why he speaks to the crowds in this way. For Matthew the parable seeks to relate the time of Jesus to the time of the church. The church may not represent the consummation of Jesus' promises of the kingdom, but certainly the dawning of the kingdom in its glory has begun.[2]

Luke does not stress the contrast between the small seed and the large plant. His point is not so much the contrast between the present and the future as the inevitability of the coming of the kingdom and the ensuing judgment—a consistent emphasis in his Gospel.

THE HISTORICAL JESUS

There is another dimension of interpretation that we have not yet considered. What is the relationship between the meanings of the parable of the mustard seed in the three synoptic Gospels and its original meaning in the ministry of Jesus? Is one of the evangelists more correct than the others in his interpretation, or are all correct? If differences are due to context we might theorize that Jesus told the parable on different occasions. This explanation would not cover outright contradictions in interpretation, however, and although it is not implausible, it does not really aid us in our interpretation of Matthew and Mark. Both place the parable in the same setting, yet their interpretations differ. The differences in the way each author concludes the parable discourse do not provide evidence of distinct historical occasions. In both Gospels a complex of events is obvious (question about family, parables, rejection at Nazareth). Modifications must be seen as evidence of editorial activity. If each evangelist has provided the literary context that is decisive for understanding the parable, however, we must still ask if one more closely approximates the original.

The issue is complicated by the use of the term *parable*. According to Mark, the parable of the mustard seed, like the parable of the sower, is one of the "riddles" Jesus told. Neither parable, however, appears to be particularly enigmatic. The point of most of Jesus' parables is quite clear. In Mark, for example, Jesus' parable about wicked tenants (12:1–10) is understood by his enemies only too clearly (12:13). The issue here is not whether Jesus' contemporaries understood his parables but whether "parable" as a form of discourse was characterized by its ability to conceal. In fact, virtually all we know about parables in the Jewish world contemporaneous with early Christianity—and about Jesus' parables— makes this "parable theory" unlikely. Most of Jesus' parables are strikingly effective communicators.

How, then, is the so-called parable theory of Mark 4:10–12 (see the versions in Matt. 13:10–17 and Luke 8:9–10) to be understood? There are few interpreters who would regard these verses as the proper historical introduction to the parable of the mustard seed provided by Jesus himself. But if the present literary context in Mark and Matthew is probably different from the original context(s), how are we to determine those original settings in Jesus' ministry so decisive for understanding the parables? The questions ought not to be clouded in advance by speaking of the "authentic voice of Jesus" in some trans-historical sense. There may be some hermeneutical legitimacy implied in such an expression, but there are hard questions that must be faced. The parables of the New Testament are narrated as parables of Jesus, and "Jesus" is not a cipher for "exalted Jesus" or the Holy Spirit. The name refers to a specific historical figure who was "born of the virgin Mary, suffered under Pontius Pilate, was crucified, dead, and buried."

Questions like these have spawned a whole history of scholarship. Among the giants in the field like Adolf Jülicher and C. H. Dodd, no one has struggled harder with the problem than Joachim Jeremias.[3] Depending largely on evidence from the New Testament, Jeremias has argued convincingly that the parables in their present form and context have undergone a history of transmission in the process of which many changes have occurred. According to Jeremias, the most far-reaching changes have occurred by providing a new setting for individual parables. If, therefore, the meaning of a specific parable is heavily dependent upon context, and if there is evidence that the present literary contexts of the parables are different from the original setting in Jesus' ministry, we have no choice but to attempt a reconstruction of that original setting if we are to recover the original meaning—however uncertain such a reconstruction might be. It would make a great difference, as Dodd has shown, if the individual parables must be understood within a ministry Jesus believed to be the time of fulfillment and harvest rather than of anticipation and sowing (see John 4:35–38).

Space does not permit a thorough consideration of this approach to interpretation of the parable of the mustard seed, since what is required to understand the individual parable is an overall view of Jesus' ministry and the place of this particular similitude in that ministry. Let me, however, give a brief sketch of one view, that of Nils A. Dahl.[4] The parables of Jesus, Dahl argues, were not told to spread information or to proclaim the gospel. Here he agrees with Jeremias and others. The parables served as weapons of debate, as answers to specific charges made against Jesus or to questions raised about his mission. The similitude about the tiny seed and the great shrub was not told by Jesus as a guarantee that one day the kingdom of God would come in all its glory. No good Jew doubted that. What many did doubt, however, was that Jesus' ministry had anything to do with that kingdom. His contemporaries undoubtedly found it difficult to believe that God's promises about the glorious age to come were finding even a provisional fulfillment in him and his small group of followers. But that, according to Dahl, is precisely what Jesus preached. His ministry did indeed mark the inauguration of the kingdom of God. The lesson to be learned from the tiny seed is that even though the minute seed and the great shrub seem incongruous, they are organically related; they are simply different stages of the same plant. Small beginnings need not rule out a link between Jesus' ministry and the kingdom of God.[5]

If Dahl's reconstruction of Jesus' message and the place of the parable is accurate, there is no great difference between the original message of Jesus and the interpretations of the evangelists. But there are differences. The parables of the kingdom, taken in isolation, do not themselves clarify when the time of consummation is expected. Did Jesus view his own time as the time of fulfillment? That seems unlikely. But was the fulfillment far off or near at hand? Did Jesus mean to portray the post-resurrection era as the glorious age, or was he looking to some time in the far-distant future? It is clear that the evangelists answered these

DONALD H. JUEL

questions differently. For Matthew the time of fruition has begun; for Mark it seems to be primarily future. The parables as narrated by Jesus do not decide the matter. That is a task for the interpreter. Even in the case of the parable of the mustard seed, the New Testament message is more than the mere continuation of Jesus' teaching. It is informed by the whole gospel of the crucified and risen Christ and by the experience of the church. This parable may not pose Bultmann's famous question about the relation of New Testament theology to the preaching of Jesus in its most poignant form, but it does at least raise it.[6]

HOMILETICAL IMPLICATIONS

Focusing on the parable as it occurs in Mark, several things might be said about proper use of the parable in preaching. When read in context, the similitude is not an example of popular wisdom. It does not seek to portray the extraordinary power of faith, as it is in Matthew 17:20; it seeks to clarify an aspect of the kingdom of God. That reality is not identical with the church, and in the New Testament as a whole it is pictured as a corporate experience with eschatological dimensions that cannot adequately be translated by individualistic categories and temporal categories that relate only to the present. The parable speaks of something more than the forgiveness of sins.

In Mark the parable of the sower attempts to make sense out of the kingdom of God in the face of the apparent absence of signs of its presence. It seeks to interpret the seeming disparity between reality and expectations or between reality and appearance. The author writes for people who perhaps find evidence of God's rule now but who face crises and times of trouble for which they are ill-prepared. They need to know that God's rule may not operate precisely as we believe it should or expect that it will. Reality and truth may be hidden from view. For those prepared for that ambiguity, trusting in the God who will one day reveal his dominion can make the absence of signs more bearable. The lesson of our parable is that God's promises will be fulfilled and the consummation of his will for all creation will come—as surely as the great shrub emerges from the tiny seed.

Interpreters of the parable of the mustard seed may discover that the need to struggle with the hiddenness of God and with disappointed expectations may be as real for us today as for Jesus' contemporaries or the readers of Mark's Gospel.

366

NOTES

1. John Dominic Crossan, *In Parables* (New York: Harper & Row, 1973); Dan Otto Via, *The Parables: Their Literary and Existential Dimensions* (Philadelphia: Fortress Press, 1967); Amos N. Wilder, *Early Christian Rhetoric: The Language of the Gospel* (Cambridge: Harvard University Press, 1971).

2. For a detailed study of the parable of the mustard seed in Matthew, see Jack Kingsbury, *The Parables of Jesus in Matthew 13* (Richmond: John Knox Press, 1969), esp. pp. 76–83.

3. Joachim Jeremias, *The Parables of Jesus*, trans. S. H. Hooke (New York: Charles Scribner's Sons, 1963).

4. Nils A. Dahl, "The Parables of Growth," in his *Jesus in the Memory of the Early Church* (Minneapolis: Augsburg Publishing House, 1976), pp. 141–66.

5. Ibid., pp. 155–56.

6. Rudolf Bultmann, *Theology of the New Testament*, trans. Kendrick Grobel (New York: Charles Scribner's Sons, 1951–55), 1:3: "The message of Jesus is a presupposition for the theology of the New Testament rather than a part of that theology itself."

Contributors

Ralph A. Bohlmann is President and Professor of Systematic Theology at Concordia Seminary, Saint Louis, Missouri.

Joseph A. Burgess is a former Assistant Professor of New Testament at Lutheran Theological Seminary, Gettysburg, Pennsylvania.

Harold H. Ditmanson is Professor of Religion at Saint Olaf College, Northfield, Minnesota.

Karlfried Froehlich is Professor of Church History at Princeton Theological Seminary, Princeton, New Jersey.

Ronald M. Hals is Professor of Old Testament at Trinity Lutheran Seminary, Columbus, Ohio.

Arland J. Hultgren is Associate Professor of New Testament at Luther Theological Seminary, Saint Paul, Minnesota.

Horace D. Hummel is Associate Professor of Exegetical Theology at Concordia Seminary, Saint Louis, Missouri.

Donald H. Juel is Assistant Professor of New Testament at Luther Theological Seminary, Saint Paul, Minnesota.

Kurt E. Marquart is Associate Professor of Systematic Theology at Concordia Theological Seminary, Fort Wayne, Indiana.

Foster R. McCurley is Professor of Old Testament and Hebrew at Lutheran Theological Seminary, Philadelphia, Pennsylvania.

Samuel H. Nafzger is Executive Secretary of the Commission on Theology and Church Relations of the Lutheran Church—Missouri Synod, Saint Louis, Missouri.

Paul D. Opsahl is Executive Director of the Division of Theological Studies of the Lutheran Council in the U.S.A., New York, New York.

Duane A. Priebe is Associate Professor of Systematic Theology at Wartburg Theological Seminary, Dubuque, Iowa.

Warren A. Quanbeck is Professor of Systematic Theology at Luther Theological Seminary, Saint Paul, Minnesota.

John Reumann is Professor of New Testament at Lutheran Theological Seminary, Philadelphia, Pennsylvania.

Martin H. Scharlemann is Graduate Professor of Exegetical Theology at Concordia Seminary, Saint Louis, Missouri.

David L. Tiede is Associate Professor of New Testament at Luther Theological Seminary, Saint Paul, Minnesota.